CANADA

THE
NORTHEAST
26–53

THE MIDWEST
84–113

THE WEST
128–155

THE SOUTHEAST
54–83

THE SOUTHWEST
114–127

MEXICO

CUBA

BAHAMAS

It's a BIG country. Learn it. Love it. Explore it.

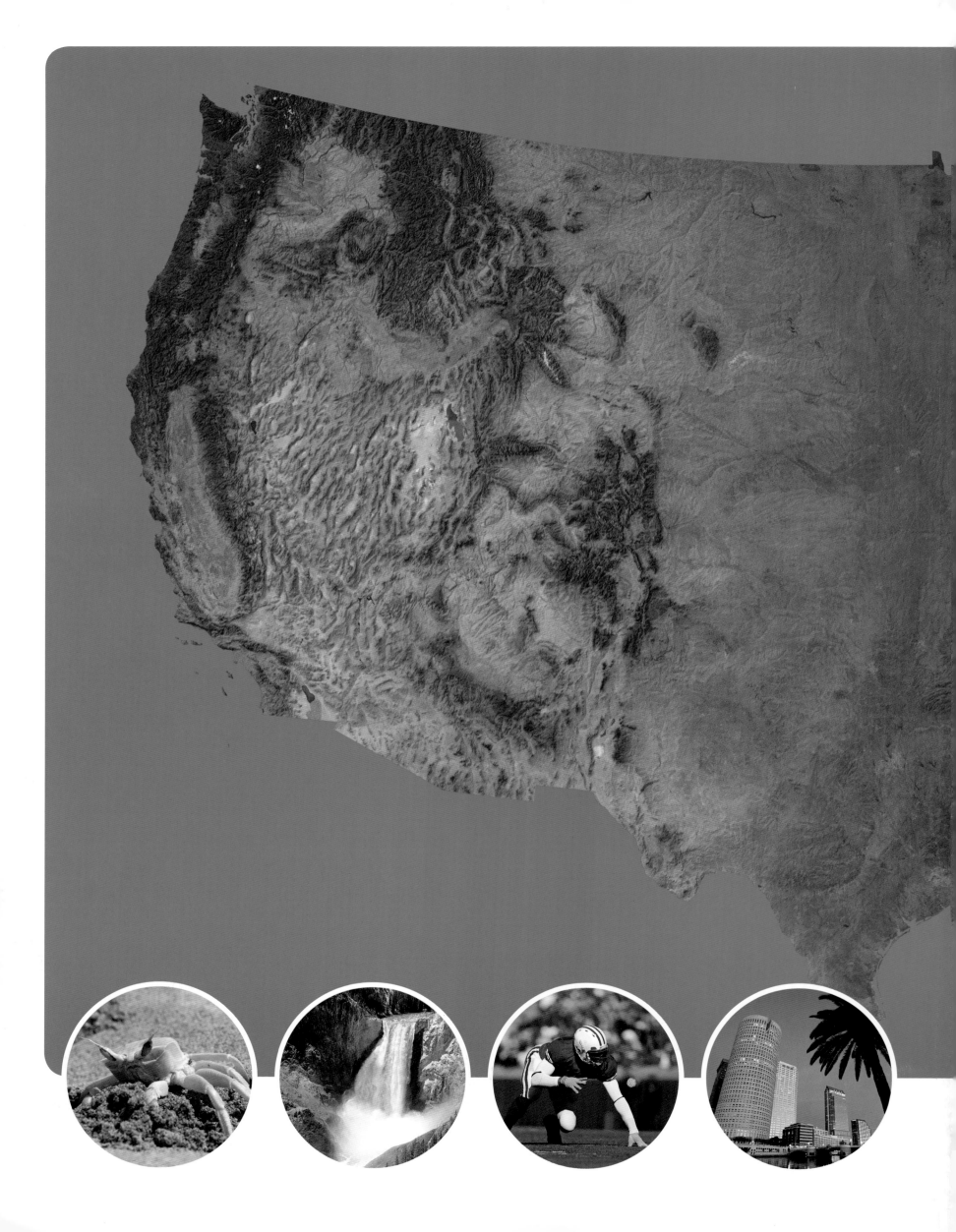

![National Geographic logo] **NATIONAL GEOGRAPHIC**

UNITED STATES
ATLAS

FOR YOUNG EXPLORERS

THIRD EDITION

NATIONAL GEOGRAPHIC

WASHINGTON, DC

TABLE OF CONTENTS

Northeast: Maine lighthouse, pp. 36–37

Southeast:
Florida manatee, p. 64

Midwest: Illinois hay field with tractor, pp. 90–91

Title page: Atlantic sand crab; Lower Falls of the Yellowstone, MT; football player; Tampa, FL; sage grouse; skyline, Seattle, WA; Organ Pipe Cactus National Monument, AZ.

Southwest: Albuquerque balloon festival, p. 122

Territories: Festival dancers, American Samoa, pp. 158–159

West: Wyoming ranch, p. 154

HOW TO USE THIS ATLAS

This atlas is much more than just another book of maps about the United States. Of course you'll find all the things you'd expect to find—country, regional, and state maps, essays, photos, flags, graphs, and fact boxes—for the country as a whole as well as for each region and state (even the territories). But there's much more. This atlas, through a specially designed Web site (see pages 8–9), not only leads you to places where you can find more information and keep up-to-date about all kinds of things, it also allows you to go beyond the flat page and experience the sights and sounds of the country through the multimedia archives of National Geographic.

STATE FACT BOX

The fact box has all the key information you need at a glance about a state, its flag and nickname, statistics about area, cities, population, ethnic and racial makeup,* statehood, industry, and agriculture, plus some fun Geo Whiz facts and the state bird and flower.

*The ethnic/racial percentages total more than 100 percent because Hispanics can be included with any race or ethnic group.

WEB LINKS

Throughout the atlas you will find black-and-yellow Web link icons for photos, videos, sounds, games, and more information. You can get to all of these links through one URL: **www.nationalgeographic.com/kids-usa-atlas.** This link will take you to the Web site specially designed to go with this atlas (see pages 8–9). Bookmark it so you can use it often.

COLOR BARS

Each section of the atlas has its own color to make it easy to move from one to another. Look for the color on the Table of Contents and across the top of the pages in the atlas. The name of the section and the title for each topic or map is in the color bar.

The Northeast
The Southeast
The Midwest
The Southwest
The West
The Territories

46 THE NORTHEAST

THE EMPIRE STATE:
NEW YORK

NEW YORK

THE BASICS
STATS
Area
54,556 sq mi (141,300 sq km)
Population
19,297,729
Capital
Albany
Population 93,919
Largest city
New York City
Population 8,214,426
Ethnic/racial groups
73.7% white; 17.4% African American; 6.9% Asian; .5% Native American; Hispanic (any race) 16.3%
Industry
Printing and publishing, machinery, computer products, finance, tourism
Agriculture
Dairy products, cattle and other livestock, vegetables, nursery stock, apples
Statehood
July 26, 1788; 11th state

GEO WHIZ
Each year at Halloween the Headless Horseman rides again through the countryside of Sleepy Hollow as residents reenact Washington Irving's *The Legend of Sleepy Hollow.*

The Erie Canal, built in the 1820s between Albany and Buffalo, helped New York City become a worldwide trading center and opened the Midwest to development by linking the Hudson River and the Great Lakes.

Cooperstown, New York, home of the National Baseball Hall of Fame, takes its name from a town established in the late 1700s by the father of James Fenimore Cooper, author of such American classics as *The Last of the Mohicans* and *The Deerslayer.*

EASTERN
BLUEBIRD
ROSE

When Englishman Henry Hudson explored New York's Hudson River Valley in 1609, the territory was already inhabited by large tribes of Native Americans, including the powerful Iroquois. In 1624 a Dutch trading company established the New Netherland colony, but after just 40 years the colony was taken over by the English and renamed for England's Duke of York. In 1788 New York became the 11th state. The state can be divided into two parts. The powerful port city of New York, center of trade and commerce and gateway to immigrants, is the largest city in the U.S. Its metropolitan area has more than 18 million people. Everything north of the city is simply referred to as "Upstate." Cities such as Buffalo and Rochester are industrial centers, while Ithaca and Syracuse boast major universities. Agriculture is also important in New York. With almost 5 million acres in cropland, the state is a major producer of dairy products, fruits, and vegetables.

⇧ LADY LIBERTY. Standing in New York Harbor, the Statue of Liberty, a gift from the people of France, is a symbol of freedom and democracy.

⇦ NATURAL WONDER. As many as 12 million tourists annually visit Niagara Falls on the U.S.-Canada border. Visitors in rain slickers trek through the mists below Bridal Veil Falls on the American side.

URBAN GIANT
8,214,426
1,549,178
2,833,321
2,144,491
1,512,986
New York
Los Angeles
Chicago
Houston
Philadelphia

Figures are based on 2000 census projections and are for population within city limits.

With more than twice the population of the next largest city, New York—known as the Big Apple—is the country's largest city.

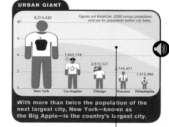

THE WEST
WEST

The West
THE HIGH FRONTIER

The western states, which make up almost half of the country's land area, have diverse landscapes and climates, ranging from the frozen heights of Denali, in Alaska, to the desolation of Death Valley, in California, and the lush, tropical islands of Hawaii. More than half the region's population lives in California, and the Los Angeles metropolitan area is second only to New York City. Yet many parts of the region are sparsely populated, and much of the land is set aside as parkland and military bases. The region also faces many natural hazards—earthquakes, landslides, wildfires, and even volcanic eruptions.

WHERE THE PICTURES ARE

WHERE ARE THE PICTURES?

If you want to know where a picture in any of the regional sections in the atlas was taken, check the map in the regional photo essay. Find the label that describes the photograph you are curious about, and follow the line to its location.

CHARTS AND GRAPHS

The photo essay for each state includes a chart or graph that highlights economic, physical, cultural, or some other type of information related to the state.

GETTING STARTED

BAR SCALE
Each map has a bar scale in miles and kilometers to help you find out how far it is from one place to another on the map.

"YOU ARE HERE"
Locator maps show you where each region and state within the region is in relation to the rest of the United States. Regions are shown in the regional color; featured states are in yellow.

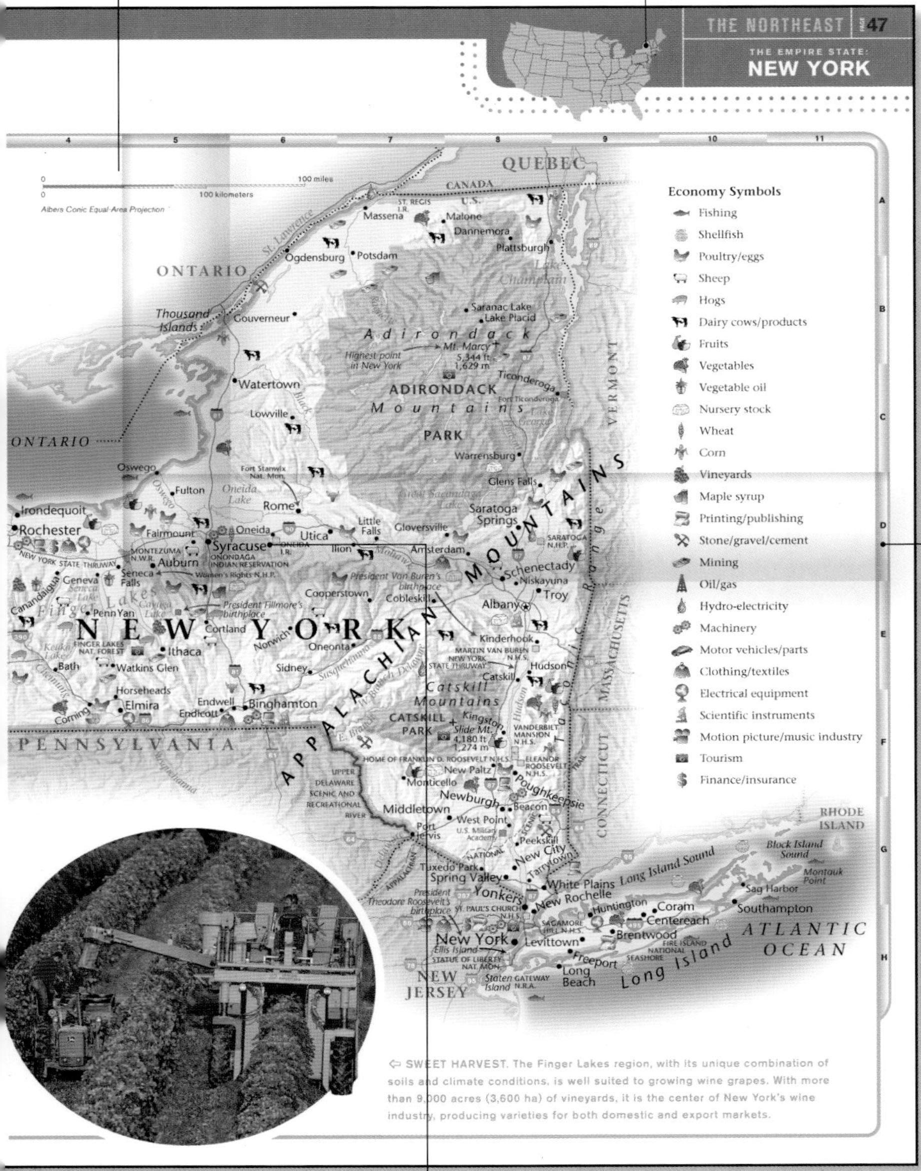
THE NORTHEAST | PAGE 47
THE EMPIRE STATE:
NEW YORK
Economy Symbols
Fishing
Shellfish
Poultry/eggs
Sheep
Hogs
Dairy cows/products
Fruits
Vegetables
Vegetable oil
Nursery stock
Wheat
Corn
Vineyards
Maple syrup
Printing/publishing
Stone/gravel/cement
Mining
Oil/gas
Hydro-electricity
Machinery
Motor vehicles/parts
Clothing/textiles
Electrical equipment
Scientific instruments
Motion picture/music industry
Tourism
Finance/insurance
QUEBEC
ONTARIO
NEW YORK
ADIRONDACK PARK
APPALACHIAN MOUNTAINS
PENNSYLVANIA
VERMONT
MASSACHUSETTS
CONNECTICUT
NEW JERSEY
ATLANTIC OCEAN
Long Island
SWEET HARVEST. The Finger Lakes region, with its unique combination of soils and climate conditions, is well suited to growing wine grapes. With more than 9,000 acres (3,600 ha) of vineyards, it is the center of New York's wine industry, producing varieties for both domestic and export markets.

Sycamore, IL **91** B4
Sycan (river), OR **149** F4
Sycan N.W.&S.R., OR **149** F4
Sylacauga, AL **61** D4
Sylvania, OH **109** A3
Syracuse, NY **47** D5
Sysladobsis Lake, ME

INDEX AND GRID
A grid system makes it easy to find places listed in the index. For example, the listing for Syracuse, New York, is followed by **47** D5. The bold type is the page number; D5 tells you the city is near the point where imaginary lines drawn from D and 5 on the grid bars meet.

MAP ICONS

Maps use symbols to stand for many physical, political, and economic features. Below is a complete list of the map symbols used in this atlas. In addition, each state map has its own key featuring symbols for major economic activities. Additional abbreviations used in this atlas as well as metric conversion tables are listed on the endsheets at the back of the book.

- Aspen .... *town of under 25,000 residents*
- Frankfort .... *town of 25,000 to 99,999*
- San Jose .... *city of 100,000 to 999,999*
- New York .... *city of 1,000,000 and over*
- National capital
- State capital
- Point of interest
- Mountain peak with elevation above sea level
- Low point with elevation below sea level
- River
- Intermittent river
- Canal
- Interstate or selected other highway
- Trail
- State or national boundary
- Continental divide
- Lake and dam
- Intermittent lake
- Dry lake
- Swamp
- Glacier
- National Wild & Scenic River, **N.W.&S.R.**
- Sand
- Lava
- Area below sea level
- Indian Reservation, **I.R.**
- State Park, **S.P.**
  State Historical Park, **S.H.P.**
  State Historic Site, **S.H.S.**
- National Battlefield, **N.B.**
  National Battlefield Park, **N.B.P.**
  National Battlefield Site, **N.B.S.**
  National Historic Site, **N.H.S.**
  National Historical Area, **N.H.A.**
  National Historical Park, **N.H.P.**
  National Lakeshore
  National Military Park, **N.M.P.**
  National Memorial, **NAT. MEM.**
  National Monument, **NAT. MON.**
  National Park, **N.P.**
  National Parkway
  National Preserve
  National Recreation Area, **N.R.A.**
  National River
  National Riverway
  National Scenic Area
  National Seashore
  National Volcanic Monument
- National Forest, **N.F.**
- National Grassland, **N.G.**
- National Wildlife Refuge, **N.W.R.**

Economy Symbols

- Fishing
- Lobster fishing
- Shellfish
- Poultry/eggs
- Sheep
- Hogs
- Dairy cows/products
- Beef cattle
- Fruits
- Vegetables
- Vegetable oil
- Peanuts
- Nursery stock
- Wheat
- Corn
- Rice
- Soybeans
- Sugarcane
- Cotton
- Tobacco
- Coffee
- Vineyards
- Maple syrup
- Timber/forest products
- Furniture
- Printing/publishing
- Stone/gravel/cement
- Mining
- Coal
- Oil/gas
- Hydro-electricity
- Machinery
- Metal manufacturing
- Metal products
- Shipbuilding
- Railroad equipment
- Motor vehicles/parts
- Rubber/plastics
- Chemistry
- Food processing
- Clothing/textiles
- Leather products
- Glass/clay products
- Jewelry
- Electrical equipment
- Computers/electronics
- Scientific instruments
- Aircraft/parts
- Aerospace
- Motion picture/music industry
- Tourism
- Finance/insurance

HOW TO USE THE ATLAS WEB SITE

As you can see by flipping through the pages, this atlas is chock full. There are photographs, statistics, quick facts, and—most of all—lots of charts and detailed maps. Plus there is a companion Web site that adds even more. You can watch videos of animals in their natural surrounds or of a volcano erupting, listen to the sounds of people, places, and animals, find lots of state information, download pictures and maps for school reports, and play games that allow you to explore the United States. You can even send e-postcards to your friends. The

Web site provides added value to specific subjects in the atlas and also helps you explore on your own, taking you deep into the resources of National Geographic and beyond. Throughout the atlas you will find these icons.

PHOTOS   VIDEO   AUDIO   GAMES   INFO

The icons are placed near pictures, on maps, or next to text. Each icon tells you that you can find more on that subject on the Web site. To follow any icon link, go to www.nationalgeographic.com/kids-usa-atlas.

⇨ **START HERE.**

There are three ways to find what you are looking for from the Home Page:

1. BY ATLAS PAGE NUMBER
2. BY TOPIC
3. BY ICON

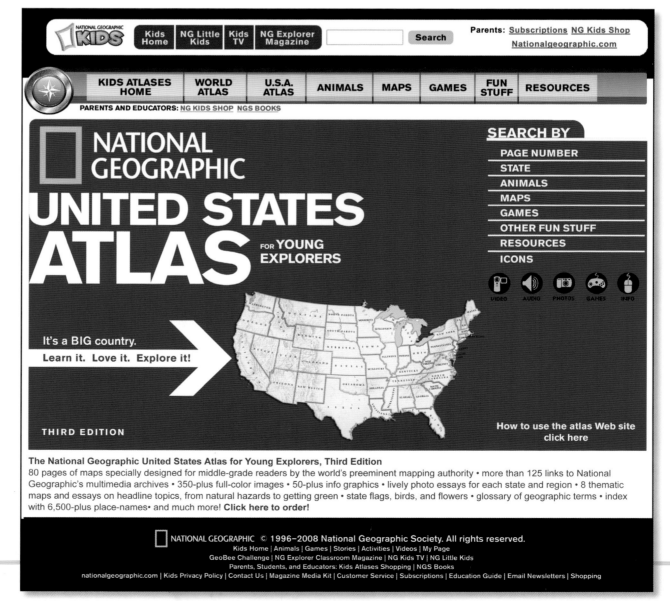

www.nationalgeographic.com/kids-usa-atlas

1. SEARCH BY ATLAS PAGE NUMBER

⇐ **PAGE NUMBER PULL-DOWN MENU.** If you find an icon in the atlas and want to go directly to that link, use the page number pull-down menu. Just drag and click.

2. SEARCH BY TOPIC

⇒ **LIST OF TOPICS.** If you want to explore a specific topic, click on the entry in the topic list. This list is your portal to vast quantities of National Geographic information, photos, videos, games, and more, all arranged by subject. Say you're interested in Animals. One click takes you to the Animals choice page (below).

⇓ **CREATURE FEATURES.** Click to go to the National Geographic Kids' animal site. Click on an animal, and you will find a full feature about it, including photos, video, a range map, and other fun info.

⇓ **CRITTERCAM.** Scientists put video cameras on animals to learn about the animal from its point of view. Click to see those videos, learn about the project, play games such as exploring the virtual world of a seal, and more.

⇐ **ANIMALS A–Z.** This choice takes you to the animal site for adults and older kids. Use the list of animals in the upper right-hand corner of the page. Clicking on an animal name takes you to the profile of that animal.

3. SEARCH BY ICON

⇐ **SELECT ONE OF FIVE ICONS.** If you want to find all the videos referenced in the atlas, or all of the audios, photos, or games, click on one of the icons. A list will drop down. Choose from the list, and you're there! Clicking on Blackbeard takes you to a trailer for a National Geographic Channel film.

THE PHYSICAL UNITED STATES

Stretching from the Atlantic in the east to the Pacific in the west, the United States is the third largest country in area in the world. Its physical diversity ranges from mountains to fertile plains and dry deserts. Shading on the map indicates changes in elevation, while colors suggest different vegetation patterns.

⇨ ALASKA AND HAWAI'I. In addition to the states located on the main landmass, the U.S. has two states—Alaska and Hawai'i—that are not directly connected to the other 48 states. If Alaska and Hawai'i were shown in their correct relative sizes and locations, the map would not fit on the page. The locator globe shows the correct relative size and location of each.

San Francisco

Coast Ranges   **Sierra Nevada**   **Great Basin**   **Rocky Mountains**

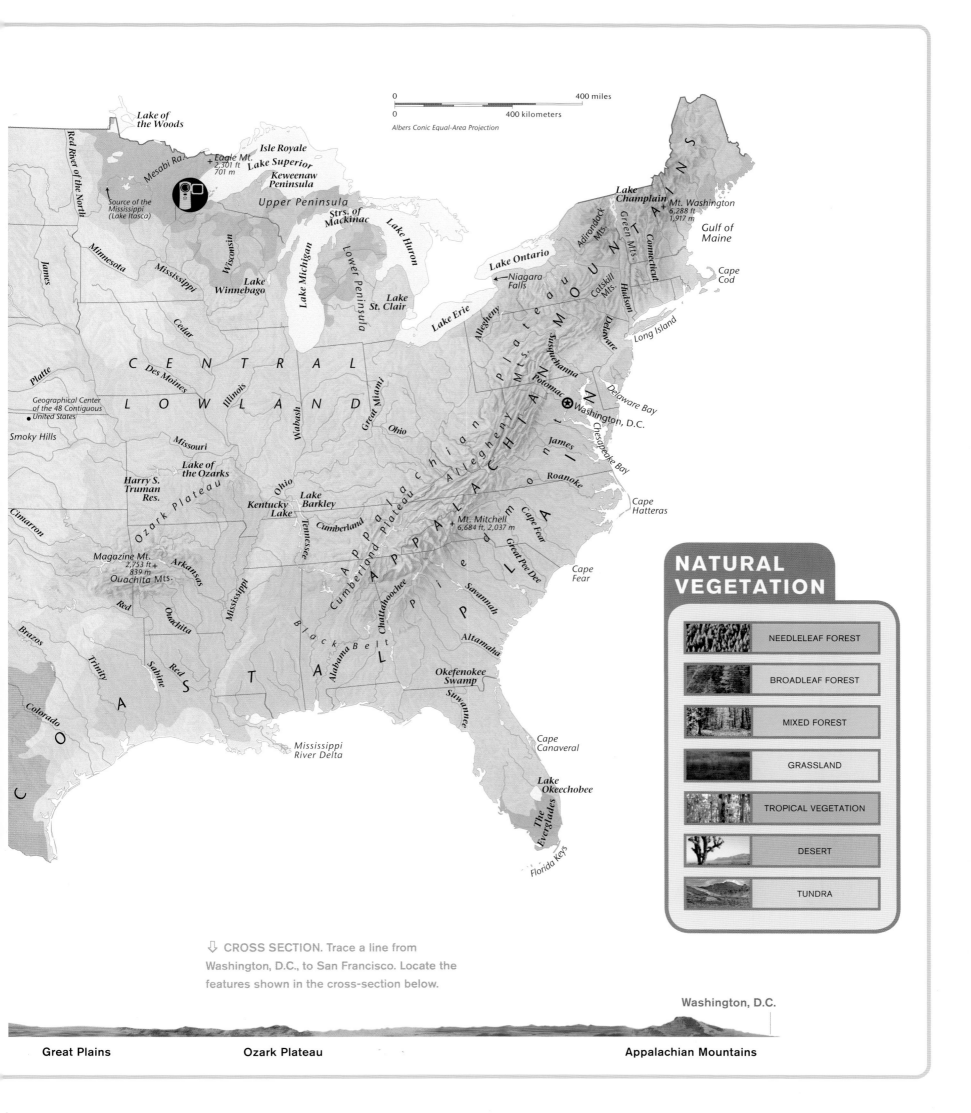

0   400 miles
0   400 kilometers
Albers Conic Equal-Area Projection

Lake of the Woods

Isle Royale

Eagle Mt.
2,301 ft
701 m
Mesabi Ra.
Lake Superior
Keweenaw Peninsula

Red River of the North

Source of the Mississippi (Lake Itasca)

Upper Peninsula

Strs. of Mackinac

Lake Huron

Minnesota

Wisconsin

James

Lake Michigan

Lower Peninsula

Lake St. Clair

Lake Champlain

ADIRONDACK MTS.

Green Mts.

Mt. Washington
6,288 ft
1,917 m

Gulf of Maine

Cape Cod

Lake Ontario

Niagara Falls

Catskill Mts.

Hudson

Connecticut

Long Island

Cedar

Lake Winnebago

Mississippi

Lake Erie

Allegheny

Plateau Mts.

Delaware

Platte

C E N T R A L

Des Moines

Illinois

Great Miami

Ohio

Susquehanna

Potomac

Washington, D.C.

Delaware Bay

Geographical Center of the 48 Contiguous United States

L O W L A N D

Wabash

James

Chesapeake Bay

Smoky Hills

Missouri

Ohio

Roanoke

A P P A L A C H I A N   M O U N T A I N S

Cimarron

Lake of the Ozarks

Harry S. Truman Res.

Ozark Plateau

Kentucky Lake

Lake Barkley

Cumberland

Tennessee

Cumberland Plateau

Mt. Mitchell
6,684 ft, 2,037 m

Cape Fear

Great Pee Dee

Cape Hatteras

Magazine Mt.
2,753 ft
839 m
Ouachita Mts.

Arkansas

Mississippi

Appalachian Plateau

P i e d m o n t

Cape Fear

Red

Ouachita

Savannah

Brazos

C O A S T A L

Black Belt

Alabama

Chattahoochee

Altamaha

Cimarron

Trinity

Sabine

Red

Okefenokee Swamp

Suwannee

Colorado

P L A I N

Cape Canaveral

Mississippi River Delta

Lake Okeechobee

The Everglades

Florida Keys

NATURAL VEGETATION

	NEEDLELEAF FOREST
	BROADLEAF FOREST
	MIXED FOREST
	GRASSLAND
	TROPICAL VEGETATION
	DESERT
	TUNDRA

⇩ CROSS SECTION. Trace a line from Washington, D.C., to San Francisco. Locate the features shown in the cross-section below.

Washington, D.C.

Great Plains   Ozark Plateau   Appalachian Mountains

NATURAL ENVIRONMENT

A big part of the natural environment of the United States is the climate. With humid areas near the coasts, dry interior regions far from any major water body, and land areas that extend from northern Alaska to southern Florida and Hawai'i, the country experiences great variation in climate. Location is the key. Distance from the Equator, nearness to water, wind patterns, temperature of nearby water bodies, and elevation are things that influence temperature and precipitation. Climate affects the types of vegetation that grow in a particular place and plays a part in soil formation.

CHANGING CLIMATE

North Pole

Summer Arctic Sea
Ice Boundary in 1979

Scientists are concerned that a recent warming trend may be more than a natural cycle and that human activity may be a contributing factor. An increase in average temperatures could result in more severe storms, changes in precipitation patterns, and the spread of deserts. Rising temperatures may also play a part in the melting of glaciers, which could lead to a rise in ocean levels and the shrinking of the Arctic ice cover. NASA satellite images indicate that Arctic ice is shrinking as much as 9 percent each decade. Many believe that this puts polar bears at risk, since they normally hunt and raise their young on ice floes.

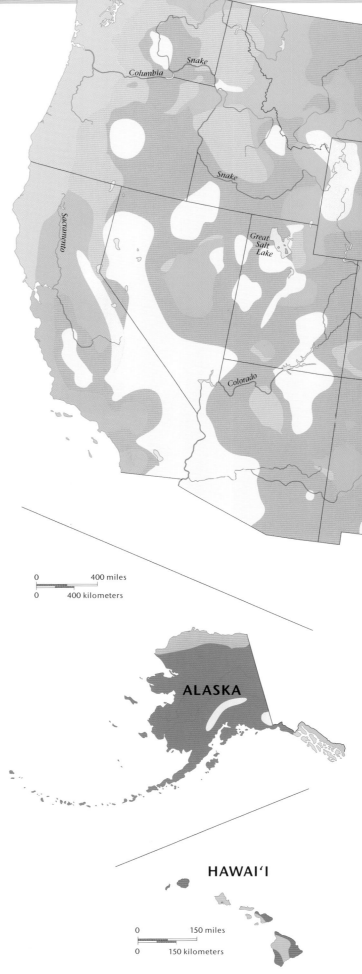

Columbia

Snake

Snake

Sacramento

Great Salt Lake

Colorado

| 0 | | 400 miles |
| 0 | | 400 kilometers |

ALASKA

HAWAI'I

| 0 | | 150 miles |
| 0 | | 150 kilometers |

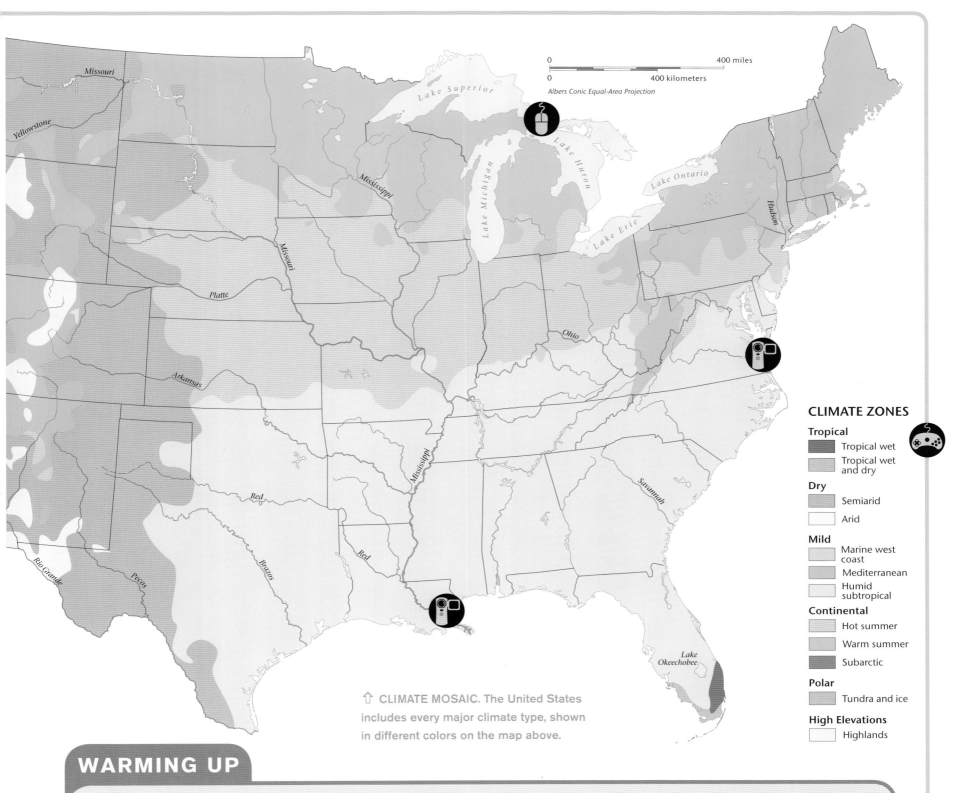

0   400 miles
0   400 kilometers
Albers Conic Equal-Area Projection

⇧ CLIMATE MOSAIC. The United States includes every major climate type, shown in different colors on the map above.

CLIMATE ZONES

Tropical
- Tropical wet
- Tropical wet and dry

Dry
- Semiarid
- Arid

Mild
- Marine west coast
- Mediterranean
- Humid subtropical

Continental
- Hot summer
- Warm summer
- Subarctic

Polar
- Tundra and ice

High Elevations
- Highlands

WARMING UP

Temperatures normally fluctuate from year to year, but evidence indicates that Earth is experiencing a warming pattern unlike any in recorded history. Data for major U.S. cities show a clear trend of rising average temperatures. The increase could be as much as 3 to 9 degrees Fahrenheit (1.7° to 5°C) by the end of the 21st century.

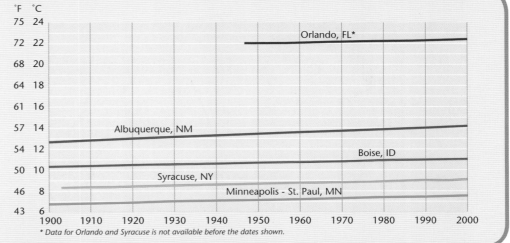

* Data for Orlando and Syracuse is not available before the dates shown.

NATURAL HAZARDS

The natural environment of the United States provides much diversity, but it also poses many dangers, especially when people locate homes and businesses in places at risk of natural disasters. Tornados bring destructive winds, and hurricanes bring strong winds, rain, and more; shifting of Earth's crust along fault lines rattles buildings; flood waters and wildfires threaten lives and property. More than one-third of the U.S. population lives in hazard-prone areas. Compare this natural disasters map to the population map on pages 18–19.

Mount Baker
Glacier Peak
North Cascades, 1872
Mount Rainier
Mount St. Helens
Columbia River, 1996
Columbia
Western fire season, 2000
Mount Hood
Three Sisters
West Coast flooding, 1982–1983, 1996–1997
Hebgen Lake, 1959
Newberry Crater
California-Oregon Coast, 1873
Medicine Lake
Snake
Mount Shasta
Tsunami, 1964
California flooding, 1995
Lassen Peak
Western fire season, 1994
Oakland firestorm, 1991
Long Valley Caldera
San Francisco, 1906
Owens Valley, 1872
Kern County, 1952
Fort Tejon, 1857
Landers, 1992
Southern California Wildfires, 1993, 2003, 2007
Colorado
Imperial Valley, 1892
Gila

ALASKA

Alaska has about 80 major volcanic centers.
More earthquakes occur in Alaska than in the other 49 states combined.

Prince William Sound, 1964
Novarupta, 1912
Tsunami, 1964
Tsunami, 1958
Tsunami, 1946, 1957

0   400 miles
0   400 kilometers

HAWAI'I

Iniki, 1992
Haleakala
Tsunami, 1946
Tsunami, 1868, 1946
Hualalai
Mauna Loa
Kilauea
Kau District, 1868
Loihi

0   150 miles
0   150 kilometers

NATURAL HAZARDS

BLIZZARD. Severe storm with bitter cold temperatures and wind-whipped snow and ice particles that reduce visibility to less than 650 feet (198 m), paralyzing transportation systems

FLOOD. Inundation of buildings or roadways caused by overflow of a river or stream swollen by heavy rainfall or rapid snowmelt; may involve displacement of people

DROUGHT. Long and continuous period of abnormally low precipitation, resulting in water shortages that negatively impact people, animals, and plant life; may result in crop loss

HURRICANE. Tropical storm in the Atlantic, Caribbean, Gulf of Mexico, or eastern Pacific with a minimum sustained wind speed of 74 miles per hour (119 kmph)

ICE STORM. Damaging accumulations of ice associated with freezing rain; may pull down trees or utility lines, causing extensive damage and creating dangerous travel conditions

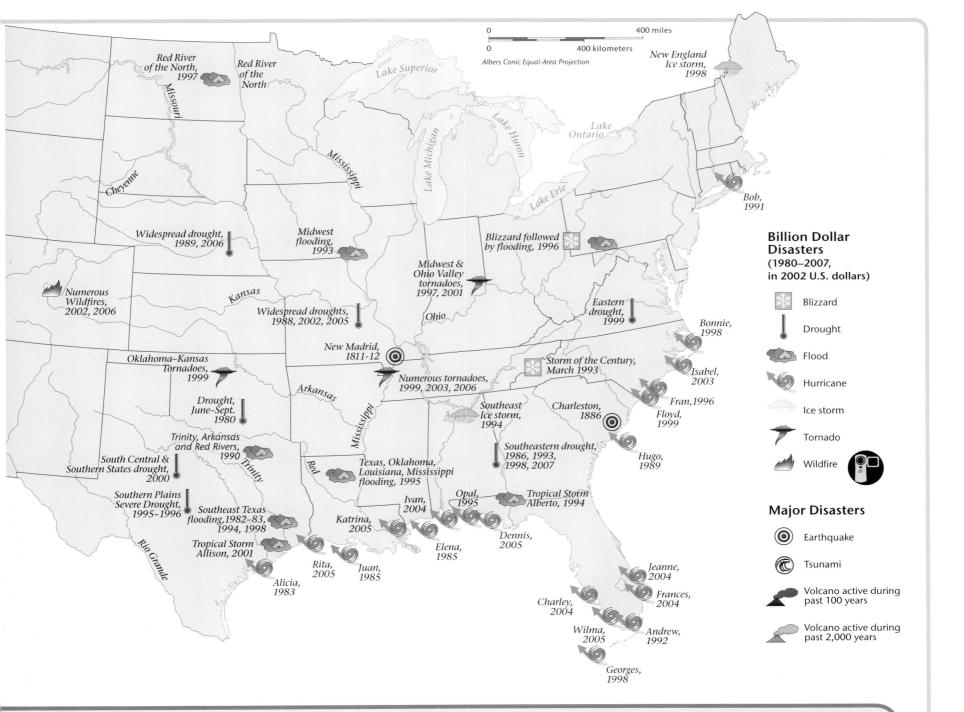

Red River
of the North,
1997

Red River
of the
North

Missouri

Lake Superior

New England
Ice storm,
1998

Cheyenne

Widespread drought,
1989, 2006

Midwest
flooding,
1993

Lake Michigan

Lake Huron

Lake
Ontario

Lake Erie

Blizzard followed
by flooding, 1996

Bob,
1991

Numerous
Wildfires,
2002, 2006

Kansas

Widespread droughts,
1988, 2002, 2005

Ohio

Midwest &
Ohio Valley
tornadoes,
1997, 2001

Eastern
drought,
1999

Bonnie,
1998

Oklahoma–Kansas
Tornadoes,
1999

New Madrid,
1811-12

Numerous tornadoes,
1999, 2003, 2006

Storm of the Century,
March 1993

Isabel,
2003

Arkansas

Drought,
June–Sept.
1980

Southeast
Ice storm,
1994

Charleston,
1886

Fran,1996

Mississippi

Floyd,
1999

Trinity, Arkansas
and Red Rivers,
1990

Trinity

Red

Texas, Oklahoma,
Louisiana, Mississippi
flooding, 1995

Southeastern drought,
1986, 1993,
1998, 2007

Hugo,
1989

South Central &
Southern States drought,
2000

Southern Plains
Severe Drought,
1995–1996

Southeast Texas
flooding,1982–83,
1994, 1998

Katrina,
2005

Ivan,
2004

Opal,
1995

Tropical Storm
Alberto, 1994

Tropical Storm
Allison, 2001

Rio Grande

Rita,
2005

Juan,
1985

Elena,
1985

Dennis,
2005

Alicia,
1983

Jeanne,
2004

Frances,
2004

Charley,
2004

Wilma,
2005

Andrew,
1992

Georges,
1998

400 miles
400 kilometers
Albers Conic Equal-Area Projection

Billion Dollar Disasters
(1980–2007,
in 2002 U.S. dollars)

- Blizzard
- Drought
- Flood
- Hurricane
- Ice storm
- Tornado
- Wildfire

Major Disasters

- Earthquake
- Tsunami
- Volcano active during past 100 years
- Volcano active during past 2,000 years

TORNADO. Violently rotating column of air that, when it reaches the ground, is the most damaging of all atmospheric phenomena; most common in the central U.S.

WILDFIRE. Free-burning, uncontained fire in a forest or grassland; may result from lightning strikes or accidental or deliberate human activity in areas where conditions are dry

EARTHQUAKE. Shaking or vibration created by the energy released by movement of Earth's crust along plate boundaries; can cause structural damage and loss of life

TSUNAMI. Series of unusually large ocean waves caused by an underwater earthquake, landslide, or volcanic eruption; very destructive in coastal areas

VOLCANO. Vent or opening in Earth's surface through which molten rock called lava, ash, and gases are released; often associated with tectonic plate boundaries

THE POLITICAL UNITED STATES

Like a giant patchwork quilt, the United States is made up of 50 states, each uniquely different but together making a national fabric held together by a Constitution and a federal government. State boundaries, outlined in various colors on the map, set apart internal political units within the country. The national capital—Washington, D.C.—is marked by a star in a double circle on the map. The capital of each state is marked by a star in a single circle.

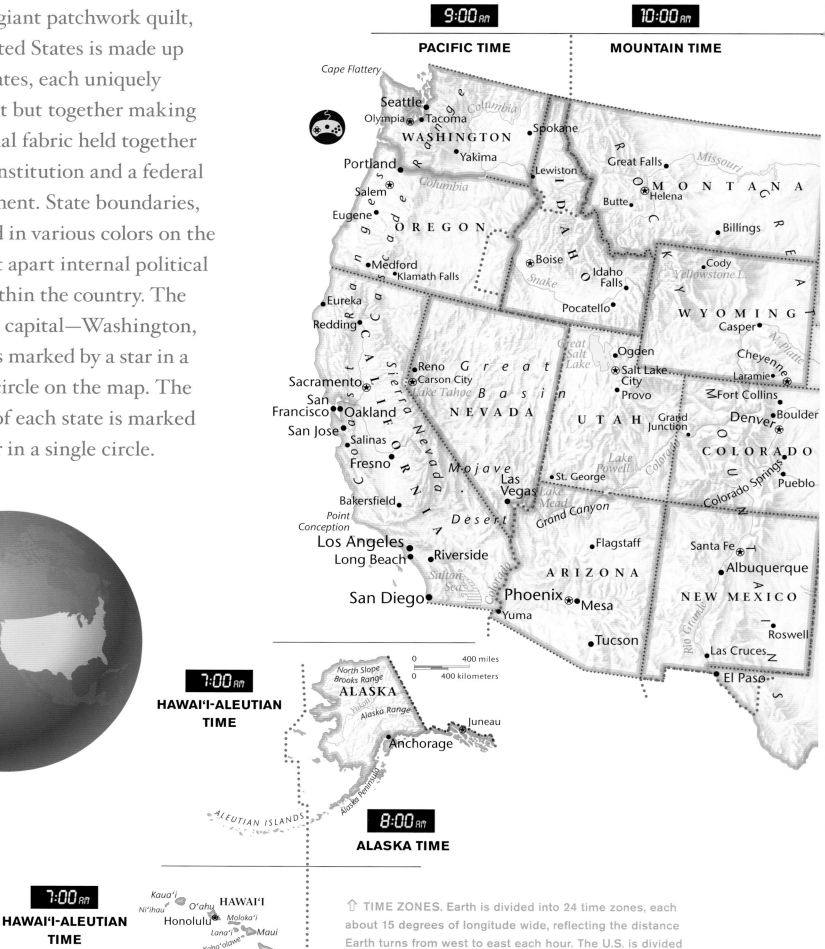

9:00 AM
PACIFIC TIME

10:00 AM
MOUNTAIN TIME

Cape Flattery

Seattle
Olympia • Tacoma
WASHINGTON
Yakima
Portland
Salem
Eugene
OREGON
Medford
Klamath Falls
Eureka
Redding
Columbia
Columbia

Spokane
Lewiston
IDAHO
Boise
Idaho Falls
Pocatello
Snake

Great Falls
Butte • Helena
MONTANA
Billings
Cody
Yellowstone L.
WYOMING
Casper
Missouri

Sacramento
San Francisco • Oakland
San Jose
Salinas
Fresno
Bakersfield
Point Conception
Los Angeles
Long Beach • Riverside
San Diego
CALIFORNIA
Sierra Nevada
Reno
Carson City
Lake Tahoe
Great Basin
NEVADA
Mojave
Desert
Las Vegas
Lake Mead
Salton Sea

Great Salt Lake
Ogden
Salt Lake City
Provo
UTAH
Grand Junction
Lake Powell
St. George
Grand Canyon
Colorado
Flagstaff
ARIZONA
Phoenix • Mesa
Yuma
Tucson

Cheyenne
Laramie
Fort Collins
Denver • Boulder
COLORADO
Colorado Springs
Pueblo
Na Platte

Santa Fe
Albuquerque
NEW MEXICO
Roswell
Las Cruces
El Paso
Rio Grande

0 — 400 miles
0 — 400 kilometers

7:00 AM
HAWAI'I-ALEUTIAN TIME

North Slope
Brooks Range
ALASKA
Yukon
Alaska Range
Juneau
Anchorage
Alaska Peninsula
ALEUTIAN ISLANDS

8:00 AM
ALASKA TIME

7:00 AM
HAWAI'I-ALEUTIAN TIME

Kaua'i
Ni'ihau • O'ahu HAWAI'I
Honolulu • Moloka'i
Lana'i • Maui
Kaho'olawe
Hilo
Hawai'i

0 — 150 mi
0 — 150 km

⇧ TIME ZONES. Earth is divided into 24 time zones, each about 15 degrees of longitude wide, reflecting the distance Earth turns from west to east each hour. The U.S. is divided into six time zones, indicated by red dotted lines on the maps. When it is noon in Boston, what is the time in Seattle?

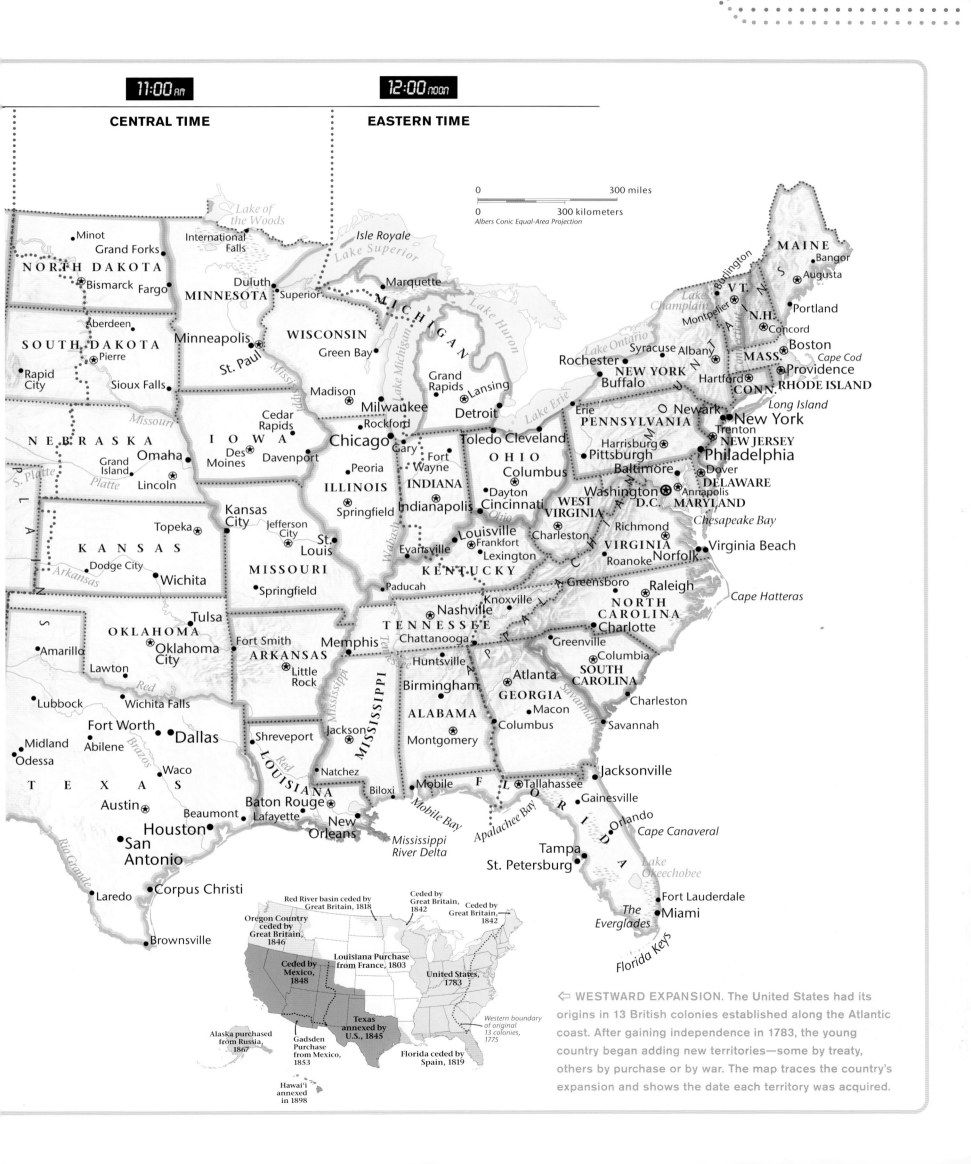

11:00 AM — **CENTRAL TIME**

12:00 noon — **EASTERN TIME**

0 ____ 300 miles
0 ____ 300 kilometers
Albers Conic Equal-Area Projection

Minot
Grand Forks
NORTH DAKOTA
Bismarck Fargo
Aberdeen
SOUTH DAKOTA
Pierre
Rapid City
Sioux Falls
International Falls
Lake of the Woods
Duluth
MINNESOTA Superior
Lake Superior
Isle Royale
MINNESOTA
Minneapolis
St. Paul
Missouri
WISCONSIN
Green Bay
Madison
MICHIGAN
Lake Michigan
Grand Rapids Lansing
Lake Huron
MAINE
Bangor
Augusta
Lake Champlain VT. N.H.
Montpelier Concord
Portland
Burlington
Syracuse Albany
Rochester
Lake Ontario
NEW YORK
Buffalo
MASS. *Cape Cod*
Hartford Providence
CONN. RHODE ISLAND

NEBRASKA
Grand Island
Lincoln
Omaha
S. Platte
Platte
IOWA
Cedar Rapids
Des Moines
Davenport
Chicago
Peoria
Rockford
Milwaukee
ILLINOIS
Springfield
INDIANA
Indianapolis
Fort Wayne
Gary
Toledo Cleveland
OHIO
Columbus
Dayton
Cincinnati
Erie
PENNSYLVANIA
Pittsburgh
Harrisburg
Newark
New York
Trenton
NEW JERSEY
Philadelphia
Baltimore Dover
DELAWARE
Washington D.C. Annapolis
MARYLAND
Long Island

Kansas City
Topeka
Jefferson City
KANSAS
Dodge City
Wichita
Arkansas
St. Louis
MISSOURI
Springfield
Louisville
Evansville
Frankfort
Lexington
KENTUCKY
Paducah
Ohio
WEST VIRGINIA
Charleston
Richmond
VIRGINIA
Roanoke
Norfolk Virginia Beach
Chesapeake Bay
Greensboro
Raleigh
Cape Hatteras

OKLAHOMA
Tulsa
Oklahoma City
Amarillo
Lawton
Fort Smith
ARKANSAS
Little Rock
Nashville
Knoxville
TENNESSEE
Chattanooga
Memphis
Huntsville
NORTH CAROLINA
Charlotte
Greenville
Columbia
SOUTH CAROLINA
Charleston

Lubbock
Wichita Falls
Fort Worth
Abilene
Dallas
Midland
Odessa
Waco
Red
Brazos
Shreveport
LOUISIANA
Jackson
MISSISSIPPI
Birmingham
ALABAMA
Montgomery
Columbus
Macon
GEORGIA
Atlanta
Savannah
Savannah

TEXAS
Austin
San Antonio
Houston
Beaumont
Lafayette
Baton Rouge
New Orleans
Natchez
Biloxi
Mobile
Mobile Bay
Tallahassee
Apalachee Bay
Jacksonville
Gainesville
Orlando
Cape Canaveral
Tampa
St. Petersburg
Lake Okeechobee
Fort Lauderdale
Miami
The Everglades
FLORIDA
Florida Keys
Mississippi River Delta

Laredo
Corpus Christi
Brownsville
Rio Grande

Red River basin ceded by Great Britain, 1818
Ceded by Great Britain, 1842
Ceded by Great Britain, 1842
Oregon Country ceded by Great Britain, 1846
Louisiana Purchase from France, 1803
United States, 1783
Ceded by Mexico, 1848
Texas annexed by U.S., 1845
Western boundary of original 13 colonies, 1775
Alaska purchased from Russia, 1867
Gadsden Purchase from Mexico, 1853
Florida ceded by Spain, 1819
Hawai'i annexed in 1898

⇐ WESTWARD EXPANSION. The United States had its origins in 13 British colonies established along the Atlantic coast. After gaining independence in 1783, the young country began adding new territories—some by treaty, others by purchase or by war. The map traces the country's expansion and shows the date each territory was acquired.

POPULATION

Three hundred million and growing! The population of the United States topped the 300 million mark in 2006, and it continues to grow by more than 2 million people each year. Before the arrival of European settlers, the population consisted of Native Americans living in tribal groups scattered across the country. In the 16th and 17th centuries, Europeans, some with slaves from Africa, settled first along the eastern seaboard and later moved westward. In 1790 the U.S. population was not quite 4 million people. Today, New York City alone has a population more than double that number. The country's population is unevenly distributed. The map shows the number of people per square mile for each county in every state. Greatest densities are in the East and along the West Coast, especially around major cities. The most rapid growth is occurring in the South and the West—an area referred to as the Sunbelt—as well as in suburban areas around cities.

⇧ COMMUTER RUSH HOUR. Crowds of people press toward trains in New York City's Grand Central station. With more than three-quarters of the population living in urban areas, commuter transportation poses a major challenge to cities in the United States.

⇨ WHERE WE LIVE. The first U.S. census in 1790 revealed that only 5 percent of people lived in towns. As industry has grown and agriculture has become increasingly mechanized, people have left farms (green), moving to urban places (blue) and their surrounding suburbs (orange).

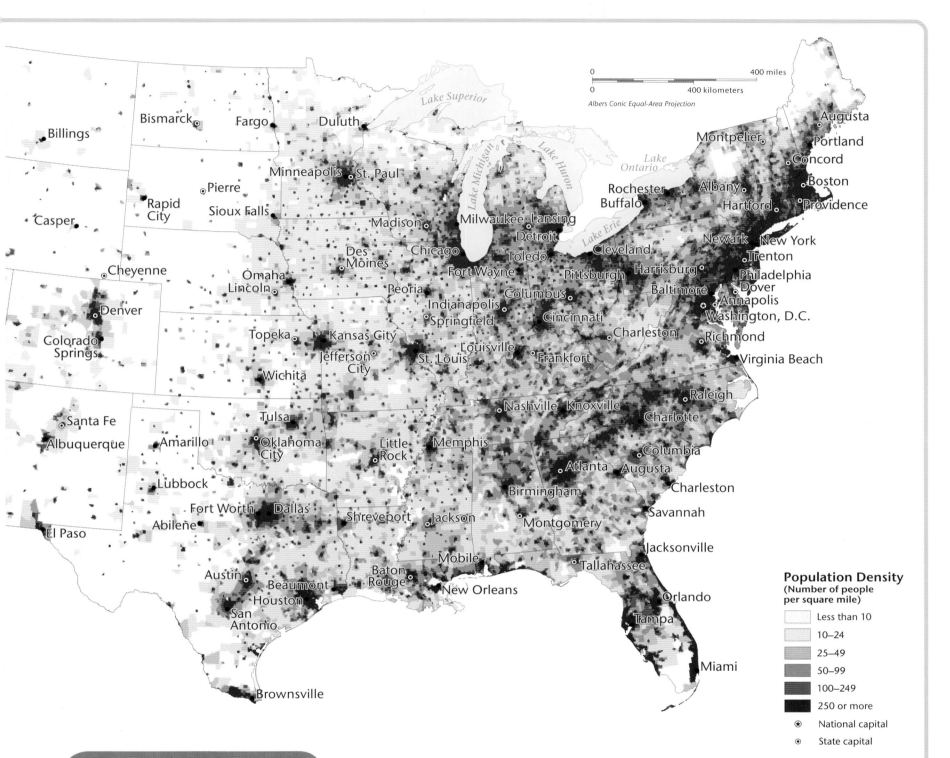

0   400 miles
0   400 kilometers
Albers Conic Equal-Area Projection

Population Density
(Number of people
per square mile)

- Less than 10
- 10–24
- 25–49
- 50–99
- 100–249
- 250 or more
- ⊛ National capital
- ⊙ State capital

HOW OLD ARE WE?

Population pyramids show the distribution of population by sex and age groups, called cohorts. In 1960 the largest cohorts, born after World War II and known as Baby Boomers, were under 15 years of age. By 2000 Baby Boomers had become middle-age. By 2040 they will reach the top of the pyramid.

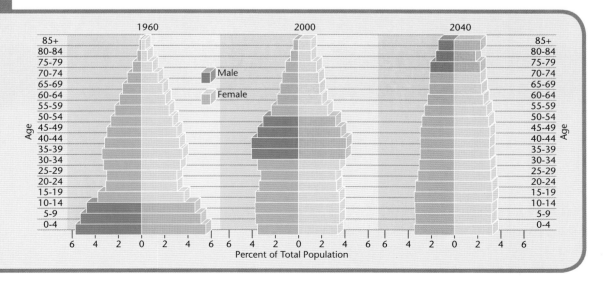

1960   2000   2040

Male

Female

Percent of Total Population

PEOPLE ON THE MOVE

From earliest human history, the land of the United States has been a focus of migration. Native peoples arrived thousands of years ago. The first European settlers came in the 16th and 17th centuries, and slave ships brought people from Africa. Today, people are still on the move. Since the mid-20th century, most international migrants have come from Latin America—especially Mexico and countries of Central America and the Caribbean—and Asia, particularly China, the Philippines, and India. While most of the population is still of European descent, certain regions have large minority concentrations, as shown on the map, that influence local cultural landscapes.

⇧ BRIDGE OF HOPE. Many Mexicans enter the U.S. (foreground) by bridges across the Rio Grande, such as this one between Nuevo Laredo, Mexico, and Laredo, Texas.

⇧ IMMIGRANT INFLUENCE. With Hispanics making up almost 15 percent of the population, signs in Spanish are popping up everywhere—even at voting areas.

⇧ SUNBELT SPRAWL. Spreading suburbs are becoming a common feature of the desert Southwest as people flock to the Sunbelt.

PEOPLE
ON THE MOVE

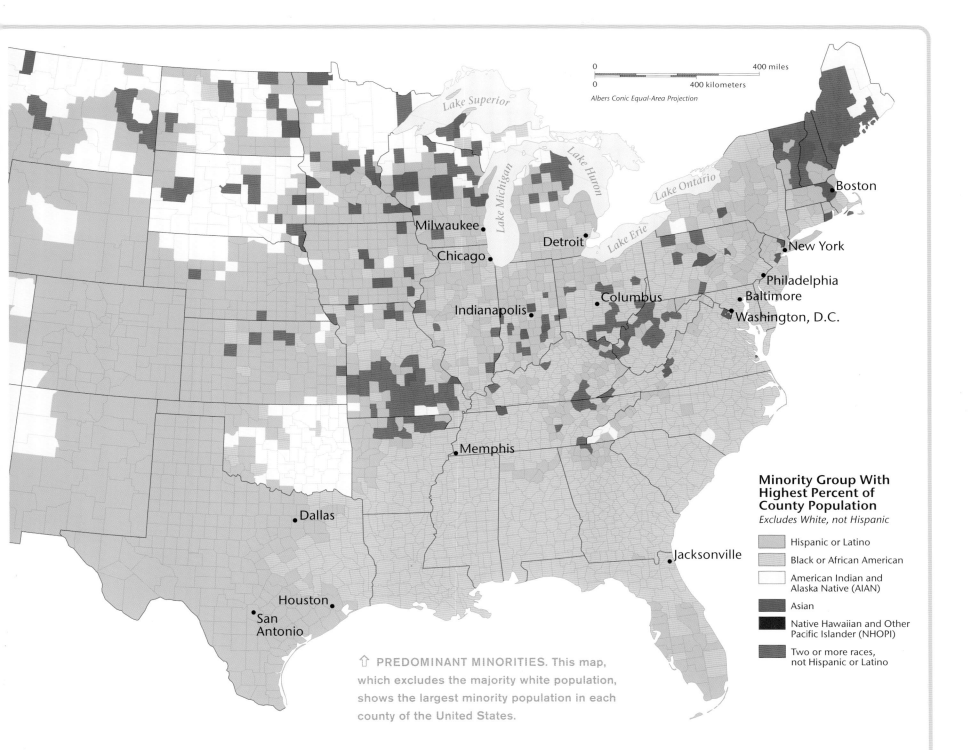

**Minority Group With
Highest Percent of
County Population**
Excludes White, not Hispanic

Hispanic or Latino

Black or African American

American Indian and
Alaska Native (AIAN)

Asian

Native Hawaiian and Other
Pacific Islander (NHOPI)

Two or more races,
not Hispanic or Latino

⇧ PREDOMINANT MINORITIES. This map,
which excludes the majority white population,
shows the largest minority population in each
county of the United States.

POPULATION SHIFT

In the last half century, people have
begun moving from the historical
industrial and agricultural regions of
the Northeast and Midwest toward
the South and West, attracted by
the promise of jobs, generally lower
living costs, and a more relaxed way
of life. This trend can be seen in the
population growth patterns, shown
in the map at right.

**Percent Change in Total Population
from 1990 to 2000 (by State)**

More than 25   13–25   Less than 13

GETTING GREEN

Every day the media is filled with stories about global warming, pollution, and dwindling resources. Headlines warn of environmental risks that may threaten our way of life. The United States is the source of a quarter of the world's greenhouse gas emissions, and Americans generate more than 250 million tons of trash each year. The average American also uses 32 times more resources than a person in the African country of Kenya. But there's a bright side to these grim statistics. We can make a positive difference to the environment by making simple lifestyle changes. Scientists and engineers have developed energy efficient appliances, cars that run on alternative fuels, and products made from recycled paper and plastics. But it is up to each of us to make changes that take advantage of these environment-friendly developments.

Columbia

Snake

Colorado

Gila

| 0 | 400 miles |
| 0 | 400 kilometers |

| 0 | 150 mi |
| 0 | 150 km |

THINGS YOU CAN DO

Each year the average American household generates more than 80 tons of carbon dioxide gases, uses 102,000 gallons (386,111 l) of water, and creates 3.3 tons of landfill waste. Improving the health of our environment begins with you. You can make a difference if you practice the 3 R's of "getting green."

- REDUCE resource consumption by turning off lights, the TV, computers, and other electronic devices when you leave the room. Close the faucet when you are not using the water. Avoid buying things you do not need.

- REUSE items whenever possible, rather than throwing things away. Consider whether a container can be used again or a pair of shoes repaired.

- RECYCLE paper, plastic, glass, and aluminum cans. Recycling makes for less landfill trash, plus it preserves resources by reusing old products to make new ones.

Visit the library or go online to learn what your community is doing to protect the environment.

Share the Road

⇧ GREEN STREETS. Biking to work or school reduces use of gasoline, a source of greenhouse gases, and it is healthy, too.

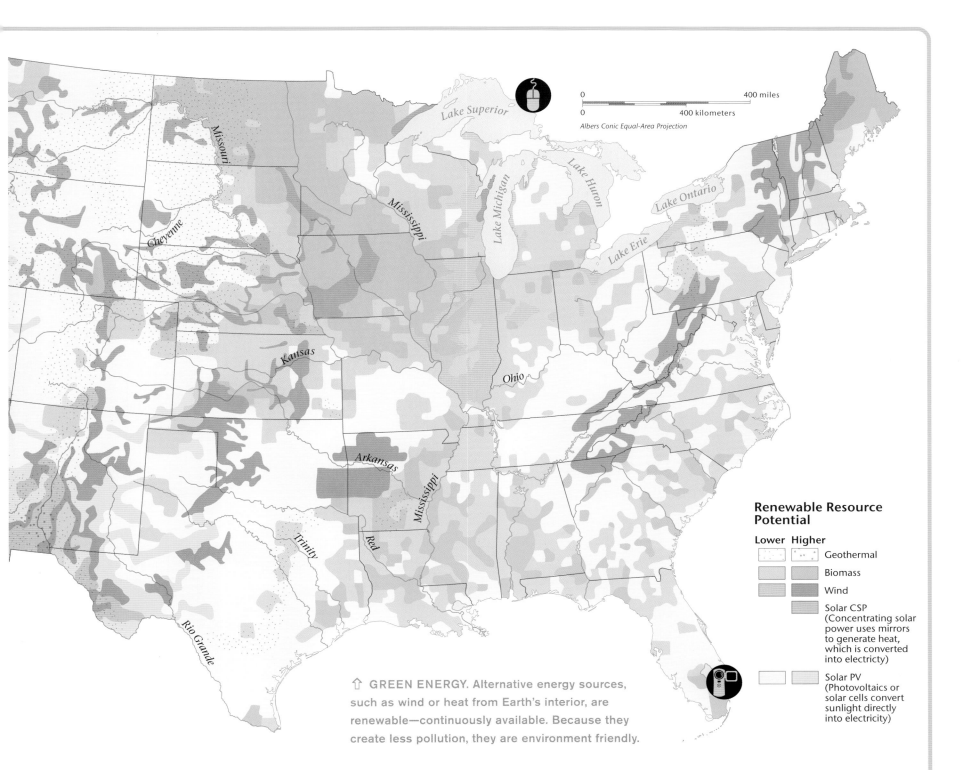

Lake Superior

0 400 miles
0 400 kilometers
Albers Conic Equal-Area Projection

Missouri

Lake Michigan

Lake Huron

Lake Ontario

Lake Erie

Cheyenne

Mississippi

Kansas

Ohio

Arkansas

Mississippi

Trinity

Red

Rio Grande

Renewable Resource Potential

Lower Higher
- Geothermal
- Biomass
- Wind
- Solar CSP (Concentrating solar power uses mirrors to generate heat, which is converted into electricty)
- Solar PV (Photovoltaics or solar cells convert sunlight directly into electricity)

⇧ GREEN ENERGY. Alternative energy sources, such as wind or heat from Earth's interior, are renewable—continuously available. Because they create less pollution, they are environment friendly.

⇐ GREEN GARDENING. An organic farmer turns a compost pile with a pitchfork. Compost is a natural fertilizer made from decayed plant material. It is good for the environment because it reuses natural materials and avoids the use of chemicals that can pollute soil and water.

⇐ RECYCLE. Bright blue trash collectors overflow with plastic containers waiting to go to a recycling center. Citizen participation is an important step toward reducing landfill waste and restoring the health of the environment.

THE NATION'S CAPITAL

THE NATION'S CAPITAL

Chosen as a compromise location between Northern and Southern interests and built on land ceded by Virginia and Maryland in the late 1700s, Washington, D.C., sits on a bank of the Potomac River. It is the seat of U.S. government and symbol of the country's history. Pierre L'Enfant, a French architect, was appointed by President George Washington to design the city, which is distinguished by a grid pattern cut by diagonal avenues. At the city's core is the National Mall, a broad park lined by monuments, museums, and stately government buildings.

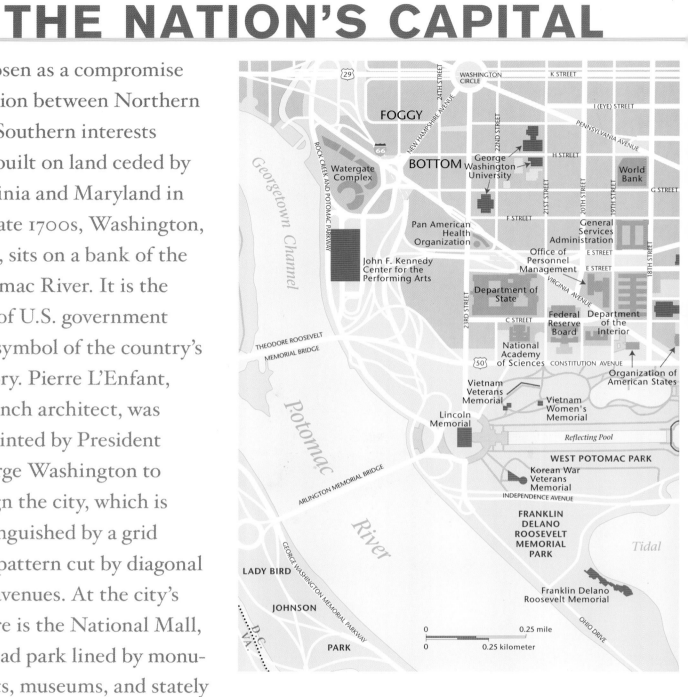

⇐ DISTRICT OF COLUMBIA. Originally on both sides of the Potomac River, the city returned land to Virginia in 1846.

⇐ GREAT LEADER. Abraham Lincoln, who was president during the Civil War and a strong opponent of slavery, is remembered in a monument that houses this seated statue at the west end of the National Mall.

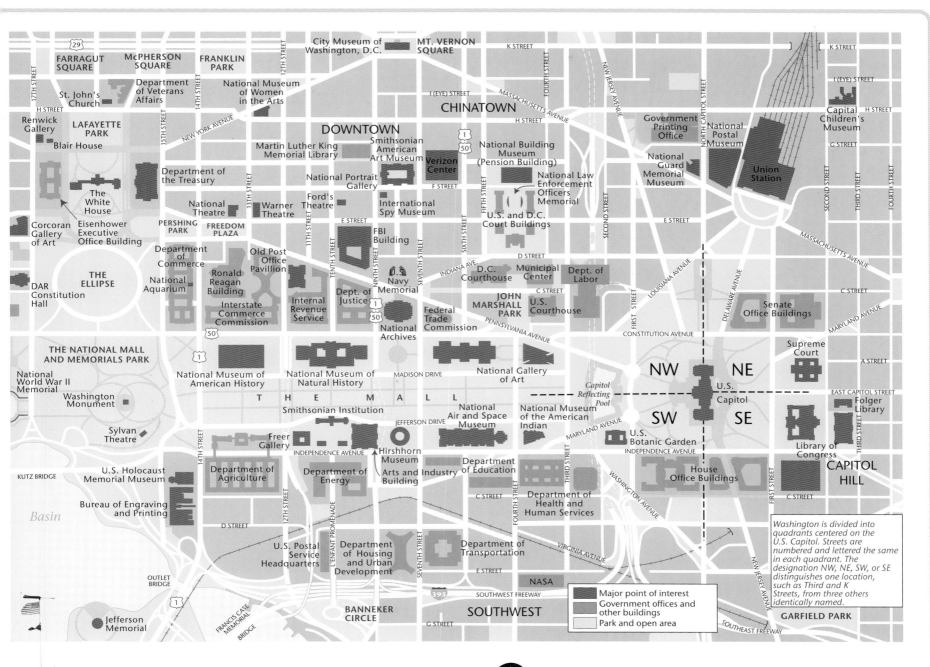

FARRAGUT
SQUARE

McPHERSON
SQUARE

FRANKLIN
PARK

City Museum of
Washington, D.C.

MT. VERNON
SQUARE

K Street

K Street

K Street

I (EYE) STREET

Capital
Children's
Museum

St. John's
Church

Department
of Veterans
Affairs

National Museum
of Women
in the Arts

CHINATOWN

H STREET

Government
Printing
Office

National
Postal
Museum

H Street

G Street

Renwick
Gallery

H STREET

LAFAYETTE
PARK

DOWNTOWN

Smithsonian
American
Art Museum

National Building
Museum
(Pension Building)

National
Guard
Memorial
Museum

Union
Station

Blair House

Martin Luther King
Memorial Library

Verizon
Center

National Law
Enforcement
Officers
Memorial

The
White
House

Department
of the Treasury

National Portrait
Gallery

F STREET

Corcoran
Gallery
of Art

Eisenhower
Executive
Office Building

National
Theatre

Warner
Theatre

Ford's
Theatre

International
Spy Museum

E STREET

U.S. and D.C.
Court Buildings

E Street

PERSHING
PARK

FREEDOM
PLAZA

FBI
Building

D STREET

DAR
Constitution
Hall

THE
ELLIPSE

Department
of Commerce

Old Post
Office
Pavillion

U.S.
Navy
Memorial

D.C.
Courthouse

Municipal
Center

Dept. of
Labor

Senate
Office Buildings

C STREET

National
Aquarium

Ronald
Reagan
Building

Internal
Revenue
Service

Dept. of
Justice

INDIANA AVE.

JOHN
MARSHALL
PARK

C Street

Supreme
Court

A STREET

THE NATIONAL MALL
AND MEMORIALS PARK

Interstate
Commerce
Commission

National
Archives

Federal
Trade
Commission

PENNSYLVANIA AVENUE

U.S.
Courthouse

CONSTITUTION AVENUE

NW | NE

EAST CAPITOL STREET

National
World War II
Memorial

National Museum of
American History

National Museum of
Natural History

MADISON DRIVE

National Gallery
of Art

Capitol
Reflecting
Pool

U.S.
Capitol

Folger
Library

Washington
Monument

THE MALL

Smithsonian Institution

JEFFERSON DRIVE

National
Air and Space
Museum

National Museum
of the American
Indian

SW | SE

Library of
Congress

Sylvan
Theatre

Freer
Gallery

Hirshhorn
Museum

INDEPENDENCE AVENUE

U.S.
Botanic Garden

INDEPENDENCE AVENUE

CAPITOL
HILL

KUTZ BRIDGE

U.S. Holocaust
Memorial Museum

Department of
Agriculture

Department of
Energy

Arts and Industry
Building

Department of
Education

Department of
Health and
Human Services

House
Office Buildings

C STREET

Basin

Bureau of Engraving
and Printing

D Street

C Street

U.S. Postal
Service
Headquarters

L'ENFANT PROMENADE

Department of
Housing and Urban
Development

Department of
Transportation

E Street

VIRGINIA AVENUE

OUTLET
BRIDGE

NASA

SOUTHWEST FREEWAY

395

SOUTHWEST

G Street

GARFIELD PARK

SOUTHEAST FREEWAY

Jefferson
Memorial

FRANCIS CASE
MEMORIAL
BRIDGE

BANNEKER
CIRCLE

Washington is divided into
quadrants centered on the
U.S. Capitol. Streets are
numbered and lettered the same
in each quadrant. The
designation NW, NE, SW, or SE
distinguishes one location,
such as Third and K
Streets, from three others
identically named.

- Major point of interest
- Government offices and other buildings
- Park and open area

KEEPER OF HISTORY. The Smithsonian
Institution, the world's largest museum, is actually
made up of 19 museums. Established in 1846,
the Smithsonian is sometimes
referred to as the nation's
attic because of its
large collections.

NATIONAL ICON. The gleaming dome of the U.S. Capitol, home
to the Senate and House of Representatives, rises above a group
of protesters on the eastern end of the National Mall.

THE REGION

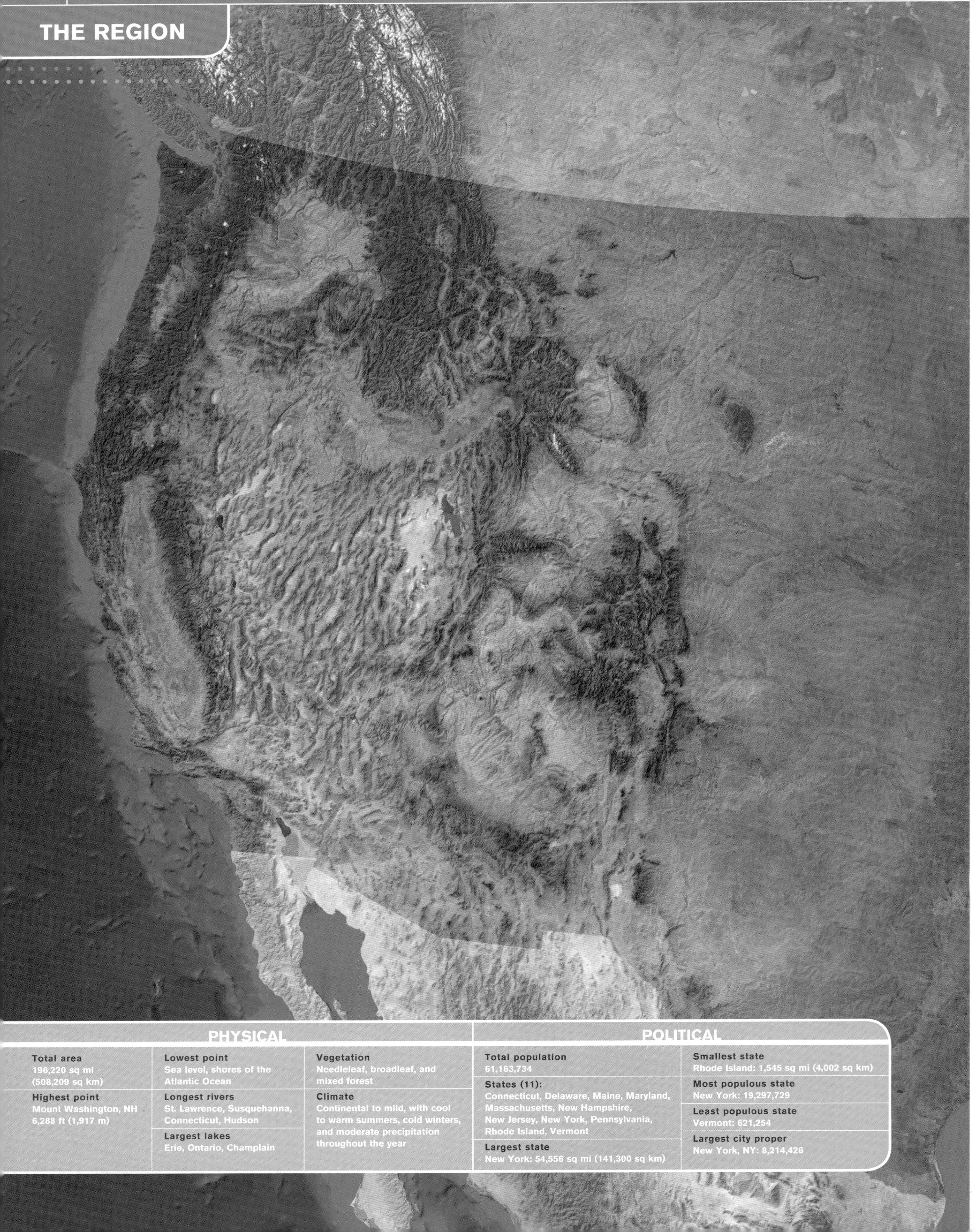

PHYSICAL

Total area
196,220 sq mi
(508,209 sq km)

Highest point
Mount Washington, NH
6,288 ft (1,917 m)

Lowest point
Sea level, shores of the
Atlantic Ocean

Longest rivers
St. Lawrence, Susquehanna,
Connecticut, Hudson

Largest lakes
Erie, Ontario, Champlain

Vegetation
Needleleaf, broadleaf, and
mixed forest

Climate
Continental to mild, with cool
to warm summers, cold winters,
and moderate precipitation
throughout the year

POLITICAL

Total population
61,163,734

States (11):
Connecticut, Delaware, Maine, Maryland,
Massachusetts, New Hampshire,
New Jersey, New York, Pennsylvania,
Rhode Island, Vermont

Largest state
New York: 54,556 sq mi (141,300 sq km)

Smallest state
Rhode Island: 1,545 sq mi (4,002 sq km)

Most populous state
New York: 19,297,729

Least populous state
Vermont: 621,254

Largest city proper
New York, NY: 8,214,426

The Northeast

NEW BRUNSWICK

NOVA SCOTIA

CANADA
U.S.

St. John

St. Croix

Bay of Fundy

Mt. Desert Island

Gulf of Maine

ATLANTIC OCEAN

Mt. Katahdin
+5,268 ft
+1,605 m

MAINE

Allagash

St. John

Penobscot

Kennebec

Saco

APPALACHIAN MOUNTAINS

Mt. Washington
6,288 ft
+1,917 m

White Mts.

N.H.

Merrimack

Cape Ann

Massachusetts Bay

Cape Cod

Nantucket Island

Martha's Vineyard

QUEBEC

Mt. Mansfield
+4,393 ft
+1,339 m

VT.

Green Mts.

Connecticut

+ Mt. Greylock
3,491 ft
1,064 m

MASSACHUSETTS

Jerimoth Hill
812 ft
+ 247 m

R.I.

Mt. Frissell
2,380 ft
725 m

CONN.

Long Island Sound

Long Island

CANADA
U.S.

Lake Champlain

Adirondack Mts.

Mt. Marcy
+ 5,344 ft
1,629 m

Hudson

High Point
1,803 ft
550 m

NEW JERSEY

Cape May

Raquette

Black

NEW YORK

APPALACHIAN

Mohawk

Oneida Lake

Catskill Mts.

Delaware

Fall Line

PINE PLAIN Barrens

COASTAL

Delaware Bay

DEL.

Delmarva Peninsula

CANADA

ST. LAWRENCE

ONTARIO

Erie Canal

Finger Lakes

Plateau

PENNSYLVANIA

PIEDMONT

448 ft
137 m

MARYLAND

D.C.

Chesapeake Bay

Lake Ontario

Genesee

Blue Ridge

Susquehanna

Niagara Falls

Lake Erie

Allegheny

Allegheny Mountains

Monongahela

Mt. Davis +
3,213 ft
919 m

Backbone Mt. +
3,360 ft
1,024 m

Ohio

Potomac

VIRGINIA

OHIO

WEST VIRGINIA

Lake Huron

100 miles

100 kilometers

Albers Conic Equal-Area Projection

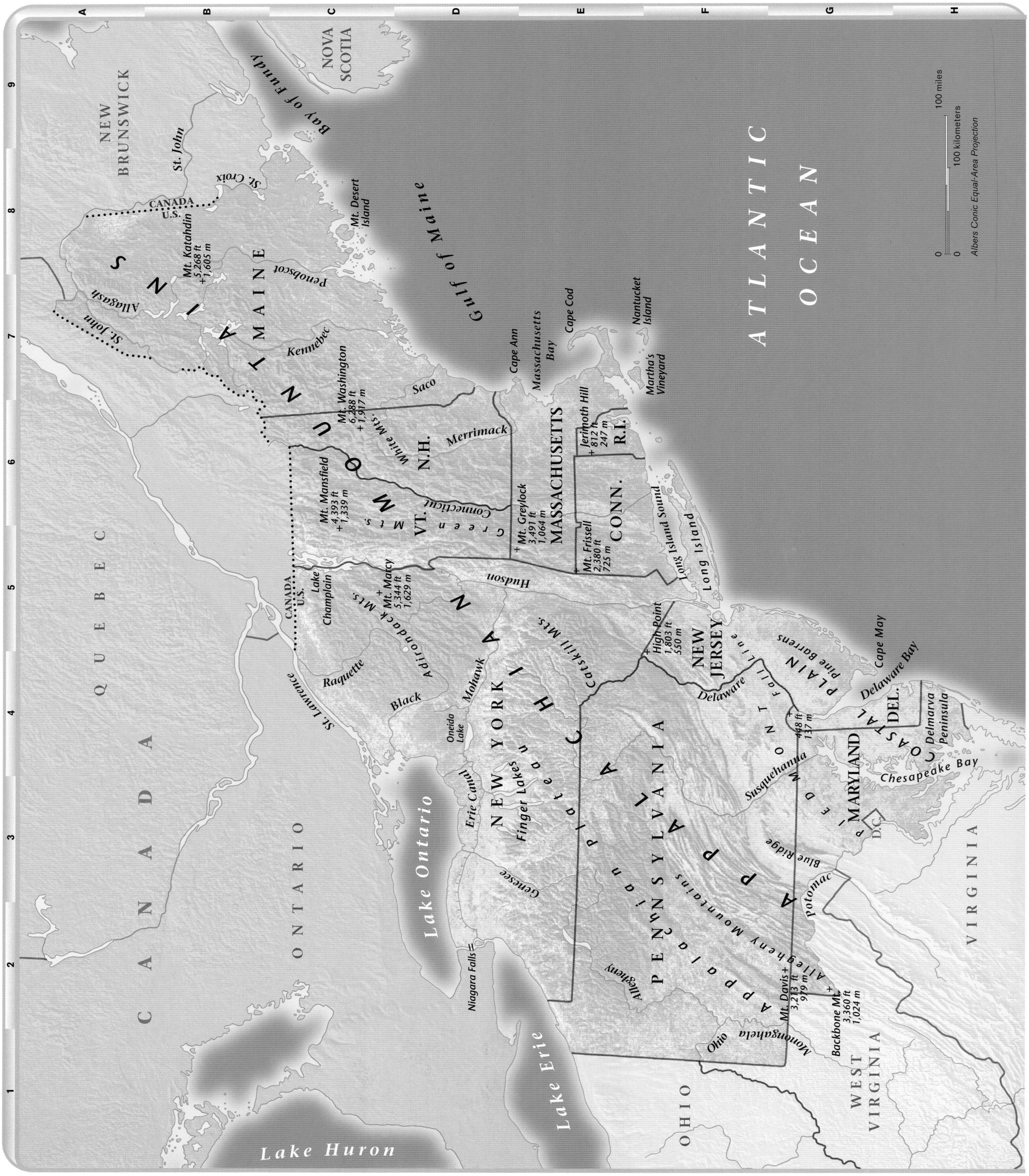

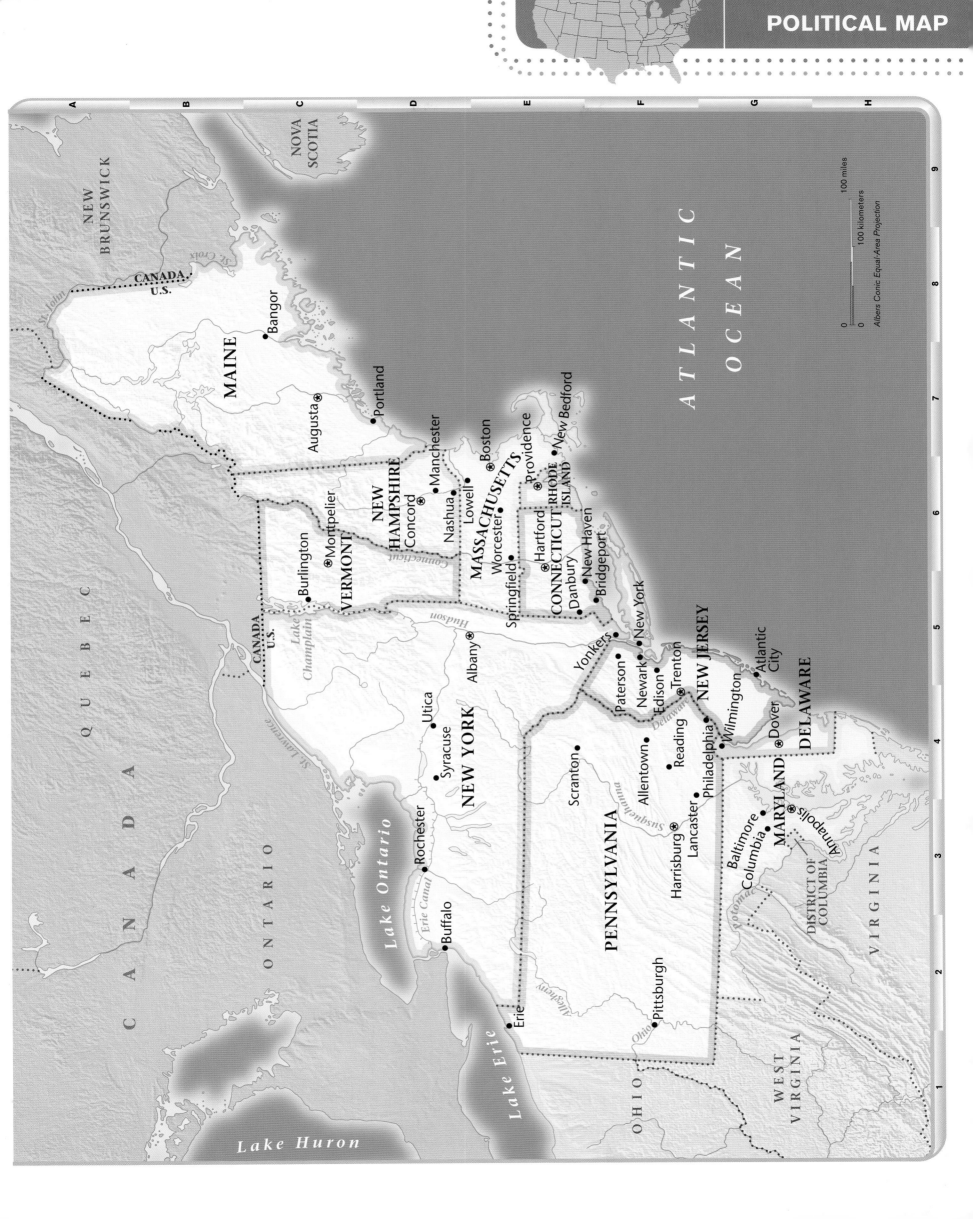

A B C D E F G H

9 8 7 6 5 4 3 2 1

100 miles
100 kilometers
Albers Conic Equal-Area Projection

NEW BRUNSWICK

NOVA SCOTIA

CANADA
U.S.

St. Croix

MAINE

• Bangor

Portland •

⊛ Augusta

QUEBEC

CANADA
U.S.

St. Lawrence

NEW HAMPSHIRE

VERMONT

Montpelier ⊛

Burlington •

Lake Champlain

Manchester •

Concord ⊛

Nashua •

Lowell •

Connecticut

MASSACHUSETTS

Worcester •

Boston ⊛

Providence ⊛

New Bedford •

RHODE ISLAND

Springfield •

Hartford ⊛

New Haven •

CONNECTICUT

Danbury •

Bridgeport •

New York •

Yonkers •

Hudson

Albany ⊛

NEW YORK

Utica •

Syracuse •

Rochester •

Buffalo •

Erie Canal

Erie •

Lake Ontario

Lake Erie

ONTARIO

CANADA

Scranton •

PENNSYLVANIA

Allentown •

Reading •

Harrisburg ⊛

Lancaster •

Pittsburgh •

Susquehanna

Allegheny

Ohio

Paterson •

Newark ⊛

Edison •

Trenton ⊛

NEW JERSEY

Atlantic City •

Delaware

Philadelphia •

Wilmington •

Dover ⊛

DELAWARE

Baltimore •

Columbia •

Annapolis ⊛

MARYLAND

Potomac

DISTRICT OF COLUMBIA

VIRGINIA

WEST VIRGINIA

OHIO

ATLANTIC OCEAN

Lake Huron

⇨ **DINNER DELICACY.** Lobsters, a favorite food for many people, turn bright red when cooked. These crustaceans live in the cold waters of the Atlantic Ocean and are caught using baited traps.

The Northeast
BIRTHPLACE OF A NATION

The United States had its beginnings in the Northeast region. Early European traders and settlers were quickly followed by immigrants from around the globe, making the region's population the most diverse in the country. The region includes the country's financial center, New York City, and its political capital, Washington, D.C. While the region boasts tranquil mountains, lakes, and rivers, its teeming cities have always been the heart of the Northeast. First there were water-powered textile mills, followed by manufacturing and shipbuilding industries. Today, service industries dominate the scene, but the economic pulse continues to beat strongly.

⇩ **MELTING POT.** From colonial times, the Northeast has been a gateway for immigration. These young girls, dressed in traditional saris and performing in an India Cultural Festival in New Jersey, reflect the rich diversity of the region.

⇨ **DEFENDER OF FREEDOM.** Rising 548 feet (167 m) above Penn Square, Philadelphia's City Hall, with its statue of William Penn, is the country's largest municipal building. Penn was founder of the Pennsylvania colony and defender of equal rights for men and women.

⇧ DAWN'S EARLY LIGHT. The lights of New York City's skyline sparkle against the early morning sky. The tall buildings of Lower Manhattan, reflected in the dark waters of the East River, are home to companies whose influence reaches around the world.

⇧ STILL WATERS. A father and son enjoy a quiet day of fishing on the smooth-as-glass waters of Lake Chocurua in New Hampshire's White Mountains. Deciduous trees turning red and gold will soon shed their leaves, and the hillsides will turn white with winter's snow, attracting skiers to the valley.

WHERE THE PICTURES ARE

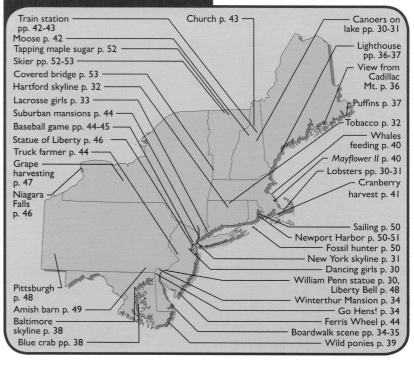

Train station pp. 42-43
Moose p. 42
Tapping maple sugar p. 52
Skier pp. 52-53
Covered bridge p. 53
Hartford skyline p. 32
Lacrosse girls p. 33
Suburban mansions p. 44
Baseball game pp. 44-45
Statue of Liberty p. 46
Truck farmer p. 44
Grape harvesting p. 47
Niagara Falls p. 46

Church p. 43

Canoers on lake pp. 30-31
Lighthouse pp. 36-37
View from Cadillac Mt. p. 36
Puffins p. 37
Tobacco p. 32
Whales feeding p. 40
Mayflower II p. 40
Lobsters pp. 30-31
Cranberry harvest p. 41
Sailing p. 50
Newport Harbor p. 50-51
Fossil hunter p. 50
New York skyline p. 31
Dancing girls p. 30
William Penn statue p. 30, Liberty Bell p. 48
Winterthur Mansion p. 34
Go Hens! p. 34
Ferris Wheel p. 44
Boardwalk scene pp. 34-35
Wild ponies p. 39

Pittsburgh p. 48
Amish barn p. 49
Baltimore skyline p. 38
Blue crab pp. 38

CONNECTICUT

As early as 1614, Dutch explorers founded trading posts along the coast of Connecticut, but the first permanent European settlements were established in 1635 by English Puritans from nearby Massachusetts. The Connecticut Fundamental Orders, which in 1639 established a democratic system of government in the colony, were an important model for the writing of the U.S. Constitution in 1787. This earned the state its nickname—Constitution State. Even in colonial times, Connecticut was an important industrial center, producing goods that competed with factories in England. During the Revolutionary War, Connecticut produced military goods for the colonial army. Today, Connecticut industries produce jet aircraft engines, helicopters, and nuclear submarines. Connecticut is home to many international corporations, but it is best known as the "insurance state." Following independence, businessmen offered to insure ship cargoes in exchange for a share of the profits. Soon after, other types of insurance were offered. Today, Connecticut is home to more than 100 insurance companies.

⇧ LEAFY HARVEST. The Connecticut River Valley is a major source of world-class premium cigar tobacco in the United States. Most of the harvest is used for cigar wrappers.

THE BASICS

STATS

Area
5,543 sq mi (14,357 sq km)

Population
3,502,309

Capital
Hartford
Population 124,512

Largest city
Bridgeport
Population 137,912

Ethnic/racial groups
84.6% white; 10.2% African American; 3.4% Asian; .4% Native American. Hispanic (any race) 11.2%.

Industry
Transportation equipment, metal products, machinery, electrical equipment, printing and publishing, scientific instruments, insurance

Agriculture
Nursery stock, dairy products, poultry, eggs, shellfish

Statehood
January 9, 1788; 5th state

GEO WHIZ

The sperm whale, Connecticut's state animal, is known for its massive head. Its brain is larger than that of any other creature known to have lived on Earth.

The first hamburgers in U.S. history were served by Louis Lassen at his New Haven lunch wagon in 1895. He didn't like to waste the excess beef left after the daily noon rush, so he ground it up, grilled it, and served it between two slices of bread.

The nuclear-powered U.S.S. *Virginia*, the world's most technologically advanced submarine, was built at Groton, home of the U.S. Naval Submarine Base.

ROBIN
MOUNTAIN LAUREL

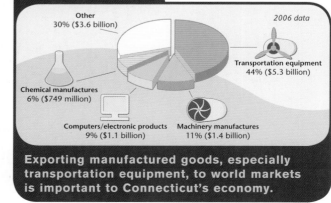

⇦ BRIGHT CITY LIGHTS. Established as a fort in the early 1600s, Hartford was one of the earliest cities of colonial America. Today, this modern state capital is a center of economic growth and cultural diversity.

GLOBAL ECONOMY

Other
30% ($3.6 billion)

2006 data

Transportation equipment
44% ($5.3 billion)

Chemical manufactures
6% ($749 million)

Computers/electronic products
9% ($1.1 billion)

Machinery manufactures
11% ($1.4 billion)

Exporting manufactured goods, especially transportation equipment, to world markets is important to Connecticut's economy.

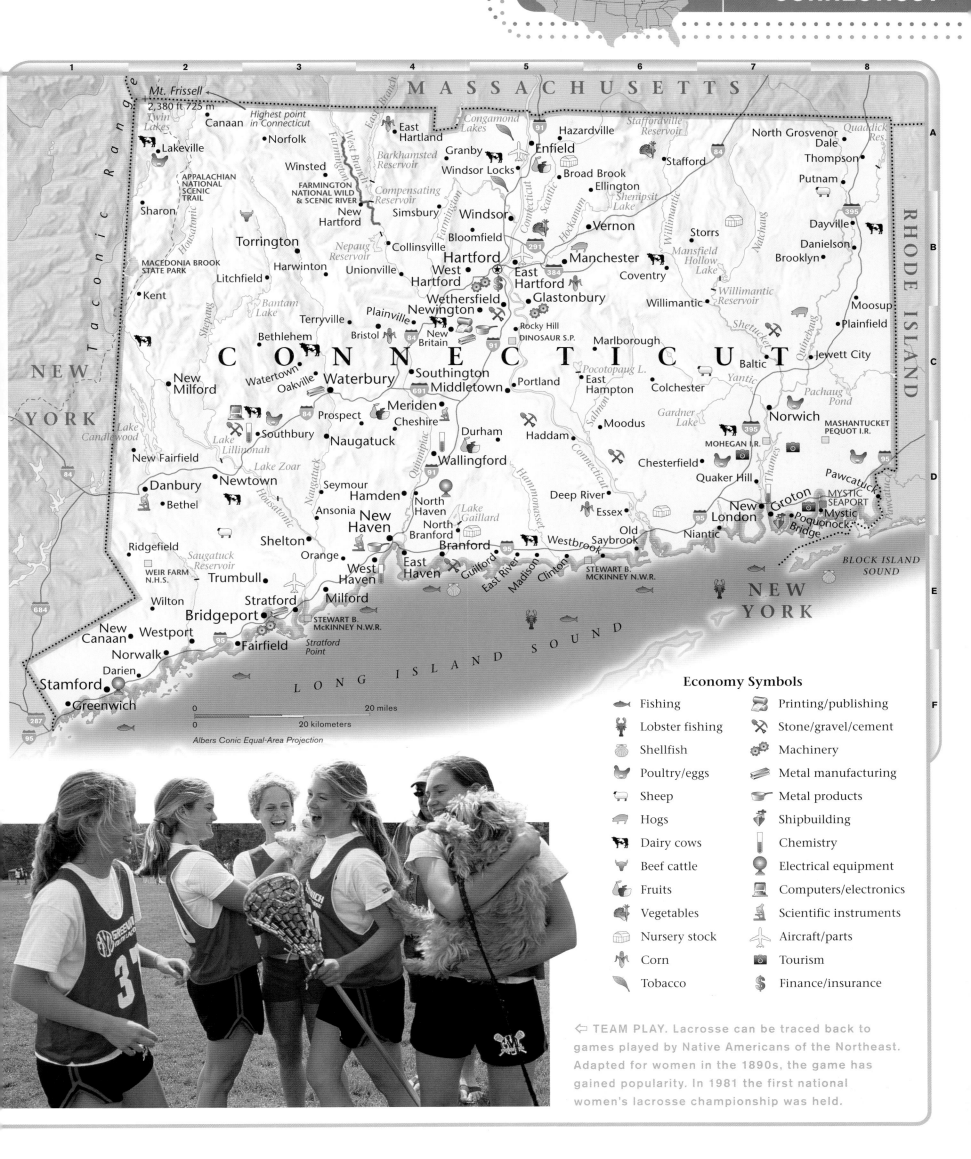

1 2 3 4 5 6 7 8

M A S S A C H U S E T T S

Mt. Frissell
2,380 ft 725 m
Highest point
in Connecticut
Twin
Lakes
Canaan
Norfolk
East
Hartland
Congamond
Lakes
Hazardville
Staffordville
Reservoir
North Grosvenor
Dale
Quaddick
Res.
Lakeville
Winsted
West Branch Farmington
Barkhamsted
Reservoir
Granby
Windsor Locks
Enfield
Broad Brook
Ellington
Stafford
Thompson
Putnam
APPALACHIAN
NATIONAL
SCENIC
TRAIL
FARMINGTON
NATIONAL WILD
& SCENIC RIVER
Compensating
Reservoir
New
Hartford
Simsbury
Windsor
Vernon
Shenipsit
Lake
Storrs
Dayville
Danielson
Sharon
Torrington
Nepaug
Reservoir
Collinsville
Bloomfield
Hartford
Manchester
Mansfield
Hollow
Lake
Brooklyn
MACEDONIA BROOK
STATE PARK
Harwinton
Unionville
West
Hartford
East
Hartford
Coventry
Willimantic
Reservoir
Moosup
Litchfield
Housatonic
Wethersfield
Glastonbury
Willimantic
Plainfield
Kent
Bantam
Lake
Terryville
Plainville
Newington
Rocky Hill
DINOSAUR S.P.
Marlborough
Shetucket
Jewett City
NEW
Bethlehem
Bristol
New
Britain
Baltic
C O N N E C T I C U T
Pocotopaug L.
Yantic
Pachaug
Pond
YORK
New
Milford
Watertown
Oakville
Waterbury
Southington
Middletown
Portland
East
Hampton
Colchester
Moodus
Norwich
MASHANTUCKET
PEQUOT I.R.
Lake
Candlewood
Prospect
Meriden
Cheshire
Durham
Haddam
Gardner
Lake
MOHEGAN I.R.
New Fairfield
Lake
Lillinonah
Southbury
Naugatuck
Wallingford
Chesterfield
Quaker Hill
Danbury
Newtown
Seymour
Hamden
North
Haven
Deep River
Essex
New
London
Groton
MYSTIC
SEAPORT
Mystic
Bethel
Ansonia
New
Haven
North
Branford
Lake
Gaillard
Old
Saybrook
Niantic
Poquonock
Bridge
Pawcatuck
Ridgefield
Saugatuck
Reservoir
Shelton
Orange
Branford
Westbrook
BLOCK ISLAND
SOUND
WEIR FARM
N.H.S.
Trumbull
West
Haven
East
Haven
Guilford
East River
Madison
Clinton
STEWART B.
MCKINNEY N.W.R.
Wilton
Stratford
Milford
NEW
Bridgeport
STEWART B.
MCKINNEY N.W.R.
YORK
New
Canaan
Westport
Fairfield
Stratford
Point
Norwalk
Darien
L O N G   I S L A N D   S O U N D
Stamford
Greenwich

NEW
YORK

RHODE ISLAND

0   20 miles
0   20 kilometers
Albers Conic Equal-Area Projection

Economy Symbols

Fishing		Printing/publishing	
Lobster fishing		Stone/gravel/cement	
Shellfish		Machinery	
Poultry/eggs		Metal manufacturing	
Sheep		Metal products	
Hogs		Shipbuilding	
Dairy cows		Chemistry	
Beef cattle		Electrical equipment	
Fruits		Computers/electronics	
Vegetables		Scientific instruments	
Nursery stock		Aircraft/parts	
Corn		Tourism	
Tobacco		Finance/insurance	

⇐ TEAM PLAY. Lacrosse can be traced back to
games played by Native Americans of the Northeast.
Adapted for women in the 1890s, the game has
gained popularity. In 1981 the first national
women's lacrosse championship was held.

DECEMBER 7, 1787

STATS

Area
2,489 sq mi (6,447 sq km)

Population
864,764

Capital
Dover
Population 32,808

Largest city
Wilmington
Population 72,051

Ethnic/racial groups
74.5% white; 20.9% African American; 2.8% Asian; .4% Native American. Hispanic (any race) 6.3%.

Industry
Food processing, chemicals, rubber and plastic products, scientific instruments, printing and publishing, financial services

Agriculture
Poultry, soybeans, nursery stock, corn, vegetables, dairy products

Statehood
December 7, 1787; 1st state

GEO WHIZ

Each year contestants bring their pumpkins and launching machines to the Punkin Chunkin World Championship in Bridgeville to see who can catapult their big, orange squash the farthest.

The Delaware Estuary is one of the four most important shorebird migration sites in the world and has the second-highest concentration of shorebirds in North America. The estuary also provides wintering and migratory habitat to many species of songbirds and raptors.

The first steam railroad to provide regular service began operations in New Castle in 1831.

BLUE HEN CHICKEN
PEACH BLOSSOM

DELAWARE

Second smallest among the states in area, Delaware has played a big role in the history of the U.S. Explored at various times by the Spanish, Portuguese, and Dutch, it was Swedes who established the first permanent European settlement in 1638 in the Delaware River Valley. In 1655 the colony fell under Dutch authority, but in 1682 the land was annexed by William Penn and the Pennsylvania colony. In 1787, Delaware was the first state to ratify the new U.S. Constitution. Delaware's Atlantic coast beaches are popular with tourists. Its fertile farmland, mainly in the south, produces soybeans, corn, dairy products, and poultry. But the state's real economic power is located in the north, around Wilmington, where factories employ thousands of workers to process food products and produce machinery and chemicals. Industry has been a source of wealth, but it also poses a danger to the environment. Protecting the environment is a high priority for Delaware.

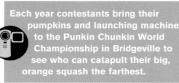

⇓ TEAM SPIRIT. Enthusiastic fans and the University of Delaware band support the "Fightin' Blue Hens." Located in Newark, the university was founded in 1743.

⇧ PAST GRANDEUR. Built in 1837 in the fashion of a British country house, Winterthur was expanded from 12 to 196 rooms by the du Ponts, chemical industry tycoons. In 1951 the house was opened to the public as a museum for the family's extensive collection of antiques and Americana.

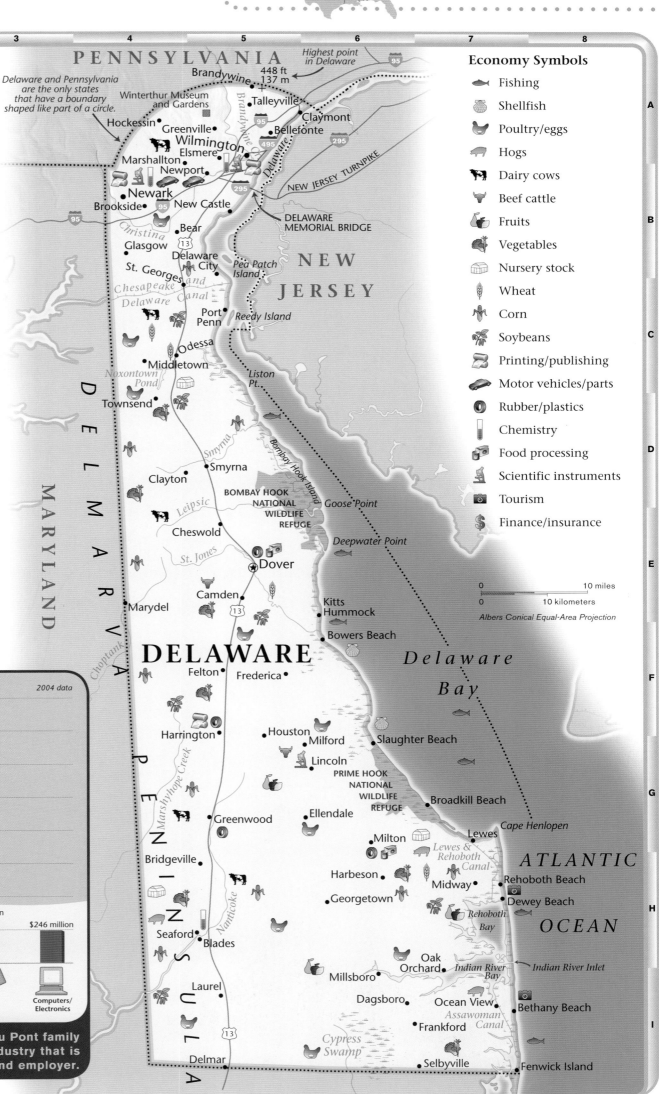

⬆ SEASIDE RETREAT. Originally established in 1873 as a church campground, Rehoboth Beach is still a popular getaway destination on Delaware's Atlantic coastline. A concrete dolphin overlooks the town's boardwalk, a popular promenade that separates shops and restaurants from the beach. The boardwalk has been destroyed on several occasions by storms.

Economy Symbols

- 🐟 Fishing
- 🐚 Shellfish
- 🐔 Poultry/eggs
- 🐖 Hogs
- 🐄 Dairy cows
- 🐂 Beef cattle
- 🍒 Fruits
- 🥬 Vegetables
- Nursery stock
- 🌾 Wheat
- 🌽 Corn
- Soybeans
- Printing/publishing
- 🚗 Motor vehicles/parts
- Rubber/plastics
- Chemistry
- Food processing
- Scientific instruments
- 📷 Tourism
- 💲 Finance/insurance

Delaware and Pennsylvania are the only states that have a boundary shaped like part of a circle.

Highest point in Delaware
448 ft
137 m

10 miles
10 kilometers
Albers Conical Equal-Area Projection

CHEMICAL GIANT

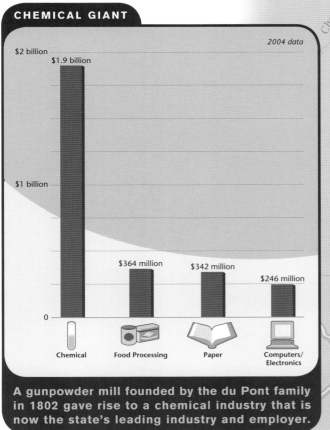

2004 data

- Chemical — $1.9 billion
- Food Processing — $364 million
- Paper — $342 million
- Computers/Electronics — $246 million

$2 billion
$1 billion
0

A gunpowder mill founded by the du Pont family in 1802 gave rise to a chemical industry that is now the state's leading industry and employer.

MAINE

Maine's story begins long before the arrival of European settlers in the 1600s. Evidence of native people dates back to at least 3000 B.C., and Leif Erikson and his Viking sailors may have explored Maine's coastline 500 years before Columbus crossed the Atlantic. English settlements were established along the southern coast in the 1620s, and in 1677 the territory of Maine came under control of Massachusetts. Following the Revolutionary War, the people of Maine pressed for separation from Massachusetts, and in 1820 Maine entered the Union as a non-slave state under the terms of the Missouri Compromise. Most of Maine's population is concentrated in towns along the coast. Famous for its rugged beauty, it is the focus of the tourist industry. Cold offshore waters contribute to a lively fishing industry, while timber from the state's mountainous interior supports wood product and paper businesses. Maine, a leader in environmental awareness, seeks a balance between economic growth and environmental protection.

THE BASICS

STATS

Area
35,385 sq mi (91,646 sq km)

Population
1,317,207

Capital
Augusta
Population 18,560

Largest city
Portland
Population 63,635

Ethnic/racial groups
96.7% white; .9% Asian; .8% African American; .6% Native American. Hispanic (any race) 1.0%.

Industry
Health services, tourism, forest products, leather products, electrical equipment, food processing, textiles

Agriculture
Seafood, potatoes, dairy products, poultry and eggs, livestock, apples, blueberries, vegetables

Statehood
March 15, 1820; 23rd state

GEO WHIZ

With world shark populations declining, some conservation-minded deep-sea fishermen in Maine have turned the idea of a shark tournament upside-down. They still compete to see who can catch the biggest fish, but then they tag and release the sharks.

Eartha, a scale model of our planet, holds the Guinness World Record as the World's Largest Revolving/Rotating Globe. It is on display in a three-story glass building in Yarmouth.

Forests cover nearly 90 percent of Maine. No wonder it is called the Pine Tree State.

Until the last ice age, Maine's coast was relatively straight. Glaciers carved hundreds of bays and inlets out of its shoreline and created some 2,000 islands off the coast.

CHICKADEE

WHITE PINE CONE AND TASSEL

⇩ ACADIA NATIONAL PARK, established in 1929, attracts thousands of tourists each year. The park includes Cadillac Mountain, the highest point along the North Atlantic coast and the site from which the earliest sunrises in the United States can be viewed from October 7 through March 6.

BLUEBERRY LEADER

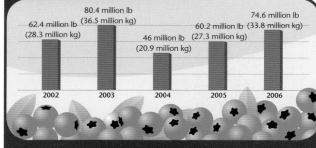

62.4 million lb (28.3 million kg) — 2002
80.4 million lb (36.5 million kg) — 2003
46 million lb (20.9 million kg) — 2004
60.2 million lb (27.3 million kg) — 2005
74.6 million lb (33.8 million kg) — 2006

In spite of a weather-related record low harvest in 2004, Maine remains the country's leading harvester of wild blueberries.

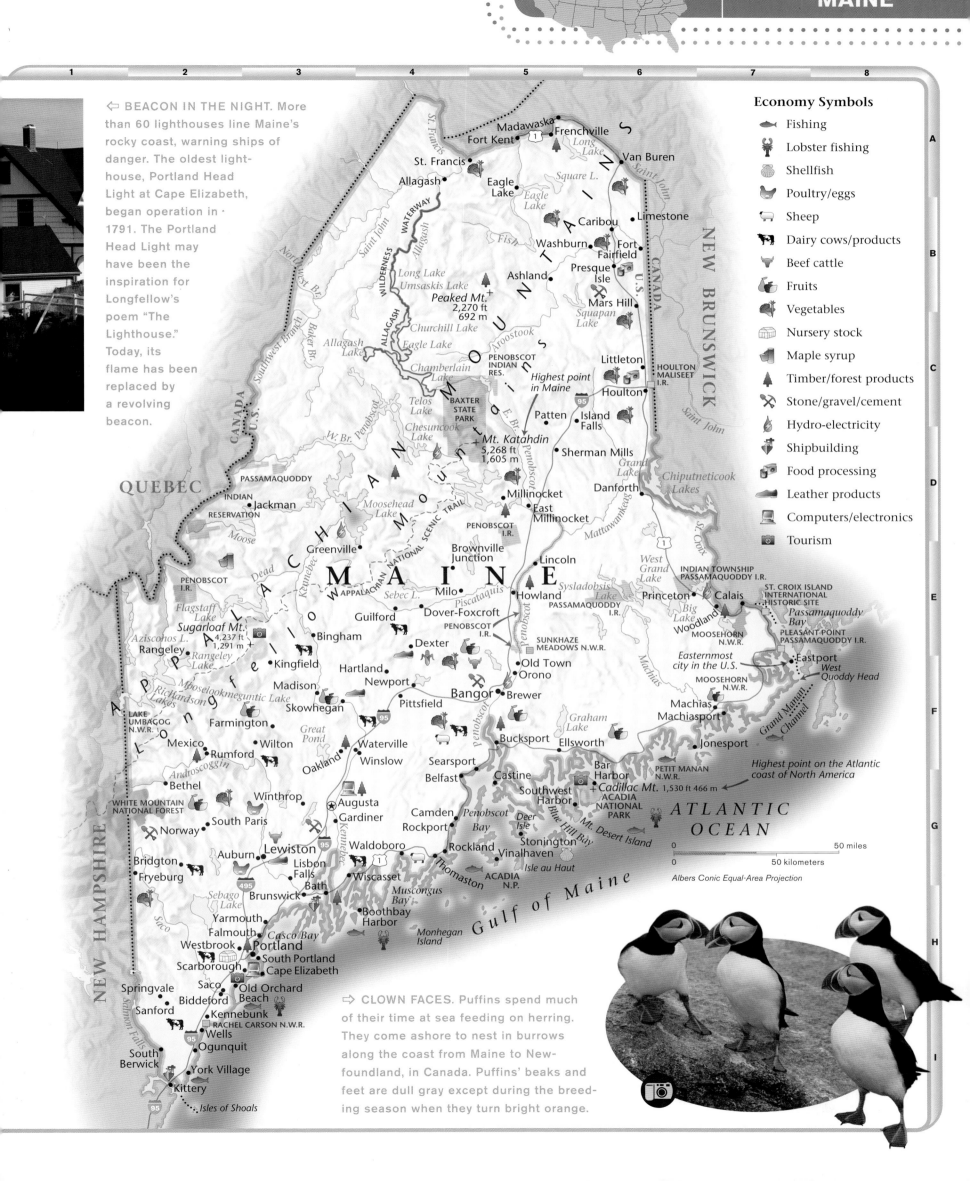

⇐ BEACON IN THE NIGHT. More than 60 lighthouses line Maine's rocky coast, warning ships of danger. The oldest lighthouse, Portland Head Light at Cape Elizabeth, began operation in 1791. The Portland Head Light may have been the inspiration for Longfellow's poem "The Lighthouse." Today, its flame has been replaced by a revolving beacon.

Economy Symbols

- 🐟 Fishing
- 🦞 Lobster fishing
- 🐚 Shellfish
- 🐔 Poultry/eggs
- 🐑 Sheep
- 🐄 Dairy cows/products
- 🐂 Beef cattle
- 🍒 Fruits
- 🥬 Vegetables
- Nursery stock
- Maple syrup
- 🌲 Timber/forest products
- Stone/gravel/cement
- Hydro-electricity
- Shipbuilding
- 📷 Food processing
- Leather products
- 💻 Computers/electronics
- 📷 Tourism

QUEBEC

NEW BRUNSWICK

St. Francis
Madawaska
Fort Kent
Frenchville
Van Buren
St. Francis
Long Lake
Allagash
Eagle Lake
Square L.
Eagle Lake
Caribou
Limestone
Washburn
Fort Fairfield
Ashland
Presque Isle
Long Lake
Umsaskis Lake
Mars Hill
Peaked Mt.
2,270 ft
692 m
Squapan Lake
Churchill Lake
Eagle Lake
Littleton
HOULTON MALISEET I.R.
PENOBSCOT INDIAN RES.
Chamberlain Lake
Highest point in Maine
Houlton
Telos Lake
BAXTER STATE PARK
Patten
Island Falls
Chesuncook Lake
Mt. Katahdin
5,268 ft
1,605 m
Sherman Mills
Danforth
Chiputneticook Lakes
PASSAMAQUODDY INDIAN RESERVATION
Jackman
Moosehead Lake
Millinocket
East Millinocket
PENOBSCOT I.R.
Grand Lake
PENOBSCOT I.R.
Greenville
Brownville Junction
Lincoln
West Grand Lake
INDIAN TOWNSHIP PASSAMAQUODDY I.R.
ST. CROIX ISLAND INTERNATIONAL HISTORIC SITE
M A I N E
Sysladobsis Lake
Princeton
Calais
Flagstaff Lake
Sugarloaf Mt.
4,237 ft
1,291 m
Milo
Sebec L.
Piscataquis
Howland
PASSAMAQUODDY I.R.
Big Lake
Woodland
MOOSEHORN N.W.R.
Passamaquoddy Bay
Aziscohos L.
Rangeley
Rangeley Lake
Guilford
Dover-Foxcroft
PENOBSCOT I.R.
SUNKHAZE MEADOWS N.W.R.
Easternmost city in the U.S.
PLEASANT POINT PASSAMAQUODDY I.R.
Eastport
West Quoddy Head
Kingfield
Bingham
Dexter
Old Town
Orono
MOOSEHORN N.W.R.
Hartland
Newport
Bangor
Brewer
Machias
Machiasport
Madison
Pittsfield
Graham Lake
Mooselookmeguntic Lake
Skowhegan
Bucksport
Ellsworth
Jonesport
LAKE UMBAGOG N.W.R.
Farmington
Great Pond
Waterville
Winslow
Searsport
Belfast
Castine
Bar Harbor
PETIT MANAN N.W.R.
Highest point on the Atlantic coast of North America
Mexico
Wilton
Oakland
Southwest Harbor
Cadillac Mt. 1,530 ft 466 m
Rumford
Bethel
Winthrop
Augusta
Gardiner
Camden
Rockport
Penobscot Bay
Deer Isle
Mt. Desert Island
ACADIA NATIONAL PARK
ATLANTIC OCEAN
WHITE MOUNTAIN NATIONAL FOREST
South Paris
Norway
Waldoboro
Rockland
Stonington
Vinalhaven
Auburn
Lewiston
Lisbon Falls
Blue Hill Bay
Isle au Haut
Bridgton
Fryeburg
Wiscasset
Bath
Thomaston
ACADIA N.P.
Brunswick
Muscongus Bay
Sebago Lake
Yarmouth
Boothbay Harbor
Monhegan Island
Gulf of Maine
Westbrook
Portland
Casco Bay
Springvale
Scarborough
South Portland
Cape Elizabeth
Sanford
Saco
Old Orchard Beach
Biddeford
Kennebunk
RACHEL CARSON N.W.R.
Wells
Ogunquit
South Berwick
York Village
Kittery
Isles of Shoals

NEW HAMPSHIRE

CANADA
U.S.

APPALACHIAN MOUNTAINS

Longfellow Mts.

ALLAGASH WILDERNESS WATERWAY

APPALACHIAN NATIONAL SCENIC TRAIL

Saint John
Fish R.
Aroostook
Saint John
St. Croix
Mattawamkeag
Penobscot
Machias
Grand Manan Channel
Northwest Br.
Baker Br.
Southwest Branch
W. Br. Penobscot
E. Br. Penobscot
Moose
Dead
Kennebec
Androscoggin
Richardson Lakes
Salmon Falls
Saco
Kennebec

0   50 miles
0   50 kilometers
Albers Conic Equal-Area Projection

⇒ CLOWN FACES. Puffins spend much of their time at sea feeding on herring. They come ashore to nest in burrows along the coast from Maine to Newfoundland, in Canada. Puffins' beaks and feet are dull gray except during the breeding season when they turn bright orange.

MARYLAND

THE BASICS

STATS

Area
12,407 sq mi (32,133 sq km)

Population
5,618,344

Capital
Annapolis
Population 36,178

Largest city
Baltimore
Population 631,366

Ethnic/racial groups
63.6% white; 29.5% African American; 4.9% Asian; .3% Native American. Hispanic (any race) 6.0%.

Industry
Real estate, federal government, health services, business services, engineering services, electrical and gas services, communications, banking, insurance

Agriculture
Poultry and eggs, dairy products, nursery stock, soybeans, corn, seafood, cattle, vegetables

Statehood
April 28, 1788; 7th state

GEO WHIZ

The Captain John Smith Chesapeake National Historic Water Trail, which traces some 3,000 miles (4,800 km) of Smith's 1607–1608 explorations of the bay, is the first national water trail in the United States.

The Naval Support Facility Thurmont, better known as Camp David, the mountain retreat of American presidents, is part of Catoctin Mountain Park in north-central Maryland.

Residents on Smith Island, in the lower Chesapeake Bay, are being robbed of their land by rising sea levels and of their traditional livelihood by dwindling blue crab harvests. They fear a major Atlantic hurricane could wipe out their island home.

The name of Baltimore's professional football team—the Ravens—may have been inspired by the title of a poem written by noted American author Edgar Allan Poe, who lived in Baltimore in the mid-1800s and whose grave is in that city.

NORTHERN (BALTIMORE) ORIOLE

BLACK-EYED SUSAN

Native Americans, who raised crops and harvested oysters from the nearby waters of Chesapeake Bay, lived on the land that would become Maryland long before early European settlers arrived. In 1608 Captain John Smith explored the waters of the bay, and in 1634 English settlers established the colony of Maryland. In 1788 Maryland became the 7th state to ratify the new U.S. Constitution. Chesapeake Bay, the largest estuary in the U.S., almost splits Maryland into two parts. East of

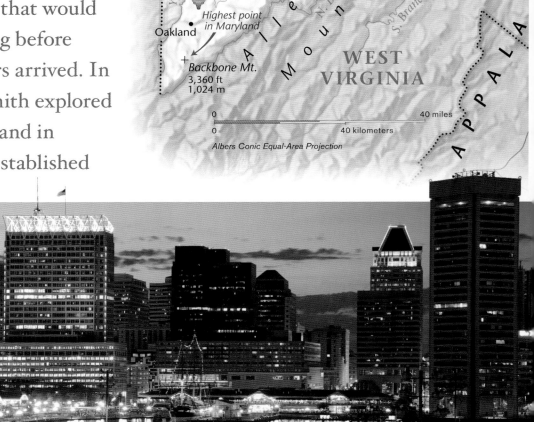

⇧ GATEWAY CITY. Since the early 1700s, Baltimore, near the upper Chesapeake Bay, has been a major seaport and focus of trade, industry, and immigration. Today, the Inner Harbor is not only a modern working port, but also the city's vibrant cultural center.

the bay lies the flat coastal plain, while to the west the land rises through the hilly piedmont and mountainous panhandle. Chesapeake Bay, the state's economic and environmental focal point, supports a busy seafood industry. It is also a major transportation artery, linking Baltimore and other Maryland ports to the Atlantic Ocean. Most of the people of Maryland live in an urban corridor between Baltimore and Washington, D.C., where jobs in government, research, and high-tech businesses provide employment.

⇦ COLORFUL CRUSTACEAN. Blue crabs, found in Maryland's Chesapeake Bay waters, were a staple in the diet of Native Americans. They have been harvested commercially since the mid-1800s, and the tasty meat is a popular menu item—especially crab cakes—in seafood restaurants throughout the area.

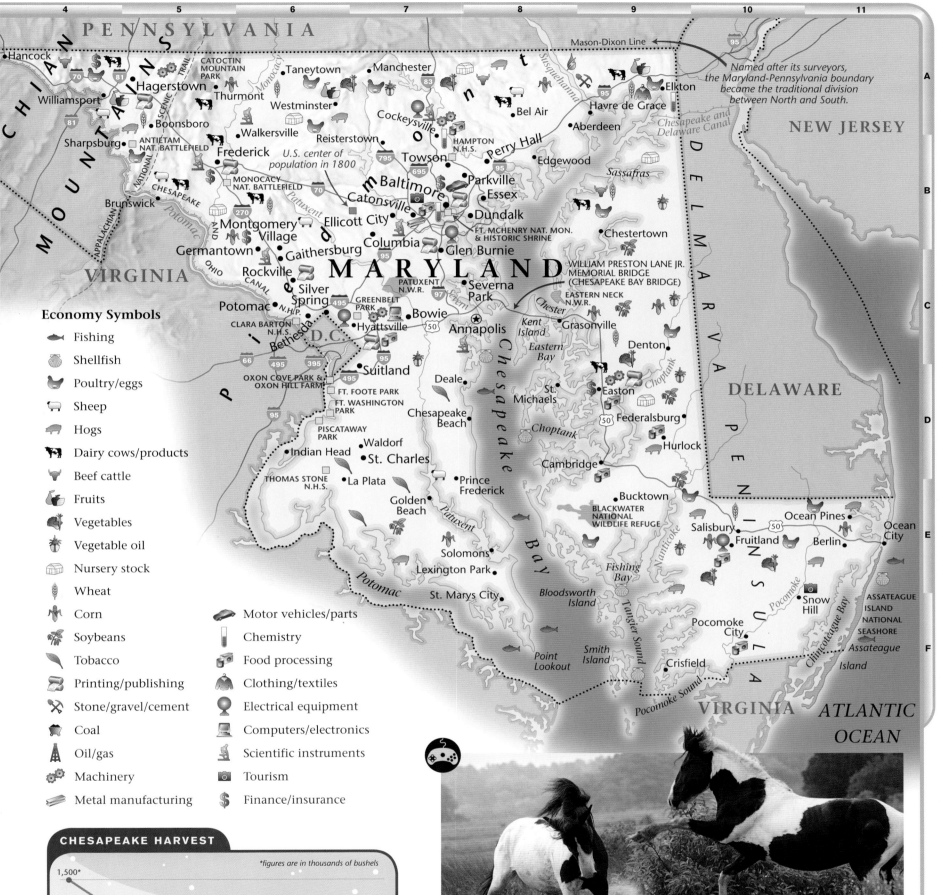

PENNSYLVANIA

Mason-Dixon Line

Named after its surveyors, the Maryland-Pennsylvania boundary became the traditional division between North and South.

NEW JERSEY

Hancock

Williamsport

Hagerstown · Thurmont

Boonsboro

Taneytown · Manchester

Westminster

Sharpsburg · ANTIETAM NAT. BATTLEFIELD

Walkersville · Reisterstown

Cockeysville

Bel Air

Elkton

Havre de Grace

Aberdeen

Chesapeake and Delaware Canal

Brunswick · CHESAPEAKE

Frederick · *U.S. center of population in 1800*

HAMPTON N.H.S.

Towson

Perry Hall

Edgewood

Sassafras

MONOCACY NAT. BATTLEFIELD

Baltimore

Parkville · Essex

Montgomery Village

Catonsville

Dundalk

Chestertown

Germantown

Ellicott City

FT. McHENRY NAT. MON. & HISTORIC SHRINE

Gaithersburg

Columbia

Glen Burnie

MARYLAND

Rockville

Silver Spring

PATUXENT N.W.R.

Severna Park

WILLIAM PRESTON LANE JR. MEMORIAL BRIDGE (CHESAPEAKE BAY BRIDGE)

DELAWARE

Potomac

GREENBELT PARK

Bowie

EASTERN NECK N.W.R.

VIRGINIA

CLARA BARTON N.H.S.

Bethesda

D.C.

Hyattsville

Annapolis

Grasonville

Denton

Kent Island

Eastern Bay

Choptank

Economy Symbols

OXON COVE PARK & OXON HILL FARM

FT. FOOTE PARK

Suitland

Deale

St. Michaels

Easton

- 🐟 Fishing
- 🐚 Shellfish
- 🐓 Poultry/eggs
- 🐑 Sheep
- 🐖 Hogs
- 🐄 Dairy cows/products
- 🐂 Beef cattle
- 🍇 Fruits
- 🥬 Vegetables
- 🌰 Vegetable oil
- 🏭 Nursery stock
- 🌾 Wheat
- 🌽 Corn
- 🌿 Soybeans
- 🍃 Tobacco
- 📰 Printing/publishing
- ⚒ Stone/gravel/cement
- 🪨 Coal
- ⛽ Oil/gas
- ⚙ Machinery
- 📦 Metal manufacturing

- 🚗 Motor vehicles/parts
- ⚗ Chemistry
- 📷 Food processing
- 👕 Clothing/textiles
- 🔦 Electrical equipment
- 💻 Computers/electronics
- 🔬 Scientific instruments
- 📷 Tourism
- 💲 Finance/insurance

FT. WASHINGTON PARK

Chesapeake Beach

Federalsburg

Hurlock

PISCATAWAY PARK

Waldorf

Choptank

Cambridge

Indian Head

St. Charles

Bucktown

THOMAS STONE N.H.S.

La Plata

Prince Frederick

BLACKWATER NATIONAL WILDLIFE REFUGE

Ocean Pines

Golden Beach

Salisbury

Berlin

Ocean City

Solomons

Fruitland

Lexington Park

Fishing Bay

ASSATEAGUE ISLAND NATIONAL SEASHORE

St. Marys City

Bloodsworth Island

Snow Hill

Assateague Island

Pocomoke City

Point Lookout

Smith Island

Crisfield

VIRGINIA

ATLANTIC OCEAN

Chesapeake Bay

Potomac

Patuxent

Pocomoke Sound

Tangier Sound

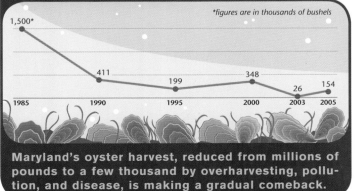

CHESAPEAKE HARVEST

figures are in thousands of bushels

1,500*

411

199

348

26

154

1985 · 1990 · 1995 · 2000 · 2003 · 2005

Maryland's oyster harvest, reduced from millions of pounds to a few thousand by overharvesting, pollution, and disease, is making a gradual comeback.

⬆ HORSEPLAY. Wild ponies have lived on Assateague Island since the 1600s. Some believe the original ponies were survivors from a Spanish galleon that sank offshore. Today, more than 300 ponies live on this Atlantic barrier island shared by Maryland and Virginia.

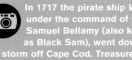

THE BASICS

STATS

Area
10,555 sq mi (27,336 sq km)

Population
6,449,755

Capital
Boston
Population 590,763

Largest city
Boston
Population 590,763

Major ethnic/racial groups
86.5% white; 6.9% African American; 4.9% Asian; .3% Native American. Hispanic (any race) 7.9%.

Industry
Electrical equipment, machinery, metal products, scientific instruments, printing and publishing, tourism

Agriculture
Fruits, nuts and berries, nursery stock, dairy products

Statehood
February 6, 1788; 6th state

GEO WHIZ

In 1717 the pirate ship *Whydah*, under the command of Captain Samuel Bellamy (also known as Black Sam), went down in a storm off Cape Cod. Treasure and artifacts recovered from the ship are on display at the Whydah Museum, in Provincetown, and are also part of a National Geographic traveling exhibit.

Massachusetts is the birthplace of several famous inventors, including Eli Whitney, Samuel Morse, and Benjamin Franklin.

The country's first lighthouse was built on Little Brewster Island in Boston Harbor in 1716. It is the last manned lighthouse in the United States. Use the online link to see what it's like to be a lighthouse keeper for Boston Light.

Cape Cod is considered one of the world's best spots for whale watching, thanks to Stellwagen Bank, a protected area at the mouth of Massachusetts Bay.

CHICKADEE
MAYFLOWER

MASSACHUSETTS

Earliest human inhabitants of Massachusetts were Native Americans who arrived more than 10,000 years ago. The first Europeans to visit Massachusetts may have been Norsemen around A.D. 1000, and later fishermen from France and Spain. But the first permanent European settlement was established in 1620 when people aboard the sailing ship *Mayflower* landed near Plymouth on the coast of Massachusetts. The Puritans arrived soon after, and by 1630 they had established settlements at Salem and Boston. By 1640 more than 16,000 people, most seeking religious freedom, had settled in Massachusetts. In the early days, the economy of Massachusetts was based on shipping, fishing, and whaling. By the 19th century, industry, taking advantage of abundant water power, had a firm foothold. Factory jobs attracted thousands of immigrants, mainly from Europe. In the late 20th century, Massachusetts experienced a boom in high-tech jobs, drawing on the state's skilled labor force and its more than 80 colleges and universities.

⇧ REMINDER OF TIMES PAST. Shrouded in morning mist, this replica of the *Mayflower* docked in Plymouth Harbor is a reminder of Massachusetts's early history.

⇨ LEVIATHANS OF THE DEEP. In the 19th century, Massachusetts was an important center for the whaling industry, with more than 300 registered whaling ships. Today, humpback whales swim in the protected waters of a marine sanctuary in Massachusetts Bay.

NEW HAMPSHIRE

ATLANTIC OCEAN

MASSACHUSETTS

Amesbury
Newburyport
Haverhill
Methuen
Lawrence
Dracut
Ipswich
PARKER RIVER N.W.R.
Lowell N.H.P.
Lowell
Chelmsford
Winchendon
Orange
Athol
Fitchburg
Gardner
Turners Falls
Greenfield
Deerfield
Leominster
OXBOW N.W.R.
SUDBURY, ASSABET & CONCORD NATIONAL WILD & SCENIC RIVER
Wilmington
Danvers
Beverly
Gloucester
Cape Ann
Salem Maritime N.H.S.
One of the ten most populous cities in the U.S. in 1790
MINUTE-MAN N.H.P.
Concord
Lexington
Peabody
Salem
Marblehead
Boston N.H.P.
Woburn
Lynn
Medford
Malden
Massachusetts
STELLWAGEN BANK NATIONAL MARINE SANCTUARY
Quabbin Reservoir
Wachusett Res.
GREAT MEADOWS N.W.R.
Cambridge
Boston
Bay
Amherst
Northampton
Marlborough
Shrewsbury
Worcester
Sudbury Res.
Framingham
Wellesley
Brookline
BOSTON HARBOR ISLANDS N.R.A.
South Hadley
Lake Quinsigamond
Milton
Quincy
Holyoke
Ludlow
Ware
Spencer
Auburn
President Kennedy's birthplace
Norwood
Weymouth
Birthplace of Presidents John Adams and John Quincy Adams
Chicopee
Springfield
Sturbridge
Southbridge
Oxford
Milford
President Bush's birthplace
Stoughton
Randolph
Rockland
Agawam
Springfield Armory N.H.S.
Webster
Bellingham
Franklin
Brockton
Whitman
Bridgewater
Silver Lake
Provincetown
CAPE COD NATIONAL SEASHORE
Plimoth Plantation
Truro
Plymouth
Wellfleet
TICUT
RHODE ISLAND
North Attleboro
Attleboro
Taunton
Middleboro
Assawompset Pond
Cape Cod Canal
Cape Cod Bay
Seekonk
Long Pond
Great Quittacus Pond
Buzzards Bay
Sandwich
Dennis
Orleans
Somerset
Fall River
New Bedford Whaling N.H.P.
Barnstable
Chatham
Hyannis
S. Yarmouth
New Bedford
Fairhaven
East Falmouth
Monomoy Island
MONOMOY N.W.R.
Woods Hole
Falmouth
Nantucket Sound
Buzzards Bay
Vineyard Haven
Oak Bluffs
NANTUCKET N.W.R.
Rhode Island Sound
Elizabeth Islands
Vineyard Sound
Edgartown
Chappaquiddick Island
Gay Head WAMPANOAG I.R.
Martha's Vineyard
Nantucket
Nomans Land
Nantucket Island

Economy Symbols

- Fishing
- Lobster fishing
- Shellfish
- Poultry/eggs
- Sheep
- Hogs
- Dairy cows/products
- Beef cattle
- Fruits
- Vegetables
- Nursery stock
- Wheat

- Tobacco
- Maple syrup
- Printing/publishing
- Stone/gravel/cement
- Hydro-electricity
- Machinery
- Metal products
- Computers/electronics
- Scientific instruments
- Aerospace
- Tourism

⇧ BIG BUSINESS. Cranberries, grown in fields called bogs, are the state's largest agricultural crop. These tiny berries, one of only three fruits native to North America, are consumed mainly in the form of juice or as a tasty accompaniment to holiday dishes. Workers flood fields to make harvesting the floating berries easier.

TRACING OUR ROOTS

Massachusetts, 2000 census data

Not Specified 12%
Multi-ancestry 33%
Single Ancestry 55%

Polish 5.1%
Portuguese 6%
French 9.9%
Italian 13.6%
English 14.5%
Irish 21%
Other 29.9%

Most new immigrants to the U.S. are from Latin America and Asia, but many people in Massachusetts trace their ancestry to Europe.

NEW HAMPSHIRE

The territory that would become the state of New Hampshire, the 9th state to approve the U.S. Constitution in 1788, began as a fishing colony established along the short 18-mile- (29-km-) long coastline in 1623. New Hampshire was named a royal colony in 1679, but as the Revolutionary War approached, it was the first colony to declare its independence from English rule.

In the early 19th century, life in New Hampshire followed two very different paths. Near the coast, villages and towns grew up around sawmills, shipyards, and warehouses. But in the forested, mountainous interior, people lived on small isolated farms, and towns provided only basic services. Today, New Hampshire is one of the fastest growing states in the Northeast. Modern industries, such as computers and electronics, and high-tech companies have brought prosperity to the state. Its natural beauty attracts tourists year-round to hike on forest trails, swim in pristine lakes, and ski on snow-covered mountain slopes.

⇧ LUMBERING GIANT. Averaging 6 feet (2 m) tall at the shoulders, moose are the largest of North America's deer. Moose are found throughout New Hampshire.

THE BASICS

STATS

Area
9,350 sq mi (24,216 sq km)

Population
1,315,828

Capital
Concord
Population 41,823

Largest city
Manchester
Population 109,497

Ethnic/racial groups
95.8% white; 1.9% Asian;
1.1% African American; .3% Native
American. Hispanic (any race) 2.3%.

Industry
Machinery, electronics, metal products

Agriculture
Nursery stock, poultry and eggs, fruits
and nuts, vegetables

Statehood
June 21, 1788; 9th state

GEO WHIZ

About ten million tourists visit New Hampshire each year, nearly ten times the number of people who live in the state.

The Granite State boasts more than 200 different kinds of rocks and minerals. Use the icon to play Rock Stars and test your knowledge.

The first potato grown in the United States was planted in 1719 in Londonderry on the Common Field, now known simply as the Commons.

Ben Kilham's unique ways of rehabilitating abandoned black bear cubs he finds in the New Hampshire woods has earned him the nickname Bear Man by residents of Lyme. He has been working with orphaned, sick, and injured cubs for more than nine years.

PURPLE FINCH
PURPLE LILAC

ROARING WINDS

F4 "devastating tornado"
207-260 mph
(333-418 km/h)

Category 5 Hurricane
wind speeds greater
than 155 mph
(249 km/h)

Mt. Washington record:
231 miles per hour
(371 km/h)
April 1934

Mount Washington holds the record for highest surface wind speed, comparable to winds in Category 5 hurricanes and F4 tornadoes.

⇨ ALL ABOARD. Tourists traveling by train through the White Mountains enjoy the cool autumn weather and the colorful fall foliage of deciduous trees that cover the mountains.

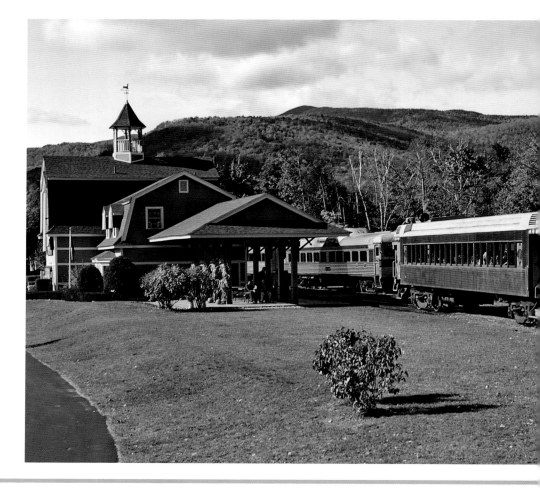

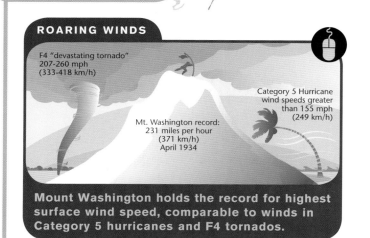

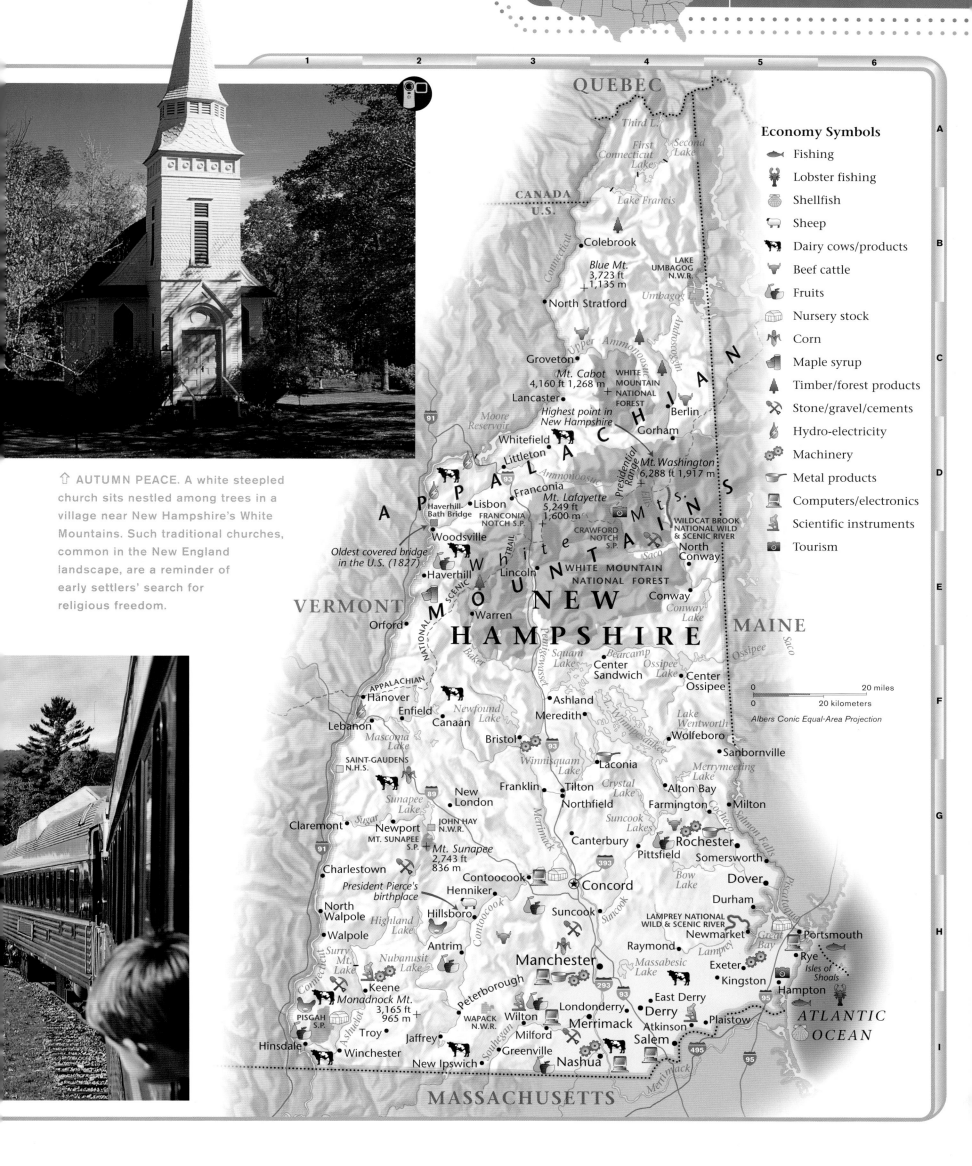

⇧ AUTUMN PEACE. A white steepled church sits nestled among trees in a village near New Hampshire's White Mountains. Such traditional churches, common in the New England landscape, are a reminder of early settlers' search for religious freedom.

Economy Symbols

- Fishing
- Lobster fishing
- Shellfish
- Sheep
- Dairy cows/products
- Beef cattle
- Fruits
- Nursery stock
- Corn
- Maple syrup
- Timber/forest products
- Stone/gravel/cements
- Hydro-electricity
- Machinery
- Metal products
- Computers/electronics
- Scientific instruments
- Tourism

QUEBEC

CANADA
U.S.

Third L.
First Connecticut Lakes
Second Lake
Lake Francis

Colebrook

Blue Mt.
3,723 ft
1,135 m

LAKE UMBAGOG N.W.R.

North Stratford

Umbagog L.

Groveton

Upper Ammonoosuc

Mt. Cabot
4,160 ft 1,268 m

WHITE MOUNTAIN NATIONAL FOREST

Lancaster

Berlin

Highest point in New Hampshire

Whitefield

Gorham

Moore Reservoir

Littleton

Ammonoosuc

Presidential Range

Mt. Washington
6,288 ft 1,917 m

Franconia

Mt. Lafayette
5,249 ft
1,600 m

Haverhill-Bath Bridge

Lisbon

FRANCONIA NOTCH S.P.

CRAWFORD NOTCH S.P.

WILDCAT BROOK NATIONAL WILD & SCENIC RIVER

Woodsville

Saco

North Conway

Oldest covered bridge in the U.S. (1827)

Lincoln

WHITE MOUNTAIN NATIONAL FOREST

Haverhill

Conway

VERMONT

Warren

Conway Lake

MAINE

Orford

Baker

NEW

Pemigewasset

Squam Lakes

Bearcamp

Ossipee

HAMPSHIRE

Center Sandwich

Ossipee Lake

Center Ossipee

Saco

APPALACHIAN

Hanover

Enfield

Newfound Lake

Ashland

Meredith

Lake Wentworth

20 miles
20 kilometers
Albers Conic Equal-Area Projection

Lebanon

Canaan

Lake Winnipesaukee

Wolfeboro

Mascoma Lake

Bristol

Sanbornville

SAINT-GAUDENS N.H.S.

Winnisquam Lake

Laconia

Merrymeeting Lake

Franklin

Tilton

Crystal Lake

Alton Bay

Milton

Claremont

Sugar

Newport

New London

Northfield

Farmington

Suncook Lakes

Sunapee Lake

MT. SUNAPEE S.P.

JOHN HAY N.W.R.

Mt. Sunapee
2,743 ft
836 m

Merrimack

Canterbury

Rochester

Somersworth

Charlestown

Contoocook

Concord

Pittsfield

Bow Lake

Dover

President Pierce's birthplace

Henniker

Suncook

Durham

North Walpole

Highland Lake

Hillsboro

Contoocook

Suncook

LAMPREY NATIONAL WILD & SCENIC RIVER

Newmarket

Great Bay

Portsmouth

Walpole

Antrim

Raymond

Lamprey

Exeter

Rye

Isles of Shoals

Nubanusit Lake

Manchester

Massabesic Lake

Kingston

Surry Mt. Lake

Keene

Monadnock Mt.
3,165 ft
965 m

Peterborough

Wilton

Londonderry

Derry

East Derry

Plaistow

Hampton

PISGAH S.P.

WAPACK N.W.R.

Merrimack

Atkinson

Salem

ATLANTIC OCEAN

Hinsdale

Troy

Winchester

Jaffrey

New Ipswich

Milford

Greenville

Nashua

MASSACHUSETTS

NEW JERSEY

Long before Europeans settled in New Jersey, the region was home to hunting and farming communities of Delaware Indians. The Dutch set up a trading post in northern New Jersey in 1618, calling it New Netherland, but yielded the land in 1664 to the English, who named it New Jersey after the English Channel Isle of Jersey. New Jersey saw more than 90 battles during the Revolutionary War. It became the 3rd U.S. state in 1787 and the first to sign the Bill of Rights. In the 19th century southern New Jersey remained largely agricultural, while the northern part of the state rapidly industrialized. Today highways and railroads link the state to urban centers along the Atlantic seaboard. Nearly 10,000 farms grow fruits and vegetables for nearby urban markets. Industries as well as services and trade are thriving. Beaches along the Atlantic coast attract thousands of tourists each year.

⇧ HOLD ON! New Jersey's Atlantic coast is lined with sandy beaches that attract vacationers from near and far. Amusement parks, such as this one in Wildwood, add to the fun.

⇨ HEADED TO MARKET. New Jersey is a leading producer of fresh fruits and vegetables. These organic vegetables are headed for urban markets in the Northeast.

⇦ SUBURBAN SPRAWL. With more than 90 percent of the state's population living in urban areas, housing developments, with close-set, look-alike houses, are a common characteristic of the suburban landscape. Residents commute to jobs in the city.

⇧ PLAY BALL! Fans pack the seats at Newark's Bear and Eagles Riverfront Stadium to watch a minor league baseball game. Built in 1999, the stadium is a part of Newark's plan to revitalize the down-town area, drawing people into the city.

Economy Symbols

- Fishing
- Shellfish
- Poultry/eggs
- Sheep
- Hogs
- Dairy cows/products
- Beef cattle
- Fruits
- Vegetables
- Nursery stock
- Wheat
- Corn
- Soybeans
- Printing/publishing
- Stone/gravel/cement
- Machinery
- Chemistry
- Food processing
- Computers/electronics
- Aerospace
- Tourism

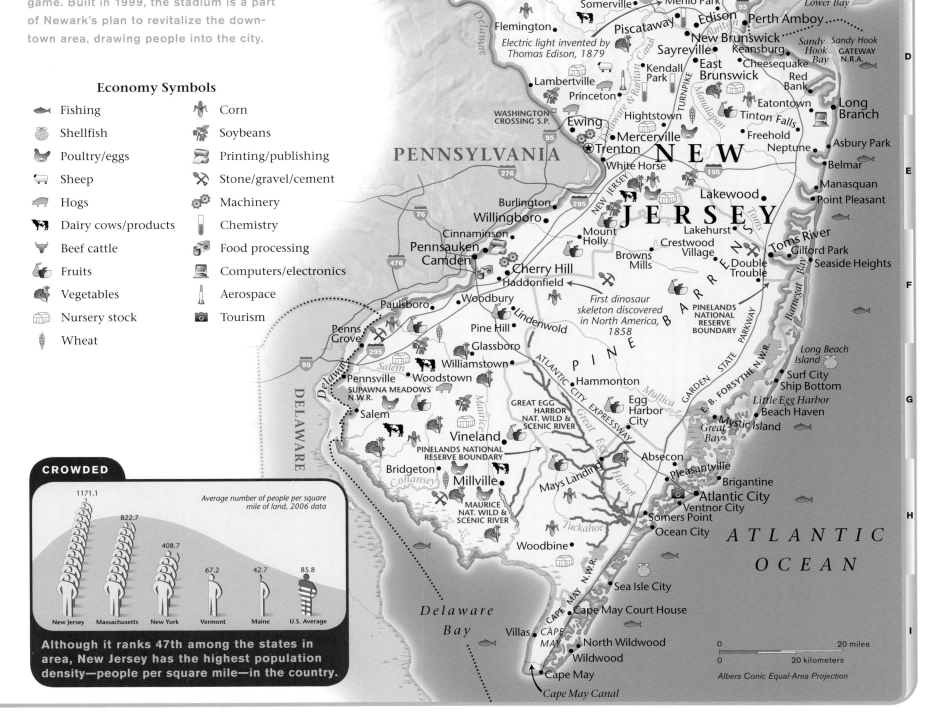

CROWDED

1171.1   822.7   408.7   67.2   42.7   85.8

Average number of people per square mile of land, 2006 data

New Jersey   Massachusetts   New York   Vermont   Maine   U.S. Average

Although it ranks 47th among the states in area, New Jersey has the highest population density—people per square mile—in the country.

NEW YORK

PENNSYLVANIA

DELAWARE

NEW JERSEY

ATLANTIC OCEAN

Delaware Bay

High Point 1,803 ft 550 m / Highest point in New Jersey

Highland Lakes
West Milford
Franklin
Ringwood
Newton
Ramsey
Sparta
Wanaque
President Cleveland's birthplace
Ridgewood
Wayne
Paramus
Hopatcong
Dover
Paterson
Clifton
Hackensack
Budd Lake
Parsippany
Caldwell
Passaic
Fort Lee
Hackettstown
Morristown
Edison N.H.S.
Newark
Union City
Washington
Bernardsville
Irvington
Jersey City
Phillipsburg
High Bridge
Berkeley Heights
Elizabeth
Bayonne
Plainfield
Rahway
Somerville
Menlo Park
Flemington
Piscataway
Edison
Perth Amboy
New Brunswick
Sayreville
Keansburg
Lambertville
Kendall Park
East Brunswick
Cheesequake
Red Bank
Princeton
Eatontown
Long Branch
Hightstown
Tinton Falls
Ewing
Mercerville
Freehold
Neptune
Asbury Park
Trenton
Belmar
White Horse
Manasquan
Burlington
Lakewood
Point Pleasant
Willingboro
Lakehurst
Cinnaminson
Mount Holly
Crestwood Village
Toms River
Pennsauken
Browns Mills
Gilford Park
Camden
Double Trouble
Seaside Heights
Cherry Hill
Haddonfield
Woodbury
Paulsboro
Lindenwold
Penns Grove
Pine Hill
Glassboro
Williamstown
Hammonton
Woodstown
Pennsville
Egg Harbor City
Surf City
Ship Bottom
Salem
Beach Haven
Vineland
Mystic Island
Bridgeton
Absecon
Millville
Pleasantville
Mays Landing
Brigantine
Atlantic City
Somers Point
Ventnor City
Ocean City
Woodbine
Sea Isle City
Cape May Court House
Villas
North Wildwood
Wildwood
Cape May
Cape May Canal

WALLKILL RIVER N.W.R.
Wanaque Reservoir
Lake Hopatcong
MORRISTOWN N.H.P.
GREAT SWAMP N.W.R.
Round Valley Res.
Ellis Island
Lower Bay
Sandy Hook Bay
Sandy Hook GATEWAY N.R.A.
DELAWARE WATER GAP N.R.A.
APPALACHIAN NATIONAL SCENIC TRAIL
Kittatinny Mountains
Musconetcong
Delaware
Raritan
Delaware & Raritan Canal
Manalapan
TURNPIKE
NEW JERSEY
PINE BARRENS
PINELANDS NATIONAL RESERVE BOUNDARY
GARDEN STATE PARKWAY
E. B. FORSYTHE N.W.R.
Long Beach Island
Little Egg Harbor
Great Bay
Mullica
ATLANTIC CITY EXPRESSWAY
GREAT EGG HARBOR NAT. WILD & SCENIC RIVER
Maurice
Great Egg Harbor
SUPAWNA MEADOWS N.W.R.
Salem
Cohansey
MAURICE NAT. WILD & SCENIC RIVER
Tuckahoe
CAPE MAY N.W.R.
CAPE MAY
Barnegat Bay
Toms
Hudson

Electric light invented by Thomas Edison, 1879

First dinosaur skeleton discovered in North America, 1858

WASHINGTON CROSSING S.P.

PINELANDS NATIONAL RESERVE BOUNDARY

0   20 miles
0   20 kilometers

Albers Conic Equal-Area Projection

THE EMPIRE STATE:
NEW YORK

NEW YORK

1   2   3

When Englishman Henry Hudson explored New York's Hudson River Valley in 1609, the territory was already inhabited by large tribes of Native Americans, including the powerful Iroquois. In 1624 a Dutch trading company established the New Netherland colony, but after just 40 years the colony was taken over by the English and renamed for England's Duke of York. In 1788 New York became the 11th state. The state can be divided into two parts. The powerful port city of New York, center of trade and commerce and gateway to immigrants, is the largest city in the U.S. Its metropolitan area has more than 18 million people. Everything north of the city is simply referred to as "Upstate." Cities such as Buffalo and Rochester are industrial centers, while Ithaca and Syracuse boast major universities. Agriculture is also important in New York. With almost 5 million acres in cropland, the state is a major producer of dairy products, fruits, and vegetables.

THE BASICS

STATS

Area
54,556 sq mi (141,300 sq km)

Population
19,297,729

Capital
Albany
Population 93,919

Largest city
New York City
Population 8,214,426

Ethnic/racial groups
73.7% white; 17.4% African American; 6.9% Asian; .5% Native American. Hispanic (any race) 16.3%.

Industry
Printing and publishing, machinery, computer products, finance, tourism

Agriculture
Dairy products, cattle and other live-stock, vegetables, nursery stock, apples

Statehood
July 26, 1788; 11th state

GEO WHIZ

Each year at Halloween the Headless Horseman rides again through the countryside of Sleepy Hollow as residents reenact Washington Irving's *The Legend of Sleepy Hollow*.

The Erie Canal, built in the 1820s between Albany and Buffalo, helped New York City become a worldwide trading center and opened the Midwest to development by linking the Hudson River and the Great Lakes.

Cooperstown, New York, home of the National Baseball Hall of Fame, takes its name from a town established in the late 1700s by the father of James Fenimore Cooper, author of such American classics as *The Last of the Mohicans* and *The Deerslayer*.

EASTERN
BLUEBIRD

ROSE

⬆ LADY LIBERTY.
Standing in New York Harbor, the Statue of Liberty, a gift from the people of France, is a symbol of freedom and democracy.

Map labels
LAKE
Niagara River
Erie Canal
Lockport
Medina
Greece
TUSCARORA I.R.
IROQUOIS N.W.R.
Gates
Niagara Falls
TONAWANDA I.R.
ONTARIO
Tonawanda
Amherst
Batavia
THEODORE ROOSEVELT INAUGURAL N.H.S.
Buffalo
Cheektowaga
W. Seneca
90
LAKE ERIE
Hamburg
Geneseo
CANADA
U.S.
Lake Erie Beach
90
CATTARAUGUS INDIAN RESERVATION
Dansville
Dunkirk
Cattaraugus Cr.
Westfield
Fredonia
OIL SPRINGS I.R.
Hornell
Chautauqua Lake
ALLEGANY INDIAN RES.
Salamanca
Wellsville
90
Jamestown
ALLEGANY STATE PARK
86
Olean
Allegheny

⬅ NATURAL WONDER.
As many as 12 million tourists annually visit Niagara Falls on the U.S.-Canada border. Visitors in rain slickers trek through the mists below Bridal Veil Falls on the American side.

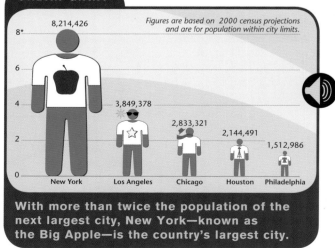

URBAN GIANT

Figures are based on 2000 census projections and are for population within city limits.

8,214,426	3,849,378	2,833,321	2,144,491	1,512,986
New York	Los Angeles	Chicago	Houston	Philadelphia

With more than twice the population of the next largest city, New York—known as the Big Apple—is the country's largest city.

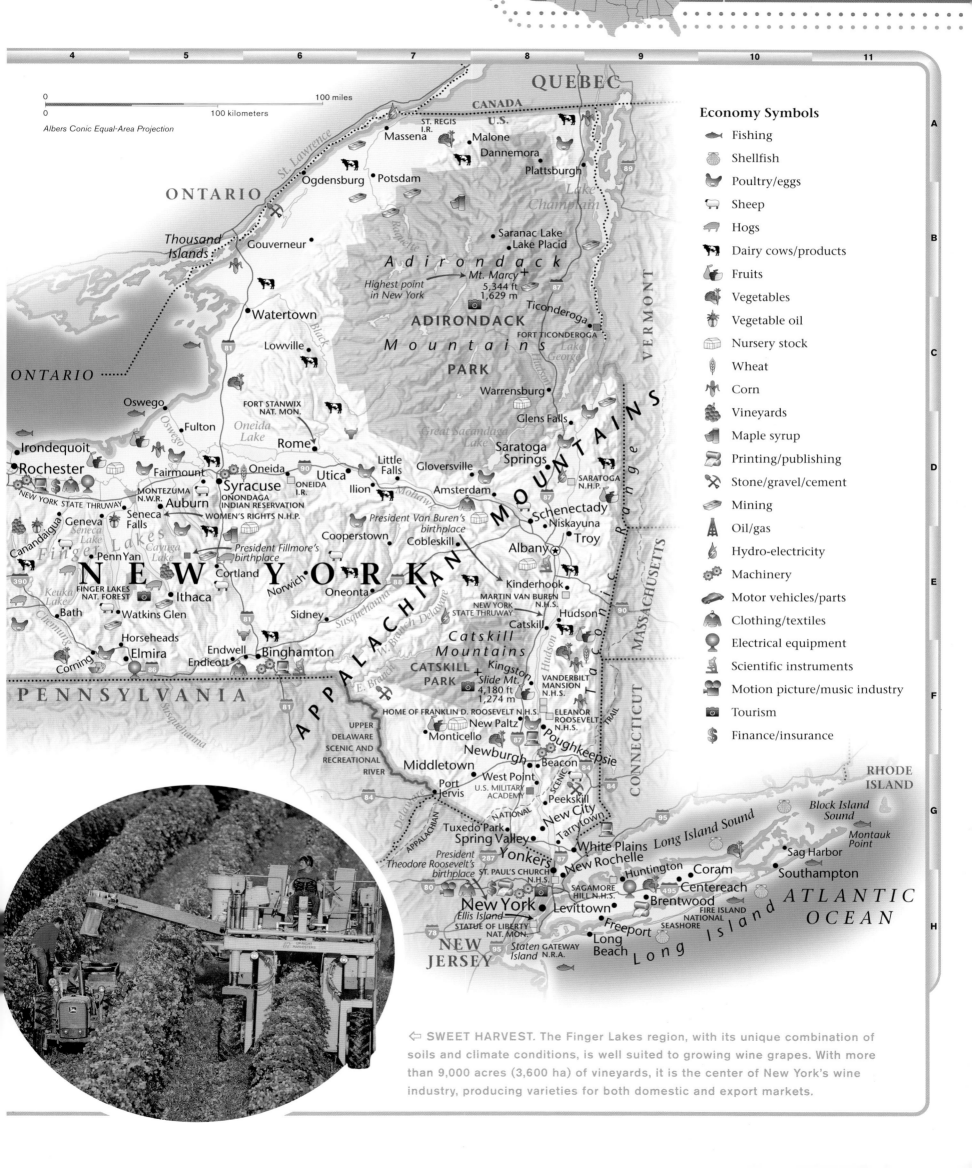

Economy Symbols

- Fishing
- Shellfish
- Poultry/eggs
- Sheep
- Hogs
- Dairy cows/products
- Fruits
- Vegetables
- Vegetable oil
- Nursery stock
- Wheat
- Corn
- Vineyards
- Maple syrup
- Printing/publishing
- Stone/gravel/cement
- Mining
- Oil/gas
- Hydro-electricity
- Machinery
- Motor vehicles/parts
- Clothing/textiles
- Electrical equipment
- Scientific instruments
- Motion picture/music industry
- Tourism
- Finance/insurance

0   100 miles
0   100 kilometers
Albers Conic Equal-Area Projection

QUEBEC
CANADA
U.S.
ONTARIO
VERMONT
MASSACHUSETTS
CONNECTICUT
RHODE ISLAND
PENNSYLVANIA
NEW JERSEY
ATLANTIC OCEAN

St. Lawrence
Thousand Islands
Lake Champlain
Lake George
Lake Ontario
Oneida Lake
Great Sacandaga Lake
Finger Lakes
Seneca Lake
Cayuga Lake
Keuka Lake

Massena
Malone
Dannemora
Plattsburgh
ST. REGIS I.R.
Ogdensburg
Potsdam
Gouverneur
Saranac Lake
Lake Placid
Ticonderoga
FORT TICONDEROGA
Watertown
Lowville
ADIRONDACK Mountains PARK
Highest point in New York
Mt. Marcy 5,344 ft 1,629 m
Warrensburg
Glens Falls
Gloversville
Saratoga Springs
SARATOGA N.H.P.
Oswego
Fulton
Irondequoit
Rochester
Fairmount
Oneida
Utica
Little Falls
FORT STANWIX NAT. MON.
Rome
ONEIDA I.R.
Ilion
Amsterdam
Schenectady
Niskayuna
Troy
Syracuse
ONONDAGA INDIAN RESERVATION
Auburn
WOMEN'S RIGHTS N.H.P.
MONTEZUMA N.W.R.
Geneva
Seneca Falls
Canandaigua
Penn Yan
President Van Buren's birthplace
Cooperstown
Cobleskill
Albany
NEW YORK STATE THRUWAY
Kinderhook
MARTIN VAN BUREN N.H.S.
NEW YORK STATE THRUWAY
Hudson
Catskill
NEW YORK
President Fillmore's birthplace
Cortland
Norwich
Oneonta
FINGER LAKES NAT. FOREST
Ithaca
Bath
Watkins Glen
Sidney
Horseheads
Elmira
Corning
Endwell
Endicott
Binghamton
Catskill Mountains
CATSKILL PARK
Slide Mt. 4,180 ft 1,274 m
Kingston
VANDERBILT MANSION N.H.S.
HOME OF FRANKLIN D. ROOSEVELT N.H.S.
ELEANOR ROOSEVELT N.H.S.
New Paltz
Monticello
Poughkeepsie
UPPER DELAWARE SCENIC AND RECREATIONAL RIVER
Newburgh
Middletown
Beacon
West Point
U.S. MILITARY ACADEMY
Port Jervis
Peekskill
New City
NATIONAL
Tuxedo Park
Spring Valley
Tarrytown
White Plains
Yonkers
New Rochelle
President Theodore Roosevelt's birthplace
ST. PAUL'S CHURCH N.H.S.
SAGAMORE HILL N.H.S.
Huntington
Coram
Centereach
Southampton
Sag Harbor
Brentwood
Long Island Sound
Block Island Sound
Montauk Point
New York
Levittown
Freeport
Long Beach
FIRE ISLAND NATIONAL SEASHORE
Ellis Island
STATUE OF LIBERTY NAT. MON.
Staten Island
GATEWAY N.R.A.

APPALACHIAN MOUNTAINS
Taconic Range
Mohawk
Hudson
Black
Raquette
Oswego
Susquehanna
W. Branch Delaware
E. Branch Delaware
Delaware
Chemung
APPALACHIAN TRAIL

← SWEET HARVEST. The Finger Lakes region, with its unique combination of soils and climate conditions, is well suited to growing wine grapes. With more than 9,000 acres (3,600 ha) of vineyards, it is the center of New York's wine industry, producing varieties for both domestic and export markets.

PENNSYLVANIA

Pennsylvania, the 12th of England's 13 American colonies, was established in 1682 by Quaker William Penn and 360 settlers seeking religious freedom and fair government. The colony enjoyed abundant natural resources—dense woodlands, fertile soils, industrial minerals, and water power—which soon attracted Germans, Scotch-Irish, and other immigrants. Pennsylvania played a central role in the move for independence from Britain, and Philadelphia served as the new country's capital from 1790 to 1800. In the 19th century Philadelphia, in the east, and Pittsburgh, in the west, became booming centers of industrial growth. Philadelphia produced ships, locomotives, and textiles, while the iron and steel industry fueled Pittsburgh's growth. Jobs in industry as well as agriculture attracted immigrants from around the world. Today, Pennsylvania's economy has shifted toward information technology, health care, financial services, and tourism, but the state remains a leader in coal and steel production.

⇑ LET FREEDOM RING. The Liberty Bell, cast in 1753 by Pennsylvania craftsmen, hangs silent in Philadelphia. Because of a crack, it is no longer rung.

THE BASICS

STATS

Area
46,055 sq mi (119,283 sq km)

Population
12,432,792

Capital
Harrisburg
Population 48,322

Largest city
Philadelphia
Population 1,448,394

Ethnic/racial groups
85.7% white; 10.7% African American; 2.4% Asian; .2% Native American. Hispanic (any race) 4.2%.

Industry
Machinery, printing and publishing, forest products, metal products

Agriculture
Dairy products, poultry and eggs, mushrooms, cattle, hogs, grains

Statehood
December 12, 1787; 2nd state

GEO WHIZ

If you are into guitars or other acoustical instruments, you will want to put the Martin Guitar Company, in Nazareth, on your list of places to visit. It has been handcrafting these instruments for musicians all over the world for more than 150 years.

For more than a century, the streets of Philadelphia have been transformed on New Year's Day as some 15,000 revelers dressed in sequined and feathered costumes "strut their stuff" to the sound of string-band music in the Mummers Parade past millions of onlookers.

RUFFED GROUSE
MOUNTAIN LAUREL

⇨ RIVER TOWN. Pittsburgh, one of the largest inland ports in the U.S., was established in 1758 where the Monongahela and Allegheny Rivers meet to form the Ohio River. Once a booming steel town, Pittsburgh is now a center of finance, medicine, and education.

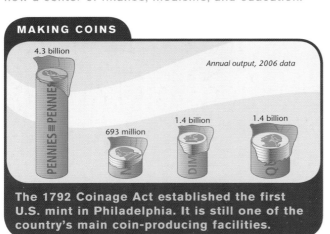

MAKING COINS

4.3 billion

Annual output, 2006 data

PENNIES

693 million

1.4 billion
DIMES

1.4 billion
QUARTERS

The 1792 Coinage Act established the first U.S. mint in Philadelphia. It is still one of the country's main coin-producing facilities.

LAKE ERIE

Erie
Millcreek
Corry
ERIE NATIONAL WILDLIFE REFUGE
Meadville
Titusville
Pymatuning Reservoir
Greenville
Oil City
OHIO
Sharon
Grove City
New Castle
Butler
Beaver Falls
Ohio
Aliquippa
McCandless
Plum
Pittsburgh
Penn Hills
McKeesport
Jeannette
Washington
Monessen
Connellsville
Waynesburg
Uniontown
FRIENDSHIP HILL N.H.S.
FT. NECESSITY NATIONAL BATTLEFIELD

WEST VIRGINIA

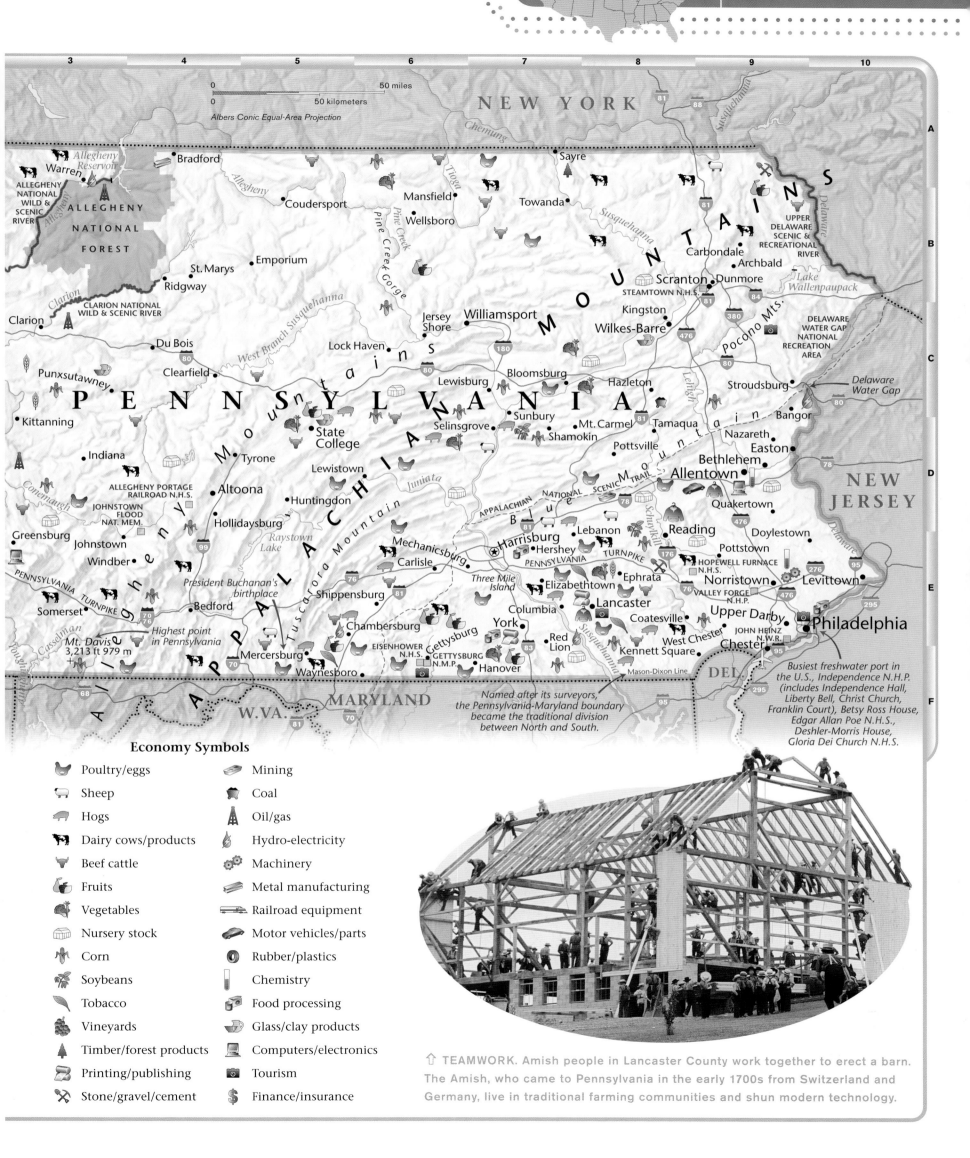

3 4 5 6 7 8 9 10

0   50 miles
0   50 kilometers
Albers Conic Equal-Area Projection

NEW YORK

Chemung

Allegheny Reservoir
Warren
ALLEGHENY NATIONAL WILD & SCENIC RIVER
ALLEGHENY NATIONAL FOREST
Bradford
Allegheny
Sayre
Mansfield
Towanda
Coudersport
Wellsboro
Pine Creek Gorge
Tioga
Susquehanna
UPPER DELAWARE SCENIC & RECREATIONAL RIVER
Carbondale
Archbald
St. Marys
Emporium
Scranton
Dunmore
STEAMTOWN N.H.S.
Lake Wallenpaupack
Ridgway
Clarion
CLARION NATIONAL WILD & SCENIC RIVER
Kingston
DELAWARE WATER GAP NATIONAL RECREATION AREA
Clarion
Du Bois
West Branch Susquehanna
Jersey Shore
Williamsport
Wilkes-Barre
Pocono Mts.
Lock Haven
Clearfield
Lewisburg
Bloomsburg
Hazleton
Stroudsburg
Delaware Water Gap
Punxsutawney
PENNSYLVANIA
Lewistown
Sunbury
Mt. Carmel
Shamokin
Pottsville
Nazareth
Bangor
Kittanning
Selinsgrove
Easton
Indiana
Tyrone
Pottsville
Bethlehem
Allentown
NEW JERSEY
ALLEGHENY PORTAGE RAILROAD N.H.S.
Altoona
Huntingdon
Juniata
APPALACHIAN NATIONAL SCENIC TRAIL
Quakertown
JOHNSTOWN FLOOD NAT. MEM.
Hollidaysburg
Raystown Lake
Mechanicsburg
Lebanon
Reading
Doylestown
Greensburg
Johnstown
Harrisburg
Hershey
PENNSYLVANIA TURNPIKE
Pottstown
Windber
Carlisle
Three Mile Island
Elizabethtown
Ephrata
HOPEWELL FURNACE N.H.S.
Norristown
Levittown
PENNSYLVANIA TURNPIKE
President Buchanan's birthplace
Shippensburg
VALLEY FORGE N.H.P.
Somerset
Bedford
Columbia
Lancaster
Upper Darby
Highest point in Pennsylvania
Chambersburg
York
Coatesville
Philadelphia
Mt. Davis 3,213 ft 979 m
Mercersburg
EISENHOWER N.H.S.
Gettysburg
Red Lion
West Chester
JOHN HEINZ N.W.R.
Chester
GETTYSBURG N.M.P.
Kennett Square
Waynesboro
Hanover
Mason-Dixon Line
DEL.
W.VA.
MARYLAND
Named after its surveyors, the Pennsylvania-Maryland boundary became the traditional division between North and South.

Busiest freshwater port in the U.S., Independence N.H.P. (includes Independence Hall, Liberty Bell, Christ Church, Franklin Court), Betsy Ross House, Edgar Allan Poe N.H.S., Deshler-Morris House, Gloria Dei Church N.H.S.

A B C D E F

Economy Symbols

- Poultry/eggs
- Sheep
- Hogs
- Dairy cows/products
- Beef cattle
- Fruits
- Vegetables
- Nursery stock
- Corn
- Soybeans
- Tobacco
- Vineyards
- Timber/forest products
- Printing/publishing
- Stone/gravel/cement

- Mining
- Coal
- Oil/gas
- Hydro-electricity
- Machinery
- Metal manufacturing
- Railroad equipment
- Motor vehicles/parts
- Rubber/plastics
- Chemistry
- Food processing
- Glass/clay products
- Computers/electronics
- Tourism
- Finance/insurance

⇧ TEAMWORK. Amish people in Lancaster County work together to erect a barn. The Amish, who came to Pennsylvania in the early 1700s from Switzerland and Germany, live in traditional farming communities and shun modern technology.

THE OCEAN STATE:
RHODE ISLAND

RHODE ISLAND

THE BASICS

STATS

Area
1,545 sq mi (4,002 sq km)

Population
1,057,832

Capital
Providence
Population 175,255

Largest city
Providence
Population 175,255

Ethnic/racial groups
88.7% white; 6.3% African American;
2.7% Asian; .6% Native American.
Hispanic (any race) 11.0%.

Industry
Health services, business services,
silver and jewelry products,
metal products

Agriculture
Nursery stock, vegetables, dairy
products, eggs

Statehood
May 29, 1790; 13th state

GEO WHIZ

Pawtucket is one of several communities in Rhode Island that have become home to a growing number of people from Cape Verde. Drought has forced people from this African country to find a new place to live. Massachusetts and North Dakota are the only other states with measurable Cape Verdean populations.

Wild coyotes are living and thriving on islands in Narragansett Bay. Researchers have outfitted some of the animals with radio collars so that their numbers and whereabouts can be tracked online—even by schoolkids.

RHODE ISLAND RED
VIOLET

In 1524 Italian navigator Giovanni Verrazzano was the first European explorer to visit Rhode Island, but place names such as Quonochontaug and Narragansett tell of an earlier Native American population. In 1636 Roger Williams, seeking greater religious freedom, left Massachusetts and established the first European settlement in what was to become the colony of Rhode Island. In the years following the Revolutionary War, Rhode Island pressed for fairness in trade, taxes, and representation in Congress, as well as greater freedom of worship, before becoming the 13th state. By the 19th century, Rhode Island had become an important center of trade and textile factories, attracting many immigrants from Europe. In addition to commercial activities, Rhode Island's coastline became a popular vacation retreat for the wealthy. Today, Rhode Island, like many other states, has seen its economy shift toward high-tech jobs and service industries. It is also promoting its coastline and bays, as well as its rich history, to attract tourists.

⇧ CLUES TO THE PAST. Fossils embedded in rocks left behind 10,000 years ago by retreating glaciers tell of Block Island's past.

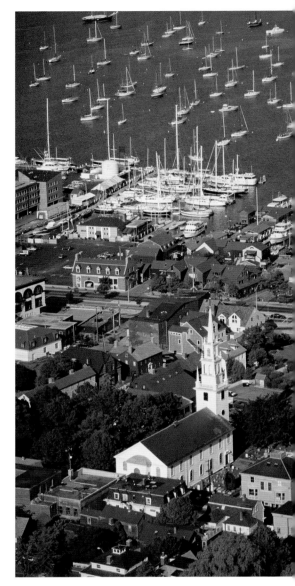

⇐ SETTING SAIL. Newport Harbor invites sailors of all ages. From 1930 to 1983, the prestigious America's Cup Yacht Race took place in the waters off Newport. Today, the town provides 900 moorings for boats of all types.

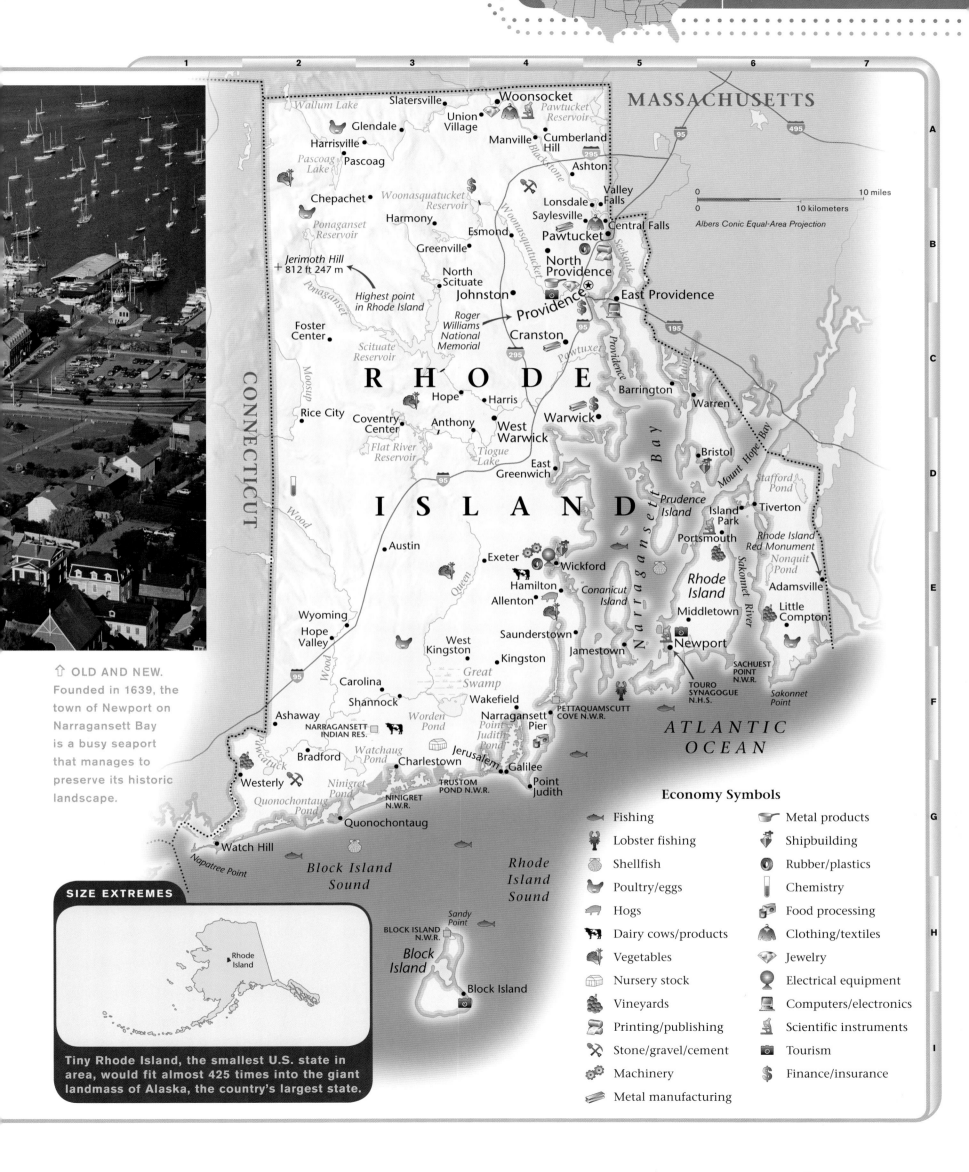

MASSACHUSETTS

Wallum Lake • Slatersville • Woonsocket
Glendale • Union Village
Harrisville Manville • Cumberland Hill
Pascoag Lake • Pascoag Ashton
Chepachet Woonasquatucket Reservoir Lonsdale Valley Falls
Ponaganset Reservoir Harmony Saylesville Central Falls
Esmond Pawtucket
Greenville North Providence
+ Jerimoth Hill North Scituate East Providence
812 ft 247 m Johnston Providence
Highest point in Rhode Island Roger Williams National Memorial Cranston
Foster Center Scituate Reservoir
R H O D E
Barrington
Moosup Hope Harris Warren
Rice City Coventry Center Anthony Warwick
Flat River Reservoir West Warwick Bristol
I S L A N D Tiogue Lake East Greenwich
Prudence Island Island Park Tiverton
Stafford Pond
Wood Austin Rhode Island Red Monument
Nonquit Pond
Exeter Portsmouth
Wickford Rhode Island Adamsville
Hamilton Conanicut Island Middletown Little Compton
Allenton
Wyoming Saunderstown Newport
Hope Valley West Kingston Jamestown Sachuest Point N.W.R.
Carolina Kingston Touro Synagogue N.H.S. Sakonnet Point
Shannock Great Swamp Wakefield Pettaquamscutt Cove N.W.R.
Ashaway Narragansett Pier ATLANTIC OCEAN
Narragansett Indian Res. Worden Pond Point Judith Pond
Bradford Watchaug Pond Jerusalem
Pawcatuck Charlestown Galilee
Westerly Ninigret Pond Trustom Pond N.W.R. Point Judith
Quonochontaug Pond Ninigret N.W.R.
Watch Hill Quonochontaug
Napatree Point Rhode Island Sound
Block Island Sound Rhode Island Sound

Connecticut

Narragansett Bay
Mount Hope Bay
Sakonnet River
Providence
Pawtuxet
Seekonk
Blackstone
Woonasquatucket
Ponaganset
Wood

Sandy Point
BLOCK ISLAND N.W.R.
Block Island
Block Island

⇧ OLD AND NEW.
Founded in 1639, the town of Newport on Narragansett Bay is a busy seaport that manages to preserve its historic landscape.

SIZE EXTREMES

Rhode Island

Tiny Rhode Island, the smallest U.S. state in area, would fit almost 425 times into the giant landmass of Alaska, the country's largest state.

Economy Symbols

🐟 Fishing		🥣 Metal products	
🦞 Lobster fishing		⚓ Shipbuilding	
🐚 Shellfish		⚫ Rubber/plastics	
🐔 Poultry/eggs		🧪 Chemistry	
🐖 Hogs		📷 Food processing	
🐄 Dairy cows/products		👕 Clothing/textiles	
🥬 Vegetables		💎 Jewelry	
Nursery stock		Electrical equipment	
🍇 Vineyards		💻 Computers/electronics	
Printing/publishing		🔬 Scientific instruments	
⚒ Stone/gravel/cement		📷 Tourism	
⚙ Machinery		$ Finance/insurance	
Metal manufacturing			

0 ——— 10 miles
0 ——— 10 kilometers
Albers Conic Equal-Area Projection

VERMONT

When French explorer Jacques Cartier arrived in Vermont in 1535, Native Americans living in woodland villages had been there for hundreds of years. Settled first by the French in 1666 and then by the English in 1724, the territory of Vermont became an area of conflict between these colonial powers. The French finally withdrew, but conflict continued between New York and New Hampshire, both of which wanted to take over Vermont. The people of Vermont declared their independence in 1777 and became the 14th U.S. state in 1791. Vermont's name, which means "Green Mountain," comes from the extensive forests that cover much of the state and that provide the basis for furniture and pulp industries. Vermont also boasts the world's largest granite quarry and the largest underground marble quarry, both of which produce valuable building materials. Tourism and recreation are also important in Vermont. Lakes, rivers, and mountain trails are popular summer attractions, while snow-covered mountains attract skiers throughout the winter.

⇧ LIQUID GOLD. In spring, sap from maple trees is collected in buckets by drilling a hole in the tree trunk—called "tapping." The sap is boiled to remove water, then filtered, and finally bottled.

THE BASICS

STATS

Area
9,614 sq mi (24,901 sq km)

Population
621,254

Capital
Montpelier
Population 7,954

Largest city
Burlington
Population 39,148

Ethnic/racial groups
96.7% white; 1.1% Asian; .7% African American; .4% Native American. Hispanic (any race) 1.1%.

Industry
Health services, tourism, finance, real estate, computer components, electrical parts, printing and publishing, machine tools

Agriculture
Dairy products, maple products, apples

Statehood
March 4, 1791; 14th state

GEO WHIZ

Barre is famous for producing granite gravestones. The tombstones of President Harry Truman, industrialist John D. Rockefeller, Sr., songwriter Stephen Foster, and fast-food-chain founder Col. Harland Sanders are all made of Barre Gray granite, as are the steps of the U.S. Capitol in Washington, D.C.

Burlington is the home of Ben & Jerry's ice cream. The company gives its leftovers to local farmers, who feed it to their hogs. The hogs seem to like every flavor except Mint Oreo.

From 1777 until it became a state in 1791, Vermont was an independent country. It had its own postal and monetary systems.

Vermont, the third-largest state in New England, is the only state in the region that does not border the Atlantic Ocean.

HERMIT THRUSH
RED CLOVER

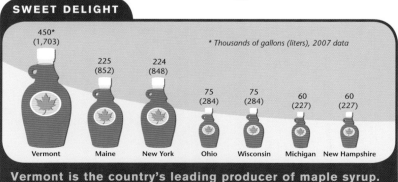

SWEET DELIGHT

450* (1,703) — Vermont
* Thousands of gallons (liters), 2007 data
225 (852) — Maine
224 (848) — New York
75 (284) — Ohio
75 (284) — Wisconsin
60 (227) — Michigan
60 (227) — New Hampshire

Vermont is the country's leading producer of maple syrup. The syrup is all natural, with no added ingredients or preservatives, just boiled sap collected from maple trees.

⇧ WINTER WONDERLAND. One of the snowiest places in the Northeast, Jay Peak averages 355 inches (900 cm) of snow each year. With 76 trails, the mountain, near Vermont's border with Canada, attracts beginner and expert skiers from near and far.

Economy Symbols

- Poultry/eggs
- Sheep
- Dairy cows/products
- Beef cattle
- Fruits
- Vegetables
- Nursery stock
- Corn
- Maple syrup
- Timber/forest products
- Printing/publishing
- Stone/gravel/cement
- Hydro-electricity
- Metal products
- Food processing
- Computers/electronics
- Tourism

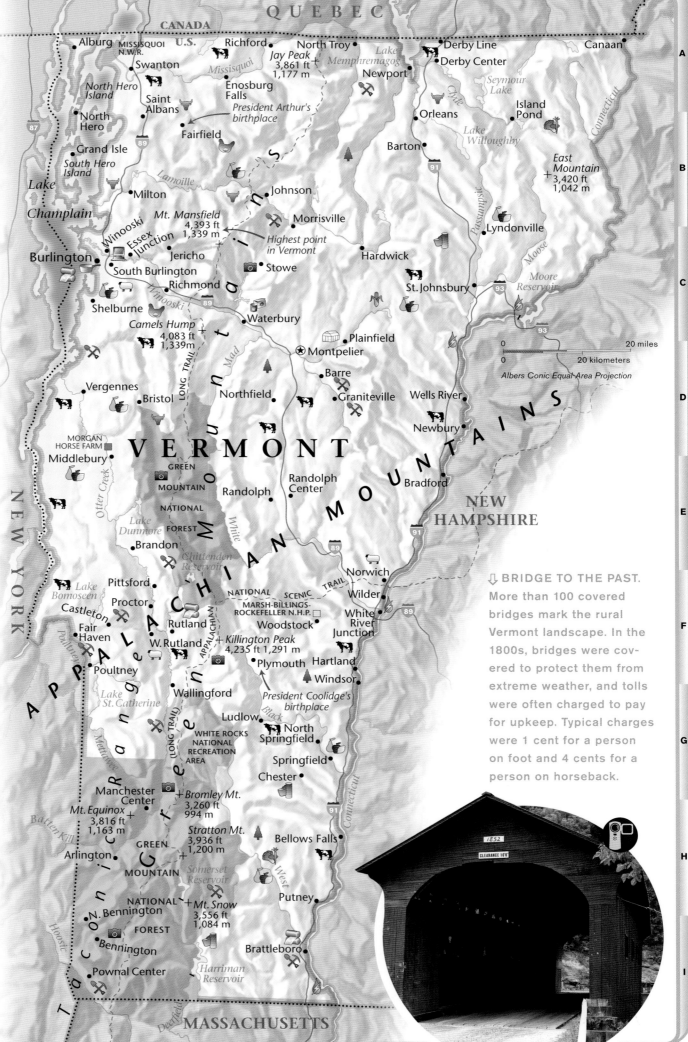

QUEBEC

CANADA
U.S.

Alburg
MISSISQUOI N.W.R.
Richford
North Troy
Jay Peak
3,861 ft
1,177 m
Derby Line
Derby Center
Canaan
Swanton
Missisquoi
Lake Memphremagog
Newport
Seymour Lake
North Hero Island
Saint Albans
Enosburg Falls
President Arthur's birthplace
Orleans
Island Pond
North Hero
Fairfield
Lake Willoughby
Barton
East Mountain
3,420 ft
1,042 m
Grand Isle
South Hero Island
Johnson
Lake Champlain
Milton
Mt. Mansfield
4,393 ft
1,339 m
Morrisville
Lyndonville
Winooski
Essex Junction
Highest point in Vermont
Hardwick
St. Johnsbury
Moore Reservoir
Burlington
Jericho
South Burlington
Richmond
Stowe
Waterbury
Shelburne
Camels Hump
4,083 ft
1,339m
Plainfield
Montpelier
Vergennes
Barre
Northfield
Graniteville
Wells River
Bristol
Newbury
Bradford
MORGAN HORSE FARM
Middlebury
VERMONT
NEW HAMPSHIRE
GREEN MOUNTAIN
Randolph
Randolph Center
NATIONAL
FOREST
Lake Dunmore
White
Brandon
Chittenden Reservoir
Norwich
Lake Bomoseen
Pittsford
TRAIL
Wilder
NEW YORK
Proctor
NATIONAL SCENIC
MARSH-BILLINGS-ROCKEFELLER N.H.P.
White River Junction
Castleton
Rutland
Woodstock
Fair Haven
Killington Peak
4,235 ft 1,291 m
W. Rutland
APPALACHIAN
Plymouth
Hartland
Poultney
Windsor
President Coolidge's birthplace
Wallingford
Lake St. Catherine
Ludlow
Black
Range
North Springfield
WHITE ROCKS NATIONAL RECREATION AREA
Springfield
Manchester Center
Chester
Bromley Mt.
3,260 ft
994 m
Mt. Equinox
3,816 ft
1,163 m
Green
Stratton Mt.
3,936 ft
1,200 m
Bellows Falls
Arlington
GREEN MOUNTAIN
Somerset Reservoir
Mountains
Range
Taconic
West
Putney
N. Bennington
FOREST
Mt. Snow
3,556 ft
1,084 m
Bennington
NATIONAL
Brattleboro
Pownal Center
Harriman Reservoir
Hoosic
Deerfield
MASSACHUSETTS

0 _____ 20 miles
0 _____ 20 kilometers
Albers Conic Equal-Area Projection

⇓ BRIDGE TO THE PAST.
More than 100 covered bridges mark the rural Vermont landscape. In the 1800s, bridges were covered to protect them from extreme weather, and tolls were often charged to pay for upkeep. Typical charges were 1 cent for a person on foot and 4 cents for a person on horseback.

THE REGION

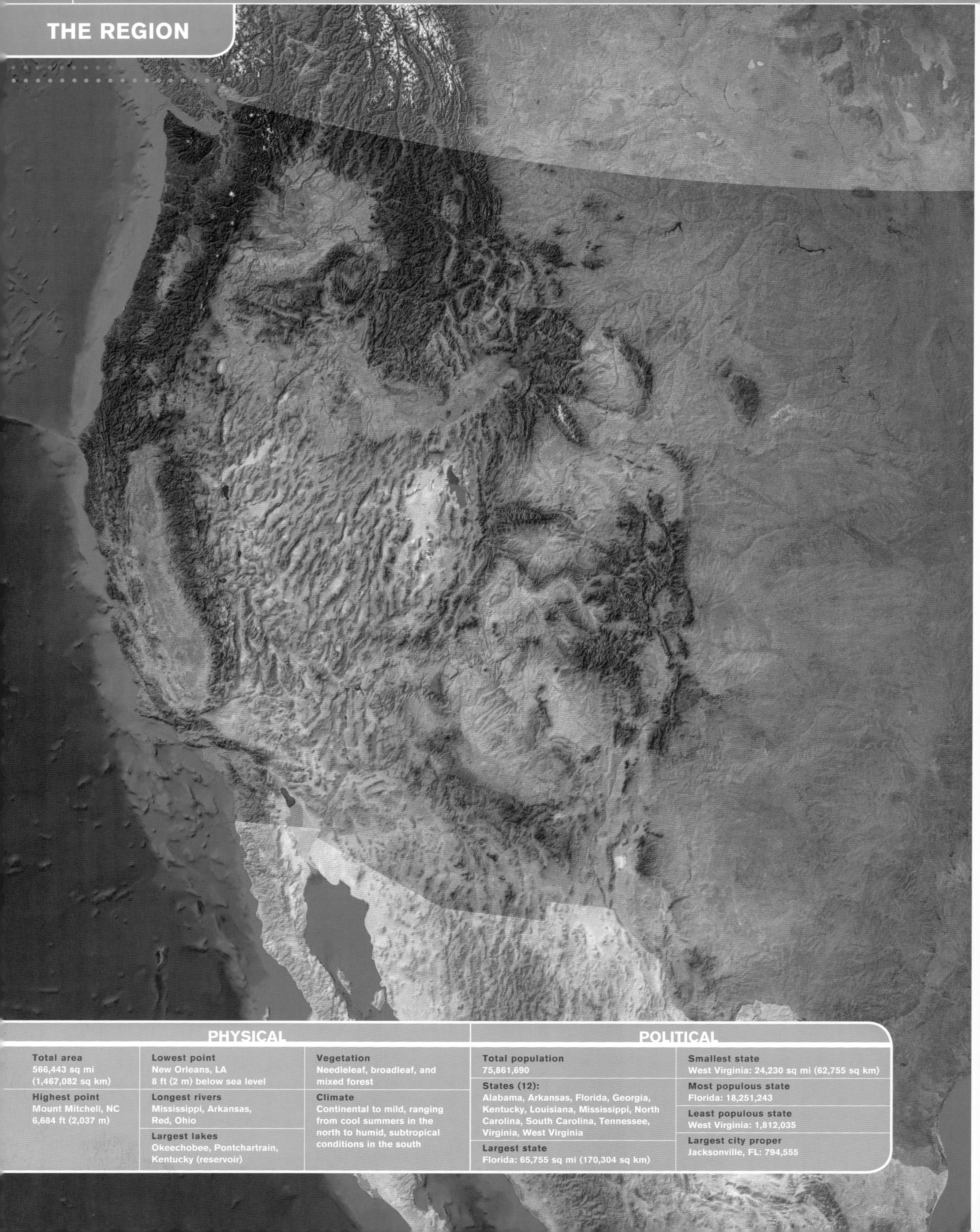

PHYSICAL

Total area
566,443 sq mi
(1,467,082 sq km)

Highest point
Mount Mitchell, NC
6,684 ft (2,037 m)

Lowest point
New Orleans, LA
8 ft (2 m) below sea level

Longest rivers
Mississippi, Arkansas,
Red, Ohio

Largest lakes
Okeechobee, Pontchartrain,
Kentucky (reservoir)

Vegetation
Needleleaf, broadleaf, and
mixed forest

Climate
Continental to mild, ranging
from cool summers in the
north to humid, subtropical
conditions in the south

POLITICAL

Total population
75,861,690

States (12):
Alabama, Arkansas, Florida, Georgia,
Kentucky, Louisiana, Mississippi, North
Carolina, South Carolina, Tennessee,
Virginia, West Virginia

Largest state
Florida: 65,755 sq mi (170,304 sq km)

Smallest state
West Virginia: 24,230 sq mi (62,755 sq km)

Most populous state
Florida: 18,251,243

Least populous state
West Virginia: 1,812,035

Largest city proper
Jacksonville, FL: 794,555

The Southeast

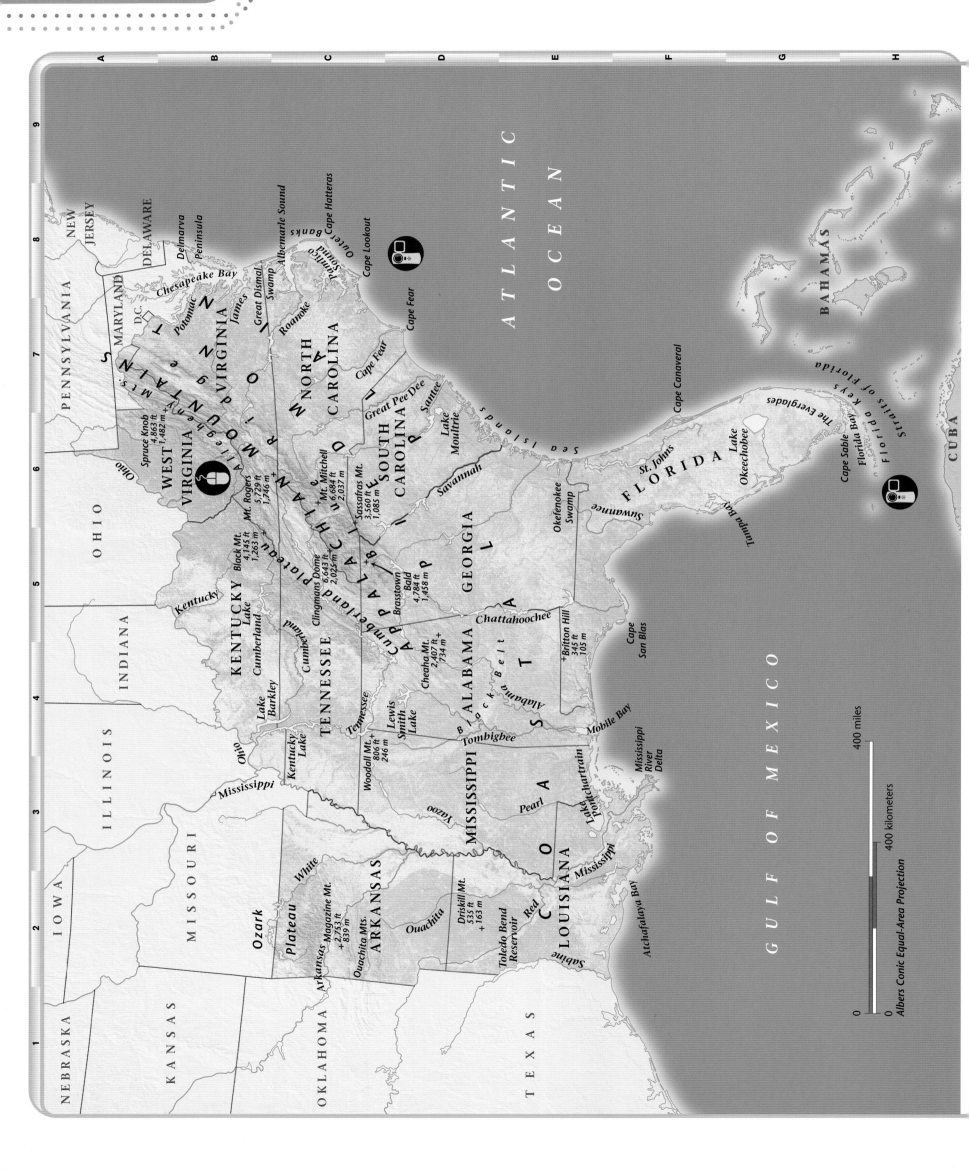

A B C D E F G H

9 8 7 6 5 4 3 2 1

NEW JERSEY

PENNSYLVANIA

DELAWARE

Delmarva Peninsula

MARYLAND

Chesapeake Bay

Great Dismal Swamp

Albemarle Sound

Outer Banks

Cape Hatteras

Cape Lookout

D.C.

Potomac

James

Roanoke

NORTH CAROLINA

Pamlico Sound

Cape Fear

VIRGINIA

WEST VIRGINIA

Spruce Knob 4,863 ft 1,482 m

Mt. Rogers 5,729 ft 1,746 m

Blue Ridge Mts.

APPALACHIAN MOUNTAINS

Mt. Mitchell 6,684 ft 2,037 m

Sassafras Mt. 3,560 ft 1,085 m

Great Pee Dee

Santee

SOUTH CAROLINA

Lake Moultrie

Cape Fear

Sea Islands

ATLANTIC OCEAN

OHIO

Ohio

KENTUCKY

Kentucky Lake

Black Mt. 4,145 ft 1,263 m

Cumberland

Cumberland Plateau

Clingmans Dome 6,643 ft 2,025 m

Brasstown Bald 4,784 ft 1,458 m

Savannah

GEORGIA

FLORIDA

St. Johns

Lake Okeechobee

The Everglades

Cape Canaveral

Florida Keys

Straits of Florida

BAHAMAS

CUBA

INDIANA

ILLINOIS

Lake Barkley

TENNESSEE

Tennessee

Cumberland

Lewis Smith Lake

Cheaha Mt. 2,407 ft 734 m

Chattahoochee

Okefenokee Swamp

Suwannee

Lake Okeechobee

Cape San Blas

Britton Hill 345 ft 105 m

Black Belt

Alabama

ALABAMA

Tampa Bay

Cape Sable

Florida Bay

IOWA

MISSOURI

KANSAS

Ozark Plateau

White

Arkansas

Magazine Mt. 2,753 ft 839 m

Ouachita Mts.

ARKANSAS

Ouachita

Driskill Mt. 535 ft 163 m

Toledo Bend Reservoir

Red

Ohio

Mississippi

Kentucky Lake

Yazoo

MISSISSIPPI

Pearl

Mississippi

Lake Pontchartrain

Tombigbee

Mobile Bay

Mississippi River Delta

LOUISIANA

Sabine

Atchafalaya Bay

GULF OF MEXICO

OKLAHOMA

TEXAS

NEBRASKA

Woodall Mt. 806 ft 246 m

400 miles

400 kilometers

Albers Conic Equal-Area Projection

0

0

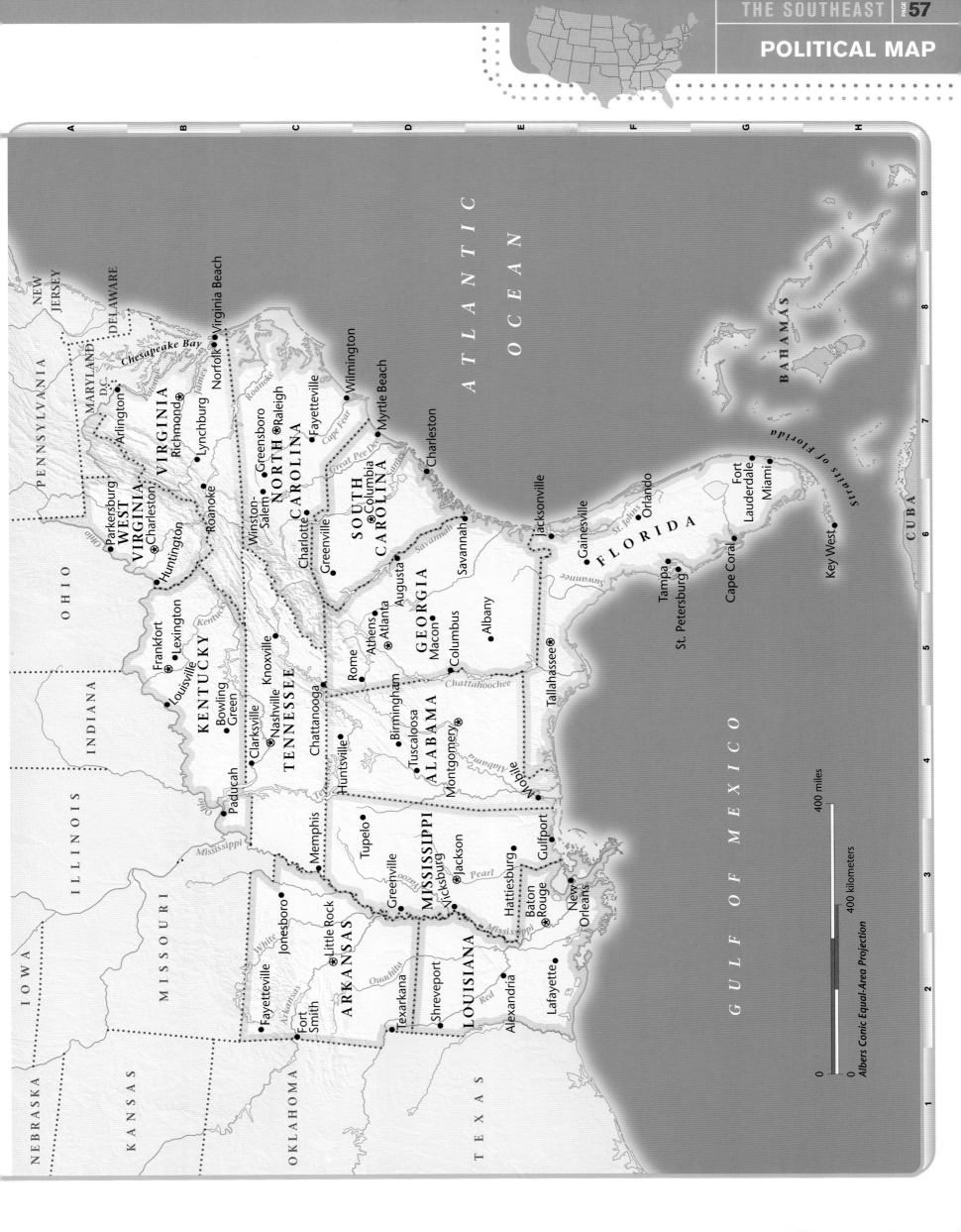

A B C D E F G H

9
8
7
6
5
4
3
2
1

NEW JERSEY

DELAWARE

PENNSYLVANIA

MARYLAND

D.C.
Arlington

Chesapeake Bay

Potomac

VIRGINIA
Richmond ⊛
Lynchburg
James
Norfolk
Virginia Beach

Roanoke

WEST VIRGINIA
Parkersburg
Charleston ⊛
Huntington
Roanoke

Ohio

Winston-Salem
Greensboro
Raleigh ⊛
NORTH CAROLINA
Fayetteville
Cape Fear
Wilmington

Great Pee Dee

Charlotte
Greenville
SOUTH CAROLINA
Columbia ⊛
Santee
Charleston

Myrtle Beach

A T L A N T I C   O C E A N

BAHAMAS

KENTUCKY
Frankfort ⊛
Lexington
Louisville
Bowling Green

Kentucky

OHIO

INDIANA

ILLINOIS

Knoxville
Clarksville
Nashville ⊛
TENNESSEE
Chattanooga
Tennessee
Huntsville
Paducah

Rome
Athens
Atlanta ⊛
Birmingham
Tuscaloosa
ALABAMA
Montgomery ⊛
Chattahoochee

GEORGIA
Macon
Columbus
Augusta
Savannah
Savannah
Albany

Jacksonville
Gainesville
St. Johns
Orlando

FLORIDA
Suwannee

Tampa
St. Petersburg

Cape Coral

Fort Lauderdale
Miami

Key West

Straits of Florida

CUBA

Tallahassee ⊛
Mobile
Alabama

MISSOURI

Memphis
Tupelo
Greenville
MISSISSIPPI
Vicksburg
Jackson ⊛
Yazoo
Pearl
Hattiesburg
Gulfport

Mississippi

Jonesboro
Little Rock ⊛
ARKANSAS
Fayetteville
Fort Smith
White
Arkansas
Ouachita

Texarkana
Shreveport
LOUISIANA
Red
Alexandria
Lafayette
Baton Rouge ⊛
New Orleans

Mississippi

G U L F   O F   M E X I C O

OKLAHOMA

TEXAS

KANSAS

NEBRASKA

IOWA

400 miles

400 kilometers

0

0

Albers Conic Equal-Area Projection

⇨ OPEN WIDE. An American alligator in Florida's Big Cypress Swamp shows off sharp teeth. These large reptiles live mainly in fresh-water swamps and marshes in coastal areas of the Southeast. Adult males average 14 feet (4 m) in length.

The Southeast
TRADITION MEETS TECHNOLOGY

From deeply weathered mountains in West Virginia to warm, humid wetlands in south Florida and the Mississippi River's sprawling delta in southern Louisiana, the Southeast is marked by great physical diversity. The region's historical roots are in agriculture—especially cotton and tobacco. The Civil War brought economic and political upheaval in the mid-19th century, but today the Southeast is part of the Sunbelt, where 3 of the top 20 metropolitan areas of the U.S. are found and where high-tech industries are redefining the way people earn a living and the way the region is connected to the global economy.

⇨ ENCHANTED KINGDOM. Fireworks light up the night sky above Cinderella's Castle at Walt Disney World near Orlando, Florida. The park, which accounts for more than 12 percent of all jobs in the Orlando area, attracts millions of tourists from around the world each year.

⇧ SOCIAL CONSCIENCE. Members of the Big Nine Social Aid and Pleasure Club of New Orleans's Lower Ninth Ward march in a parade through a neighborhood devastated by Hurricane Katrina. Such clubs, which date back to late 19th-century benevolent societies, bring support and hope to communities in need.

WHERE THE PICTURES ARE

Banjo playing p. 69
River rafting p. 83
Coal miner p. 82
Horse race p. 68
Cyclists on outcrop pp. 58-59
Black bear family p. 78
Harpers Ferry p. 82
Motorboats p. 79
Luray Caverns p. 80
Grand Ole Opry p. 79
Indian Woman p. 75
Cyclists pp. 80-81
Space camp p. 60
Dice p. 80
Race car p. 59
Rockclimber p. 62
Bird-watchers p. 62
Wright Brothers Memorial p. 74
Blackbeard's cannon p. 59
Diamond hunter p. 63
Boys playing basketball p. 74
Paddleboat p. 72
Beach scene p. 76
Blues guitarist p. 72
Wild turkey p. 77
Catfish p. 73
Historic Charleston pp. 76-77
Atlanta p. 66
Oak Alley Plantation p. 70
Oil rig p. 60
Aerial of Sea Islands p. 66
Peanuts p. 66
Manatee p. 64
Shuttle launch pp. 64-65
Katrina parade p. 58
Cinderella's Castle p. 58, Girl in parade p. 64
Shrimp fisherman p. 70
Alligator p. 58

⇧ VIEW FROM ABOVE. Cyclists look out from a rocky ledge across West Virginia's Germany Valley. The area took its name from German immigrants who moved there in the mid-1700s from North Carolina and Pennsylvania and established farming villages.

⇨ CAR STARS. For more than 50 years, auto racing has been a leading sport in the U.S., especially in the Southeast. The International Motorsports Hall of Fame, located adjacent to the Talledega Superspeedway in Alabama, features racing cars, motorcycles, and vintage cars.

⇦ PIRATE'S DEFENSE. This 4.5-foot (1.4-m) cast-iron cannon was recovered from the wreck of the *Queen Anne's Revenge* off North Carolina's coast. The vessel, which probably belonged to the notorious pirate Blackbeard, grounded on a sandbar and sank in 1718 near Cape Lookout.

THE HEART OF DIXIE STATE:
ALABAMA

THE BASICS

STATS

Area
52,419 sq mi (135,765 sq km)

Population
4,627,851

Capital
Montgomery
Population 201,998

Largest city
Birmingham
Population 229,424

Ethnic/racial groups
71.2% white; 26.3% African American;
.9% Asian; .5% Native American.
Hispanic (any race) 2.5%.

Industry
Retail and wholesale trade, services,
government, finance, insurance, real
estate, transportation, construction,
communication

Agriculture
Fruits and vegetables, dairy products,
cattle, forest products, commercial
fishing

Statehood
December 14, 1819; 22nd state

GEO WHIZ

Condoleezza Rice, the first African-
American woman to serve as U.S.
Secretary of State, and Rosa
Parks, whose refusal to give up
her seat on a Montgomery bus
earned her the title "mother of the
modern-day civil rights movement,"
were both born in Alabama: Rice in
Birmingham and Parks in Tuskegee.

Russell Cave, near Bridgeport, was home
to prehistoric peoples for more than
10,000 years. In 1961 a national monument was established on land donated
by the National Geographic Society.
Today, visitors can take guided tours of
the cave and see the kinds of tools and
weapons its early inhabitants used.

In 2004 Hurricane Ivan, one of
the worst storms to batter
Alabama's Gulf coast
since 1900, struck
Orange Beach.

NORTHERN
FLICKER

CAMELLIA

ALABAMA

Alabama has a colorful story. The French established the first permanent European settlement at Mobile Bay in 1702, but different groups—British, Native Americans, and U.S. settlers—struggled over control of the land for more than 100 years. In 1819 Alabama became the 22nd state, but in 1861 it joined the Confederacy. During the Civil War, Montgomery was the capital of the secessionist South for a time. After the war Alabama struggled to rebuild its agriculture-based economy. By 1900 the state was producing more than one million bales of cotton annually. In the mid-20th century, Alabama was at the center of the civil rights movement, which pressed for equal rights for all people regardless of race or social status. Key players included Martin Luther King, Jr., and Rosa Parks. Modern industries, including the NASA space program, have given the state's economy a big boost. In 2002 assembly plants built by automakers from Asia created thousands of new jobs.

⇧ UNDERWATER RESOURCE. A massive drill descends from an offshore oil rig to tap petroleum deposits beneath the water of the Gulf of Mexico off Alabama's shore.

⇧ ROCKET POWER. Students inspect giant booster rockets during Space Camp at Marshall Space Flight Center, in Huntsville, Alabama. The center is one of NASA's largest installations, providing support to space shuttle missions and the International Space Station.

ON THE ROAD

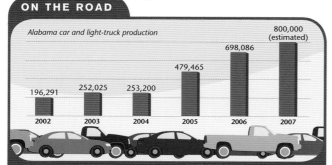

Alabama car and light-truck production

2002	2003	2004	2005	2006	2007
196,291	252,025	253,200	479,465	698,086	800,000 (estimated)

Since the first vehicles rolled off the assembly line in 1993, Alabama has risen to #5 in national automotive production.

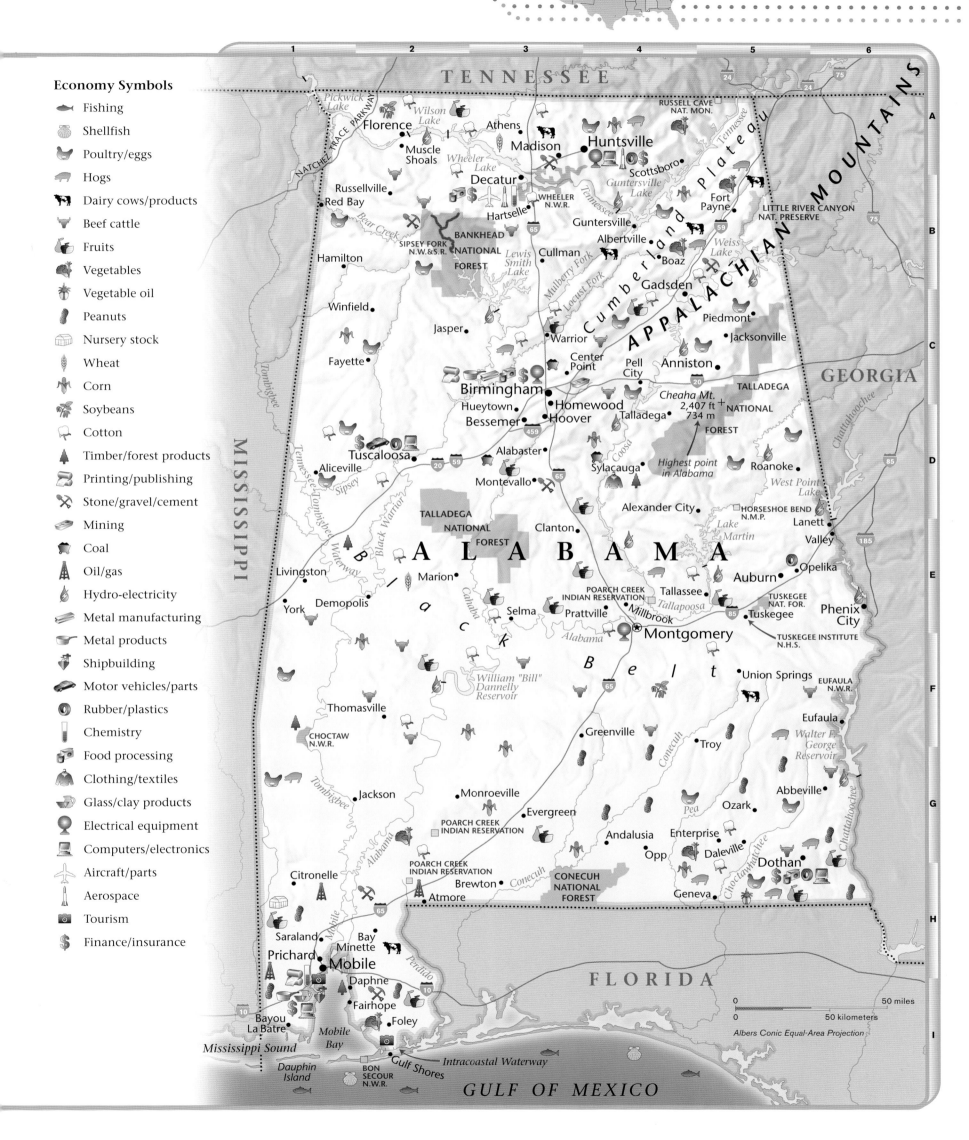

Economy Symbols

- Fishing
- Shellfish
- Poultry/eggs
- Hogs
- Dairy cows/products
- Beef cattle
- Fruits
- Vegetables
- Vegetable oil
- Peanuts
- Nursery stock
- Wheat
- Corn
- Soybeans
- Cotton
- Timber/forest products
- Printing/publishing
- Stone/gravel/cement
- Mining
- Coal
- Oil/gas
- Hydro-electricity
- Metal manufacturing
- Metal products
- Shipbuilding
- Motor vehicles/parts
- Rubber/plastics
- Chemistry
- Food processing
- Clothing/textiles
- Glass/clay products
- Electrical equipment
- Computers/electronics
- Aircraft/parts
- Aerospace
- Tourism
- Finance/insurance

THE NATURAL STATE:
ARKANSAS

ARKANSAS

THE BASICS

STATS

Area
53,179 sq mi (137,732 sq km)

Population
2,834,797

Capital
Little Rock
Population 184,422

Largest city
Little Rock
Population 184,422

Ethnic/racial groups
81.1% white; 15.7% African American;
1.0% Asian; .8% Native American.
Hispanic (any race) 5.0%.

Industry
Services, food processing, paper products, transportation, metal products,
machinery, electronics

Agriculture
Poultry and eggs, rice, soybeans,
cotton, wheat

Statehood
June 15, 1836; 25th state

GEO WHIZ

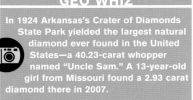

In 1924 Arkansas's Crater of Diamonds
State Park yielded the largest natural
diamond ever found in the United
States—a 40.23-carat whopper
named "Uncle Sam." A 13-year-old
girl from Missouri found a 2.93 carat
diamond there in 2007.

Since 1936 Stuttgart has been the site
of the annual World Championship
Duck Calling Contest. The first winner
took home a grand total of $6.60.
Today, the prize package is worth
more than $15,000.

The city of Texarkana is
divided by the Arkansas-
Texas border. It has two
governments, one for
each state.

MOCKINGBIRD
APPLE BLOSSOM

ARKANSAS

The land that is Arkansas was explored by the Spanish in 1541 and later by the French, but it came under U.S. control with the Louisiana Purchase in 1803. As settlers arrived, Native Americans were pushed out, and cotton fields spread across the fertile valleys of the Arkansas and Mississippi Rivers. Arkansas became the 25th state in 1836, but joined the Confederacy in 1861. Following the war, Arkansas faced hard times, and many people moved away in search of jobs. Today, agriculture remains an important part of the economy. Rice has replaced cotton as the state's main crop, and poultry and grain production are also important. Natural gas, in the northwestern part of the state, and petroleum, along the southern border with Louisiana, are key mining products in Arkansas. The state is headquarters for Wal-Mart, the world's largest retail chain, and tourism is growing as visitors are attracted to the natural beauty of the Ozark and Ouachita Mountains.

⇧ HOLD ON! A rock climber clings to a sandstone cliff in northwest Arkansas, where the Ozark and Ouachita Mountains make up the Interior Highlands of the United States. The Ouachita are folded mountains, but the Ozarks are really a deeply eroded plateau.

⇦ BIRDWATCHERS. Biologists and volunteers scan the treetops for a rare ivory-billed woodpecker in the White River National Wildlife Refuge. Established in 1935 along the White River near where it joins the Mississippi, the refuge provides a protected habitat for migratory birds.

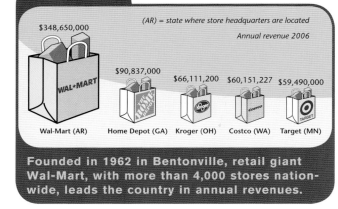

SUPERSTORE

(AR) = state where store headquarters are located

Annual revenue 2006

$348,650,000

$90,837,000 $66,111,200 $60,151,227 $59,490,000

Wal-Mart (AR) Home Depot (GA) Kroger (OH) Costco (WA) Target (MN)

Founded in 1962 in Bentonville, retail giant Wal-Mart, with more than 4,000 stores nation-wide, leads the country in annual revenues.

MISSOURI

1 2 3 4 5 6 7 8

OZARK PLATEAU

Bella Vista
Bentonville
PEA RIDGE N.M.P.
Eureka Springs
Berryville
MAMMOTH SPRING S.P.
Corning
Rogers
Siloam Springs
Beaver Lake
Mountain Home
Cherokee Village
Pocahontas
Paragould
Springdale
OZARK N.F.
Harrison
Norfork Lake
Horseshoe Bend
Spring
Walnut Ridge
BIG LAKE N.W.R.
Blytheville
Fayetteville
OZARK N.F.
BUFFALO NATIONAL RIVER
OZARK NATIONAL FOREST
White
Jonesboro
Manila
Boston Mountains
HURRICANE CREEK NAT. W.&S.R.
NORTH SYLAMORE CREEK NAT. WILD & SCENIC RIVER
Mountain View
Batesville
Black
Tuckerman
Trumann
Osceola
BUFFALO NAT. W.&S.R.
RICHLAND CREEK NAT. WILD & SCENIC RIVER
Buffalo
OZARK NATIONAL FOREST
MULBERRY NAT. WILD & SCENIC RIVER
BIG PINEY CREEK NATIONAL WILD & SCENIC RIVER
Fairfield Bay
Newport
Marked Tree
FORT SMITH N.H.S.
Mulberry
Clinton
Greers Ferry Lake
White
WAPANOCCA N.W.R.
Van Buren
Ozark
Clarksville
Heber Springs
Little Red
Earle
Fort Smith
Arkansas
Lake Dardanelle
Russellville
Bald Knob
Wynne
CACHE RIVER NATIONAL WILDLIFE REFUGE
West Memphis
Paris
Greenbrier
Searcy
Cache
Big Piney
Mississippi
Greenwood
Magazine Mt. 2,753 ft+ 839 m
Highest point in Arkansas
OZARK N.F.
Dardanelle
Morrilton
HOLLA BEND N.W.R.
Conway
Beebe
Forrest City
Brinkley
Booneville
Cabot
Marianna
ARKANSAS
Maumelle
Jacksonville
Waldron
OUACHITA NATIONAL MOUNTAINS FOREST
North Little Rock
ST. FRANCIS NATIONAL FOREST
Ouachita
Little Rock
LITTLE ROCK CENTRAL HIGH SCHOOL N.H.S.
WHITE
Lake Ouachita
Bryant
Benton
England
RIVER
West Helena
Helena
Mena
HOT SPRINGS NATIONAL PARK
Hot Springs
Stuttgart
NATIONAL
LITTLE MISSOURI N.W.&S.R.
De Gray Lake
Malvern
Sheridan
De Witt
WILDLIFE
COSSATOT NAT. WILD & SCENIC RIVER
Lake Greeson
Arkadelphia
Pine Bluff
White
Arkansas
REFUGE
Cossatot
Murfreesboro
CRATER OF DIAMONDS S.P.
Gurdon
ARKANSAS POST NAT. MEM.
DeQueen
Little Missouri
Saline
Bayou Bartholomew
COSSATOT N.W.R.
Nashville
Fordyce
Dumas
Millwood Lake
Prescott
White Oak Lake
Warren
Monticello
McGehee
Little
Ashdown
Hope
Camden
Ouachita
Dermott
Mississippi
Red
Birthplace of President Bill Clinton
Texarkana
Stamps
Smackover
Lake Village
Magnolia
El Dorado
FELSENTHAL N.W.R.
Hamburg
Lake Erling
Lake Jack Lee
Crossett
Eudora
OVERFLOW N.W.R.

TEXAS

OKLAHOMA

TENNESSEE

MISSISSIPPI

LOUISIANA

0 50 miles
0 50 kilometers
Albers Conic Equal-Area Projection

A B C D E F G

DIRTY WORK. Hoping to find diamonds, a man hauls buckets of mud from the eroded surface of an ancient, gem-bearing volcanic pipe at Crater of Diamonds State Park.

Economy Symbols

- Poultry/eggs
- Sheep
- Hogs
- Dairy cows/products
- Beef cattle
- Fruits
- Vegetables
- Nursery stock
- Wheat
- Corn
- Rice
- Soybeans
- Cotton
- Vineyards
- Timber/forest products
- Stone/gravel/cement
- Oil/gas
- Hydro-electricity
- Machinery
- Metal manufacturing
- Metal products
- Motor vehicles/parts
- Chemistry
- Food processing
- Electrical equipment
- Computers/electronics
- Aircraft/parts
- Tourism

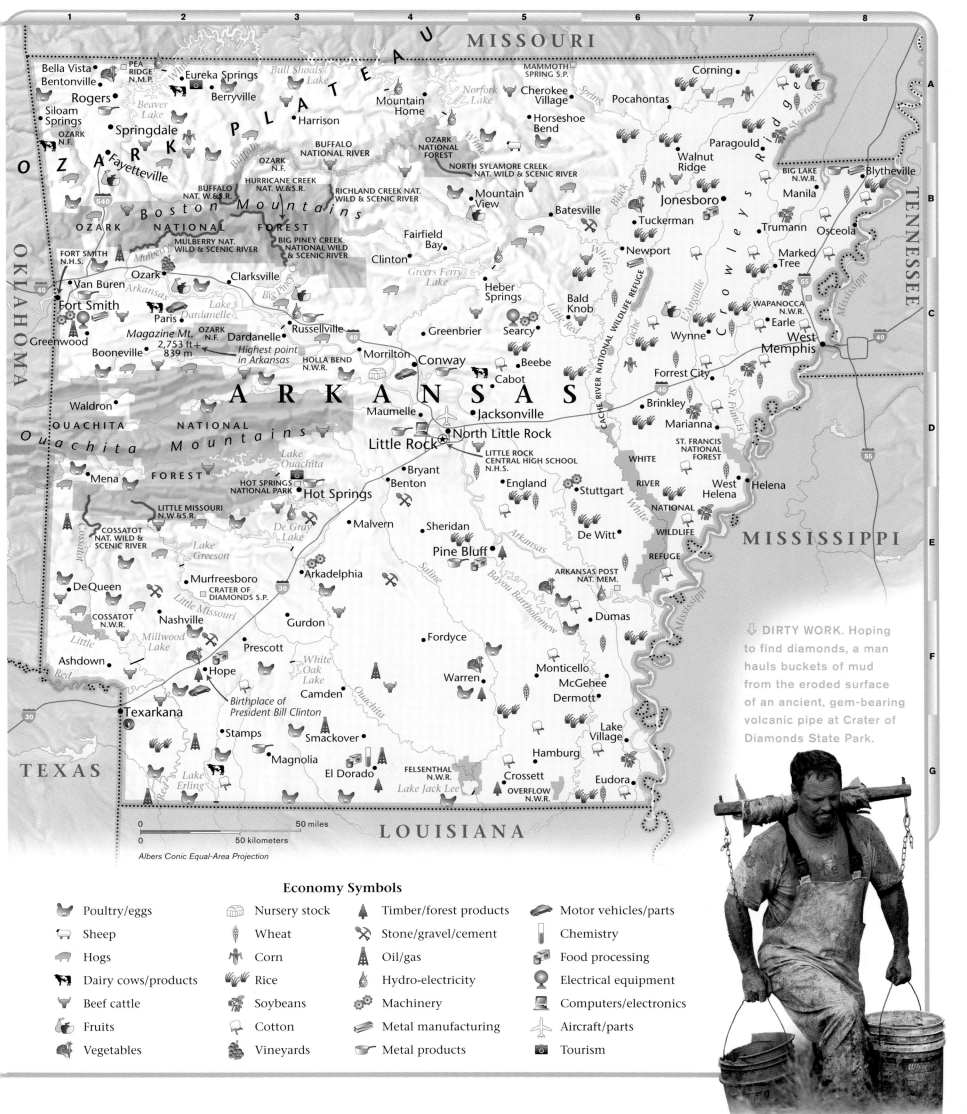

THE SUNSHINE STATE:
FLORIDA

FLORIDA

Florida is home to St. Augustine, the country's oldest permanent European settlement, established by the Spanish in 1565. But native peoples had called Florida home long before then. Florida became a U.S. territory in 1821 and a state in 1845. The state's turbulent early history included the Civil War and three wars with Native Americans over control of the land. Railroads opened Florida to migration from the northern states as early as the 1890s. The mild climate and sandy beaches attracted people seeking to escape cold winters in the north. This trend continues today and includes both tourists and retirees. South Florida has a large Hispanic population that has migrated from all over Latin America—especially from nearby Cuba. Florida is working to solve many challenges: competition between city-dwellers and farmers for limited water resources; the annual risk of tropical storms; and the need to preserve its natural environment, including the vast Everglades wetland.

THE BASICS

STATS

Area
65,755 sq mi (170,304 sq km)

Population
18,251,243

Capital
Tallahassee
Population 159,012

Largest city
Jacksonville
Population 794,555

Ethnic/racial groups
80.2% white; 15.8% African American; 2.2% Asian; .4% Native American. Hispanic (any race) 20.2%.

Industry
Tourism, health services, business services, communications, banking, electronic equipment, insurance

Agriculture
Citrus fruits, vegetables, field crops, nursery stock, cattle, dairy products

Statehood
March 3, 1845; 27th state

GEO WHIZ

 Key West, the southernmost point in the continental U.S., is just 90 miles (145 km) from Cuba.

In 1937 Amelia Earhart and her navigator took off from Miami with the goal of making an around-the-world flight, but disappeared over the Pacific Ocean and were never seen again. You can read all about this famous flying ace in our children's book *Sky Pioneer*, by Corine Szabo.

Everglades National Park, the largest subtropical wilderness in the United States, is home to rare and endangered species such as the American crocodile, Florida panther, and West Indian manatee.

Britton Hill, Florida's highest point, is only 345 feet (105 m) above sea level.

 Lightning strikes occur more often in Florida than in any other U.S. state.

MOCKINGBIRD
ORANGE BLOSSOM

⬆ CULTURAL PRIDE. A young girl marches in Orlando's Puerto Rican Parade, a celebration of the music, dance, and culture of this U.S. island territory.

ALABAMA

☐ POARCH CREEK I.R.
Perdido
Highest point in Florida
✚ Britton Hill 345 ft 105 m
Crestview •
Niceville •
Fort Walton Beach
Pensacola •
FORT PICKENS
GULF ISLANDS NATIONAL SEASHORE
Choctawhatchee
Intracoastal Waterway

⇨ LIFTOFF! Crowds watch as a space shuttle rises amid clouds of steam at NASA's Kennedy Space Center on Florida's Atlantic coast. The center has been the launch site for all U.S. human space flight missions.

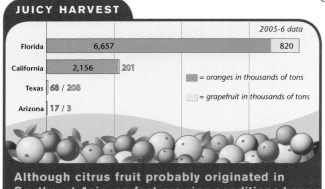

JUICY HARVEST

		2005-6 data
Florida	6,657	820
California	2,156	201
Texas	68	208
Arizona	17	3

■ = oranges in thousands of tons
▨ = grapefruit in thousands of tons

Although citrus fruit probably originated in Southeast Asia, perfect growing conditions have made Florida the leading producer in the U.S.

⇨ GENTLE GIANT. The manatee, which is closely related to the elephant, is Florida's state marine mammal. Averaging 10 feet (3 m) in length and 1,000 pounds (453 kg), these endangered animals live on a diet of sea grasses.

THE SUNSHINE STATE:
FLORIDA

THE EMPIRE STATE OF THE SOUTH:
GEORGIA

GEORGIA

THE BASICS

STATS

Area
59,425 sq mi (153,910 sq km)

Population
9,544,750

Capital
Atlanta
Population 486,411

Largest city
Atlanta
Population 486,411

Ethnic/racial groups
65.8% white; 29.9% African American; 2.8% Asian; .3% Native American. Hispanic (any race) 7.5%.

Industry
Textiles and clothing, transportation equipment, food processing, paper products, chemicals, electrical equipment, tourism

Agriculture
Poultry and eggs, cotton, peanuts, vegetables, sweet corn, melons, cattle

Statehood
January 2, 1788; 4th state

GEO WHIZ

The Okefenokee Swamp, the largest swamp in North America, is home to many meat-eating plants, which capture animals for food. The swamp was also the setting for the adventures of Pogo the Possum, Albert the Alligator, and other characters created by cartoonist Walt Kelly.

The Georgia Aquarium in Atlanta, the world's largest, features more than 100,000 animals in more than 8 million gallons (30.3 million liters) of water.

Stone Mountain near Atlanta is famous for its enormous carving of three historic figures from the Confederate States of America: Stonewall Jackson, Robert E. Lee, and Jefferson Davis. It is one of the largest single masses of exposed granite in the world.

BROWN THRASHER
CHEROKEE ROSE

⇧ CASH CROP. Peanuts are a big moneymaker in Georgia, where almost half the U.S. crop is grown—about half of which is used to make peanut butter.

When Spanish explorers arrived in the mid-1500s in what would become Georgia, they found the land already occupied by Cherokees, Creeks, and other native peoples. Georgia was the frontier separating Spanish Florida and English South Carolina, but in 1733 James Oglethorpe founded a new colony on the site of present-day Savannah. Georgia became the 4th state in 1788 and built an economy based on agriculture and slave labor. The state suffered widespread destruction during the Civil War and endured a long period of poverty in the years that followed. Modern-day Georgia is part of the fast-changing Sunbelt region. Agriculture—especially poultry, cotton, and forest products—remains important. Atlanta has emerged as a regional center of banking, telecommunications, and transportation, and Savannah is a major container port near the Atlantic coast, linking the state to the global economy. Historic sites, sports, and beaches draw thousands of tourists to the state every year.

⇧ LIGHT SHOW. Busy Interstate traffic appears as ribbons of light below Atlanta's nighttime skyline. Atlanta is a center of economic growth, leading all cities in the region with 12 Fortune 500 companies. Its metropolitan area leads the country in population growth, adding almost one million people since 2000.

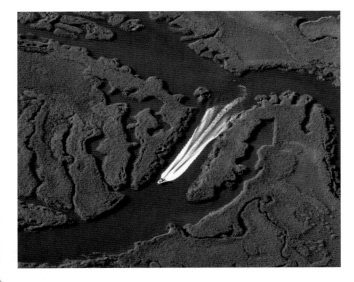

⇦ PAST MEETS PRESENT. Georgia's 100-mile (160-km) coastline is laced with barrier islands, wetlands, and winding streams. In the 19th century plantations grew Sea Island cotton here. Today, tourists are attracted to the area's natural beauty and beaches.

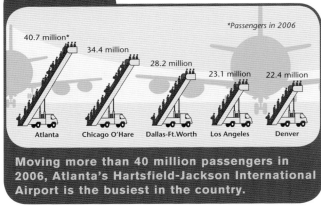

FLYING HIGH

40.7 million*
34.4 million
28.2 million
23.1 million
22.4 million

Atlanta | Chicago O'Hare | Dallas-Ft.Worth | Los Angeles | Denver

*Passengers in 2006

Moving more than 40 million passengers in 2006, Atlanta's Hartsfield-Jackson International Airport is the busiest in the country.

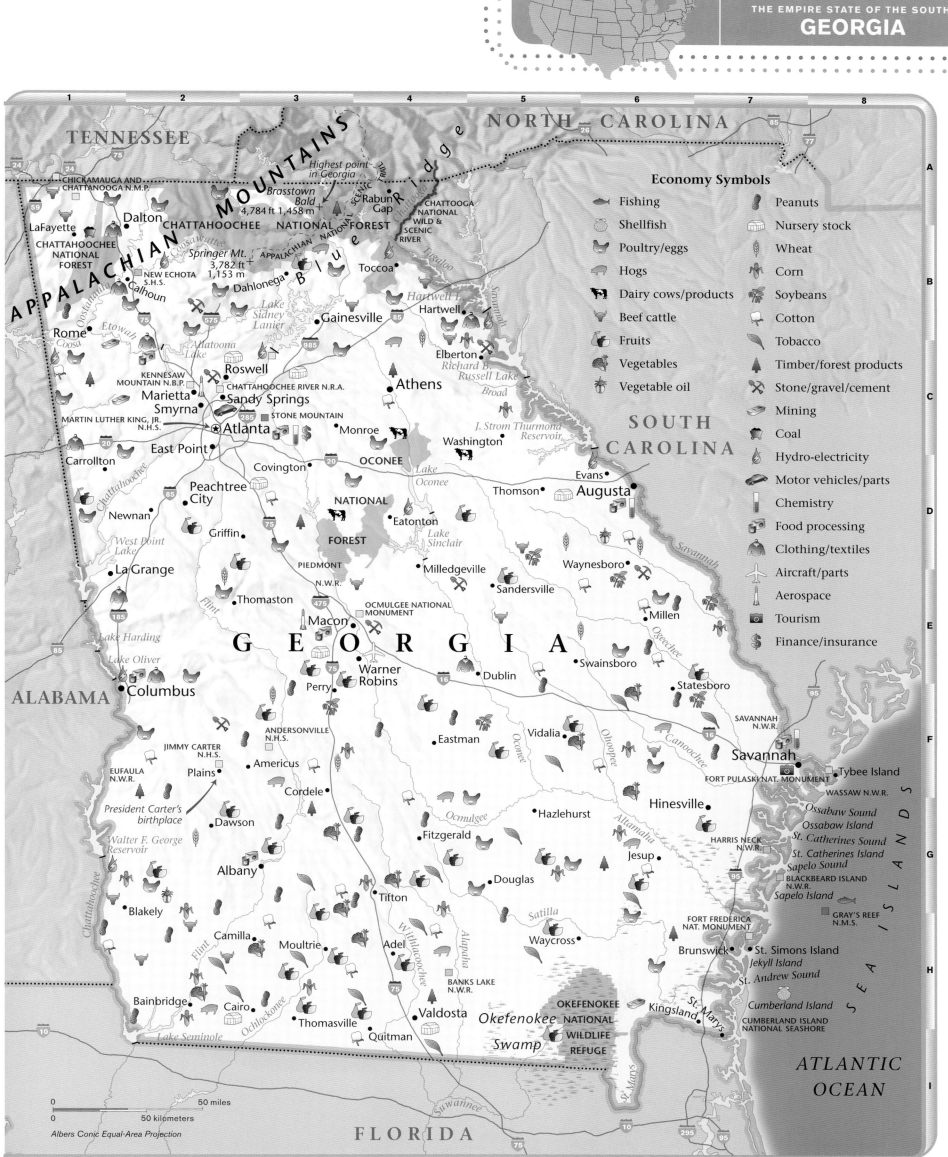

THE BASICS

STATS

Area
40,409 sq mi (104,659 sq km)

Population
4,241,474

Capital
Frankfort
Population 27,408

Largest city
Louisville Metro
Population 701,500

Ethnic/racial groups
90.2% white; 7.5% African American;
1.0% Asian; .2% Native American.
Hispanic (any race) 2.0%.

Industry
Manufacturing, services, government,
finance, insurance, real estate, retail
trade, transportation, wholesale trade,
construction, mining

Agriculture
Horses, tobacco, cattle, corn, dairy
products

Statehood
June 1, 1792; 15th state

GEO WHIZ

A favorite Kentucky dessert is Derby
Pie, a rich chocolate-and-walnut
pastry that was first created by George
Kern, manager of the Melrose Inn, in
Prospect, in the 1950s. It became so
popular that the name was registered
with the U.S. Patent Office and the
Commonwealth of Kentucky.

Pleasant Hill, near Lexington, was
the site of a Shaker religious
community. It is now a National
Historic Site where visitors can
tour the living history museum.

The song "Happy Birthday to You,"
one of the most popular songs in the
English language, was the creation of
two Louisville sisters in 1893.

Post-it notes are manufactured
exclusively in Cynthiana. Millions
of self-stick notes in 27 sizes
and 57 colors are produced
each year.

CARDINAL

GOLDENROD

KENTUCKY

1   2   3

The original inhabitants of the area known today as Kentucky were
Native Americans, but a treaty with the Cherokees, signed in 1775, opened
the territory to settlers—including the legendary Daniel Boone—from
the soon-to-be independent eastern colonies. In 1776 Kentucky became
a western county of the state of Virginia. In 1792 it became the 15th state
of the young U.S. Eastern Kentucky is a part of Appalachia, a region
rich in soft bituminous coal but burdened with environmental
problems that often accompany the mining industry.
The region is known for crafts and music that can
be traced back to Scotch-Irish immigrants who
settled there. In central Kentucky, the
Bluegrass region produces some of the
finest Thoroughbred horses in the
world, and the Kentucky Derby, held
in Louisville, is a part of racing's
coveted Triple Crown. In western
Kentucky, coal found near the
surface is strip mined, leaving
scars on the landscape, but
federal laws now require that
the land be restored.

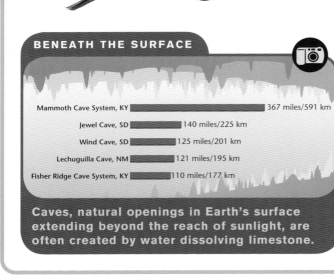

BENEATH THE SURFACE

Mammoth Cave System, KY	367 miles/591 km
Jewel Cave, SD	140 miles/225 km
Wind Cave, SD	125 miles/201 km
Lechuguilla Cave, NM	121 miles/195 km
Fisher Ridge Cave System, KY	110 miles/177 km

Caves, natural openings in Earth's surface
extending beyond the reach of sunlight, are
often created by water dissolving limestone.

⇧ THEY'RE OFF! Riders and horses press for the finish line at Churchill
Downs, in Louisville. Kentucky is a major breeder of Thoroughbred race
horses, and horses are the leading source of farm income in the state.

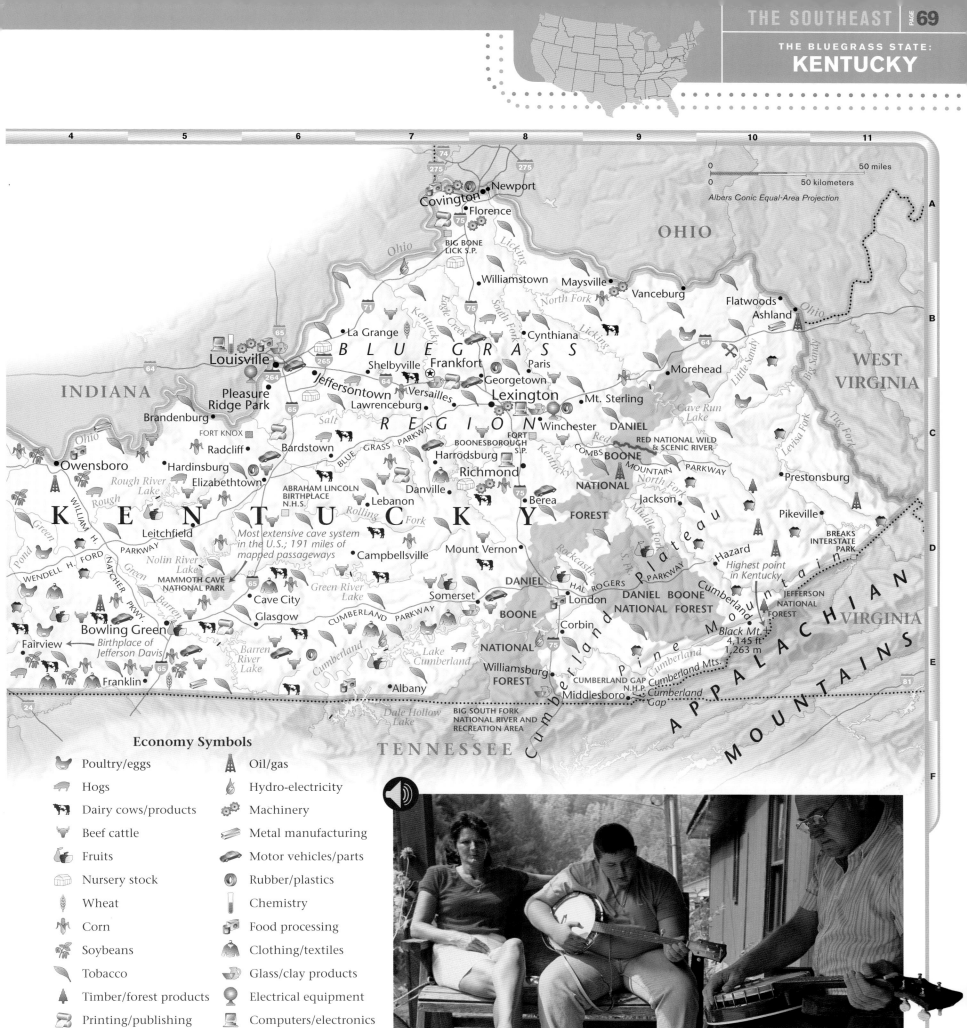

OHIO

WEST VIRGINIA

INDIANA

B L U E G R A S S

R E G I O N

K E N T U C K Y

VIRGINIA

APPALACHIAN MOUNTAINS

TENNESSEE

Newport
Covington
Florence
BIG BONE LICK S.P.
Williamstown
Maysville
Vanceburg
Flatwoods
Ashland
La Grange
Cynthiana
Louisville
Shelbyville
Frankfort
Paris
Morehead
Jeffersontown
Versailles
Georgetown
Lexington
Mt. Sterling
Pleasure Ridge Park
Lawrenceburg
Winchester
DANIEL
Brandenburg
FORT KNOX
Radcliff
Bardstown
Harrodsburg
FORT BOONESBOROUGH S.P.
BOONE
RED NATIONAL WILD & SCENIC RIVER
Prestonsburg
Owensboro
Hardinsburg
Richmond
NATIONAL
Elizabethtown
Danville
Berea
FOREST
Jackson
Pikeville
ABRAHAM LINCOLN BIRTHPLACE N.H.S.
Lebanon
BREAKS INTERSTATE PARK
Leitchfield
Most extensive cave system in the U.S.; 191 miles of mapped passageways
Campbellsville
Mount Vernon
Hazard
Highest point in Kentucky
JEFFERSON NATIONAL FOREST
MAMMOTH CAVE NATIONAL PARK
DANIEL
Somerset
DANIEL BOONE NATIONAL FOREST
Cave City
London
Black Mt. 4,145 ft 1,263 m
Bowling Green
Glasgow
BOONE
Corbin
Fairview
Birthplace of Jefferson Davis
NATIONAL
Williamsburg
CUMBERLAND GAP N.H.P.
Franklin
FOREST
Albany
Middlesboro
Cumberland Gap
BIG SOUTH FORK NATIONAL RIVER AND RECREATION AREA

50 miles
50 kilometers
Albers Conic Equal-Area Projection

Economy Symbols

Poultry/eggs		Oil/gas	
Hogs		Hydro-electricity	
Dairy cows/products		Machinery	
Beef cattle		Metal manufacturing	
Fruits		Motor vehicles/parts	
Nursery stock		Rubber/plastics	
Wheat		Chemistry	
Corn		Food processing	
Soybeans		Clothing/textiles	
Tobacco		Glass/clay products	
Timber/forest products		Electrical equipment	
Printing/publishing		Computers/electronics	
Stone/gravel/cement		Aerospace	
Coal			

⇨ STRUMMING A TUNE. Music is an important part of Kentucky's cultural heritage, especially in remote mountain areas where a banjo can become the focus of a family gathering.

THE PELICAN STATE:
LOUISIANA

LOUISIANA

Louisiana's Native American heritage is evident in place-names such as Natchitoches and Opelousas. Spanish sailors explored the area in 1528, but the French, traveling down the Mississippi River, established permanent settlements in the mid-17th century and named the region for King Louis XIV. The U.S. gained possession of the territory as part of the Louisiana Purchase in 1803, and Louisiana became the 18th state in 1812. New Orleans and the Port of South Louisiana, located near the delta of the Mississippi River, are Louisiana's main ports. Trade from the interior of the U.S. moves through these ports and out to world markets. Oil and gas are drilled in the Mississippi Delta area, and coastal waters are an important source of seafood. Louisiana is vulnerable to tropical storms. In late August 2005 Hurricane Katrina roared in off the Gulf of Mexico, flooding towns, breaking through levees, and changing forever the lives of everyone in southern Louisiana.

THE BASICS

STATS

Area
51,840 sq mi (134,265 sq km)

Population
4,293,204

Capital
Baton Rouge
Population 229,553

Largest city
Baton Rouge
Population 229,553

Ethnic/racial groups
65.4% white; 31.7% African American; 1.4% Asian; .6% Native American. Hispanic (any race) 2.9%.

Industry
Chemicals, petroleum products, food processing, health services, tourism, oil and natural gas extraction, paper products

Agriculture
Forest products, poultry, marine fisheries, sugarcane, rice, dairy products, cotton, cattle, aquaculture

Statehood
April 30, 1812; 18th state

GEO WHIZ

The brown pelican, the state bird of Louisiana, was placed on the endangered species list in 1970. The species has made a remarkable recovery in the Atlantic coastal states, but it is still considered endangered in the Gulf Coast area.

The magnolia, Louisiana's state flower, is the oldest flowering plant in the world. Some species are believed to be 100 million years old.

Cajuns, people whose French-speaking ancestors were exiled by the British from Acadia, in what is now Canada, live primarily in the bayou region of Louisiana. Their distinctive music and spicy food have become popular throughout the country.

BROWN PELICAN
MAGNOLIA

⇑ TASTY HARVEST. Louisiana produces almost half of all shrimp caught in the U.S. Most of this harvest comes from the Barataria-Terrebonne region, an estuary at the mouth of the Mississippi River that supports shrimp, oysters, crabs, and fish.

KISATCHIE NATIONAL FOREST

•Vivian
Caddo Lake
Springhill
Red
•Minden
Shreveport •Bossier City
Lake Bistineau
Mansfield•
Red
•Natchitoches
CANE RIVER CREOLE N.H.P. AND HERITAGE AREA
•Many
Toledo Bend Reservoir
Leesville•
TEXAS
Rosepine•
De Ridder•
Sabine
•De Quincy
Sulphur•
Intracoastal
Lake Charles
CAMERON PRAIRIE N.W.R.
Calcasieu Lake
Sabine Lake SABINE NAT. WILDLIFE REFUGE

⇐ AVENUE TO THE PAST. Stately live oaks, believed to be 300 years old, frame Oak Alley Plantation on the banks of the Mississippi River west of New Orleans. Built in 1839, the house has been restored to its former grandeur and is open to the public for tours and private events.

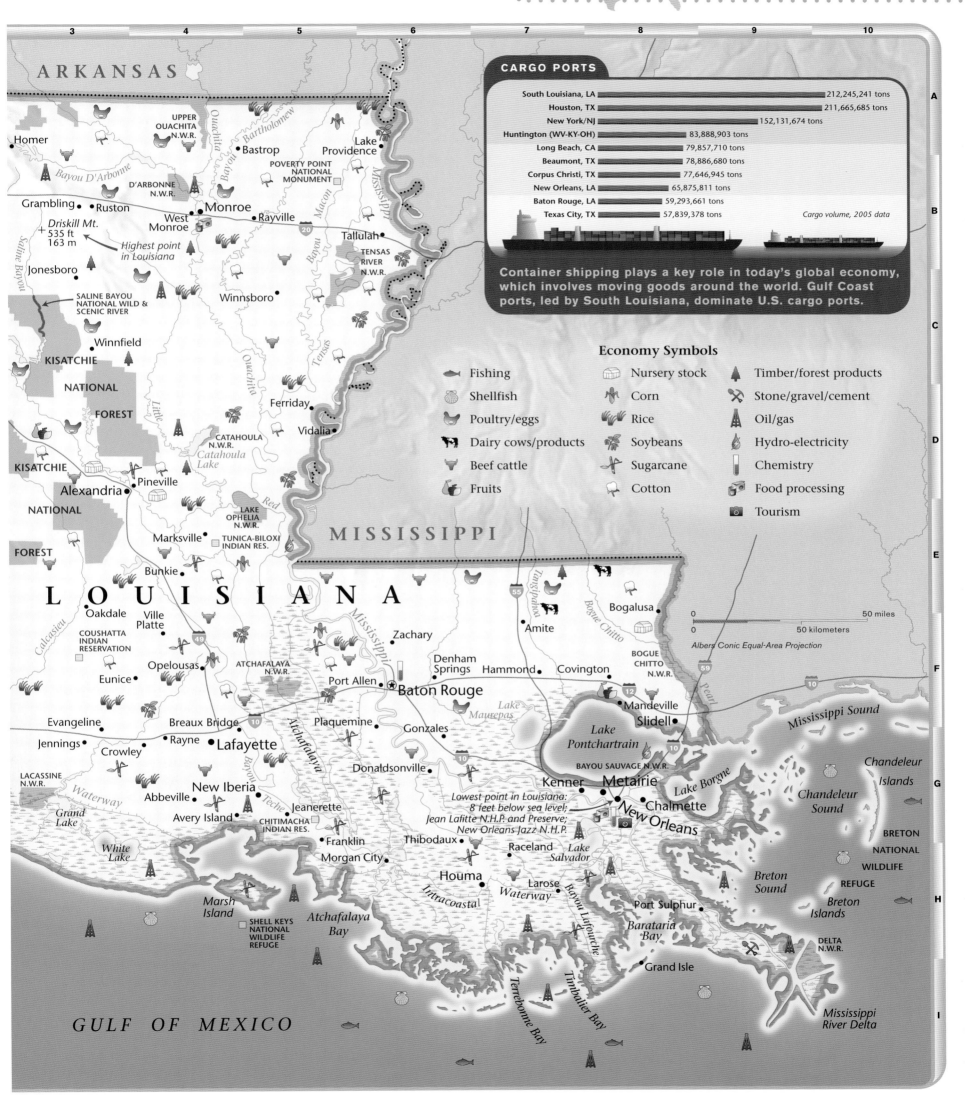

ARKANSAS

Homer

UPPER OUACHITA N.W.R.

Bastrop

Lake Providence

POVERTY POINT NATIONAL MONUMENT

Bayou D'Arbonne

D'ARBONNE N.W.R.

Grambling • Ruston

Monroe

West Monroe • Rayville

Tallulah

Driskill Mt. + 535 ft 163 m
Highest point in Louisiana

Jonesboro

Saline Bayou

TENSAS RIVER N.W.R.

SALINE BAYOU NATIONAL WILD & SCENIC RIVER

Winnsboro

Winnfield

KISATCHIE

NATIONAL

FOREST

Ferriday

Vidalia

KISATCHIE

CATAHOULA N.W.R.
Catahoula Lake

Alexandria
Pineville

LAKE OPHELIA N.W.R.

NATIONAL

Marksville

TUNICA-BILOXI INDIAN RES.

FOREST

Bunkie

MISSISSIPPI

CARGO PORTS

South Louisiana, LA	212,245,241 tons
Houston, TX	211,665,685 tons
New York/NJ	152,131,674 tons
Huntington (WV-KY-OH)	83,888,903 tons
Long Beach, CA	79,857,710 tons
Beaumont, TX	78,886,680 tons
Corpus Christi, TX	77,646,945 tons
New Orleans, LA	65,875,811 tons
Baton Rouge, LA	59,293,661 tons
Texas City, TX	57,839,378 tons

Cargo volume, 2005 data

Container shipping plays a key role in today's global economy, which involves moving goods around the world. Gulf Coast ports, led by South Louisiana, dominate U.S. cargo ports.

Economy Symbols

- Fishing
- Shellfish
- Poultry/eggs
- Dairy cows/products
- Beef cattle
- Fruits
- Nursery stock
- Corn
- Rice
- Soybeans
- Sugarcane
- Cotton
- Timber/forest products
- Stone/gravel/cement
- Oil/gas
- Hydro-electricity
- Chemistry
- Food processing
- Tourism

L O U I S I A N A

Oakdale

Ville Platte

COUSHATTA INDIAN RESERVATION

Zachary

Opelousas

Amite

Bogalusa

BOGUE CHITTO N.W.R.

Eunice

ATCHAFALAYA N.W.R.

Denham Springs

Hammond

Covington

Evangeline

Breaux Bridge

Port Allen

Baton Rouge

Mandeville

Slidell

0   50 miles
0   50 kilometers

Albers Conic Equal-Area Projection

Jennings

Rayne

Plaquemine

Gonzales

Lake Maurepas

Lake Pontchartrain

Mississippi Sound

Crowley

Lafayette

LACASSINE N.W.R.

Donaldsonville

BAYOU SAUVAGE N.W.R.

Lake Borgne

Chandeleur Islands

New Iberia

Kenner

Metairie

Chandeleur Sound

Abbeville

Avery Island

Jeanerette

CHITIMACHA INDIAN RES.

Lowest point in Louisiana: 8 feet below sea level; Jean Lafitte N.H.P. and Preserve; New Orleans Jazz N.H.P.

Chalmette

New Orleans

BRETON

NATIONAL

Grand Lake

Franklin

Thibodaux

Raceland

Lake Salvador

WILDLIFE

White Lake

Morgan City

Houma

Larose

Breton Sound

REFUGE

Breton Islands

Marsh Island

SHELL KEYS NATIONAL WILDLIFE REFUGE

Atchafalaya Bay

Intracoastal

Waterway

Port Sulphur

Barataria Bay

DELTA N.W.R.

Grand Isle

GULF OF MEXICO

Terrebonne Bay

Timbalier Bay

Mississippi River Delta

THE MAGNOLIA STATE:
MISSISSIPPI

MISSISSIPPI

STATS

Area
48,430 sq mi (125,434 sq km)

Population
2,918,785

Capital
Jackson
Population 176,614

Largest city
Jackson
Population 176,614

Ethnic/racial groups
60.9% white; 37.1% African American; .8% Asian; .5% Native American. Hispanic (any race) 1.8%.

Industry
Petroleum products, health services, electronic equipment, transportation, banking, forest products, communications

Agriculture
Poultry and eggs, cotton, catfish, soybeans, cattle, rice, dairy products

Statehood
December 10, 1817; 20th state

GEO WHIZ

The Windsor Ruins, located near Port Gibson, are 23 monolithic columns that once made up the largest antebellum mansion in the state. The mansion survived the Civil War but was destroyed by a fire in 1890.

The Marine Life Oceanarium in Gulfport was almost completely destroyed by Hurricane Katrina in 2005. Eight of its 14 bottlenose dolphins were swept into the Gulf of Mexico by a 40-foot (12-m) wave. These animals and two sea lions named Splash and Elliot were eventually rescued. Others were not so lucky.

Greenville is the birthplace of Jim Henson, creator of Kermit the Frog, Miss Piggy, Big Bird, and other famous Muppets.

MOCKINGBIRD
MAGNOLIA

Mississippi is named for the river that forms its western boundary. The name comes from the Chippewa words *mici zibi,* meaning "great river." Indeed it is a great river, draining much of the interior U.S. and providing a trade artery to the world. Explored by the Spanish in 1540 and claimed by the French in 1699, the territory of Mississippi passed to the U.S. in 1783 and became the 20th state in 1817. For more than a hundred years following statehood, Mississippi was the center of U.S. cotton production and trade. The fertile soils and mild climate of the delta region in northwestern Mississippi provided a perfect environment for cotton, a crop that depended on slave labor. When the Civil War broke out, it took a heavy toll on the state. Today, poverty, especially in rural areas, is a major challenge for the state where agriculture—poultry, cotton, soybeans, and rice—is still the base of the economy.

⇧ SINGING THE BLUES. B.B. King sings the soulful sounds of the blues, a music form that traces its roots to Mississippi's cotton fields and the sorrows of West Africans traveling on slave ships to the Americas.

GONE FISHIN'

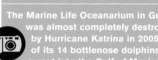

2006 data

Mississippi	215 million
Alabama	71 million
Arkansas	56.5 million
Louisiana	10.8 million
North Carolina	4.6 million

The Southeast, especially Mississippi, is the leading producer of pond-raised catfish. Mississippi also tops all other states in revenue for catfish sales.

⇨ BIG WHEEL TURNING. Now popular with tourists, paddlewheel boats made the Mississippi River a major artery for trade and travel in the 19th century.

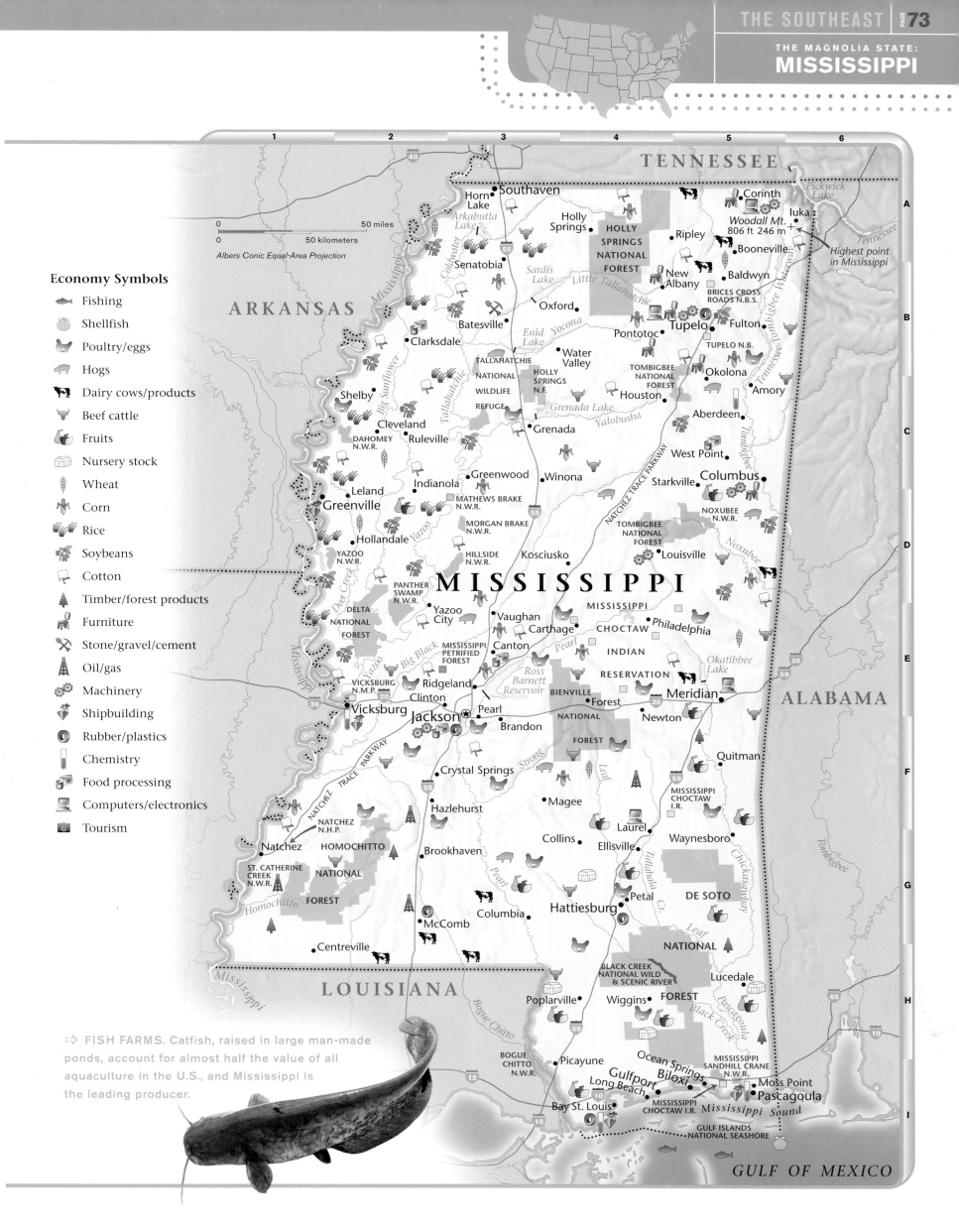

Economy Symbols

- Fishing
- Shellfish
- Poultry/eggs
- Hogs
- Dairy cows/products
- Beef cattle
- Fruits
- Nursery stock
- Wheat
- Corn
- Rice
- Soybeans
- Cotton
- Timber/forest products
- Furniture
- Stone/gravel/cement
- Oil/gas
- Machinery
- Shipbuilding
- Rubber/plastics
- Chemistry
- Food processing
- Computers/electronics
- Tourism

⇨ FISH FARMS. Catfish, raised in large man-made ponds, account for almost half the value of all aquaculture in the U.S., and Mississippi is the leading producer.

TENNESSEE

ARKANSAS

LOUISIANA

ALABAMA

GULF OF MEXICO

MISSISSIPPI

0   50 miles
0   50 kilometers
Albers Conic Equal-Area Projection

Woodall Mt.
806 ft 246 m
Highest point in Mississippi

Southaven
Horn Lake
Holly Springs
Corinth
Iuka
Ripley
Booneville
HOLLY SPRINGS NATIONAL FOREST
New Albany
Baldwyn
Senatobia
BRICES CROSS ROADS N.B.S.
Oxford
Pontotoc
Tupelo
Fulton
TUPELO N.B.
Batesville
Clarksdale
Water Valley
Okolona
Amory
TALLAHATCHIE NATIONAL WILDLIFE REFUGE
HOLLY SPRINGS N.F.
Houston
Aberdeen
Shelby
Grenada
TOMBIGBEE NATIONAL FOREST
West Point
Cleveland
Ruleville
Columbus
DAHOMEY N.W.R.
Starkville
Winona
NOXUBEE N.W.R.
Greenwood
Indianola
Leland
MATHEWS BRAKE N.W.R.
Louisville
Greenville
MORGAN BRAKE N.W.R.
TOMBIGBEE NATIONAL FOREST
Hollandale
HILLSIDE N.W.R.
Kosciusko
YAZOO N.W.R.
PANTHER SWAMP N.W.R.
MISSISSIPPI
Philadelphia
MISSISSIPPI CHOCTAW
DELTA NATIONAL FOREST
Yazoo City
Vaughan
Carthage
INDIAN RESERVATION
MISSISSIPPI PETRIFIED FOREST
Canton
Meridian
VICKSBURG N.M.P.
Ridgeland
Clinton
BIENVILLE NATIONAL FOREST
Newton
Vicksburg
Jackson
Pearl
Brandon
Quitman
Crystal Springs
MISSISSIPPI CHOCTAW I.R.
NATCHEZ TRACE PARKWAY
Hazlehurst
Magee
Laurel
Natchez
NATCHEZ N.H.P.
HOMOCHITTO
Collins
Ellisville
Waynesboro
ST. CATHERINE CREEK N.W.R.
NATIONAL FOREST
Brookhaven
DE SOTO
McComb
Columbia
Hattiesburg
Petal
Centreville
NATIONAL FOREST
BLACK CREEK NATIONAL WILD & SCENIC RIVER
Lucedale
Poplarville
Wiggins
FOREST
BOGUE CHITTO N.W.R.
Picayune
Ocean Springs
MISSISSIPPI SANDHILL CRANE N.W.R.
Moss Point
Gulfport
Biloxi
Pascagoula
Long Beach
Bay St. Louis
MISSISSIPPI CHOCTAW I.R.
Mississippi Sound
GULF ISLANDS NATIONAL SEASHORE

Pickwick Lake
Arkabutla Lake
Sardis Lake
Enid Lake
Grenada Lake
Ross Barnett Reservoir
Okatibbee Lake

NORTH CAROLINA

1   2   3

Before European contact, the land that became North Carolina was inhabited by numerous Native American groups. Early attempts to settle the area met with strong resistance, and one early colony established in 1587 on Roanoke Island disappeared without a trace. More attempts at settlement came in 1650, and in 1663 King Charles granted a charter for the Carolina colony, which included present-day North Carolina, South Carolina, and part of Georgia. In 1789 North Carolina became the 12th state, but in 1861 it joined the Confederacy, supplying more men and equipment to the Southern cause than any other state. In 1903 the Wright brothers piloted the first successful airplane near Kitty Hawk, foreshadowing the change and growth coming to the Tar Heel State. Traditional industries included agriculture, textiles, and furniture making. Today, these, plus high-tech industries and education in the Raleigh-Durham Research Triangle area, as well as banking and finance in Charlotte, are important to the economy.

THE BASICS

STATS

Area
53,819 sq mi (139,390 sq km)

Population
9,061,032

Capital
Raleigh
Population 356,321

Largest city
Charlotte
Population 630,478

Ethnic/racial groups
74.0% white; 21.7% African American; 1.9% Asian; 1.3% Native American. Hispanic (any race) 6.7%.

Industry
Real estate, health services, chemicals, tobacco products, finance, textiles

Agriculture
Poultry, hogs, tobacco, nursery stock, cotton, soybeans

Statehood
November 21, 1789; 12th state

GEO WHIZ

The University of North Carolina at Chapel Hill, which opened its doors in 1795, is the oldest state university in the United States.

The Biltmore estate in Asheville is the largest private residence in the United States. Built to resemble a French chateau, the mansion is still owned by descendants of Cornelius Vanderbilt, who made the family's original fortune in the late 1800s.

Standing 208 feet (63 m) high, Cape Hatteras Light is the tallest lighthouse in the U.S. Its beacon can be seen some 20 miles (32 km) out to sea and has warned sailors for more than a century about the shallow waters around a group of treacherous sandbars called Diamond Shoals.

CARDINAL

FLOWERING DOGWOOD

⇨ FAVORITE PASTIME. With four of the state's major schools represented in the powerful Atlantic Coast Conference, it is not surprising that basketball is a popular sport among all ages, whether on the court or in the backyard.

⇦ TAKING FLIGHT. The Wright Brothers Memorial on Kill Devil Hill, near Kitty Hawk on North Carolina's Outer Banks, marks the site of the first successful airplane flight in 1903.

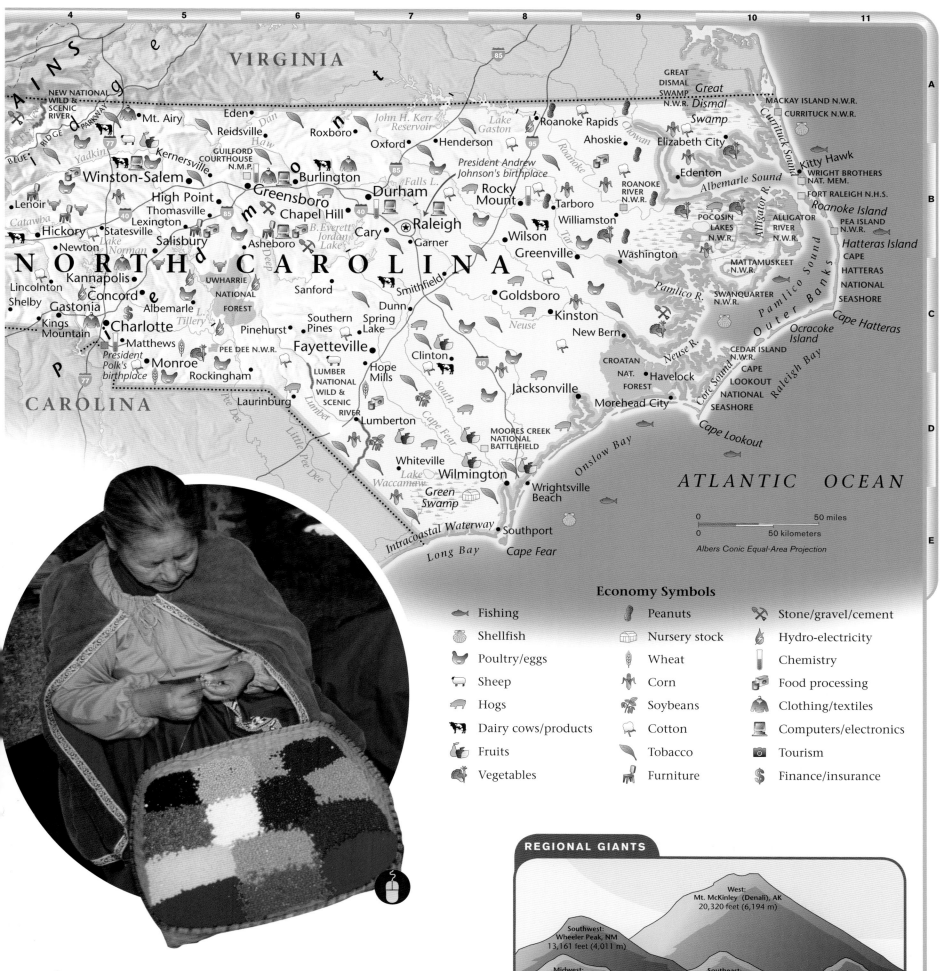

Economy Symbols

- 🐟 Fishing
- 🐚 Shellfish
- 🐔 Poultry/eggs
- 🐑 Sheep
- 🐖 Hogs
- 🐄 Dairy cows/products
- 🍎 Fruits
- 🥬 Vegetables

- Peanuts
- Nursery stock
- 🌾 Wheat
- 🌽 Corn
- Soybeans
- Cotton
- Tobacco
- 🪑 Furniture

- ✖️ Stone/gravel/cement
- Hydro-electricity
- Chemistry
- Food processing
- Clothing/textiles
- 💻 Computers/electronics
- 📷 Tourism
- $ Finance/insurance

⇧ **SKILLED ARTISAN.** A Cherokee woman sews a beaded belt in Oconaluftee Indian Village in western North Carolina. Cherokees in this mountainous region are descendants of Indians who hid in the hills to avoid the forced migration known as the Trail of Tears. The village preserves traditional 18th-century crafts, customs, and lifestyles.

REGIONAL GIANTS

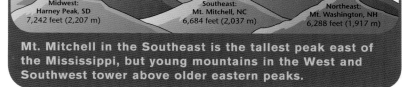

West:
Mt. McKinley (Denali), AK
20,320 feet (6,194 m)

Southwest:
Wheeler Peak, NM
13,161 feet (4,011 m)

Midwest:
Harney Peak, SD
7,242 feet (2,207 m)

Southeast:
Mt. Mitchell, NC
6,684 feet (2,037 m)

Northeast:
Mt. Washington, NH
6,288 feet (1,917 m)

Mt. Mitchell in the Southeast is the tallest peak east of the Mississippi, but young mountains in the West and Southwest tower above older eastern peaks.

SOUTH CAROLINA

Attempts in the 16th century by the Spanish and the French to colonize the area that would become South Carolina met fierce resistance from local Native American groups, but in 1670 the English were the first to establish a permanent European settlement at present-day Charleston. The colony prospered by relying on slave labor to produce first cotton, then rice and indigo. South Carolina became the 8th state in 1788 and the first to leave the Union just months before the first shots of the Civil War were fired on Fort Sumter in 1861. After the war, South Carolina struggled to rebuild its economy.

Early in the 20th century, textile mills introduced new jobs. Today, agriculture remains important, manufacturing and high-tech industries are expanding along interstate highway corridors, and tourists and retirees are drawn to the state's Atlantic coastline. But these coastal areas are not without risk. In 1989 Hurricane Hugo's 135-mile-per-hour (217-kmph) winds left a trail of destruction.

⇧ GLOW OF DAWN. The rising sun reflects off the water along the Atlantic coast. Beaches attract visitors year-round, contributing to tourism, the state's largest industry.

⇩ SOUTHERN CHARM. Twilight settles over antebellum homes in the historic district of Charleston. The city, established in 1670, is an important port located where the Ashley and Cooper Rivers merge before flowing to the Atlantic Ocean.

THE BASICS

STATS

Area
32,020 sq mi (82,932 sq km)

Population
4,407,709

Capital
Columbia
Population 119,961

Largest city
Columbia
Population 119,961

Ethnic/racial groups
68.5% white; 29.0% African American; 1.1% Asian; .4% Native American. Hispanic (any race) 3.5%.

Industry
Service industries, tourism, chemicals, textiles, machinery, forest products

Agriculture
Chickens, tobacco, nursery stock, beef cattle, dairy products, cotton

Statehood
May 23, 1788; 8th state

GEO WHIZ

The loggerhead sea turtle, South Carolina's state reptile, is threatened throughout its range. These turtles weigh between 200–450 pounds (90–204 kg).

North America's largest remnant of old-growth bottomland hardwood forest towers above the Congaree River and is protected as a 22,000-acre (8,903-ha) refuge called Congaree National Park.

Sweetgrass basketmaking, a traditional art form of African origin, has been a part of the Mount Pleasant community for more than 300 years. The baskets were originally used by slaves in the planting and processing of rice in coastal lowland regions.

Bobcats are thriving on Kiawah Island, a resort community southeast of Charleston. The elusive, nocturnal cats, which are about twice the size of an average house cat, play an important role in controlling the island's deer population.

CAROLINA WREN
YELLOW JESSAMINE

Map labels

Highest point in South Carolina
Blue Ridge
CHATTOOGA NATIONAL WILD & SCENIC RIVER
SUMTER
Sassafras Mt. 3,560 ft 1,085 m
Lake Keowee
Greenville
Easley
Gantt
NATIONAL FOREST
Chattooga
Tugaloo
Seneca
Clemson
85
Belton
Anderson
Hartwell Lake
Savannah
Richard B. Russell Lake
Abbeville
J. Strom Thurmond Reservoir
1
2

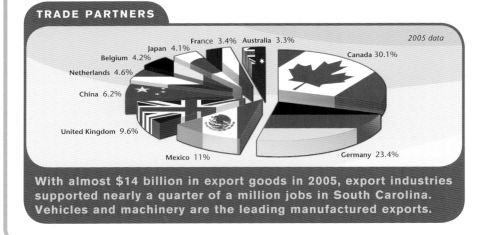

TRADE PARTNERS

France 3.4%
Australia 3.3%
Japan 4.1%
Belgium 4.2%
Netherlands 4.6%
China 6.2%
United Kingdom 9.6%
Mexico 11%
Canada 30.1%
Germany 23.4%
2005 data

With almost $14 billion in export goods in 2005, export industries supported nearly a quarter of a million jobs in South Carolina. Vehicles and machinery are the leading manufactured exports.

3 4 5 6 7 8 9 10

0   50 miles
0   50 kilometers
Albers Conic Equal-Area Projection

→ SHOWING OFF. Feathers extended, a male
wild turkey struts through Francis Beidler
Forest, a wildlife sanctuary and the world's
largest virgin cypress-tupelo swamp forest.

A
B
C
D
E
F
G
H

COWPENS N.B.
Gaffney
Greer
Taylors
Spartanburg
Mauldin
Simpsonville
Union
Laurens
Clinton
SUMTER
NATIONAL
FOREST
Greenwood
Newberry
SUMTER
NINETY SIX N.H.S.
NATIONAL
FOREST
Edgefield
Batesburg-Leesville
West Columbia
Cayce
Aiken
North Augusta
Clearwater
Williston
Bamberg
Barnwell
Allendale
Hampton

KINGS MOUNTAIN N.M.P.
York
Rock Hill
Fort Mill
CATAWBA I.R.
Chester
Lancaster
Cheraw
Bennettsville
CAROLINA SANDHILLS N.W.R.
Hartsville
Dillon
Winnsboro
Camden
Darlington
Florence
Mullins
Marion
Loris
Lake Murray
Irmo
Forest Acres
Columbia
SOUTH
Lake City
Conway
North Myrtle Beach
Sumter
Manning
Kingstree
Myrtle Beach
Socastee
Surfside Beach
Garden City
CAROLINA
Orangeburg
SANTEE N.W.R.
Georgetown
Lake Marion
Santee Dam
Lake Moultrie
North Island
Moncks Corner
FRANCIS MARION NATIONAL FOREST
Cape Island
Summerville
Goose Creek
Hanahan
Ladson
CAPE ROMAIN N.W.R.
North Charleston
Charleston
Mt. Pleasant
CHARLES PINCKNEY N.H.S.
FT. SUMTER NAT. MON.
ACE BASIN N.W.R.
Walterboro
Burton
Beaufort
Port Royal
St. Helena Sound
St. Helena Island
Edisto Island
SAVANNAH NATIONAL WILDLIFE REFUGE
PINCKNEY ISLAND N.W.R.
Parris Island
Port Royal Sound
Hilton Head Island
Daufuskie Island

NORTH CAROLINA
GEORGIA
ATLANTIC OCEAN
Long Bay
SEA ISLANDS

Wylie Lake
Broad
Catawba
Wateree Lake
Great Pee Dee
Little Pee Dee
Saluda
Lake Murray
Congaree
Wateree
CONGAREE NATIONAL PARK
Lynches
Black
S. Fork Edisto
N. Fork Edisto
Edisto
Savannah
Coosawhatchie
Combahee
Santee
Cooper
Waccamaw
Intracoastal Waterway

Economy Symbols

Fishing		Soybeans	
Shellfish		Cotton	
Poultry/eggs		Tobacco	
Hogs		Timber/forest products	
Dairy cows/products		Stone/gravel/cement	
Fruits		Hydro-electricity	
Vegetables		Machinery	
Peanuts		Rubber/plastics	
Nursery stock		Chemistry	
Wheat		Clothing/textiles	
Corn		Tourism	

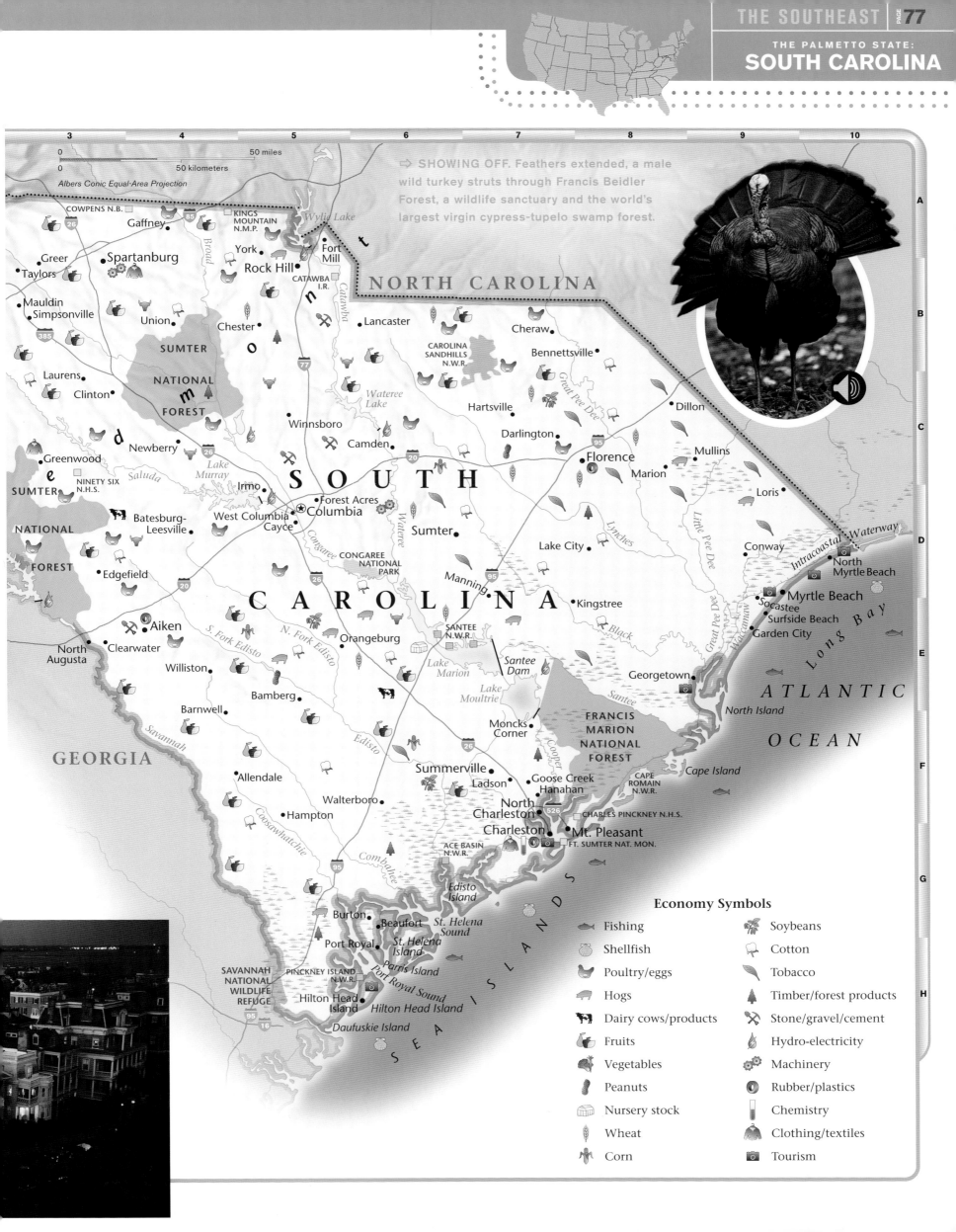

TENNESSEE

Following the last ice age, Native Americans moved onto the fertile lands of Tennessee. The earliest Europeans in Tennessee were Spanish explorers who passed through in 1541. In 1673 both the English and French made claims on the land, hoping to develop trade with the power-ful Cherokees, whose town, called *Tanasi,* gave the state its name. Originally part of North Carolina, Tennessee was ceded to the federal government and became the 16th state in 1796. Tennessee was the last state to join the Confederacy and endured years of hardship after the war. Beginning in the 1930s, the federally funded Tennessee Valley Authority (TVA) set a high stan-dard in water management in the state, and the hydropower it generated supported major industrial development. Tennessee played a key role in the civil rights movement of the 1960s. Today, visitors to Tennessee are drawn to national parks, Nashville's country music, and the mournful sound of the blues in Memphis.

THE BASICS

STATS

Area
42,143 sq mi (109,151 sq km)

Population
6,156,719

Capital
Nashville
Population 552,120

Largest city
Memphis
Population 670,902

Ethnic/racial groups
80.4% white; 16.9% African American; 1.3% Asian; .3% Native American. Hispanic (any race) 3.2%.

Industry
Service industries, chemicals, transportation equipment, processed foods, machinery

Agriculture
Cattle, cotton, dairy products, hogs, poultry, nursery stock

Statehood
June 1, 1796; 16th state

GEO WHIZ

Twenty-seven species of salamanders live in Great Smoky Mountains National Park, earning it the nickname Salamander Capital of the World. Among the species are the spotted, the Jordans, which is found nowhere else, and the five-foot- (1.5-m-) long hellbender.

The New Madrid Earthquakes of 1811–1812, some of the largest earthquakes in the history of the U.S., created Reelfoot Lake in northwestern Tennessee. It is the state's only large, natural lake; others were created by damming waterways.

The Tennessee-Tombigbee Waterway is a 234-mile (376-km) artificial waterway that connects the Tennessee and Tombigbee Rivers. This water transportation route provides inland ports with an outlet to the Gulf of Mexico.

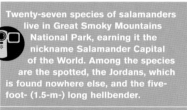

MOCKINGBIRD
IRIS

◁ OUT FOR A STROLL. Black bear cubs are usually born in January and remain with their mother for about 18 months. The Great Smoky Mountains National Park is one of the few remaining natural habitats for black bears in the eastern U.S.

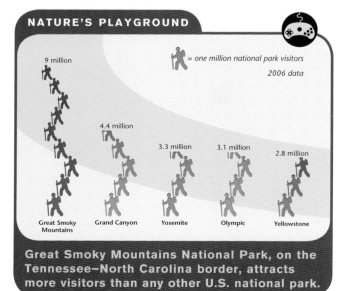

NATURE'S PLAYGROUND

= one million national park visitors
2006 data

9 million — Great Smoky Mountains
4.4 million — Grand Canyon
3.3 million — Yosemite
3.1 million — Olympic
2.8 million — Yellowstone

Great Smoky Mountains National Park, on the Tennessee–North Carolina border, attracts more visitors than any other U.S. national park.

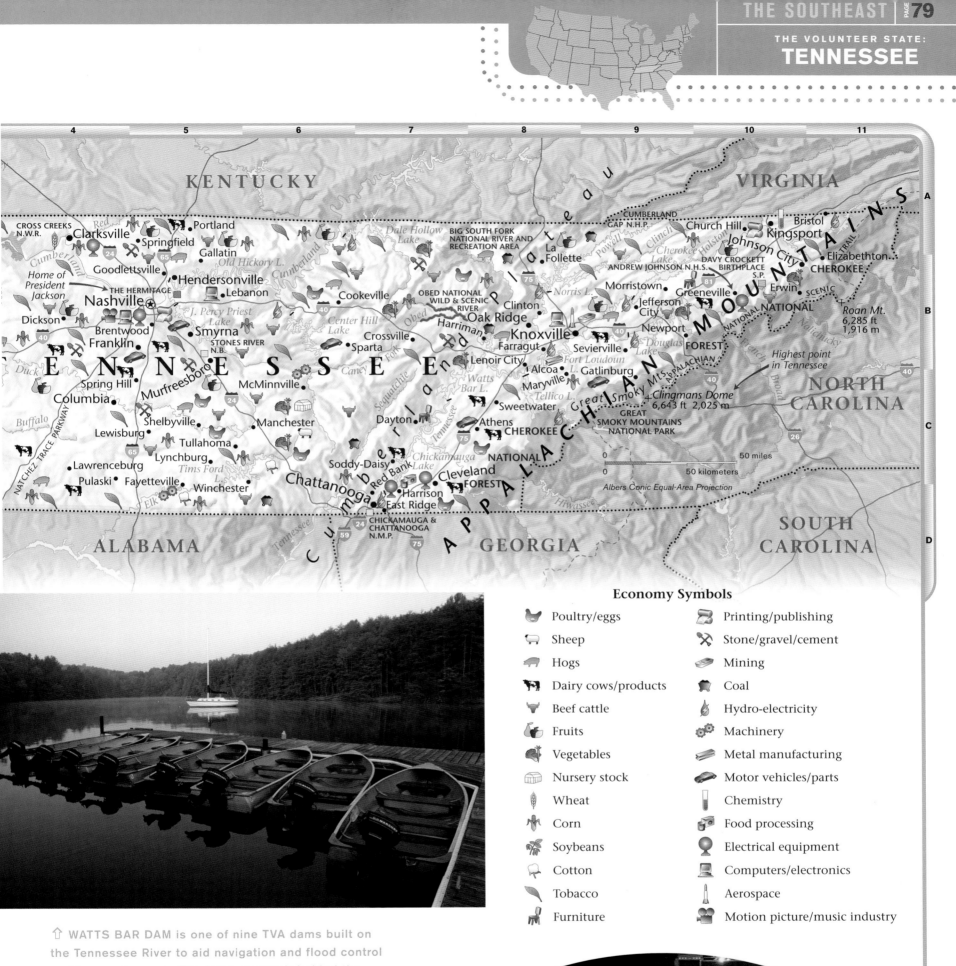

KENTUCKY

VIRGINIA

4 **5** **6** **7** **8** **9** **10** **11**

CROSS CREEKS N.W.R.
Clarksville
Portland
Springfield
Gallatin
Goodlettsville
Old Hickory L.
Hendersonville
Home of President Jackson
THE HERMITAGE
Lebanon
Dickson
Nashville
J. Percy Priest Lake
Brentwood
Franklin
Smyrna
STONES RIVER N.B.
Dale Hollow Lake
BIG SOUTH FORK NATIONAL RIVER AND RECREATION AREA
Cumberland
Center Hill Lake
Crossville
Sparta
La Follette
Cumberland
Plateau
OBED NATIONAL WILD & SCENIC RIVER
Obed
Clinton
Oak Ridge
Harriman
Norris L.
CUMBERLAND GAP N.H.P.
Powell
Clinch
Church Hill
Kingsport
Bristol
Johnson City
ANDREW JOHNSON N.H.S.
DAVY CROCKETT BIRTHPLACE S.P.
Elizabethton
CHEROKEE
Cherokee Lake
Holston
Morristown
Greeneville
Erwin
NATIONAL SCENIC
Jefferson City
Newport
FOREST
Roan Mt. 6,285 ft 1,916 m
Knoxville
Farragut
Sevierville
Douglas Lake
Gatlinburg
Spring Hill
Columbia
Murfreesboro
McMinnville
TENNESSEE
Duck
Lenoir City
Alcoa
Maryville
Fort Loudoun
L. Tellico L.
Watts Bar L.
Clingmans Dome 6,643 ft 2,025 m
Highest point in Tennessee
APPALACHIAN
Smoky Mts.
French
Broad
NORTH CAROLINA
Shelbyville
Lewisburg
Tullahoma
Manchester
Caney Fork
Sequatchie
Sweetwater
Athens
CHEROKEE
GREAT SMOKY MOUNTAINS NATIONAL PARK
Great Smoky Mts.
Lawrenceburg
Lynchburg
Tims Ford L.
Dayton
Tennessee
NATIONAL
50 miles
50 kilometers
Natchez Trace Parkway
Pulaski
Fayetteville
Winchester
Soddy-Daisy
Red Bank
Chickamauga Lake
Cleveland
FOREST
Albers Conic Equal-Area Projection
Buffalo
Chattanooga
Harrison
East Ridge
SOUTH CAROLINA
Elk
ALABAMA
CHICKAMAUGA & CHATTANOOGA N.M.P.
GEORGIA
Hiwassee
Tennessee

Economy Symbols

Symbol	Type	Symbol	Type
🐔	Poultry/eggs		Printing/publishing
🐑	Sheep		Stone/gravel/cement
🐖	Hogs		Mining
🐄	Dairy cows/products		Coal
🐂	Beef cattle		Hydro-electricity
	Fruits		Machinery
	Vegetables		Metal manufacturing
	Nursery stock		Motor vehicles/parts
	Wheat		Chemistry
	Corn		Food processing
	Soybeans		Electrical equipment
	Cotton		Computers/electronics
	Tobacco		Aerospace
	Furniture		Motion picture/music industry

⬆ WATTS BAR DAM is one of nine TVA dams built on the Tennessee River to aid navigation and flood control and to supply power. The large reservoir behind the dam provides a recreation area that attracts millions of vacationers each year. Without the dam, cities such as Chattanooga would face devastating floods.

⇨ SOUTHERN TRADITION. Nashville's Grand Ole Opry is the home of country music. Originally a 1925 radio show called "Barn Dance," the Opry now occupies a theater with a seating capacity of 4,400 and the largest broadcasting studio in the world. Country music, using mainly stringed instruments, evolved from traditional folk tunes of the Appalachians.

THE OLD DOMINION STATE:
VIRGINIA

VIRGINIA

1   2   3   4

Long before Europeans arrived in present-day Virginia, Native Americans populated the area. Early Spanish attempts to establish a colony failed, but in 1607 merchants established the first permanent English settlement in North America at Jamestown. Virginia became a prosperous colony, growing tobacco using slave labor. Virginia played a key role in the drive for independence, and the final battle of the Revolutionary War was at Yorktown, near Jamestown. In 1861 Virginia joined the Confederacy and became a major battleground of the Civil War, which

⬆ EARLY ENTERTAINMENT. Dating back to ancient Greece and Rome, dice made of bone, ivory, or lead were popular during colonial times.

left the state in financial ruin. Today, Virginia has a diversified economy. Farmers still grow tobacco, along with other crops. The Hampton Roads area, near the mouth of Chesapeake Bay, is a center for shipbuilding and home to major naval bases. Northern Virginia, across the Potomac River from Washington, D.C., boasts federal government offices and high-tech businesses. And the state's natural beauty and many historic sites attract tourists from around the world.

KENTUCKY
Bluefield   77
Tazewell
Richlands   APPALACHIAN
Norton   Clinch
Lebanon   Mountain   Wytheville
Big Stone Gap   JEFFERSON   NATIONAL   FOREST
CUMBERLAND GAP N.H.P.   Clinch   Marion   MT. ROGERS RECREATION
Powell   North Fork   Mt. Rogers
Abingdon   5,729 ft
Bristol   1,746 m
Holston   Highest point in Virginia
TENNESSEE   S. Fork   APPALACHIA

➡ NATURAL WONDER. Winding under the Appalachian Mountains, Luray Caverns formed as water dissolved limestone rocks and precipitated calcium deposits to form stalactites and stalagmites.

⇓ PAST AND PRESENT. Cyclists speed past a statue of Confederate General Robert E. Lee on Richmond's Monument Avenue. The street has drawn criticism for recognizing leaders of the Confederacy.

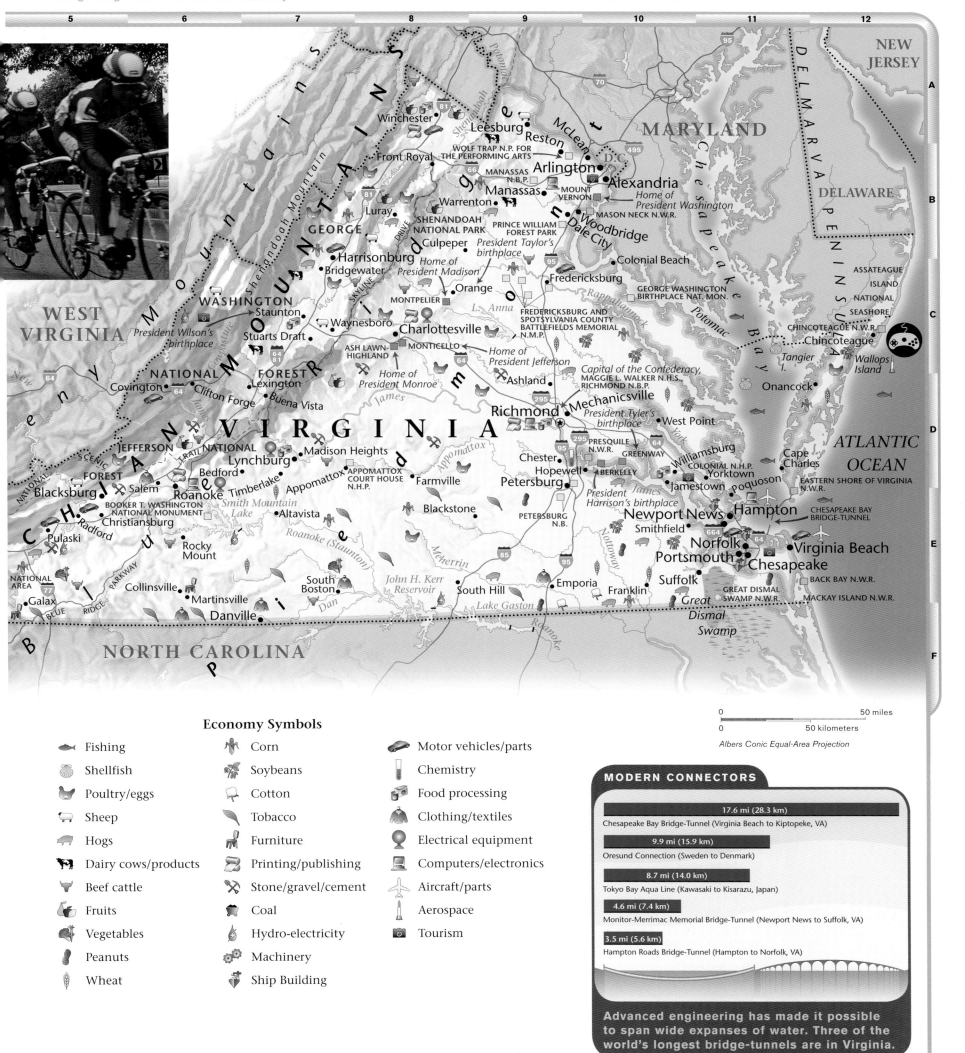

Economy Symbols

- Fishing
- Shellfish
- Poultry/eggs
- Sheep
- Hogs
- Dairy cows/products
- Beef cattle
- Fruits
- Vegetables
- Peanuts
- Wheat

- Corn
- Soybeans
- Cotton
- Tobacco
- Furniture
- Printing/publishing
- Stone/gravel/cement
- Coal
- Hydro-electricity
- Machinery
- Wheat

- Motor vehicles/parts
- Chemistry
- Food processing
- Clothing/textiles
- Electrical equipment
- Computers/electronics
- Aircraft/parts
- Aerospace
- Tourism
- Ship Building

0   50 miles
0   50 kilometers
Albers Conic Equal-Area Projection

MODERN CONNECTORS

| 17.6 mi (28.3 km) |
Chesapeake Bay Bridge-Tunnel (Virginia Beach to Kiptopeke, VA)

| 9.9 mi (15.9 km) |
Oresund Connection (Sweden to Denmark)

| 8.7 mi (14.0 km) |
Tokyo Bay Aqua Line (Kawasaki to Kisarazu, Japan)

| 4.6 mi (7.4 km) |
Monitor-Merrimac Memorial Bridge-Tunnel (Newport News to Suffolk, VA)

| 3.5 mi (5.6 km) |
Hampton Roads Bridge-Tunnel (Hampton to Norfolk, VA)

Advanced engineering has made it possible to span wide expanses of water. Three of the world's longest bridge-tunnels are in Virginia.

THE BASICS

STATS

Area
24,230 sq mi (62,755 sq km)

Population
1,812,035

Capital
Charleston
Population 51,394

Largest city
Charleston
Population 51,394

Ethnic/racial groups
94.9% white; 3.3% African American; .6% Asian; .2% Native American. Hispanic (any race) .9%.

Industry
Tourism, coal mining, chemicals, metal manufacturing, forest products, stone, clay, oil, glass products

Agriculture
Poultry and eggs, cattle, dairy products, apples

Statehood
June 20, 1863; 35th state

GEO WHIZ

 The FBI crime data center in Clarksburg has the largest collection of fingerprints in the world. The center processes some 50,000 fingerprints each day.

The city of Weirton is nestled in the panhandle between Ohio and Pennsylvania. It is the only city in the U.S. that sits in one state and borders two others.

 Bridge Day, held each October, is the only day of the year when it is legal to jump off the 876-foot- (267-m-) high New River Gorge Bridge using bungee cords, parachutes, or other equipment.

The first rural free mail delivery in the United States started in Charles Town on October 1, 1896.

CARDINAL
RHODODENDRON

WEST VIRGINIA

1   2

Mountainous West Virginia was first settled by Native Americans who favored the wooded region for hunting. The first Europeans to settle in what originally was an extension of Virginia were Germans and Scotch-Irish, who came through mountain valleys of Pennsylvania in the early 1700s. Because farms in West Virginia did not depend upon slaves, residents opposed secession during the Civil War and broke away from Virginia, becoming the 35th state in 1863. In the early 1800s West Virginia harvested forest products and mined salt, but it was the exploitation of vast coal deposits that brought industrialization to the state. Coal fueled steel mills, steamboats, and trains, and jobs in the mines attracted immigrants from far and near. However, poor work conditions resulted in a legacy of poverty, illness, and environmental degradation—problems the state continues to face. Today, the state is working to build a tourist industry based on its natural beauty and mountain crafts and culture.

⬆ HARD LABOR. Coal miners work under difficult conditions. In 2006 West Virginia mined more than 152 million tons of coal, or 13 percent of U.S. production.

OHIO

Point Pleasant

Hurricane
Kenova • Huntington • Nitro
St. Albans

Madison

Logan

Williamson

KENTUCKY

⬅ STRATEGIC LOCATION. Founded in 1751 by Robert Harper, who built a ferry to cross the Shenandoah River, Harpers Ferry was a departure point for pioneers heading West as well as the site of many battles during the Civil War.

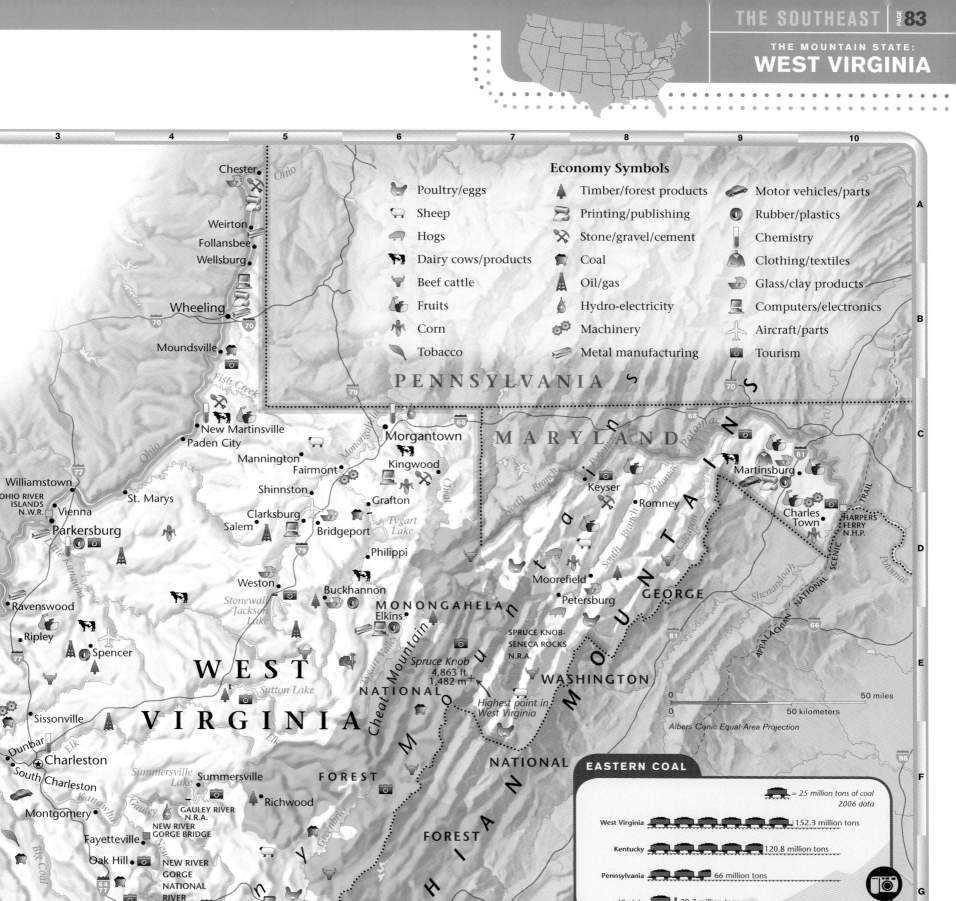

Economy Symbols

- Poultry/eggs
- Sheep
- Hogs
- Dairy cows/products
- Beef cattle
- Fruits
- Corn
- Tobacco
- Timber/forest products
- Printing/publishing
- Stone/gravel/cement
- Coal
- Oil/gas
- Hydro-electricity
- Machinery
- Metal manufacturing
- Motor vehicles/parts
- Rubber/plastics
- Chemistry
- Clothing/textiles
- Glass/clay products
- Computers/electronics
- Aircraft/parts
- Tourism

PENNSYLVANIA

MARYLAND

OHIO

WEST VIRGINIA

Chester
Weirton
Follansbee
Wellsburg
Wheeling
Moundsville
New Martinsville
Paden City
Mannington
Fairmont
Kingwood
Shinnston
Grafton
Clarksburg
Salem
Bridgeport
Williamstown
OHIO RIVER ISLANDS N.W.R.
Vienna
St. Marys
Parkersburg
Philippi
Weston
Buckhannon
Stonewall Jackson Lake
MONONGAHELA
Elkins
Ravenswood
Ripley
Spencer
Sutton Lake
NATIONAL
Cheat Mountain
Spruce Knob
4,863 ft
1,482 m
Highest point in West Virginia
SPRUCE KNOB-SENECA ROCKS N.R.A.
Sissonville
Dunbar
Charleston
South Charleston
Summersville Lake
Summersville
FOREST
Richwood
Montgomery
GAULEY RIVER N.R.A.
Fayetteville
NEW RIVER GORGE BRIDGE
Oak Hill
NEW RIVER GORGE NATIONAL RIVER
Beckley
Lewisburg
White Sulphur Springs
Hinton
Mullens
BLUESTONE NATIONAL SCENIC RIVER
Welch
Bluestone Lake
Princeton
Bluefield
JEFFERSON
NATIONAL
VIRGINIA
FOREST
APPALACHIAN
Allegheny
Mountains
Keyser
Romney
Moorefield
Petersburg
WASHINGTON
GEORGE
Martinsburg
Charles Town
HARPERS FERRY N.H.P.
APPALACHIAN NATIONAL SCENIC TRAIL
Shenandoah

EASTERN COAL

= 25 million tons of coal
2006 data

West Virginia	152.3 million tons
Kentucky	120.8 million tons
Pennsylvania	66 million tons
Virginia	29.7 million tons

Deep in the Appalachian Mountains are large deposits of coal, a major source of energy for industry and power generation.

0 — 50 miles
0 — 50 kilometers
Albers Conic Equal-Area Projection

⇨ THRILL SEEKERS. West Virginia's mountain rivers offer some of the best white-water rafting in the eastern U.S. The gorge of the New River is called the Grand Canyon of the East, while the Gauley River is called the Beast of the East.

THE REGION

PHYSICAL			POLITICAL	
Total area 821,739 sq mi (2,128,287 sq km)	**Lowest point** St. Francis River, MO 230 ft (70 m)	**Vegetation** Grassland; broadleaf, needleleaf, and mixed forest	**Total population** 66,388,795	**Smallest state** Indiana: 36,418 sq mi (94,322 sq km)
Highest point Harney Peak, SD 7,242 ft (2,207 m)	**Longest rivers** Mississippi, Missouri, Arkansas, Ohio	**Climate** Continental to mild, ranging from cold winters and cool summers in the north to mild winters and humid summers in the south	**States (12):** Illinois, Indiana, Iowa, Kansas, Michigan, Minnesota, Missouri, Nebraska, North Dakota, Ohio, South Dakota, Wisconsin	**Most populous state** Illinois: 12,852,548
	Largest lakes Superior, Michigan, Huron, Erie		**Largest state** Michigan: 96,716 sq mi (250,495 sq km)	**Least populous state** North Dakota: 639,715
				Largest city proper Chicago, IL: 2,833,321

The Midwest

QUEBEC

PENNSYLVANIA

ONTARIO

WEST VIRGINIA

VIRGINIA

NORTH CAROLINA

SOUTH CAROLINA

CANADA

200 miles

200 kilometers

Albers Conic Equal-Area Projection

0

0

Lake Erie

Lake Huron

Lake Superior

Upper Peninsula

Keweenaw Peninsula

Isle Royale

M I C H I G A N

Lower Peninsula

Strs. of Mackinac

Saginaw Bay

Muskegon

Grand

Lake St. Clair

N

Ohio

O H I O

Campbell Hill
1,550 ft
472 m

Scioto

Muskingum

Great Miami

Maumee

KENTUCKY

TENNESSEE

ALABAMA

GEORGIA

MISSISSIPPI

Mt. Arvon +
1,979 ft
603 m

Eagle Mt. +
2,301 ft
701 m

CANADA
U.S.

Lake Winnibigoshish

Mille Lacs Lake

Lake Michigan

Green Bay

Door Pen.

Menominee

WISCONSIN

Lake Winnebago

Timms Hill +
1,951 ft
595 m

Wisconsin

Fox

Rock

Charles Mound +
1,235 ft
376 m

Illinois

I L L I N O I S

Wabash

White

I N D I A N A

1,257 ft
383 m

Ohio

C E N T R A L

Mississippi

St. Francis

Taum Sauk
Mt. + 1,772 ft
540 m

Lake of
the Ozarks

Osage

O z a r k   P l a t e a u

Table Rock Lake

ARKANSAS

Rainy L.

Upper Red Lake

Leech Lake

Lower Red Lake

Lake of the Woods

M I N N E S O T A

Mississippi

Cedar

Iowa

Des Moines

I O W A

L O W L A N D

Minnesota

Hawkeye Point +
1,670 ft
509 m

Little Sioux

MISSOURI

Missouri

Harry S.
Truman
Reservoir

Neosho

Red River of the North

Big Sioux

Missouri

Souris

Lake Sakakawea

N O R T H   D A K O T A

Lake Oahe

James

L. Sharpe

Lake Francis Case

S O U T H   D A K O T A

Cheyenne

Niobrara

Sand Hills

N E B R A S K A

P l a t t e

Platte

North Platte

South Platte

Republican

Smoky Hill

Smoky Hills

K A N S A S

Arkansas

Flint Hills

Red Hills

Cimarron

Kansas

MANITOBA

SASKATCHEWAN

CANADA
U.S.

Missouri

G R E A T

White Butte
3,506 ft
1,069 m

Little Missouri

Badlands

Black Hills

Harney Peak +
7,242 ft
2,207 m

White

Panorama Point
5,423 ft
1,653 m

Mt. Sunflower +
4,039 ft
1,231 m

P L A I N S

MONTANA

WYOMING

COLORADO

NEW MEXICO

OKLAHOMA

TEXAS

H i g h

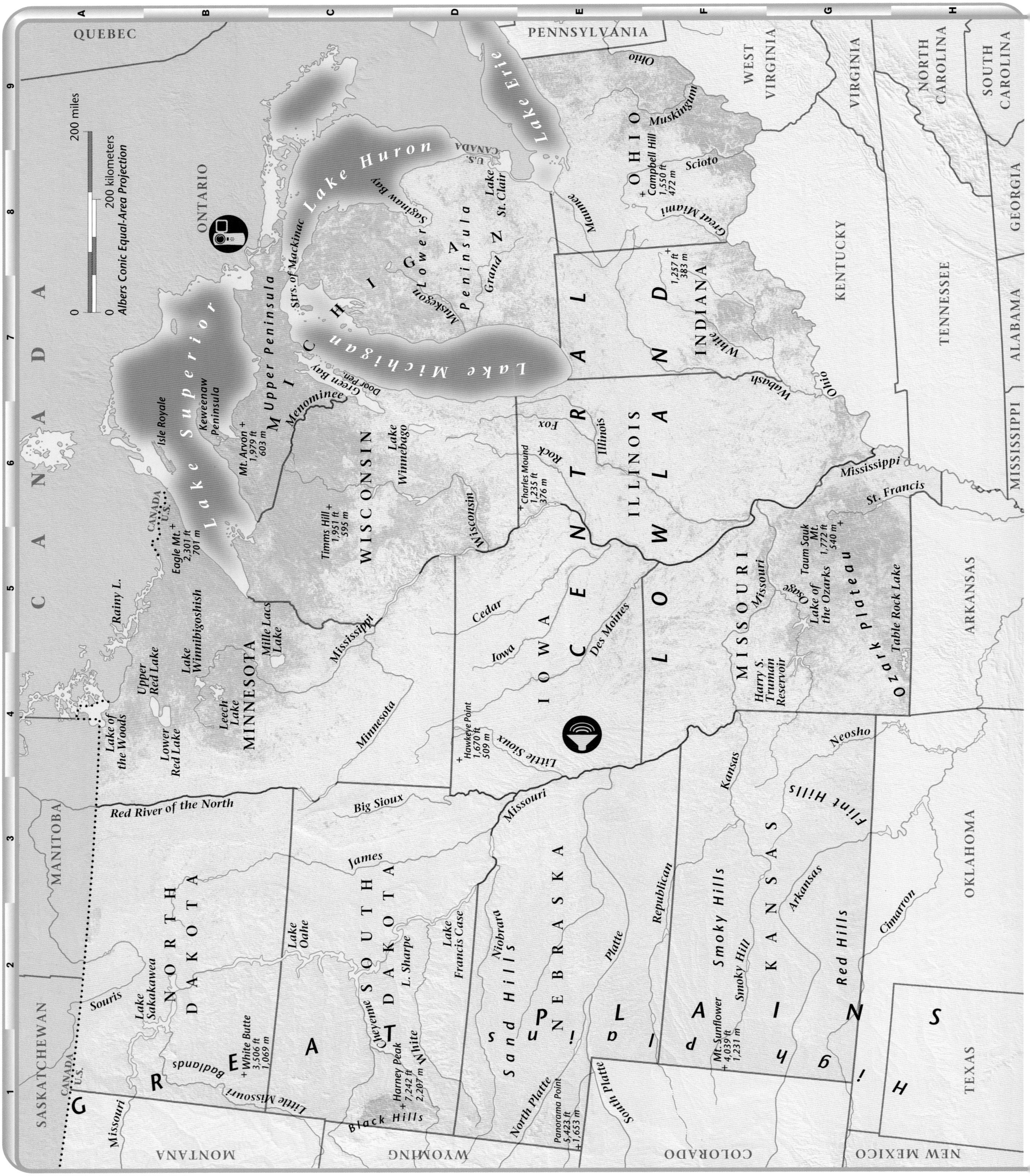

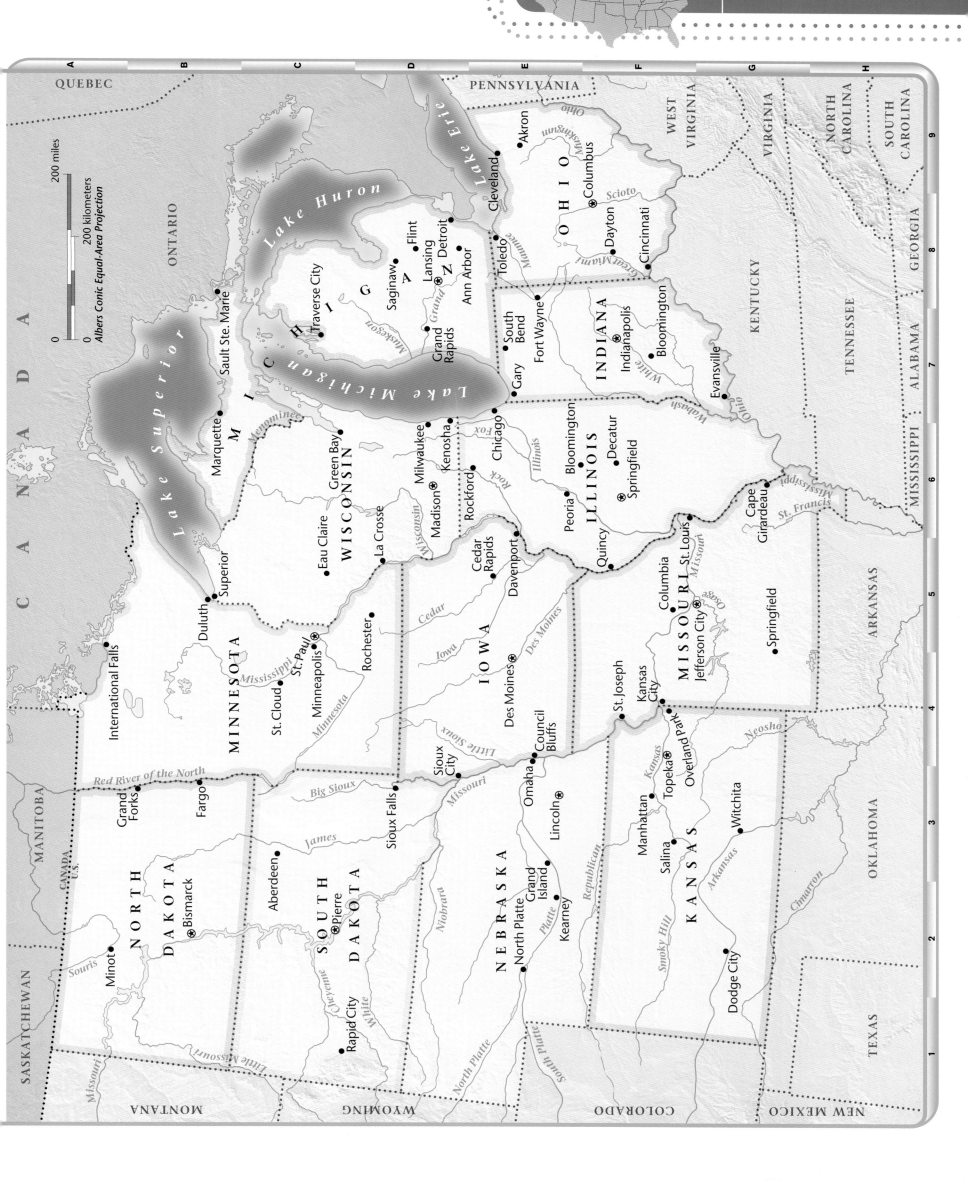

200 miles

200 kilometers

Albers Conic Equal-Area Projection

QUEBEC

PENNSYLVANIA

CANADA

ONTARIO

Lake Superior

Lake Huron

Lake Erie

Lake Michigan

Ohio

WEST VIRGINIA

VIRGINIA

NORTH CAROLINA

SOUTH CAROLINA

Akron

Cleveland

O H I O

Columbus

Scioto

Dayton

Cincinnati

Muskingum

KENTUCKY

TENNESSEE

GEORGIA

Great Miami

Flint

Lansing

Detroit

Saginaw

M I C H I G A N

Ann Arbor

Toledo

Maumee

Grand

Traverse City

Grand Rapids

Muskegon

South Bend

Fort Wayne

I N D I A N A

Indianapolis

Bloomington

White

Evansville

ALABAMA

MISSISSIPPI

Sault Ste. Marie

Marquette

Menominee

Green Bay

Milwaukee

Kenosha

Chicago

Fox

Rock

Illinois

Gary

Bloomington

Decatur

Springfield

I L L I N O I S

Wabash

Ohio

Eau Claire

W I S C O N S I N

La Crosse

Wisconsin

Madison

Rockford

Peoria

Quincy

Cape Girardeau

Mississippi

St. Francis

ARKANSAS

Superior

Duluth

Cedar Rapids

Davenport

St. Louis

Columbia

Missouri

Springfield

International Falls

Rochester

Cedar

I O W A

Des Moines

Iowa

Des Moines

M I S S O U R I

Jefferson City

Osage

St. Cloud

St. Paul

Minneapolis

M I N N E S O T A

Minnesota

Sioux City

Council Bluffs

St. Joseph

Kansas City

Overland Park

Neosho

Mississippi

Little Sioux

Red River of the North

Fargo

Grand Forks

Big Sioux

Missouri

Omaha

Lincoln

Manhattan

Topeka

Salina

Wichita

Kansas

MANITOBA

CANADA
U.S.

Minot

Souris

N O R T H
D A K O T A

Bismarck

Aberdeen

James

S O U T H
D A K O T A

Pierre

Cheyenne

White

Rapid City

Little Missouri

Niobrara

N E B R A S K A

North Platte

Grand Island

Kearney

Platte

Republican

Smoky Hill

K A N S A S

Arkansas

Dodge City

Cinnaron

OKLAHOMA

SASKATCHEWAN

Missouri

MONTANA

WYOMING

North Platte

South Platte

COLORADO

NEW MEXICO

TEXAS

A B C D E F G H

9 8 7 6 5 4 3 2 1

⇨ FIERCE GIANT. Students in Chicago's Field Museum eye the skeleton of *Tyrannosaurus rex*, a dinosaur that roamed North America's plains 65 million years ago.

The Midwest
GREAT LAKES, GREAT RIVERS

The Midwest's early white settlers emigrated from eastern states or Europe, but recent immigrants come from all parts of the world. Hispanics, for example, are settling in communities large and small throughout the region, while many Arabs reside in Dearborn, Michigan. Drained by three mighty rivers—the Mississippi, Missouri, and Ohio—the Midwestern lowlands and plains are one of the world's most bountiful farmlands. Though the number of farmers has declined, new technologies and equipment have made farms larger and more productive. Meanwhile, industrial cities of the Rust Belt are adjusting to an economy focused more on information and services than on manufacturing.

⇩ CROP CIRCLES. Much of the western part of the region receives less than 20 inches (50 cm) of rain yearly—not enough to support agriculture. Large circular center-pivot irrigation systems draw water from underground reserves called aquifers to provide life-giving water to crops.

⇩ DAIRY HEARTLAND. Dairy cows, such as these in Wisconsin, are sometimes treated with growth hormones to increase milk production. These animals play an important role in the economy of the Midwest, which supplies much of the country's milk, butter, and cheese.

▬ MIDWEST URBAN HUB. Chicago, the third largest urban area in the U.S., with almost 10 million people, is the economic and cultural core of the Midwest and a major transportation hub.

⇨ PRESERVING THE PAST. A young Cherokee man, dressed in beaded costume and feathered headband, dances at a powwow in Milwaukee. Such gatherings provide Indians from across the country with a chance to share their traditions.

⇧ NATURE'S MOST VIOLENT STORMS. Parts of the midwestern U.S. have earned the nickname Tornado Alley because these destructive, swirling storms, which develop in association with thunderstorms along eastward-moving cold fronts, occur here more than any other place on Earth.

WHERE THE PICTURES ARE

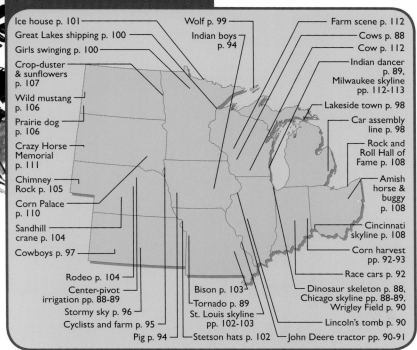

Ice house p. 101
Great Lakes shipping p. 100
Girls swinging p. 100
Crop-duster & sunflowers p. 107
Wild mustang p. 106
Prairie dog p. 106
Crazy Horse Memorial p. 111
Chimney Rock p. 105
Corn Palace p. 110
Sandhill crane p. 104
Cowboys p. 97
Rodeo p. 104
Center-pivot irrigation pp. 88-89
Stormy sky p. 96
Cyclists and farm p. 95
Pig p. 94
Wolf p. 99
Indian boys p. 94
Bison p. 103
Tornado p. 89
St. Louis skyline pp. 102-103
Stetson hats p. 102
Farm scene p. 112
Cows p. 88
Cow p. 112
Indian dancer p. 89, Milwaukee skyline pp. 112-113
Lakeside town p. 98
Car assembly line p. 98
Rock and Roll Hall of Fame p. 108
Amish horse & buggy p. 108
Cincinnati skyline p. 108
Corn harvest pp. 92-93
Race cars p. 92
Dinosaur skeleton p. 88, Chicago skyline pp. 88-89, Wrigley Field p. 90
Lincoln's tomb p. 90
John Deere tractor pp. 90-91

THE LAND OF LINCOLN STATE:
ILLINOIS

ILLINOIS

ILLINOIS

Two rivers that now form the borders of Illinois aided the state's early white settlement. Frenchmen first explored the area in 1673 by traveling down the Mississippi, and the Ohio brought many 19th-century settlers to southern Illinois. Most Indians were forced out by the 1830s, more than a decade after Illinois became the 21st state. Ethnically diverse Chicago, the most populous city in the Midwest, is an economic giant and one of the country's busiest rail, highway, and air transit hubs. Barges from its port reach the Gulf of Mexico via rivers and canals, while ships reach the Atlantic Ocean via the Great Lakes and St. Lawrence Seaway. Flat terrain and fertile prairie soils in the northern and central regions help make the state a top producer of corn and soybeans. The more rugged, forested south has deposits of bituminous coal. Springfield, capital of the Land of Lincoln, welcomes tourists visiting the home and tomb of the country's 16th president.

THE BASICS

STATS

Area
57,914 sq mi (149,998 sq km)

Population
12,852,548

Capital
Springfield
Population 116,482

Largest city
Chicago
Population 2,833,321

Ethnic/racial groups
79.3% white; 15.0% African American; 4.2% Asian; .3% Native American. Hispanic (any race) 14.7%.

Industry
Industrial machinery, electronic equipment, food processing, chemicals, metals, printing and publishing, rubber and plastics, motor vehicles

Agriculture
Corn, soybeans, hogs, cattle, dairy products, nursery stock

Statehood
December 3, 1818; 21st state

GEO WHIZ

A giant fossilized rain forest has been unearthed in an eastern Illinois coal mine near the town of Danville. Scientists believe an earthquake buried the entire forest 300 million years ago.

The Great Chicago fire of 1871 destroyed the city's waterworks, so firemen had to drag water in buckets from Lake Michigan and the Chicago River. The fire burned out of control for two days until rain finally put it out.

CARDINAL
VIOLET

⇧ REMEMBERING A PRESIDENT. Dedicated in 1874, the National Lincoln Monument in Springfield honors Abraham Lincoln, who was assassinated in 1865. A special vault holds the remains of the slain president, who led the country during the Civil War.

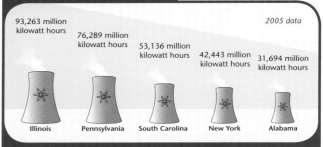

ALTERNATIVE ENERGY

2005 data

93,263 million kilowatt hours — Illinois
76,289 million kilowatt hours — Pennsylvania
53,136 million kilowatt hours — South Carolina
42,443 million kilowatt hours — New York
31,694 million kilowatt hours — Alabama

Illinois ranks first among the 31 states that produce nuclear power. The state has 6 nuclear power plants with 11 reactors.

WRIGLEY FIELD
HOME OF
CHICAGO CUBS

PIRATES 1 — TOP 9TH — CUBS 4

⇧ PLAY BALL! Wrigley Field, home to the Chicago Cubs baseball team, is affected by wind conditions more than any other major league park due to its location near Lake Michigan.

⇧ FIELDS OF GRAIN. Illinois has long been a major grain producer, but farming today is highly mechanized. Above, a tractor moves bales of rolled hay.

Economy Symbols

- Poultry/eggs
- Sheep
- Hogs
- Dairy cows/products
- Beef cattle
- Vegetables
- Nursery stock
- Wheat
- Corn
- Soybeans
- Printing/publishing
- Stone/gravel/cement
- Mining
- Coal
- Oil/gas
- Machinery
- Metal products
- Motor vehicles/parts
- Rubber/plastics
- Chemistry
- Food processing
- Computers/electronics
- Motion picture/music industry
- Tourism
- Finance/insurance

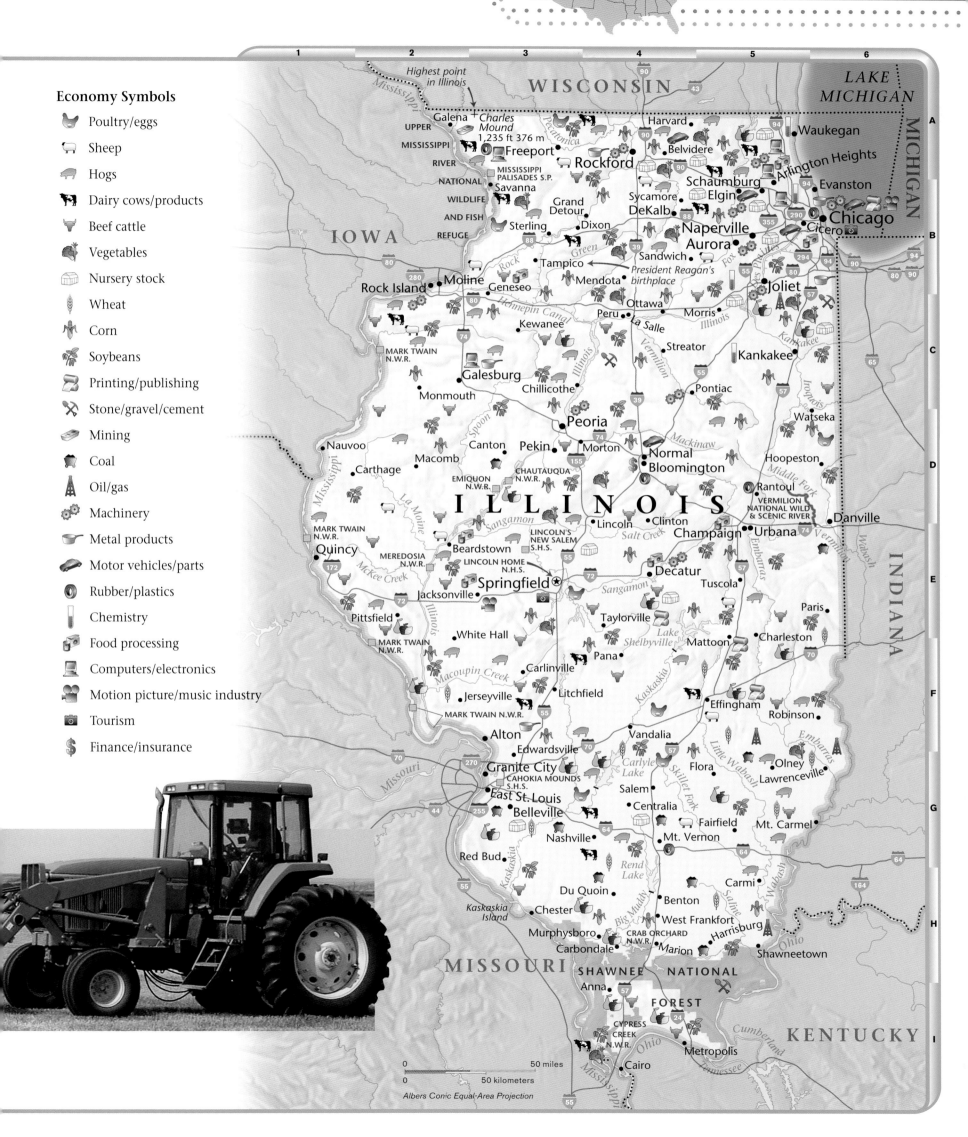

THE HOOSIER STATE:
INDIANA

INDIANA

Indiana's name, meaning "Land of the Indians," honors the tribes who lived in the region before the arrival of Europeans. The first permanent white settlement was Vincennes, established by the French in the early 1700s. Following statehood in 1816, most Indians were forced out to make way for white settlement. Lake Michigan, in the state's northwest corner, brings economic and recreational opportunities. The lakefront city of Gary anchors a major industrial region. Nearby, the natural beauty and shifting sands of the Indiana Dunes National Lakeshore attract many visitors. Corn, soybeans, and hogs are the most important products from Indiana's many farms. True to the state motto, "The Crossroads of America," highways from all directions converge at Indianapolis. Traveling at a much higher speed are cars on that city's famed Motor Speedway, home to the Indy 500 auto race since 1911. Cheering for a favorite high school or college team is a favorite pastime for many Hoosiers who catch basketball fever.

⇧ START YOUR ENGINES. The Indianapolis Motor Speedway seats 250,000 sports fans. Nicknamed the Brickyard, its track was once paved with 3.2 million bricks.

THE BASICS

STATS

Area
36,418 sq mi (94,322 sq km)

Population
6,345,289

Capital
Indianapolis
Population 795,484

Largest city
Indianapolis
Population 795,484

Ethnic/racial groups
88.3% white; 8.9% African American; 1.3% Asian; .3% Native American. Hispanic (any race) 4.8%.

Industry
Transportation equipment, steel, pharmaceutical and chemical products, machinery, petroleum, coal

Agriculture
Corn, soybeans, hogs, poultry and eggs, cattle, dairy products

Statehood
December 11, 1816; 19th state

GEO WHIZ

Every July during Circus Festival, in Peru, a couple hundred local kids and a couple thousand volunteers put on a three-ring circus complete with clowns, snow cones, and standing ovations from sellout crowds. The city is home to the International Circus Hall of Fame.

Every year Fort Wayne hosts the Johnny Appleseed Festival to honor John Chapman, the man who planted apple orchards from Pennsylvania to Illinois.

The Indianapolis Children's Museum, in partnership with National Geographic and the Environmental Research Systems Institute, has created an international traveling exhibit to teach children and parents that maps are tools of adventure.

CARDINAL
PEONY

⇨ FUEL FARMING. Indiana farming is undergoing dramatic changes as corn is used in the production of ethanol, a non-fossil fuel energy source that is increasingly popular.

HEAVY INDUSTRY

Indiana	27.34 million tons
Ohio	15.76 million tons
Pennsylvania	6.9 million tons
Michigan	6.44 million tons

2004 data

Steel production was the core of early U.S. industrialization. Indiana leads in steel production, but the U.S. also imports steel from other countries.

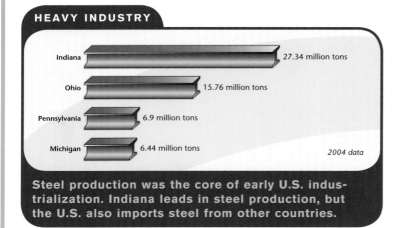

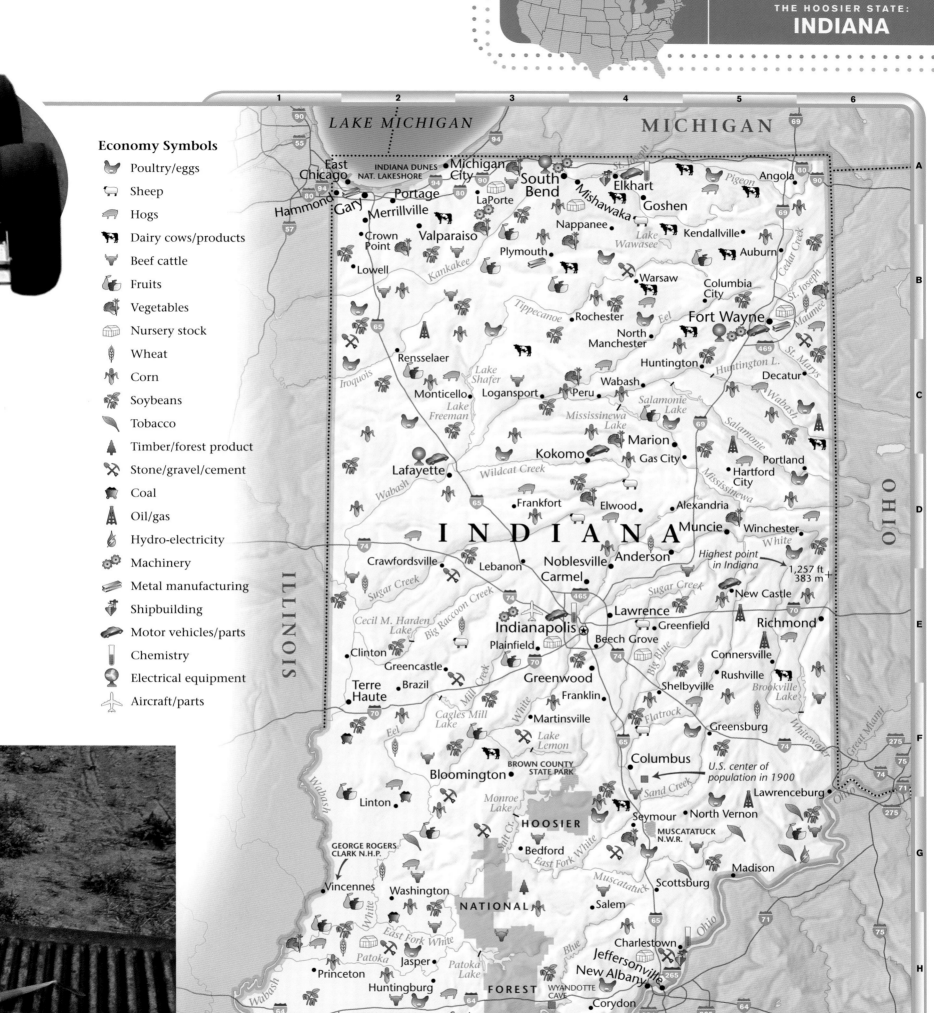

Economy Symbols

- Poultry/eggs
- Sheep
- Hogs
- Dairy cows/products
- Beef cattle
- Fruits
- Vegetables
- Nursery stock
- Wheat
- Corn
- Soybeans
- Tobacco
- Timber/forest product
- Stone/gravel/cement
- Coal
- Oil/gas
- Hydro-electricity
- Machinery
- Metal manufacturing
- Shipbuilding
- Motor vehicles/parts
- Chemistry
- Electrical equipment
- Aircraft/parts

LAKE MICHIGAN

MICHIGAN

OHIO

ILLINOIS

KENTUCKY

INDIANA

East Chicago
Hammond
Gary
Portage
Merrillville
Crown Point
Lowell
Valparaiso
INDIANA DUNES NAT. LAKESHORE
Michigan City
LaPorte
South Bend
Mishawaka
Elkhart
Goshen
Nappanee
Plymouth
Kendallville
Auburn
Angola
Lake Wawasee
Warsaw
Columbia City
Fort Wayne
Rochester
North Manchester
Huntington
Decatur
Rensselaer
Monticello
Lake Shafer
Logansport
Peru
Wabash
Lake Freeman
Mississinewa Lake
Salamonie Lake
Marion
Gas City
Portland
Hartford City
Kokomo
Lafayette
Wildcat Creek
Frankfort
Elwood
Alexandria
Muncie
Winchester
Crawfordsville
Lebanon
Noblesville
Anderson
Highest point in Indiana 1,257 ft 383 m
Carmel
New Castle
Sugar Creek
Indianapolis
Lawrence
Greenfield
Richmond
Plainfield
Beech Grove
Connersville
Clinton
Greencastle
Greenwood
Rushville
Brookville Lake
Terre Haute
Brazil
Franklin
Shelbyville
Martinsville
Greensburg
Bloomington
BROWN COUNTY STATE PARK
Columbus
U.S. center of population in 1900
Linton
Lawrenceburg
Monroe Lake
HOOSIER
Seymour
North Vernon
MUSCATATUCK N.W.R.
Bedford
Madison
GEORGE ROGERS CLARK N.H.P.
Vincennes
Washington
NATIONAL
Salem
Scottsburg
Charlestown
Jeffersonville
New Albany
Jasper
Princeton
Huntingburg
FOREST
WYANDOTTE CAVE
Corydon
NEW HARMONY S.H.S.
LINCOLN BOYHOOD NATIONAL MEMORIAL
Santa Claus
Mount Vernon
Boonville
Evansville
Tell City

0   100 miles
0   100 kilometers
Albers Equal-Area Projection Projection

THE HAWKEYE STATE:
IOWA

IOWA

IOWA

THE BASICS

STATS

Area
56,272 sq mi (145,743 sq km)

Population
2,988,046

Capital
Des Moines
Population 193,886

Largest city
Des Moines
Population 193,886

Ethnic/racial groups
94.6% white; 2.5% African
American; 1.6% Asian;
.4% Native American. Hispanic
(any race) 3.8%.

Industry
Real estate, health services,
industrial machinery, food processing,
construction

Agriculture
Hogs, corn, soybeans, oats, cattle,
dairy products

Statehood
December 28, 1846; 29th state

GEO WHIZ

The most famous house in Iowa and
one of the most famous houses in
America is in Eldon. It was immor-
talized in Grant Wood's famous
painting "American Gothic." The
stern-faced, pitchfork-holding farmer
and his wife shown in the art were not
farmers at all. Wood's sister and his
dentist posed for the painting.

Effigy Mounds National Monument,
in the northeast corner of Iowa, is the
only place in the country with such
a large collection of mounds in the
shapes of mammals, birds, and reptiles.
Of the 191 mounds, 29 are shaped
like animals. Eastern Woodland
Indians built these mounds from
about B.C. 500 to 1300 A.D.

Iowa, along with California
and Texas, is one
of the country's
leading producers
of wind energy.

AMERICAN
GOLDFINCH

WILD ROSE

Iowa's prehistoric inhabitants built earthen mounds—
some shaped like birds and bears—that are visible in
the state's northeast. Nineteenth-century white
settlers found rolling prairies covered
by a sea of tall grasses that soon yielded
to the plow. A decade after statehood in
1846, a group of religious German immigrants
established the Amana Colonies, a communal
society that still draws visitors. Blessed with
ample precipitation and rich soils, Iowa
is the heart of one of the world's most
productive farming regions. The state is the
country's top producer of corn, soybeans,
hogs, and eggs. Food processing
and manufacturing machinery are two of the
biggest industries. Much of the grain crop
feeds livestock destined to reach
dinner plates in the U.S. and around
the world. An increasing amount of
corn is used to make ethanol, which
is mixed with gasoline to fuel cars
and trucks. Des Moines,
the capital and largest
city, is a center of
insurance and publishing.

⇧ PIG BUSINESS.
Hogs outnumber
people five to one in
Iowa. The state raises
25 percent of the
nation's hogs, making
it the leading producer.

GREEN ENERGY

		*2007 production capacity in millions of gallons (liters)		
3,357 (12,709)*	1,745 (6,607)	1,172 (4,436)	1,102 (4,172)	985 (3,729)
Iowa	Nebraska	Illinois	Minnesota	South Dakota

Iowa is the leading producer of ethanol fuel,
a clean-burning, renewable, non-fossil fuel
energy source made mainly from corn.

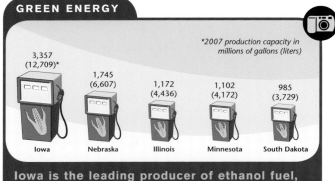

⇨ LEGACY OF THE
PAST. Young boys
dressed in colorful
outfits participate in
a traditional dance
ceremony, calling
to mind Iowa's rich
Native American heritage.

SOUTH DAKOTA

Hawkeye Point +
1,670 ft
509 m
Highest point
in Iowa

Sioux
Center

Sheldon

Orange
City

Le Mars

Cherokee

Big Sioux

Floyd

29

Sioux City

Missouri

Little Sioux

Onawa

DE SOTO N.W.R.

NEBRASKA

680

680

Council
Bluffs

80

Glenwood

Missouri

29

1   2

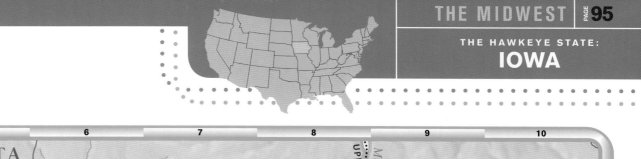

THE HAWKEYE STATE:
IOWA

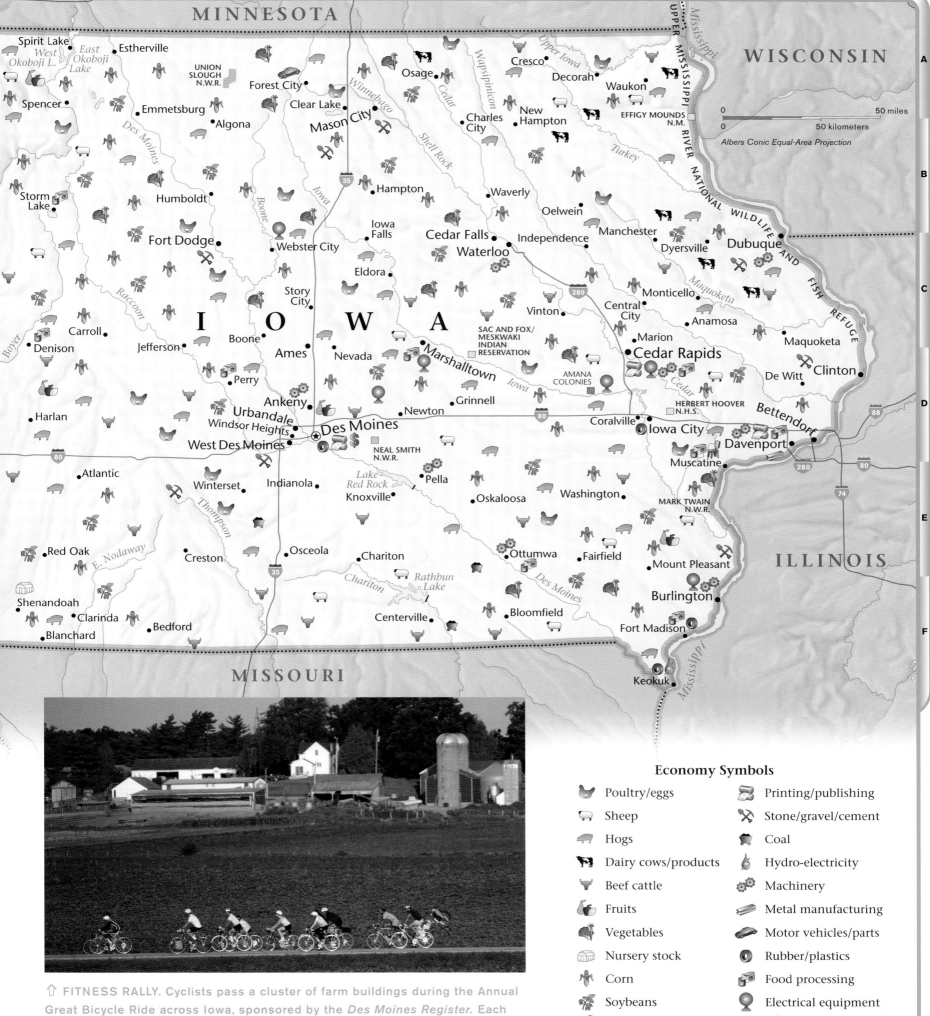

↑ FITNESS RALLY. Cyclists pass a cluster of farm buildings during the Annual Great Bicycle Ride across Iowa, sponsored by the *Des Moines Register*. Each year more than 10,000 riders participate in this event.

Economy Symbols

Poultry/eggs		Printing/publishing	
Sheep		Stone/gravel/cement	
Hogs		Coal	
Dairy cows/products		Hydro-electricity	
Beef cattle		Machinery	
Fruits		Metal manufacturing	
Vegetables		Motor vehicles/parts	
Nursery stock		Rubber/plastics	
Corn		Food processing	
Soybeans		Electrical equipment	
Furniture		Finance/insurance	

THE SUNFLOWER STATE:
KANSAS

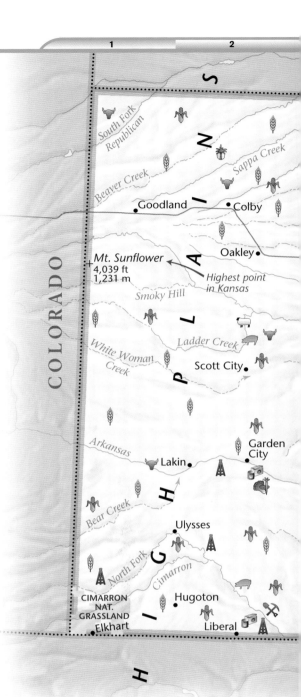

KANSAS

1   2

COLORADO

HIGH PLAINS

South Fork Republican

Beaver Creek

Sappa Creek

• Goodland   • Colby

Mt. Sunflower
4,039 ft
1,231 m   • Oakley   Highest point in Kansas

Smoky Hill

White Woman Creek

Ladder Creek

Scott City •

Arkansas   • Lakin   Garden City

Bear Creek

North Fork   • Ulysses   Cimarron

CIMARRON NAT. GRASSLAND
Elkhart   • Hugoton   • Liberal

THE BASICS

STATS

Area
82,277 sq mi (213,097 sq km)

Population
2,775,997

Capital
Topeka
Population 122,113

Largest city
Wichita
Population 357,698

Ethnic/racial groups
89.1% white; 6.0% African American; 2.2% Asian; 1.0% Native American. Hispanic (any race) 8.6%.

Industry
Aircraft manufacturing, transportation equipment, construction, food processing, printing and publishing, health care

Agriculture
Cattle, wheat, sorghum, soybeans, hogs, corn

Statehood
January 29, 1861; 34th state

GEO WHIZ

Plesiosaur skeletons and many other marine reptile fossils have been unearthed in Kansas. In 2007 National Geographic released the IMAX film *Sea Monsters*, which explores the kinds of animals that lived in the prehistoric sea that covered Kansas and much of North America 82 million years ago.

The Tallgrass Prairie National Preserve, the nation's last great expanse of tallgrass prairie, anchors a world renewed by fire. It is in the Flint Hills of Kansas.

Lindsborg is proud of its Swedish heritage and the fact that it is home to the Anatoly Karpov International School of Chess. The school is named for the Russian player who succeeded American Bobby Fischer as world champion in 1975.

WESTERN MEADOWLARK
SUNFLOWER

Considered by whites to be unsuitable for settlement, Kansas was made part of Indian Territory—a vast tract of land between Missouri and the Rockies—in the 1830s. By the 1850s whites were fighting Indians for more land and among themselves over the issue of slavery. In 1861 Kansas entered the Union as a free state. After the Civil War, cowboys drove Texas cattle to railheads in the Wild West towns of Abilene and Dodge City, where waiting trains hauled cattle to slaughterhouses in the East. Today, the state remains a major beef producer and the country's top wheat grower. Oil and natural gas wells dot the landscape, while factories in Wichita, the largest city, make aircraft equipment. A preserve in the Flint Hills boasts one of the few tallgrass prairies to escape farmers' plows. Heading west toward the Rockies, elevations climb slowly, and the climate gets drier. Threats of fierce thunderstorms accompanied by tornados have many Kansans keeping an eye on the sky.

⇧ OMINOUS SKY. Lightning splits the sky as black clouds of a thunderstorm roll across a field of wheat. Such storms bring heavy rain and often spawn dangerous tornados.

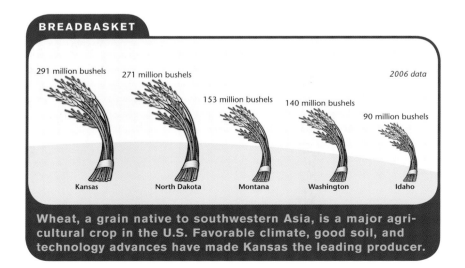

BREADBASKET

291 million bushels   271 million bushels   *2006 data*

153 million bushels   140 million bushels

90 million bushels

Kansas   North Dakota   Montana   Washington   Idaho

Wheat, a grain native to southwestern Asia, is a major agricultural crop in the U.S. Favorable climate, good soil, and technology advances have made Kansas the leading producer.

NEBRASKA

3   4   5   6   7   8   9   10

Oberlin   Norton   Phillipsburg   Lebanon

Geographic center of the 48 contiguous states

Washington   Belleville   Marysville   Seneca

SAC AND FOX I.R.   IOWA I.R.

Hiawatha

Prairie Dog Creek

North Fork Solomon

Kirwin Reservoir   KIRWIN N.W.R.

Waconda Lake   Concordia   Beloit

Clay Center

Little Blue   Big Blue

KICKAPOO INDIAN RESERVATION

Holton

Atchison

NICODEMUS N.H.S.   Plainville

South Fork Solomon

Smoky Hills

Solomon

Tuttle Creek Lake

POTAWATOMI INDIAN RESERVATION

Leavenworth   Lansing

Perry Lake

Kansas City

Minneapolis   Manhattan   Wamego

Bonne Springs

WaKeeney

Wilson Lake   Saline

Abilene   Junction City

Kansas

Topeka   Overland Park

Hays   Russell

Cedar Bluff Reservoir

Smoky Hill

Smoky Hill

Salina

BROWN V. BOARD OF EDUCATION N.H.S.

Lawrence   Olathe

K A N S A S

Ellsworth   Kanopolis Lake

Council Grove

Neosho

Ottawa   Hillsdale Lake   Paola

Hoisington   Lindsborg

Ness City   Walnut Creek

Cheyenne Bottoms

Marion Lake

TALLGRASS PRAIRIE NATIONAL PRESERVE

Osage City   Osawatomie

Emporia

Great Bend   McPherson   Hillsboro

Pawnee

Larned   Lyons

Arkansas

FLINT HILLS N.W.R.

John Redmond Reservoir

Burlington

Garnett

Marais des Cygnes

FORT LARNED N.H.S.

Buckner Creek

QUIVIRA N.W.R.

Hesston   Newton

FORT SCOTT N.H.S.

Kinsley   Hutchinson

El Dorado Lake

Iola   Fort Scott

Dodge City

Cheney Reservoir   Wichita

El Dorado

Verdigris

Chanute

Greensburg   Pratt   Kingman

Augusta

Fredonia

Neosho

Pittsburg

Derby   Mulvane

Fall

Elk City Lake

Parsons

Columbus

Red Hills

Medicine Lodge   Medicine Lodge

Wellington

Winfield

Flint Hills

Elk

Independence

Baxter Springs

Meade

Crooked Creek

Cimarron

Anthony

Arkansas City   Coffeyville

Caney

Arkansas

OKLAHOMA

0   50 miles
0   50 kilometers

Alber Conic Equal-Area Projection

MISSOURI

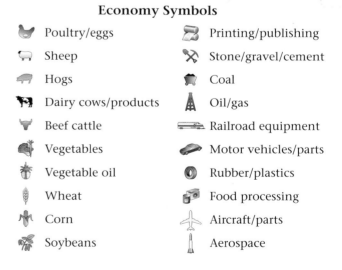

Economy Symbols

- Poultry/eggs
- Sheep
- Hogs
- Dairy cows/products
- Beef cattle
- Vegetables
- Vegetable oil
- Wheat
- Corn
- Soybeans
- Printing/publishing
- Stone/gravel/cement
- Coal
- Oil/gas
- Railroad equipment
- Motor vehicles/parts
- Rubber/plastics
- Food processing
- Aircraft/parts
- Aerospace

← MODERN-DAY COWBOYS. Dodge City traces its history to Fort Dodge, built on the Santa Fe Trail in 1865 to protect pioneer wagon trains and the mail service from Indian attacks. Frequented by cattle herders and buffalo hunters, the town was known for its lawlessness.

THE GREAT LAKE STATE:
MICHIGAN

MICHIGAN

THE BASICS

STATS

Area
96,716 sq mi (250,495 sq km)

Population
10,071,822

Capital
Lansing
Population 114,276

Largest city
Detroit
Population 871,121

Ethnic/racial groups
81.2% white; 14.3% African American; 2.4% Asian; .6% Native American. Hispanic (any race) 3.9%.

Industry
Motor vehicles and parts, machinery, metal products, office furniture, tourism, chemicals

Agriculture
Dairy products, cattle, vegetables, hogs, corn, nursery stock, soybeans, hay, fruit

Statehood
January 26, 1837; 26th state

GEO WHIZ

Researchers at the Seney National Wildlife Refuge near Seney, Michigan, have discovered that male loons change the sound of their call when they move to a new territory. The reason is still a mystery, but it does explain why people say that loons sound different on different lakes.

The Keweenaw Peninsula is an adventurer's paradise. There's a 100-mile (161-km) water trail for canoers, scores of wrecks for divers, 14 miles (23 km) of forested bike paths, and more than 150 miles (240 km) of hiking trails on nearby Isle Royale National Park.

Climate change is causing Lake Michigan and the other Great Lakes to shrink, a fact that is very costly to shipping. For every inch (2.5 cm) of draft that a ship loses, a freighter must lighten its cargo by as much as 270 tons to keep from running aground. The collective annual cost can be in the billions of dollars.

ROBIN

APPLE BLOSSOM

Indians had friendly relations with early French fur traders who came to what is now Michigan, but they waged battles with the British who later assumed control. Completion of New York's Erie Canal in 1825 made it easier for settlers to reach the area, and statehood came in 1837. Michigan consists of two large peninsulas that border four of the five Great Lakes— Erie, Huron, Michigan, and Superior.

⇧ ROLLING OFF THE ASSEMBLY LINE. Motor vehicle production is the largest manufacturing sector in the U.S., and Michigan is the center of the industry. At Chrysler's Sterling Heights assembly plant, more than 700 robots speed production by making it possible to build different car models on the same assembly line.

Most of the population is on the state's Lower Peninsula, while the Upper Peninsula, once a productive mining area, now is popular among vacationing nature lovers. The five-mile- (8-km-) long Mackinac Bridge has linked the peninsulas since 1957. In the 20th century Michigan became the center of the American auto industry, and the state's fortunes have risen and fallen with those of the Big Three car companies. Though it remains a big producer of cars and trucks, the state is working to diversify its economy. Michigan's farms grow crops ranging from grains to fruits and vegetables.

⇧ REFLECTION OF THE PAST. Victorian-style summer homes, built on Mackinac Island in the late 19th century by wealthy railroad families, now welcome vacationers to the island. To protect the environment, cars are not allowed.

WINTER SPORT

*Registered snowmobiles 2006–2007 data

302,000* — Michigan
277,290 — Minnesota
232,320 — Wisconsin
146,662 — New York
53,400 — Alaska

Snowmobiling has become a popular winter sport. Michigan and other states of the upper Midwest lead in number of registered snowmobiles.

1 2 3 4 5 6 7 8

ONTARIO

CANADA
U.S.

MINNESOTA

L A K E   S U P E R I O R

CANADA
U.S.

ISLE ROYALE
NATIONAL
PARK
Isle Royale

⇐ SOLEMN PREDA-
TOR. Wolves on Isle
Royale, in upper
Lake Superior,
live in packs that
hunt moose in
this isolated
national park.

KEWEENAW
N.H.P. Laurium
*Keweenaw
Peninsula*

Soo Canals: among the busiest ship
canals in the Western Hemisphere

ONTONAGON
INDIAN
RESERVATION
Houghton

HURON
N.W.R.

Sault Sainte Marie
SAULT SAINTE MARIE I.R.

PORCUPINE MTS.
S.P.
ONTONAGON
N.W.& S.R.
L'Anse
Mt. Arvon
1,979 ft
+603 m

STURGEON
N.W.&
S.R.
L'ANSE
I.R.

YELLOW DOG N.W.&S.R.

OTTAWA
N.F.

Marquette
GRAND ISLAND
N.R.A.

PICTURED
ROCKS
NATIONAL
LAKESHORE

TAHQUAMENON
FALLS S.P.
*Whitefish
Bay*

BAY
MILLS
I.R.

St. Mary's

BAY MILLS I.R.

ONTARIO

BLACK
N.W.&S.R.
OTTAWA

NAT.

FOREST

*Highest point
in Michigan*

Ishpeming

Munising

SENEY
N.W.R.

TAHQUAMENON
(EAST BRANCH)
N.W.&S.R.

St. Ignace

HARBOR ISLAND N.W.R.

Ironwood

PRESQUE
ISLE
N.W.&S.R.

PAINT
N.W.&S.R.

LAC VIEUX DESERT I.R.

U P P E R   P E N I N S U L A

Brule

Ford

WHITEFISH
N.W.&
S.R.

INDIAN
N.W.&
S.R.

HIAWATHA   NATIONAL   FOREST

Manistique

CARP N.W.&S.R.

FATHER MARQUETTE
NATIONAL MEMORIAL

Mackinac I.

Straits of Mackinac

Drummond
Island

Bois Blanc I.

HANNAHVILLE
I.R.

Gladstone

STURGEON N.W.&S.R.

Cheboygan

Economy Symbols

Iron
Mountain

Escanaba

*Garden
Peninsula*

*Beaver
I.*

Burt
Lake

Mullett
L.

L A K E   H U R O N

🐟 Fishing

🐔 Poultry/eggs

🐖 Hogs

Menominee

Menominee

*Site of at least
50 shipwrecks*

*Manitou
Islands*

Grand Traverse Bay

GRAND
TRAVERSE
I.R.

Petoskey

Boyne
City

Rogers City

Pigeon

Alpena

Thunder Bay

🐄 Dairy cows/products

🐂 Beef cattle

WISCONSIN

Green Bay

Cedar

SLEEPING
BEAR DUNES
NAT. LAKESHORE

Gaylord

Hubbard L.

Thunder Bay

🍎 Fruits

M I C H I G A N

Manitou Passage

Kalkaska

Au Sable

HURON

Mio

AU SABLE
N.W.&S.R.

🥬 Vegetables

Traverse City

Manistee

*Houghton
Lake*

NAT.

🌱 Nursery stock

BEAR CREEK
N.W.&
S.R.

Cadillac

Houghton
Lake

FOREST

Rifle

Tawas
City

🌾 Wheat

LITTLE RIVER I.R.

PINE
N.W.&S.R.

🌽 Corn

Manistee

MANISTEE N.W.&S.R.

ISABELLA I.R.

🌿 Soybeans

MANISTEE

L O W E R

*Saginaw
Bay*

Bad Axe

Harbor
Beach

🌲 Timber/forest products

Ludington

PERE
MARQUETTE
N.W.&S.R.

NATIONAL

Muskegon

Big Rapids

ISABELLA
I.R.

Midland

Bay City

Caro

Cass

Black

🪑 Furniture

🔨 Stone/gravel/cement

FOREST

Fremont

Mt. Pleasant

Alma

SHIAWASSEE
N.W.R.

Saginaw

Sandusky

⛏ Mining

FLAT
N.W.&
S.R.

🛢 Oil/gas

Greenville

P E N I N S U L A

💧 Hydro-electricity

Muskegon

Belding

Ionia

St. Johns Owosso

Flint

Port
Huron

⚙ Machinery

Grand Haven

Grand

Looking Glass

Burton

St. Clair

🍳 Metal products

Grand Rapids

Kentwood

East Lansing

Flint

🚗 Motor vehicles/parts

Holland Zeeland

Lansing

Pontiac

Warren

St. Clair
Shores

🧪 Chemistry

Hastings

Charlotte

Mason

Troy

Livonia

*Lake
St. Clair*

🥘 Food processing

South Haven

Kalamazoo

Battle
Creek

Jackson

Ann Arbor

Detroit

ONTARIO

📷 Tourism

Kalamazoo

Marshall

Albion

Raisin

Ypsilanti

Dearborn

Benton Harbor

Portage

St. Joseph

Tecumseh

Monroe

CANADA
U.S.

St. Joseph

Dowagiac

Coldwater

Adrian

L A K E

Niles

Three Rivers

Sturgis

Hillsdale

Lambertville

Temperance

E R I E

Kalamazoo

ILLINOIS

INDIANA

OHIO

THE GOPHER STATE:
MINNESOTA

MINNESOTA

French fur traders began arriving in present-day Minnesota in the mid-17th century. Statehood was established in 1858, and most remaining Indians were forced from the state after a decisive battle in 1862. During the late 1800s large numbers of Germans, Scandinavians, and other immigrants settled a land rich in wildlife, timber, minerals, and fertile soils. Today, farming is concentrated in the south and west. In the northeast, the Mesabi Range's open-pit mines make the state the country's source of iron ore. Most of the ore is shipped from Duluth. It, along with Superior, in nearby Wisconsin (see p. 113), is the leading Great Lakes port. Ships from the port reach the Atlantic Ocean via the St. Lawrence Seaway. Scattered across the state's landscape are thousands of lakes—ancient footprints of retreating glaciers—that draw anglers and canoeists. One of those lakes, Lake Itasca, is the source of the mighty Mississippi River, which flows through the Twin Cities of Minneapolis and St. Paul.

THE BASICS

STATS

Area
86,939 sq mi (225,172 sq km)

Population
5,197,621

Capital
St. Paul
Population 273,535

Largest city
Minneapolis
Population 372,833

Ethnic/racial groups
89.3% white; 4.5% African American; 3.5% Asian; 1.2% Native American. Hispanic (any race) 3.8%.

Industry
Health services, tourism, real estate, banking and insurance, industrial machinery, printing and publishing, food processing, scientific equipment

Agriculture
Corn, soybeans, dairy products, hogs, cattle, turkeys, wheat

Statehood
May 11, 1858; 32nd state

GEO WHIZ

Nett Lake on the Bois Forte Chippewa reservation, in northern Minnesota, is the largest contiguous wild rice lake in the world. Native people have been gathering what the Indians call *manoomin* for thousands of years.

The Mayo Clinic, a world-famous medical research center founded in 1889 by Dr. William W. Mayo, is in Rochester.

The Boundary Waters Canoe Area Wilderness, along the Minnesota-Ontario border, was the first wilderness area in the U.S. to be set aside for canoeing.

COMMON LOON

SHOWY LADY'S SLIPPER

⇧ SUMMER FUN. Young girls play on a rope swing near Leech Lake in northern Minnesota. The state's many lakes are remnants of the last ice age, when glaciers gouged depressions that filled with water as the ice sheets retreated.

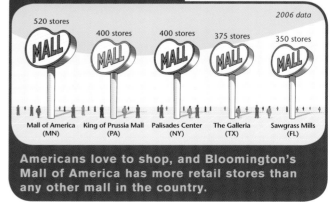

SHOPPER'S PARADISE

2006 data

520 stores — MALL — Mall of America (MN)
400 stores — MALL — King of Prussia Mall (PA)
400 stores — MALL — Palisades Center (NY)
375 stores — MALL — The Galleria (TX)
350 stores — MALL — Sawgrass Mills (FL)

Americans love to shop, and Bloomington's Mall of America has more retail stores than any other mall in the country.

⇦ INLAND PORT. Duluth, on the northern shore of Lake Superior, is the westernmost deep-water port on the St. Lawrence Seaway. Barges and container ships move products such as iron ore and grain along the Great Lakes to the Atlantic Ocean and to markets around the world.

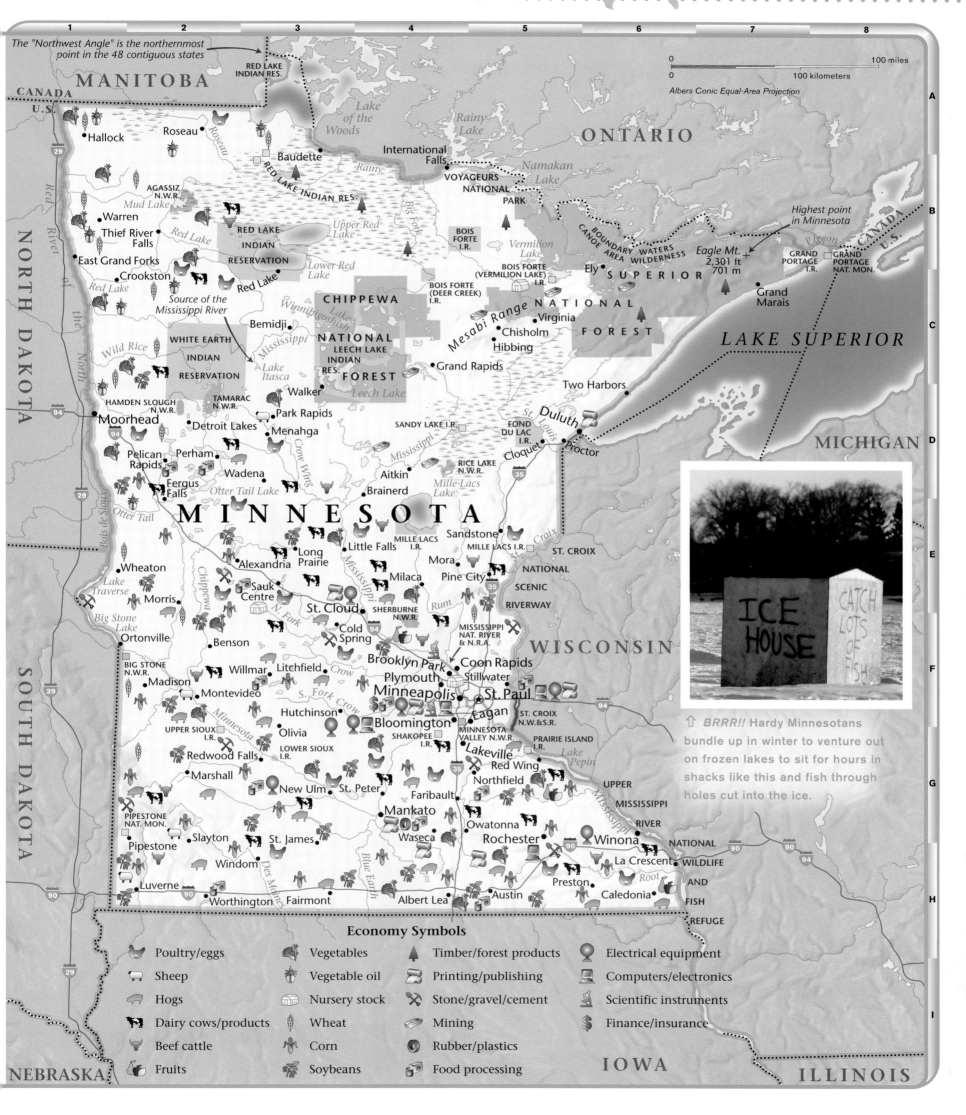

The "Northwest Angle" is the northernmost point in the 48 contiguous states

MANITOBA

CANADA
U.S.

Hallock
Roseau
Baudette
RED LAKE INDIAN RES.

Lake of the Woods

Rainy Lake

International Falls

ONTARIO

VOYAGEURS NATIONAL PARK

Namakan Lake

RED LAKE INDIAN RES.

Roseau

Rainy

Warren
AGASSIZ N.W.R.
Mud Lake

Upper Red Lake

Big Fork

BOIS FORTE I.R.

Vermilion Lake

BOUNDARY WATERS
CANOE AREA WILDERNESS

Highest point in Minnesota

CANADA
U.S.

Thief River Falls
Red Lake
RED LAKE INDIAN RESERVATION
Lower Red Lake

BOIS FORTE (VERMILION LAKE) I.R.

Ely
SUPERIOR

Eagle Mt. +
2,301 ft
701 m

GRAND PORTAGE I.R.
GRAND PORTAGE NAT. MON.

East Grand Forks
Crookston

Red Lake

Source of the Mississippi River

BOIS FORTE (DEER CREEK) I.R.

NATIONAL

Grand Marais

Virginia

Red Lake

CHIPPEWA
NATIONAL

Mesabi Range

Chisholm
Hibbing

FOREST

LAKE SUPERIOR

Bemidji
Winnibigoshish

WHITE EARTH INDIAN RESERVATION

Wild Rice

LEECH LAKE INDIAN RES.

Grand Rapids

Two Harbors

Lake Itasca
Walker

Leech Lake

FOREST

Mississippi

HAMDEN SLOUGH N.W.R.

TAMARAC N.W.R.

Park Rapids

SANDY LAKE I.R.

St. Louis

Duluth

MICHIGAN

Moorhead
Detroit Lakes
Menahga

FOND DU LAC I.R.

Cloquet
Proctor

Pelican Rapids
Perham
Wadena

Mississippi

Mille Lacs Lake

RICE LAKE N.W.R.

Fergus Falls

Aitkin

Brainerd

Otter Tail Lake

Crow Wing

MINNESOTA

St. Croix

Wheaton

Long Prairie
Little Falls

MILLE LACS I.R.

Sandstone

Alexandria

MILLE LACS I.R.

ST. CROIX

Lake Traverse

Sauk Centre

Mississippi

Milaca
Mora

Pine City

NATIONAL

Morris

Chippewa

N. Fork

Rum

SCENIC

Big Stone Lake

St. Cloud

SHERBURNE N.W.R.

RIVERWAY

Ortonville

Cold Spring

Benson

MISSISSIPPI NAT. RIVER & N.R.A.

WISCONSIN

BIG STONE N.W.R.

Willmar
Litchfield

Crow

Brooklyn Park
Plymouth

Coon Rapids
Stillwater

Madison
Montevideo

S. Fork Crow

Minneapolis
St. Paul

ICE HOUSE

CATCH LOTS OF FISH

Hutchinson

UPPER SIOUX I.R.

Olivia

Minnesota

Bloomington

Eagan

ST. CROIX N.W.&S.R.

⇧ BRRR!! Hardy Minnesotans bundle up in winter to venture out on frozen lakes to sit for hours in shacks like this and fish through holes cut into the ice.

Redwood Falls

LOWER SIOUX I.R.

SHAKOPEE I.R.

MINNESOTA VALLEY N.W.R.

PRAIRIE ISLAND I.R.

Marshall

New Ulm
St. Peter

Lakeville

Red Wing

Lake Pepin

Faribault

Northfield

UPPER MISSISSIPPI

PIPESTONE NAT. MON.

Mankato

Owatonna

Mississippi

RIVER

Slayton
St. James

Waseca

Rochester

Winona

NATIONAL

Pipestone

Windom

Blue Earth

Des Moines

La Crescent

WILDLIFE

SOUTH DAKOTA

Luverne

Worthington
Fairmont

Albert Lea

Austin

Preston

Caledonia

Root

AND

FISH

REFUGE

NEBRASKA

IOWA

ILLINOIS

Economy Symbols

- Poultry/eggs
- Sheep
- Hogs
- Dairy cows/products
- Beef cattle
- Fruits
- Vegetables
- Vegetable oil
- Nursery stock
- Wheat
- Corn
- Soybeans
- Timber/forest products
- Printing/publishing
- Stone/gravel/cement
- Mining
- Rubber/plastics
- Food processing
- Electrical equipment
- Computers/electronics
- Scientific instruments
- Finance/insurance

0   100 miles
0   100 kilometers
Albers Conic Equal-Area Projection

MISSOURI

The Osage people were among the largest tribes in present-day Missouri when the French began establishing permanent settlements in the 1700s. The U.S. obtained the territory in the 1803 Louisiana Purchase, and Lewis and Clark began exploring the vast wilderness by paddling up the Missouri River from the St. Louis area. Missouri entered the Union as a slave state in 1821. Though it remained in the Union during the Civil War, sympathies were split between the North and South. For much of the 1800s the state was the staging ground for pioneers traveling to western frontiers on the Santa Fe and Oregon Trails. Today, Missouri leads the country in lead mining. Farmers raise cattle, hogs, poultry, corn, and soybeans. Cotton and rice are grown in the southeastern Bootheel region. Cross-state river-port rivals St. Louis and Kansas City are centers of transportation, manufacturing, and finance. Lakes, caves, scenic views, and Branson's country music shows bring many tourists to the Ozarks.

⇧ TALL HATS. Since its founding in 1865 in St. Joseph, the Stetson Company has been associated with western hats worn by men and women around the world.

THE BASICS

STATS

Area
69,704 sq mi (180,534 sq mi)

Population
5,878,415

Capital
Jefferson City
Population 37,550

Largest city
Kansas City
Population 447,306

Ethnic/racial groups
85.1% white; 11.5% African American; 1.4% Asian; .5% Native American. Hispanic (any race) 2.8%.

Industry
Transportation equipment, food processing, chemicals, electrical equipment, metal products

Agriculture
Cattle, soybeans, hogs, corn, poultry and eggs, dairy products

Statehood
August 10, 1821; 24th state

GEO WHIZ

Camp Wood, near St. Louis, was the starting point for Lewis and Clark's Corps of Discovery, commissioned by President Thomas Jefferson to seek a water route to the Pacific. Along the way their encounters included hundreds of new species of plants and animals, nearly 50 Indian tribes, and the Rocky Mountains.

In Ash Grove, near Springfield, Father Moses Berry has turned his family history into a museum for slavery education. His family was one of the few who didn't flee the area after three falsely accused black men were lynched in 1906. The museum is the only one of its kind in the Ozark region.

EASTERN BLUEBIRD
HAWTHORN

HISTORICAL MARKERS

630 feet (192 m) — Gateway Arch (MO)
570 feet (174 m) — San Jacinto Monument (TX)
555 feet (169 m) — Washington Monument (DC)
352 feet (107 m) — Perry's Victory and International Peace Memorial (OH)
351 feet (107 m) — Jefferson Davis Monument (KY)

The tallest of all monuments in the U.S. is Gateway Arch in St. Louis, which marks the departure point for westward-bound pioneers during the 19th century.

⇨ HEADING WEST. The 630-foot (192-m) Gateway Arch honors the role St. Louis played in U.S. westward expansion. Trams carry one million tourists to the top of the arch each year.

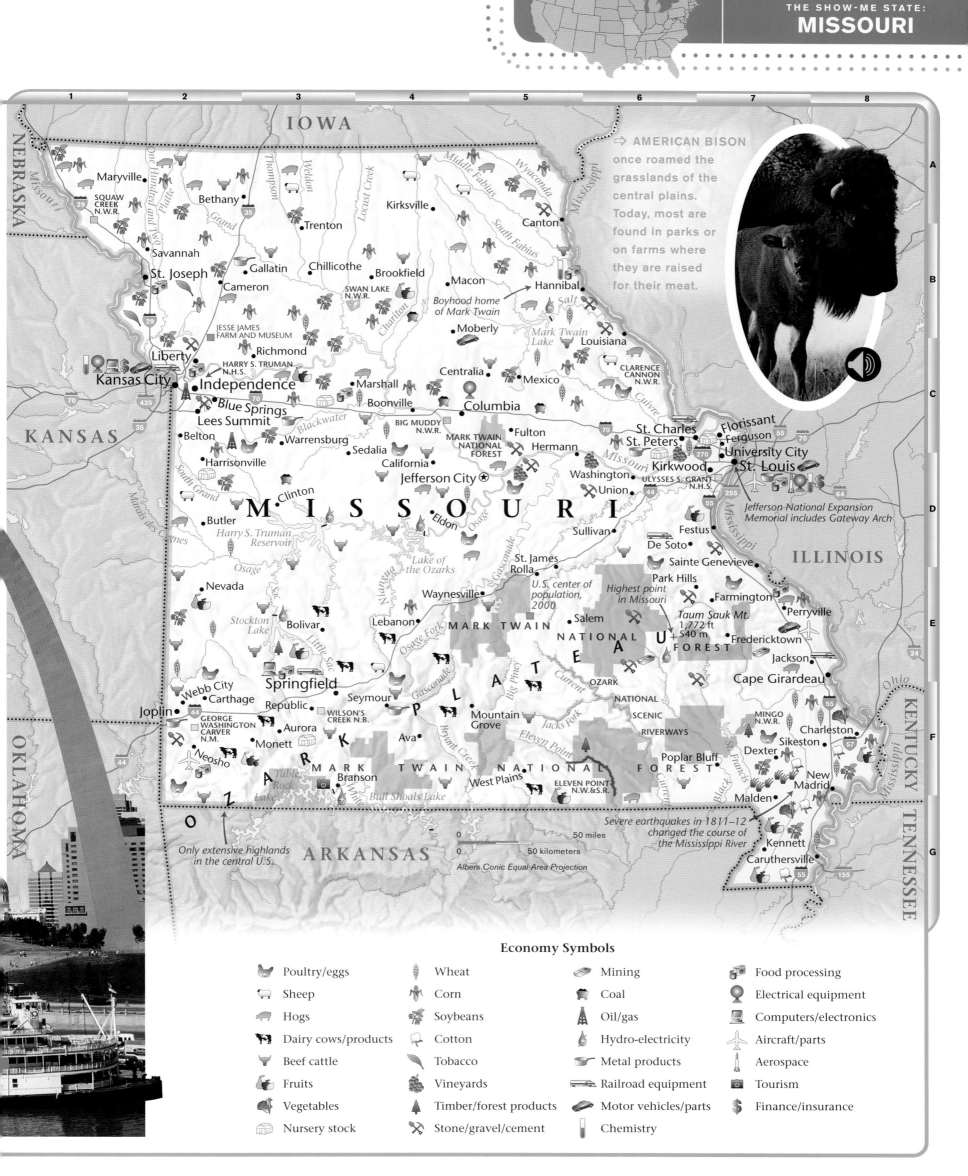

⇨ **AMERICAN BISON** once roamed the grasslands of the central plains. Today, most are found in parks or on farms where they are raised for their meat.

IOWA

NEBRASKA

Maryville
SQUAW CREEK N.W.R.
Bethany
Trenton
Kirksville
Canton
Savannah
Gallatin
Chillicothe
Brookfield
Macon
St. Joseph
Cameron
SWAN LAKE N.W.R.
Hannibal
Boyhood home of Mark Twain
Moberly
Louisiana
JESSE JAMES FARM AND MUSEUM
Liberty
Richmond
Centralia
Mexico
CLARENCE CANNON N.W.R.
Mark Twain Lake
Salt
HARRY S. TRUMAN N.H.S.
Kansas City
Independence
Marshall
Boonville
Columbia
St. Charles
Florissant
Ferguson
Blue Springs
Lees Summit
Blackwater
BIG MUDDY N.W.R.
Fulton
Hermann
St. Peters
Kirkwood
University City
St. Louis
Belton
Warrensburg
Sedalia
MARK TWAIN NATIONAL FOREST
Washington
Union
ULYSSES S. GRANT N.H.S.
Harrisonville
California
Jefferson City ★
Jefferson National Expansion Memorial includes Gateway Arch

KANSAS

MISSOURI

Clinton
Eldon
Osage
Sullivan
Festus
De Soto
Butler
Harry S. Truman Reservoir
Lake of the Ozarks
Gasconade
St. James
Rolla
Sainte Genevieve
ILLINOIS
Nevada
Waynesville
U.S. center of population, 2000
Park Hills
Highest point in Missouri
Farmington
Perryville
Stockton Lake
Bolivar
Lebanon
Salem
Taum Sauk Mt. 1,772 ft 540 m
Fredericktown
Jackson
MARK TWAIN
NATIONAL FOREST
Cape Girardeau
Springfield
Seymour
Gasconade
Big Piney
OZARK
NATIONAL
SCENIC
MINGO N.W.R.
Webb City
Carthage
Republic
WILSON'S CREEK N.B.
Mountain Grove
Jacks Fork
RIVERWAYS
Charleston
Joplin
GEORGE WASHINGTON CARVER N.M.
Aurora
Ava
Current
Sikeston
Dexter
Monett
Eleven Point
Poplar Bluff
Neosho
Table Rock Lake
Branson
West Plains
ELEVEN POINT N.W.&S.R.
New Madrid
Malden
OZARK
MARK TWAIN NATIONAL FOREST
Bull Shoals Lake
Severe earthquakes in 1811–12 changed the course of the Mississippi River
Kennett

OKLAHOMA

Only extensive highlands in the central U.S.

ARKANSAS

Caruthersville

KENTUCKY

TENNESSEE

0 50 miles
0 50 kilometers
Albers Conic Equal-Area Projection

Economy Symbols

Poultry/eggs	Wheat	Mining	Food processing
Sheep	Corn	Coal	Electrical equipment
Hogs	Soybeans	Oil/gas	Computers/electronics
Dairy cows/products	Cotton	Hydro-electricity	Aircraft/parts
Beef cattle	Tobacco	Metal products	Aerospace
Fruits	Vineyards	Railroad equipment	Tourism
Vegetables	Timber/forest products	Motor vehicles/parts	Finance/insurance
Nursery stock	Stone/gravel/cement	Chemistry	

THE CORNHUSKER STATE:
NEBRASKA

THE BASICS

STATS

Area
77,354 sq mi (200,346 sq km)

Population
1,774,571

Capital
Lincoln
Population 241,167

Largest city
Omaha
Population 419,545

Ethnic/racial groups
91.8% white; 4.4% African American; 1.7% Asian; 1.0% Native American. Hispanic (any race) 7.4%.

Industry
Food processing, machinery, electrical equipment, printing and publishing

Agriculture
Cattle, corn, hogs, soybeans, wheat, sorghum

Statehood
March 1, 1867; 37th state

GEO WHIZ

Many of Nebraska's early settlers were called sodbusters because they cut chunks of the grassy prairie (sod) to build their houses. These building blocks became known as "Nebraska marble."

Nebraska's state fossil is the mammoth. Fossils of these prehistoric elephants have been found in all 93 counties. The state estimates that as many as 10 mammoths are buried beneath an average square mile of territory.

Boys Town, founded in 1917 as a home for troubled boys, has provided a haven for girls since 1979. They now make up about half the population of 500 kids in this village-style community near Omaha.

WESTERN MEADOWLARK
GOLDENROD

NEBRASKA

For thousands of westbound pioneers on the Oregon and California Trails, Scotts Bluff and Chimney Rock were unforgettable landmarks, towering above the North Platte River. Once reserved for Indians by the government, Nebraska was opened for white settlement in 1854. Following statehood in 1867, ranchers clashed with farmers in an unsuccessful bid to preserve open rangelands. Before white settlers arrived, Indians hunted bison and grew corn, pumpkins, beans, and squash. Today, farms and ranches cover nearly all of the state. Ranchers graze beef cattle on the grass-covered Sand Hills, while farmers grow corn, soybeans, and wheat elsewhere. The vast underground Ogallala Aquifer feeds center-pivot irrigation systems needed to water crops in areas that do not receive enough rain. Processing the state's farm products, especially meatpacking, is a big part of the economy. Omaha, which sits along the Missouri River, is a center of finance, insurance, and agribusiness. Lincoln, the state capital, has the only unicameral, or one-house, legislature in the United States.

⬆ TAKING FLIGHT. Migratory Sandhill cranes pass through Nebraska in late winter, stopping in the Platte River Valley to feed and rest.

OGLALA NATIONAL GRASSLAND
White
Chadron
Crawford
Rushville
Pine Ridge
NEBRASKA NATIONAL FOREST
AGATE FOSSIL BEDS NAT. MON.
Fossils of extinct mammals that lived here about 20 million years ago
NORTH PLATTE N.W.R.
Alliance
Scottsbluff
Gering
SCOTTS BLUFF N.M.
CHIMNEY ROCK N.H.S.
Bridgeport
Pumpkin Creek
North Platte
Highest point in Nebraska
Kimball
Lodgepole Cr.
Sidney
Panorama Point +5,423 ft, 1,653 m

WYOMING

COLORADO

⬇ RIDER DOWN. The Big Rodeo is an annual event in tiny Burwell (population 1,130) in Nebraska's Sand Hills. The town, sometimes called "the place where the Wild West meets the 21st century," has hosted the rodeo for more than 80 years.

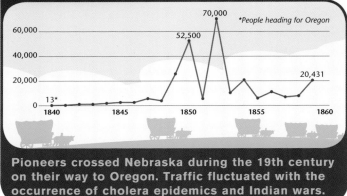

WESTWARD BOUND

People heading for Oregon

70,000
60,000
52,500
40,000
20,000
20,431
13*
1840   1845   1850   1855   1860

Pioneers crossed Nebraska during the 19th century on their way to Oregon. Traffic fluctuated with the occurrence of cholera epidemics and Indian wars.

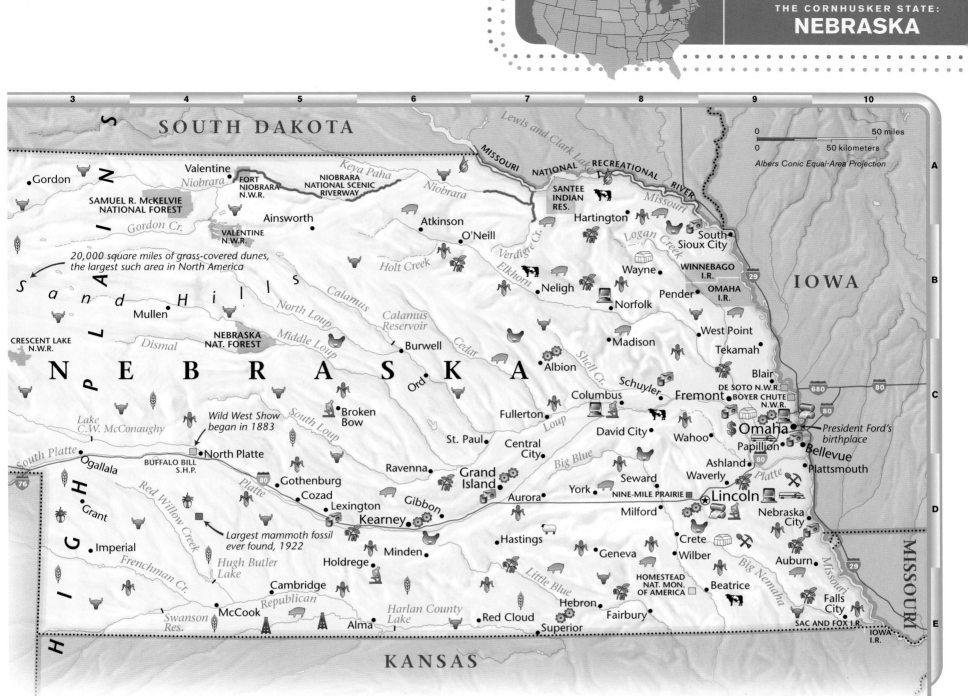

SOUTH DAKOTA

3   4   5   6   7   8   9   10

0 ___ 50 miles
0 ___ 50 kilometers
Albers Conic Equal-Area Projection

Gordon

Valentine
Niobrara
FORT
NIOBRARA
N.W.R.

SAMUEL R. McKELVIE
NATIONAL FOREST

Gordon Cr.

VALENTINE
N.W.R.

NIOBRARA
NATIONAL SCENIC
RIVERWAY

Keva Paha

Niobrara

Lewis and Clark Lake

MISSOURI NATIONAL RECREATIONAL RIVER

SANTEE
INDIAN
RES.

Hartington

South
Sioux City

IOWA

Ainsworth

Atkinson

O'Neill

Holt Creek

Verdigre Cr.

Neligh

Wayne

Pender

WINNEBAGO
I.R.

OMAHA
I.R.

29

*20,000 square miles of grass-covered dunes,
the largest such area in North America*

Elkhorn

Norfolk

West Point

Logan Creek

Calamus

Madison

Tekamah

S a n d   H i l l s

Mullen

North Loup

*Calamus
Reservoir*

NEBRASKA
NAT. FOREST

Middle Loup

Burwell

Dismal

Cedar

Albion

Schuyler

Blair

DE SOTO N.W.R.

P L A I N S

CRESCENT LAKE
N.W.R.

N   E   B   R   A   S   K   A

Ord

Shell Cr.

Columbus

Fremont

BOYER CHUTE
N.W.R.

680

80

*Lake
C.W. McConaughy*

*Wild West Show
began in 1883*

Broken
Bow

Fullerton

Loup

David City

Wahoo

Omaha

President Ford's
birthplace

80

St. Paul

Central
City

Papillion

Bellevue

South Loup

South Platte

Ogallala

76

BUFFALO BILL
S.H.P.

North Platte

80

Gothenburg

Cozad

Lexington

Ravenna

Gibbon

Grand
Island

Aurora

York

Big Blue

NINE-MILE PRAIRIE

Seward

Ashland

Waverly

Platte

Lincoln

Plattsmouth

H   I   G   H

Grant

Red Willow Creek

*Largest mammoth fossil
ever found, 1922*

Kearney

Minden

Hastings

Milford

Crete

Nebraska
City

Imperial

Frenchman Cr.

*Hugh Butler
Lake*

Holdrege

Geneva

Wilber

Auburn

Big Nemaha

Cambridge

Republican

*Harlan County
Lake*

Little Blue

HOMESTEAD
NAT. MON.
OF AMERICA

Beatrice

*Swanson
Res.*

McCook

Alma

Red Cloud

Superior

Hebron

Fairbury

Falls
City

SAC AND FOX I.R.

IOWA
I.R.

MISSOURI

KANSAS

⟸ THE WAY WEST. Longhorn cattle and a bison
stand knee-deep in grass below Chimney Rock,
which rises more than 300 feet (91 m) above western
Nebraska's rolling landscape. An important landmark
on the Oregon Trail for 19th-century westbound
pioneers and now a national historic site, the
formation is being worn away by forces of erosion.

Economy Symbols

🐔 Poultry/eggs

🐑 Sheep

🐖 Hogs

🐄 Dairy cows/products

🐂 Beef cattle

Vegetables

Vegetable oil

Nursery stock

🌾 Wheat

🌽 Corn

Soybeans

Printing/publishing

Stone/gravel/cement

Oil/gas

Hydro-electricity

⚙ Machinery

Railroad equipment

Food processing

💻 Computers/electronics

Scientific instruments

$ Finance/insurance

THE BASICS

STATS

Area
70,700 sq mi (183,113 sq km)

Population
639,715

Capital
Bismarck
Population 56,344

Largest city
Fargo
Population 91,484

Ethnic/racial groups
91.9% white; 5.4% Native
American; .8% African American;
.7% Asian. Hispanic (any race) 1.7%.

Industry
Services, government, finance,
construction, transportation, oil and gas

Agriculture
Wheat, cattle, sunflowers, barley,
soybeans

Statehood
November 2, 1889; 39th state

GEO WHIZ

Teenage Indian guide Sakakawea (also
known as Sacagawea) joined the
Lewis and Clark expedition in the
spring of 1805 after the explorers
spent the winter in the Mandan-
Hidatsa villages near present-day
Washburn. Today, the state's largest
reservoir is named in her honor.

Devils Lake has earned the title Perch
Capital of the World for the large
number of walleye—a kind of perch—
that anglers catch there.

North Dakota's landscape boasts some
of the world's largest outdoor animal
sculptures, including Salem Sue, the
world's largest Holstein cow; a 60-ton
buffalo; a 40-by-60-foot (12-by-18-m)
grasshopper; a giant snowmobiling
turtle; and Wally the Giant Walleye.

WESTERN
MEADOWLARK

WILD PRAIRIE ROSE

NORTH DAKOTA

During the winter of 1804–05, Lewis and Clark camped at a Mandan village where they met Sacagawea, the Shoshone woman who helped guide them through the Rockies and onto the Pacific Ocean. White settlement of the vast grassy plains coincided with the growth of railroads, and statehood was gained in 1889. The geographic center of North America is southwest of Rugby. The state's interior location helps give it a huge annual temperature range. A record low temperature of -60°F (-51°C) and record high of 121°F (49°C) were recorded in 1936. Fargo, located on the northward flowing Red River of the North, is the state's largest city. Garrison Dam, on the Missouri River, generates electricity and provides water for irrigation. The state leads the country in the production of flax-seed, canola, sunflowers, and barley, but it is wheat, cattle, and soybeans that provide the greatest income. Oil and lignite coal are impor-tant in the western part of the state.

↑ VIGILANT LOOKOUT.
A black-tailed prairie
dog watches for signs
of danger. This member
of the squirrel family
lives in burrows in the
Great Plains.

OIL FROM SEEDS

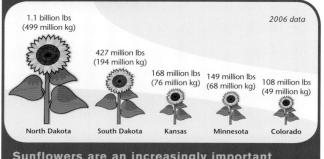

2006 data

1.1 billion lbs
(499 million kg)

427 million lbs
(194 million kg)

168 million lbs
(76 million kg)

149 million lbs
(68 million kg)

108 million lbs
(49 million kg)

North Dakota | South Dakota | Kansas | Minnesota | Colorado

**Sunflowers are an increasingly important
source of seeds and edible oil obtained by
crushing the seeds of the flower.**

⇨ RUNNING FREE. A wild horse runs through a landscape
dramatically eroded by the Little Missouri River in Theodore
Roosevelt National Park in North Dakota's Badlands region.

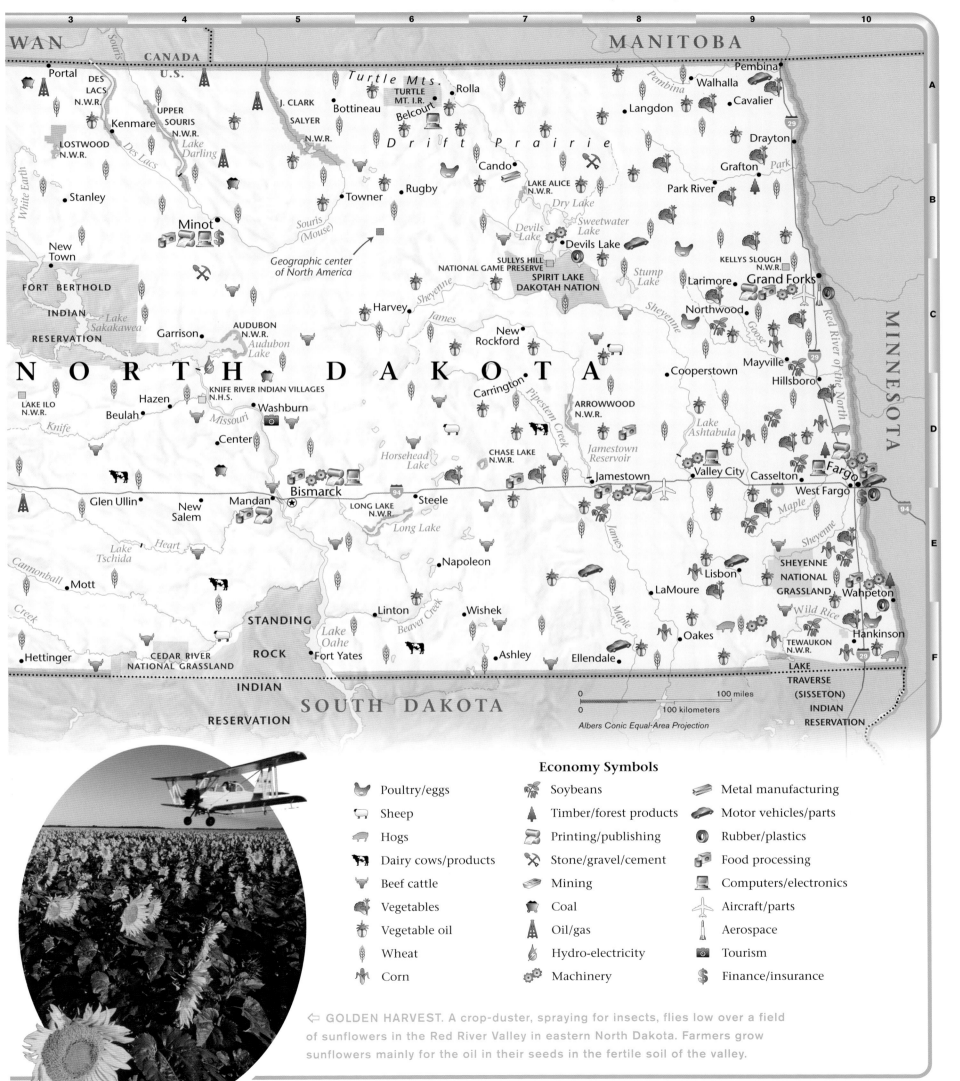

MANITOBA

CANADA
U.S.

WAN

Portal
DES
LACS
N.W.R.
J. CLARK
SALYER
N.W.R.
UPPER
SOURIS
N.W.R.
Kenmare
LOSTWOOD
N.W.R.
Lake
Darling
Des Lacs
Stanley
White Earth
Minot
New
Town
FORT BERTHOLD
INDIAN
RESERVATION
Lake
Sakakawea
Garrison
AUDUBON
N.W.R.
Audubon
Lake
LAKE ILO
N.W.R.
Hazen
Beulah
KNIFE RIVER INDIAN VILLAGES
N.H.S.
Knife
Washburn
Center
Glen Ullin
New
Salem
Mandan
Bismarck
Lake
Tschida
Heart
Cannonball
Mott
Hettinger
Creek
CEDAR RIVER
NATIONAL GRASSLAND

Turtle Mts.
TURTLE
MT. I.R.
Belcourt
Rolla
Bottineau
Drift Prairie
Souris (Mouse)
Towner
Rugby
Geographic center
of North America
Sheyenne
Harvey
James
NORTH DAKOTA
Horsehead
Lake
Missouri
New
Rockford
Carrington
CHASE LAKE
N.W.R.
Pipestem Creek
94
Steele
LONG LAKE
N.W.R.
Long Lake
Napoleon
Linton
Wishek
Beaver Creek
Lake
Oahe
Fort Yates
Ashley
STANDING
ROCK
INDIAN
RESERVATION

Langdon
Cando
LAKE ALICE
N.W.R.
Dry Lake
Devils
Lake
Devils Lake
SULLYS HILL
NATIONAL GAME PRESERVE
SPIRIT LAKE
DAKOTAH NATION
Sweetwater
Lake
Stump
Lake
Park River
Larimore
Northwood
Cooperstown
ARROWWOOD
N.W.R.
Jamestown
Reservoir
Jamestown
Valley City
Casselton
Lake
Ashtabula
Lisbon
LaMoure
Oakes
Ellendale
Maple
James

Pembina
Walhalla
Cavalier
Drayton
Grafton
Park
29
KELLYS SLOUGH
N.W.R.
Grand Forks
Mayville
Hillsboro
Red River of the North
Goose
Sheyenne
West Fargo
Fargo
94
Maple
Sheyenne
SHEYENNE
NATIONAL
GRASSLAND
Wild Rice
Wahpeton
TEWAUKON
N.W.R.
Hankinson
29
LAKE
TRAVERSE
(SISSETON)
INDIAN
RESERVATION
MINNESOTA

Pembina

SOUTH DAKOTA

0   100 miles
0   100 kilometers
Albers Conic Equal-Area Projection

Economy Symbols

Poultry/eggs	Soybeans	Metal manufacturing
Sheep	Timber/forest products	Motor vehicles/parts
Hogs	Printing/publishing	Rubber/plastics
Dairy cows/products	Stone/gravel/cement	Food processing
Beef cattle	Mining	Computers/electronics
Vegetables	Coal	Aircraft/parts
Vegetable oil	Oil/gas	Aerospace
Wheat	Hydro-electricity	Tourism
Corn	Machinery	Finance/insurance

← GOLDEN HARVEST. A crop-duster, spraying for insects, flies low over a field
of sunflowers in the Red River Valley in eastern North Dakota. Farmers grow
sunflowers mainly for the oil in their seeds in the fertile soil of the valley.

THE BUCKEYE STATE:
OHIO

THE BASICS

STATS

Area
44,825 sq mi (116,097 sq km)

Population
11,466,917

Capital
Columbus
Population 733,203

Largest city
Columbus
Population 733,203

Ethnic/racial groups
84.9% white; 12.0% African American;
1.5% Asian; .2% Native American.
Hispanic (any race) 2.3%.

Industry
Transportation equipment, metal
products, machinery, food processing,
electrical equipment

Agriculture
Soybeans, dairy products, corn, hogs,
cattle, poultry and eggs

Statehood
March 1, 1803; 17th state

GEO WHIZ

Cedar Point Amusement Park,
in Sandusky, is known as the
Rollercoaster Capital of the World.
Top Thrill Dragster, claimed to be
the tallest and fastest rollercoaster on
Earth, is 420 feet (128 m) high with a top
speed of 120 miles per hour (193 kmph)!

Ohio's state tree is the buckeye,
so-called because the nut it produces
resembles the eye of a buck. A buck
is a male deer.

Ohio's state insect is the ladybird
beetle, more commonly known
as the ladybug. Use of these
beetles to control
plant-eating pests
greatly reduces the
need for chemical
pesticides.

CARDINAL

SCARLET CARNATION

OHIO

Ohio and the rest of the Northwest Territory became part of the United States after the Revolutionary War. The movement of white settlers into the region led to conflicts with the native inhabitants until 1794 when Indian resistance was defeated at Fallen Timbers. Ohio entered the Union nine years later. Lake Erie in the north and the Ohio River in the south, along with canals and railroads, provided transportation links that spurred early immigration and commerce. The state became an industrial giant, producing steel, machinery, rubber, and glass. From 1869 to 1923, 7 of 12 U.S. presidents were Ohioans. With 20 electoral votes, sixth highest in the country, Ohio is still a big player in presidential elections. Education, government, and finance employ many people in Columbus, the capital and largest city. Manufacturing in Cleveland, Toledo, Cincinnati, and other cities remains a vital segment of the state's economy. Farmers on Ohio's western, glaciated plains grow soybeans and corn, the two largest cash crops.

⇑ INLAND URBAN CENTER. Cincinnati's skyline sparkles in the red glow of twilight. Founded in 1788, the modern city boasts education and medical centers as well as headquarters for companies such as Procter & Gamble.

⇓ TRADITIONAL TRAVEL. Horse and buggy are a familiar sight in central Ohio, location of the world's largest Amish population.

⇑ SOUND OF MUSIC. Colorful guitars mark the entrance to the Rock and Roll Hall of Fame in downtown Cleveland. The museum, through its Rockin' the School's program, attracts more than 50,000 students annually to experience the sounds of rock and roll music and learn about its history.

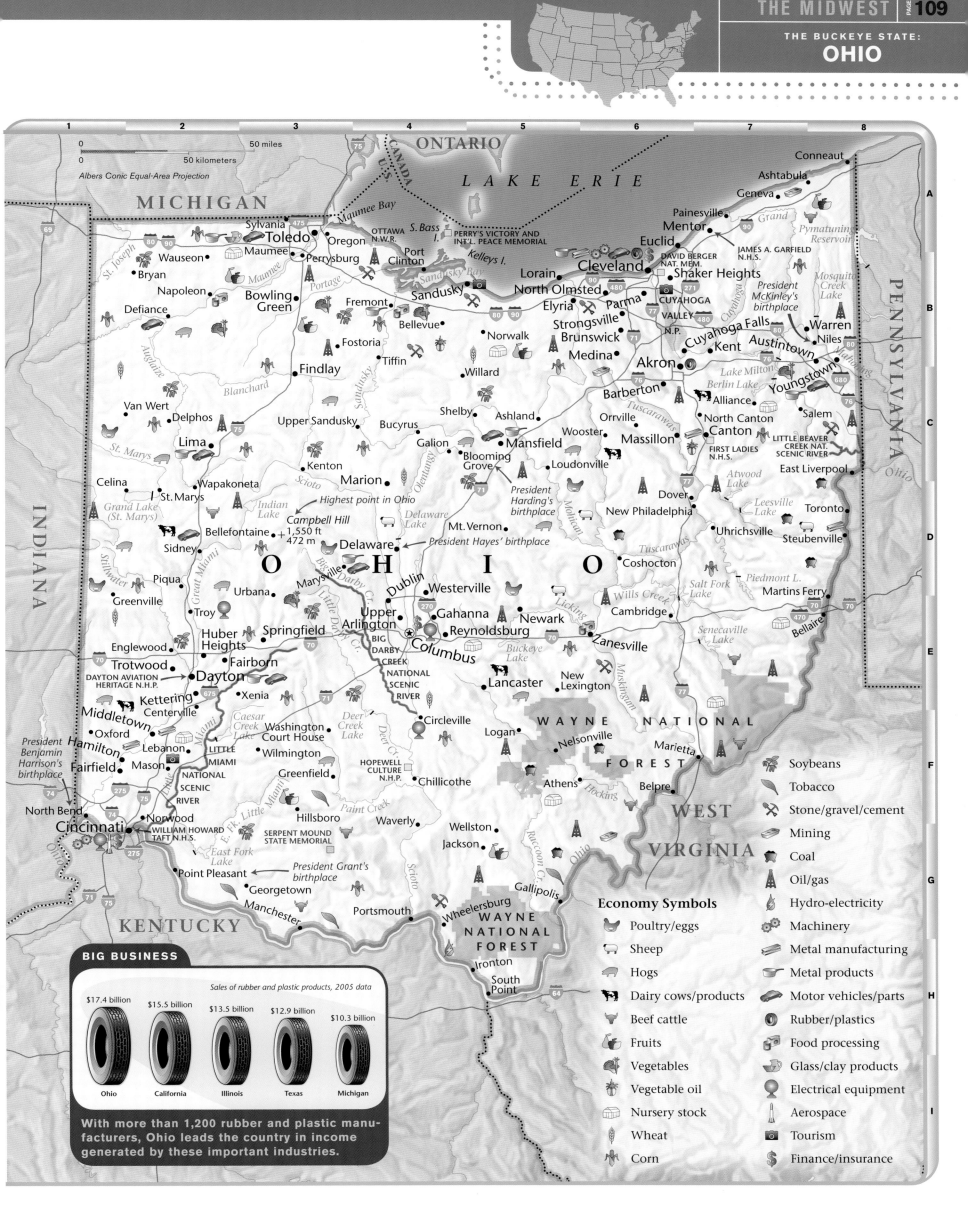

SOUTH DAKOTA

After the discovery of Black Hills gold in 1874, prospectors poured in and established lawless mining towns such as Deadwood. Indians fought this invasion but were defeated, and statehood came in 1889. Today, South Dakota has several reservations, and nearly nine percent of the state's people are Native Americans. The Missouri River flows through the center of the state, creating two distinct regions. To the east, farmers grow corn and soybeans on the fertile, rolling prairie. To the west, where it is too dry for most crops, farmers grow wheat and graze cattle and sheep on the vast plains. In the southwest, the Black Hills, named for the dark coniferous trees blanketing their slopes, are still a rich source of gold. Millions of tourists visit the area to see Mount Rushmore and a giant sculpture of Crazy Horse that has been in the works since 1948. Nearby, the fossil-rich Badlands, a region of eroded buttes and pinnacles, dominate the landscape.

THE BASICS

STATS

Area
77,117 sq mi (199,732 sq km)

Population
796,214

Capital
Pierre
Population 14,095

Largest city
Sioux Falls
Population 142,396

Ethnic/racial groups
88.4% white; 8.5% Native American; .9% African American; .7% Asian. Hispanic (any race) 2.1%.

Industry
Finance, services, manufacturing, government, retail trade, transportation and utilities, wholesale trade, construction, mining

Agriculture
Cattle, corn, soybeans, wheat, hogs, hay, dairy products

Statehood
November 2, 1889; 40th state

GEO WHIZ

Thirty years ago, black-footed ferrets were on the brink of extinction. Now, thanks to captive breeding programs, the world's largest wild black-footed ferret population is thriving in a black-tailed prairie dog colony in south-central South Dakota.

Called Shrine of Democracy by its creator Gutzon Borglum, Mount Rushmore National Monument features the faces of George Washington, Thomas Jefferson, Abraham Lincoln, and Theodore Roosevelt. Each is 60 feet (18 m) tall.

The Black Hills Institute of Geological Research in Hill City has been involved in digging up eight *Tyrannosaurus rex* skeletons, including Sue, Stan, Bucky, and WREX. In addition to research work, the institute prepares museum-quality reproductions.

RING-NECKED PHEASANT

PASQUEFLOWER

⇨ HONORING AGRICULTURE. The face of the Corn Palace in Mitchell is renewed each year using thousands of bushels of grain to create pictures depicting the role of agriculture in the state's history.

ALTERNATIVE BEEF

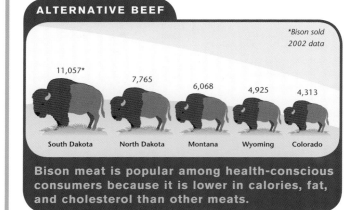

*Bison sold 2002 data

11,057* — South Dakota
7,765 — North Dakota
6,068 — Montana
4,925 — Wyoming
4,313 — Colorado

Bison meat is popular among health-conscious consumers because it is lower in calories, fat, and cholesterol than other meats.

MITCHELL CORN PALACE — LIFE ON THE FARM 2005

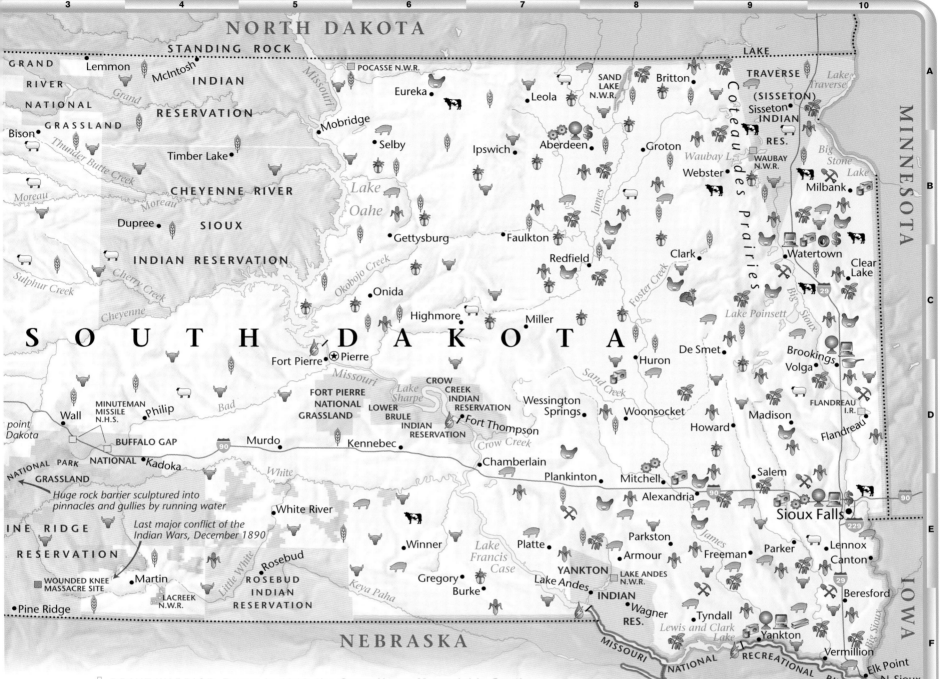

NORTH DAKOTA

STANDING ROCK

GRAND RIVER NATIONAL GRASSLAND

Lemmon • McIntosh
Bison •

INDIAN RESERVATION

Timber Lake • Mobridge • Selby • Eureka • Leola
SAND LAKE N.W.R.
POCASSE N.W.R.
Britton
TRAVERSE (SISSETON) INDIAN RES.
Lake Traverse

CHEYENNE RIVER

Dupree •
Moreau
SIOUX
INDIAN RESERVATION

Lake Oahe
Ipswich • Aberdeen • Groton
Webster
WAUBAY N.W.R.
Milbank
Big Stone Lake

MINNESOTA

Gettysburg • Faulkton
Redfield • Clark
Watertown
Clear Lake

SOUTH DAKOTA

Fort Pierre • Pierre
Onida • Highmore • Miller • Huron • De Smet
Brookings • Volga
Lake Poinsett

Missouri
Lake Sharpe
CROW CREEK INDIAN RESERVATION
FORT PIERRE NATIONAL GRASSLAND
LOWER BRULE INDIAN RESERVATION
Fort Thompson
Wessington Springs • Woonsocket
Madison
Howard
FLANDREAU I.R.
Flandreau

Wall • Philip
MINUTEMAN MISSILE N.H.S.
BUFFALO GAP
Murdo • Kennebec
Chamberlain
Plankinton • Mitchell
Salem
Alexandria
point Dakota
NATIONAL PARK
NATIONAL GRASSLAND • Kadoka
White
Huge rock barrier sculptured into pinnacles and gullies by running water

Sioux Falls

White River
Winner • Platte • Parkston
Armour • Freeman • Parker
Lennox • Canton

PINE RIDGE RESERVATION
Last major conflict of the Indian Wars, December 1890
Martin
WOUNDED KNEE MASSACRE SITE
Pine Ridge
LACREEK N.W.R.
Rosebud
ROSEBUD INDIAN RESERVATION
Gregory • Burke
Lake Francis Case
YANKTON
Lake Andes
LAKE ANDES N.W.R.
INDIAN RES.
Wagner • Tyndall
Lewis and Clark Lake
Yankton
Beresford
Vermillion
Elk Point
N. Sioux City

IOWA

NEBRASKA

MISSOURI NATIONAL RECREATIONAL RIVER

↓ BRAVE WARRIOR. Begun in 1948, the Crazy Horse Memorial in South Dakota's Black Hills honors the culture, tradition, and living heritage of North American Indians. In the background sculptors are recreating the statue of the Lakota chief and his horse in the mountainside.

Economy Symbols

Poultry/eggs		Hydro-electricity	
Sheep		Machinery	
Hogs		Metal manufacturing	
Dairy cows/products		Metal products	
Beef cattle		Rubber/plastics	
Vegetable oil		Food processing	
Wheat		Jewelry	
Corn		Electrical equipment	
Soybeans		Computers/electronics	
Stone/gravel/cement		Tourism	
Mining		Finance/insurance	
Oil/gas			

WISCONSIN

1848

THE BASICS

STATS

Area
65,498 sq mi (169,639 sq km)

Population
5,601,640

Capital
Madison
Population 223,389

Largest city
Milwaukee
Population 573,358

Ethnic/racial groups
90.0% white; 6.0% African American; 2.0% Asian; .9% Native American. Hispanic (any race) 4.7%.

Industry
Industrial machinery, paper products, food processing, metal products, electronic equipment, transportation

Agriculture
Dairy products, cattle, corn, poultry and eggs, soybeans

Statehood
May 29, 1848; 30th state

GEO WHIZ

The Indian Community School in Milwaukee offers courses in native languages, history, and rituals. In all of its programs—from math to tribal creation stories—seven core values are stressed: bravery, love, truth, wisdom, humility, loyalty, and respect.

Bogs left by retreating ice-age glaciers provide excellent conditions for raising cranberries. Wisconsin leads the nation in cranberry farming, producing more than half of the estimated 575 million pounds (261 million kg) consumed by Americans annually.

Wisconsin is nicknamed the Badger State, not for the animal but for the men who mined lead in the state during the 1820s. They dug living spaces by burrowing like badgers into the hillside.

ROBIN
WOOD VIOLET

WISCONSIN

Frenchman Jean Nicolet was the first European to reach present-day Wisconsin when he stepped ashore from Green Bay in 1634. After decades of getting along, relations with the region's Indians soured as the number of settlers increased. The Black Hawk War in 1832 ended the last major Indian resistance, and statehood came in 1848. Many Milwaukee residents are descendants of German immigrants who labored in the city's breweries and meatpacking plants. Even as the economic importance of health care and other services has increased, food processing and the manufacture of machinery and metal products remains significant for the state. More than one million dairy cows graze in America's Dairyland, as the state is often called. It leads the country in cheese production, and is the second-largest producer of milk and butter. Other farmers grow crops ranging from corn and soybeans to potatoes and cranberries. Northern Wisconsin is sparsely populated but heavily forested, and is the source of paper and paper products produced by the state.

⇧ CITY BY THE LAKE. Milwaukee, on the shore of Lake Michigan, derives its name from the Algonquian word for "beautiful land." The city, known for brewing and manufacturing, also has a growing service sector.

⇧ TASTY GRAZING. The largest concentration of Brown Swiss cows in the U.S. is in Wisconsin, where the milk of this breed is prized by cheese manufacturers.

⇦ RURAL ECONOMY. The dairy industry is an important part of Wisconsin's rural economy, and dairy farmers control most of the state's farmland.

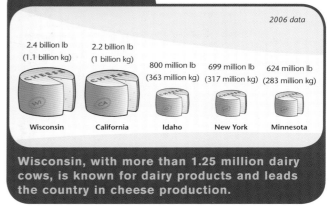

DAIRY HEARTLAND

2006 data

2.4 billion lb (1.1 billion kg)	2.2 billion lb (1 billion kg)	800 million lb (363 million kg)	699 million lb (317 million kg)	624 million lb (283 million kg)
Wisconsin	California	Idaho	New York	Minnesota

Wisconsin, with more than 1.25 million dairy cows, is known for dairy products and leads the country in cheese production.

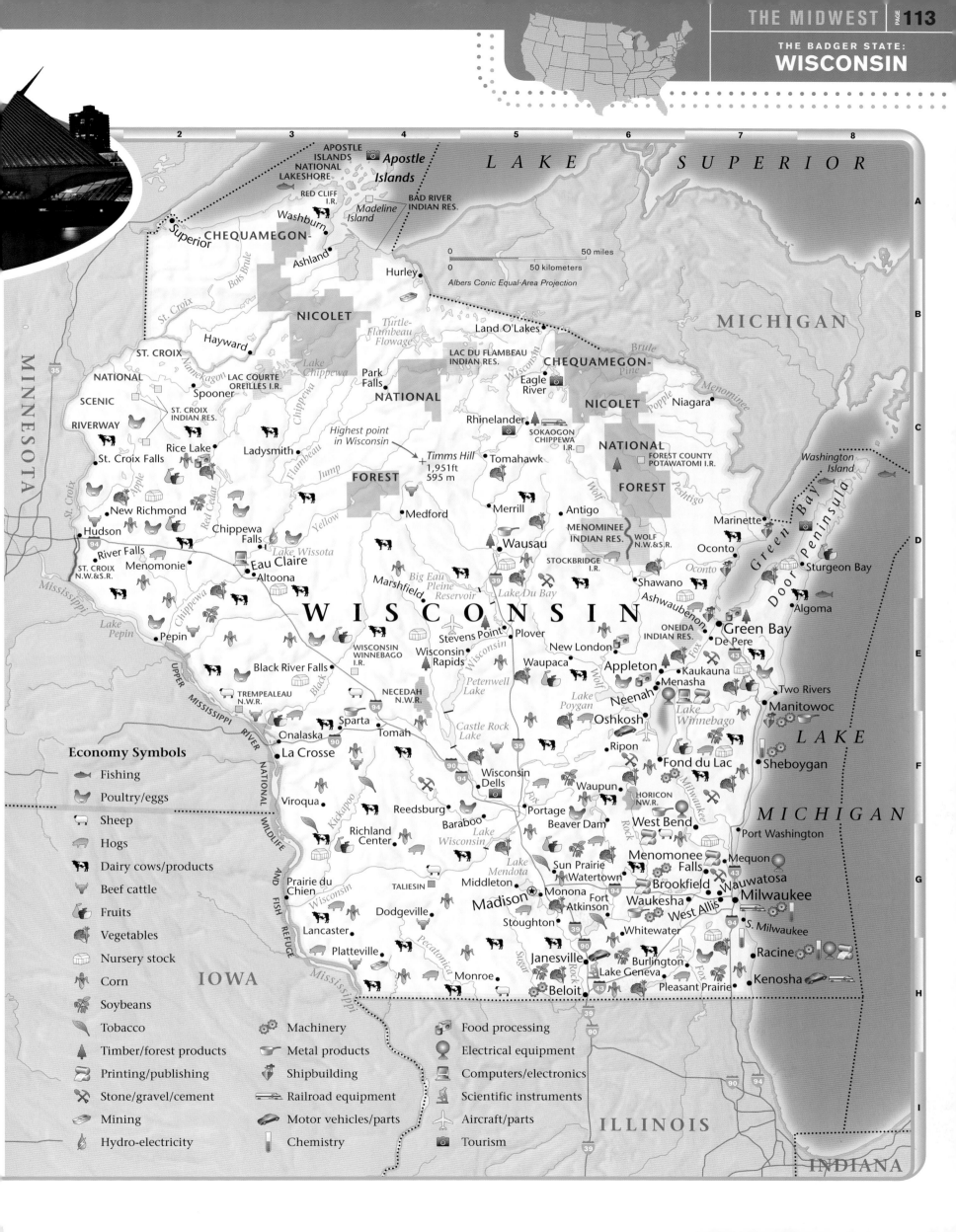

LAKE SUPERIOR

2 3 4 5 6 7 8

A
B
C
D
E
F
G
H
I

APOSTLE ISLANDS NATIONAL LAKESHORE
Apostle Islands
RED CLIFF I.R.
Washburn
Madeline Island
BAD RIVER INDIAN RES.
Superior
CHEQUAMEGON-
Ashland
Hurley

0   50 miles
0   50 kilometers
Albers Conic Equal-Area Projection

NICOLET
Bois Brule
Turtle-Flambeau Flowage
Land O'Lakes
MICHIGAN
Hayward
St. Croix
Brule
Namekagon
LAC DU FLAMBEAU INDIAN RES.
Wisconsin
Pine
ST. CROIX
Lake Chippewa
Park Falls
Eagle River
Popple
CHEQUAMEGON-
Menominee
NATIONAL
LAC COURTE OREILLES I.R.
Spooner
NATIONAL
Rhinelander
SOKAOGON CHIPPEWA I.R.
Niagara
NICOLET
SCENIC
ST. CROIX INDIAN RES.
Chippewa
FOREST
Peshtigo
FOREST COUNTY POTAWATOMI I.R.
Washington Island
RIVERWAY
Rice Lake
Ladysmith
Highest point in Wisconsin
Timms Hill 1,951ft 595 m
Tomahawk
NATIONAL
St. Croix Falls
Flambeau
Jump
FOREST
Merrill
Antigo
Marinette
New Richmond
Red Cedar
Yellow
Medford
Wolf
FOREST
Oconto
Green Bay
Hudson
Chippewa Falls
Lake Wissota
Wausau
MENOMINEE INDIAN RES.
WOLF N.W.&S.R.
Sturgeon Bay
River Falls
Eau Claire
Big Eau Pleine Reservoir
Lake Du Bay
STOCKBRIDGE I.R.
Shawano
Door Peninsula
ST. CROIX N.W.&S.R.
Menomonie
Altoona
Marshfield
Oconto
Ashwaubenon
Algoma
WISCONSIN
ONEIDA INDIAN RES.
Green Bay
De Pere
Mississippi
Chippewa
Lake Pepin
Pepin
WISCONSIN WINNEBAGO I.R.
Stevens Point
Plover
New London
Appleton
Kaukauna
Two Rivers
Black River Falls
Wisconsin Rapids
Wisconsin
Waupaca
Menasha
Neenah
Manitowoc
Black
Petenwell Lake
Lake Poygan
Oshkosh
LAKE
TREMPEALEAU N.W.R.
NECEDAH N.W.R.
Castle Rock Lake
Lake Winnebago
Sparta
Ripon
UPPER
Onalaska
Tomah
Fond du Lac
Sheboygan
Economy Symbols
La Crosse
Wisconsin Dells
Waupun
HORICON N.W.R.
MICHIGAN
🐟 Fishing
MISSISSIPPI
Viroqua
Reedsburg
Portage
West Bend
Port Washington
🐓 Poultry/eggs
Kickapoo
Baraboo
Beaver Dam
Rock
🐑 Sheep
RIVER
Richland Center
Lake Wisconsin
Milwaukee
Menomonee Falls
Mequon
🐖 Hogs
NATIONAL
Lake Mendota
Sun Prairie
Brookfield
Wauwatosa
🐄 Dairy cows/products
Prairie du Chien
TALIESIN
Middleton
Watertown
Waukesha
Milwaukee
🐂 Beef cattle
WILDLIFE
Wisconsin
Madison
Monona
Fort Atkinson
West Allis
🍎 Fruits
Dodgeville
Stoughton
Whitewater
S. Milwaukee
🥬 Vegetables
AND
Lancaster
Racine
🏠 Nursery stock
FISH
Platteville
Pecatonica
Janesville
Burlington
Lake Geneva
Kenosha
🌽 Corn
REFUGE
IOWA
Monroe
Beloit
Pleasant Prairie
🌿 Soybeans
Mississippi
Sugar
Rock
Fox
🍃 Tobacco
🌲 Timber/forest products
⚙️ Machinery
📦 Food processing
🖨️ Printing/publishing
🍽️ Metal products
💡 Electrical equipment
⚒️ Stone/gravel/cement
🚢 Shipbuilding
💻 Computers/electronics
🚂 Railroad equipment
🔬 Scientific instruments
⛏️ Mining
🚗 Motor vehicles/parts
✈️ Aircraft/parts
💧 Hydro-electricity
🧪 Chemistry
📷 Tourism
ILLINOIS
INDIANA
MINNESOTA
35
94
39
90
94
43
39
90

THE REGION

PHYSICAL

Total area 574,067 sq mi (1,486,833 sq km)	**Lowest point** Sea level, shores of the Gulf of Mexico	**Vegetation** Mixed, broadleaf, and needleleaf forest; grassland; desert
Highest point Wheeler Peak, NM 13,161 ft (4,011 m)	**Longest rivers** Rio Grande, Arkansas, Colorado	**Climate** Humid subtropical, semiarid and arid, with warm to hot summers and cool winters
	Largest lakes Toledo Bend, Sam Rayburn, Eufaula (all reservoirs)	

POLITICAL

Total population 35,830,366	**Smallest state** Oklahoma: 69,898 sq mi (181,036 sq km)
States (4): Arizona, New Mexico, Oklahoma, Texas	**Most populous state** Texas: 23,904,380
	Least populous state New Mexico: 1,969,915
Largest state Texas: 268,581 sq mi (695,624 sq km)	**Largest city proper** Houston, TX: 2,144,491

The
Southwest

A B C D E F G H

MISSOURI

ARKANSAS

LOUISIANA

Red

Sabine

Neches

Sabine Lake

Toledo Bend Reservoir

Sam Rayburn Reservoir

Lake Livingston

Galveston Bay

GULF OF MEXICO

Neosho

Lake O' The Cherokees

Eufaula Lake

Matagorda Bay

Corpus Christi Bay

Padre Island

KANSAS

Arkansas

Arkansas

OKLAHOMA

Lake Texoma

Trinity

Brazos

Colorado

C O A S T A L

P L A I N

TAMAULIPAS

Red

T E X A S

Edwards Plateau

NUEVO LEÓN

Falcon Reservoir

COLORADO

G R E A T

P L A I N S

Canadian

+ Black Mesa
4,973 ft
1,516 m

Llano Estacado

Pecos

Red Bluff Lake

Amistad Reservoir

U.S.
MEXICO

Rio Grande

COAHUILA

Colorado

R O C K Y

Wheeler Peak
+ 13,161 ft
4,011 m

N E W   M E X I C O

M O U N T A I N S

Guadalupe Peak +
8,749 ft
2,667 m

M E X I C O

CHIHUAHUA

DURANGO

Colorado

UTAH

San Juan

Navajo Reservoir

Rio Grande

Elephant Butte Reservoir

200 miles

200 kilometers
Albers Conic Equal-Area Projection

Lake Powell

Colorado

Plateau

Mogollon Rim

Gila

Humphreys Peak
+ 12,633 ft
3,851 m

Salt

A R I Z O N A

Theodore Roosevelt Lake

SONORA

U.S.
MEXICO

0

0

Grand Canyon

Lake Mead

Lake Mohave

Lake Havasu

NEVADA

S o n o r a n   D e s e r t

Gila

CALIFORNIA

Colorado

BAJA CALIFORNIA

BAJA CALIFORNIA SUR

GULF OF CALIFORNIA

SINALOA

PACIFIC OCEAN

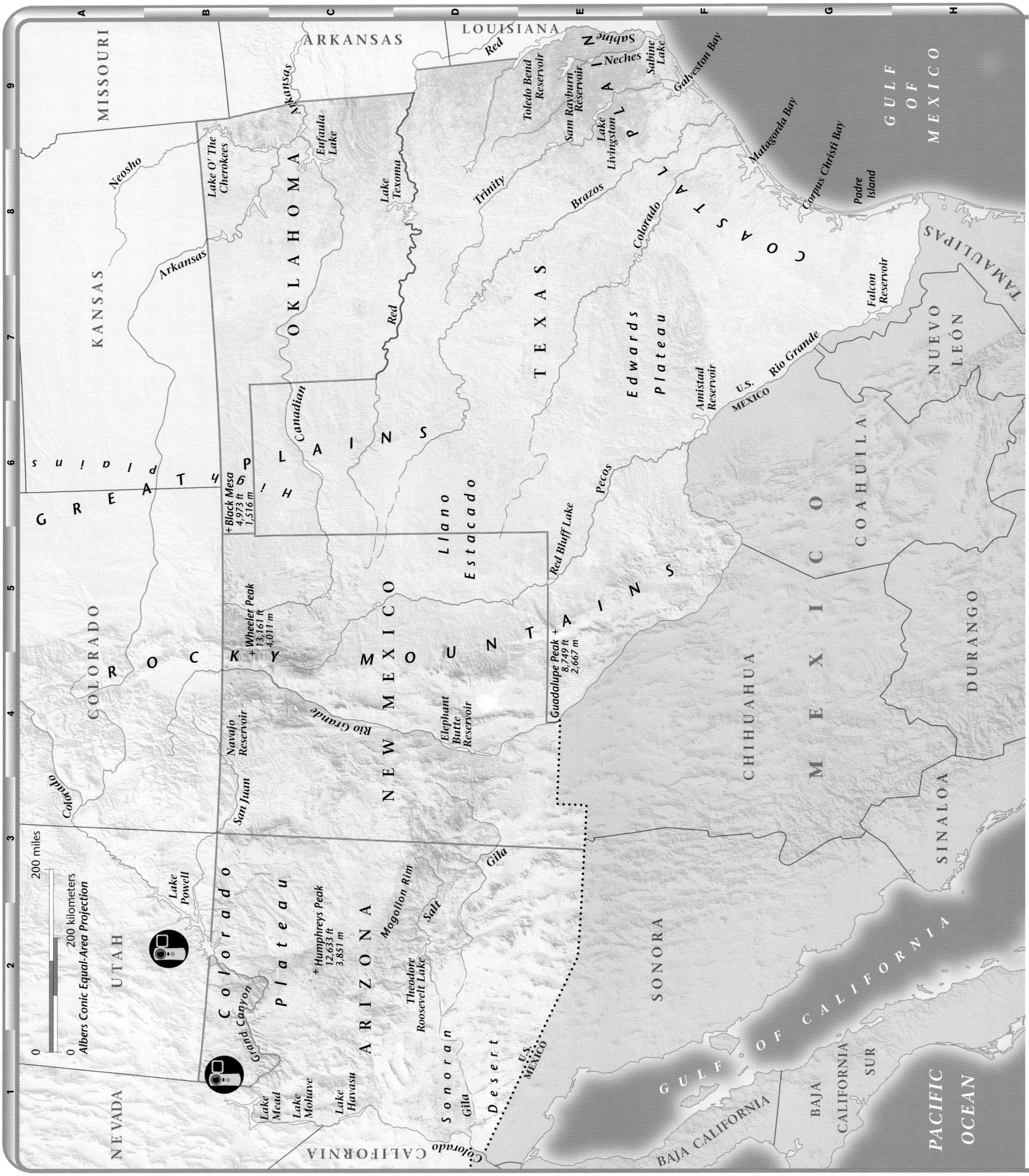

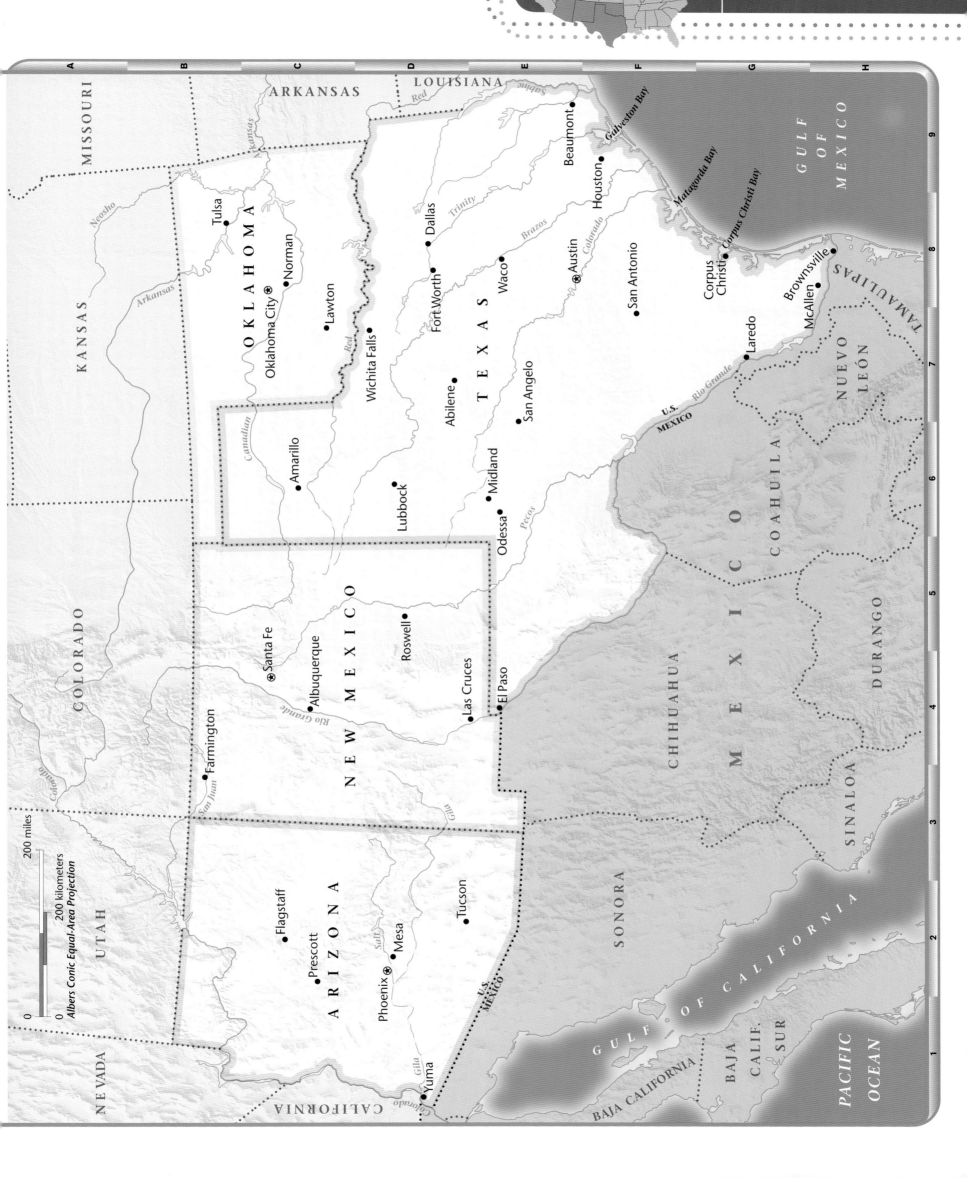

⇨ SKY STONE. According to Indian legend, turquoise stole its color from the sky. This Zuni woman is wearing turquoise jewelry for a festival in Phoenix. Zuni Indians, whose reservation is in western New Mexico, have made jewelry for more than one thousand years.

The Southwest
FROM CANYONS TO GRASSLANDS

Legendary cities of gold lured Spanish conquistadors to the Southwest in the 1500s. Today, the promise of economic opportunities brings people from other states as well as immigrants, both legal and illegal, from countries south of the border. This part of the Sunbelt region boasts future-oriented cities while preserving Wild West tales and Native American traditions. Stretching from the humid Gulf Coast to Arizona's deserts, the landscape is as diverse as its climate, ranging from sprawling plains in the east to plateaus cut by dramatic canyons in the west. Water is a major concern in the Southwest, one of the country's fastest-growing regions.

⇩ HIGH SOCIETY. Dressed in an elegant ball gown, a young woman participates in the Society of Martha Washington Pageant in Laredo, Texas. This event presents daughters of wealthy and long-established Hispanic families to the local community.

⇑ MODERN METROPOLIS. Lights sparkle in the skyline of Dallas, Texas. Although incorporated as a town in 1856, it was not until 1930 that it experienced explosive growth and prosperity due to the discovery of oil. Today, Dallas is a center of the U.S. oil industry and a leader in technology-based industries.

⇑ DEADLY VIPER. Shaking the rattles on the tip of its tail, this diamondback rattlesnake—coiled for attack—warns intruders to stay away. Common throughout the arid Southwest, the snake eats mainly small rodents.

⇐ STANDING TALL. The saguaro cactus, which often rises more than 30 feet (9 m) above the shrubs of the Sonoran Desert, frequently has several branches and produces creamy-white flowers that bloom at night. The Sonoran, hottest desert in North America, is located in the borderlands of southern Arizona and California and extends into northern Mexico.

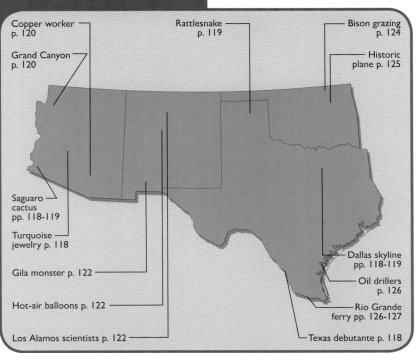

WHERE THE PICTURES ARE

Copper worker p. 120

Grand Canyon p. 120

Rattlesnake p. 119

Bison grazing p. 124

Historic plane p. 125

Saguaro cactus pp. 118-119

Turquoise jewelry p. 118

Gila monster p. 122

Hot-air balloons p. 122

Los Alamos scientists p. 122

Dallas skyline pp. 118-119

Oil drillers p. 126

Rio Grande ferry pp. 126-127

Texas debutante p. 118

THE GRAND CANYON STATE:
ARIZONA

ARIZONA

The Europeans to first visit what is now Arizona were the Spanish in the 1500s. The territory passed from Spain to Mexico and then to the United States over the next three centuries. In the 1800s settlers clashed with the Apache warriors Cochise and Geronimo—and with one another in lawless towns like Tombstone. Youngest of the 48 contiguous states, statehood arrived in 1912. Arizona's economy was long based on the Five C's—copper, cattle, cotton, citrus, and climate—but manufacturing and service industries have gained prominence. A fast-growing population, sprawling cities, and agricultural irrigation strain limited water supplies in this dry state, which depends on water from the Colorado River and underground aquifers. Tourists flock to the Colorado Plateau in the north to see stunning vistas of the Grand Canyon, Painted Desert, and Monument Valley. To the south, the Sonoran Desert's unique ecosystem includes the giant saguaro cactus. Indian reservations scattered around the state offer outsiders the chance to learn about tribal history and culture.

↑ HOT WORK. A man in protective clothing works near a furnace that melts and refines copper ore at Magma Copper Company near Tucson. Arizona is one of the largest copper-producing regions in the world.

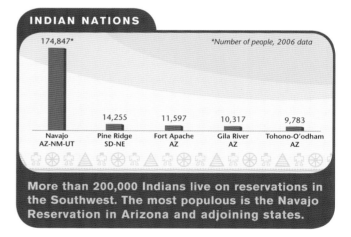

INDIAN NATIONS

174,847*   *Number of people, 2006 data

Navajo AZ-NM-UT	Pine Ridge SD-NE	Fort Apache AZ	Gila River AZ	Tohono-O'odham AZ
174,847*	14,255	11,597	10,317	9,783

More than 200,000 Indians live on reservations in the Southwest. The most populous is the Navajo Reservation in Arizona and adjoining states.

⇩ NATURAL WONDER. Carved by the rushing waters of the Colorado River, the Grand Canyon's geologic features and fossil record reveal almost two billion years of Earth's history. Archaeological evidence indicates human habitation dating back 12,000 years.

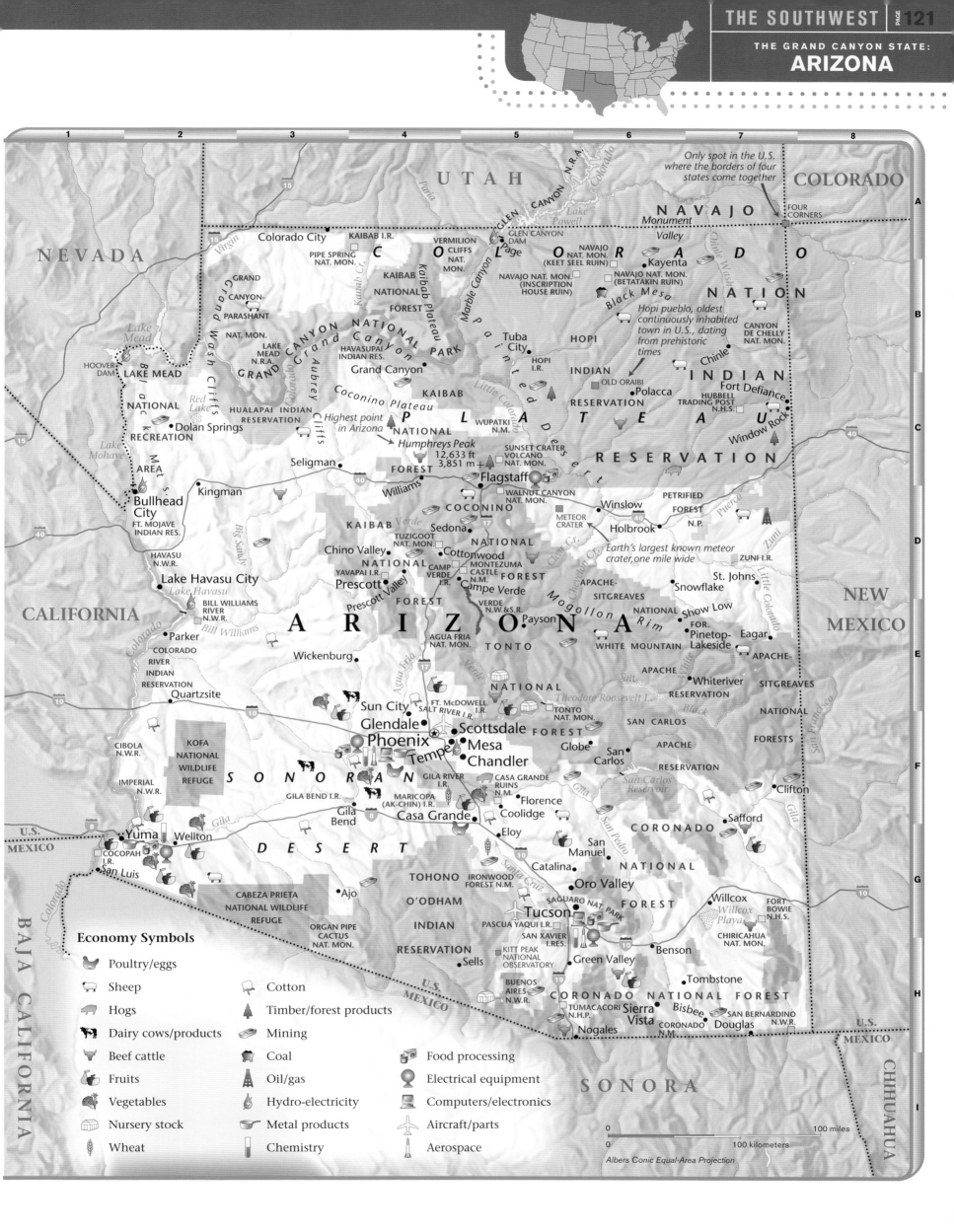

UTAH
COLORADO

NEVADA

Only spot in the U.S. where the borders of four states come together

FOUR CORNERS

Virgin
Colorado

Colorado City
KAIBAB I.R.
PIPE SPRING NAT. MON.
VERMILION CLIFFS NAT. MON.
GLEN CANYON N.R.A.
Lake Powell
GLEN CANYON DAM
Page
NAVAJO NAT. MON. (KEET SEEL RUIN)
Kayenta
NAVAJO
Monument Valley

GRAND CANYON-PARASHANT NAT. MON.

Lake Mead

KAIBAB
Kanab Cr.
KAIBAB NATIONAL FOREST
Kaibab Plateau
Marble Canyon
NAVAJO NAT. MON. (INSCRIPTION HOUSE RUIN)
Black Mesa
NAVAJO NAT. MON. (BETATAKIN RUIN)

Chinle Wash

NATION

HOOVER DAM
LAKE MEAD
BLACK
GRAND CANYON NATIONAL PARK
Havasupai Indian Res.
Tuba City
HOPI
Hopi pueblo, oldest continuously inhabited town in U.S., dating from prehistoric times
CANYON DE CHELLY NAT. MON.

LAKE MEAD N.R.A.
Grand Canyon
Coconino Plateau
Little Colorado
HOPI I.R.
INDIAN
OLD ORAIBI
Polacca
Chinle
INDIAN

Red Lake
NATIONAL
HUALAPAI INDIAN RESERVATION
KAIBAB
RESERVATION
HUBBELL TRADING POST N.H.S.
Fort Defiance

Lake Mohave
Dolan Springs
RECREATION
Cliffs
Highest point in Arizona
NATIONAL
Humphreys Peak 12,633 ft 3,851 m
WUPATKI N.M.
PLATEAU
Window Rock
RESERVATION

AREA
Black Mts.
Aubrey
Seligman
FOREST
SUNSET CRATER VOLCANO NAT. MON.
Flagstaff
WALNUT CANYON NAT. MON.
Winslow
PETRIFIED FOREST N.P.
Puerco

Bullhead City
Kingman
FT. MOJAVE INDIAN RES.
Williams
40
COCONINO
17
METEOR CRATER
Holbrook
Earth's largest known meteor crater, one mile wide
Zuni

HAVASU N.W.R.
Big Sandy
KAIBAB
Verde
Sedona
NATIONAL
TUZIGOOT NAT. MON.
Little Colorado
ZUNI I.R.

Lake Havasu City
Bill Williams
Chino Valley
Cottonwood
CAMP VERDE
MONTEZUMA CASTLE N.M.
FOREST
St. Johns
Snowflake
NEW MEXICO

CALIFORNIA
BILL WILLIAMS RIVER N.W.R.
NATIONAL
YAVAPAI I.R.
Prescott
Prescott Valley
I.R.
Campe Verde
APACHE-SITGREAVES

Lake Havasu
Colorado
FOREST
VERDE N.W.&S.R.
Mogollon Rim
NATIONAL
Show Low
FOR.
Pinetop-Lakeside
Eagar

Parker
COLORADO RIVER INDIAN RESERVATION
ARIZONA
AGUA FRIA NAT. MON.
Payson
WHITE MOUNTAIN
APACHE-

Quartzsite
Wickenburg
TONTO
Clear Cr.
Salt
APACHE
Whiteriver
RESERVATION
SITGREAVES

10
Agua Fria
17
NATIONAL
Theodore Roosevelt L.
Black
NATIONAL
San Francisco

CIBOLA N.W.R.
KOFA NATIONAL WILDLIFE REFUGE
Sun City
FT. McDOWELL I.R.
SALT RIVER I.R.
FORESTS

IMPERIAL N.W.R.
SONORAN
Glendale
Phoenix
Scottsdale
Mesa
Chandler
Globe
San Carlos
APACHE
Clifton

Tempe
GILA RIVER I.R.
CASA GRANDE RUINS N.M.
RESERVATION

Gila
MARICOPA (AK-CHIN) I.R.
Florence
Gila
San Carlos Reservoir
CORONADO
Safford
Gila

U.S.
8
Yuma
Wellton
Gila Bend I.R.
Gila Bend
8
Casa Grande
Coolidge
Eloy
San Manuel
San Pedro
NATIONAL

MEXICO
DESERT
Catalina
NATIONAL
10
G

COCOPAH I.R.
TOHONO
IRONWOOD FOREST N.M.
Oro Valley
FOREST
Willcox
FORT BOWIE N.H.S.

San Luis
CABEZA PRIETA NATIONAL WILDLIFE REFUGE
Ajo
O'ODHAM
SAGUARO NAT. PARK
Willcox Playa
CHIRICAHUA NAT. MON.

ORGAN PIPE CACTUS NAT. MON.
INDIAN
Tucson
PASCUA YAQUI I.R.
10
Benson

BAJA CALIFORNIA
RESERVATION
SAN XAVIER I.RES.
10

Sells
KITT PEAK NATIONAL OBSERVATORY
Green Valley
Tombstone

BUENOS AIRES N.W.R.
19
Sierra Vista
Bisbee
SAN BERNARDINO N.W.R.

CORONADO NATIONAL FOREST

TUMACACORI N.H.P.
CORONADO N.M.
Nogales
Douglas

U.S.
MEXICO
SONORA
CHIHUAHUA

Economy Symbols

- Poultry/eggs
- Sheep
- Hogs
- Dairy cows/products
- Beef cattle
- Fruits
- Vegetables
- Nursery stock
- Wheat
- Cotton
- Timber/forest products
- Mining
- Coal
- Oil/gas
- Hydro-electricity
- Metal products
- Chemistry
- Food processing
- Electrical equipment
- Computers/electronics
- Aircraft/parts
- Aerospace

0   100 miles
0   100 kilometers

Albers Conic Equal-Area Projection

NEW MEXICO

New Mexico is among the youngest states—statehood was established in 1912—but its capital city is the country's oldest. The Spanish founded Santa Fe in 1610, a decade before the *Mayflower* reached America. Beginning in the 1820s, the Santa Fe Trail brought trade and settlers, and the United States acquired all the territory from Mexico by 1853. Most large cities are in the center of the state, along the Rio Grande. The Rocky Mountains divide the plains in the east from eroded mesas and canyons in the west. Cattle and sheep ranching on the plains is the chief agricultural activity, but hay, onions, and chili peppers are also important. Copper, potash, and natural gas produce mineral wealth. Cultural richness created by the historic interaction of Indian, Hispanic, and Anglo peoples abounds. Visitors experience this unique culture in the state's spicy cuisine, the famous art galleries of Taos, and the crafts made by Indians on the state's many reservations.

THE BASICS

STATS

Area
121,590 sq mi (314,917 sq km)

Population
1,969,915

Capital
Santa Fe
Population 66,476

Largest city
Albuquerque
Population 504,949

Ethnic/racial groups
84.6% white; 9.8% Native American; 2.5% African American; 1.3% Asian. Hispanic (any race) 44.0%.

Industry
Electronic equipment, state and local government, real estate, business services, federal government, oil and gas extraction, health services

Agriculture
Cattle, dairy products, hay, chili peppers, onions

Statehood
January 6, 1912; 47th state

GEO WHIZ

Carlsbad Caverns National Park has more than a hundred caves, including the deepest limestone cavern in the U.S. From May through October, visitors can watch hundreds of thousands of Mexican free-tailed bats emerge from the cavern on their nightly search for food.

Taos Pueblo, in north-central New Mexico, has been continuously inhabited by Pueblo people for more than 1,000 years. When Spanish explorers reached it in 1540, they thought they had found one of the fabled golden cities of Cibola.

In 2007 voters in a county in south-central New Mexico approved a tax to help fund construction of a spaceport where rockets will launch tourists into space.

ROADRUNNER

YUCCA

⇧ PAINFUL BITE. The strikingly patterned gila monster, the most poisonous lizard native to the United States, lives in desert areas of the Southwest.

⇧ FLYING HIGH. Brightly colored balloons rise into a brilliant blue October sky during Albuquerque's annual International Balloon Fiesta, the largest such event in the world. During the 9-day festival more than 700 hot-air balloons drift on variable air currents created by surrounding mountains.

SPICY HOT!

2006 data

2.5 million hundredweight	1.6 million hundredweight	460,000 hundredweight	140,000 hundredweight
New Mexico	California	Arizona	Texas

Chili peppers help give Southwestern food its distinctive taste. New Mexico leads the country in production of this fiery flavor enhancer.

⇦ NUCLEAR MYSTERIES. Scientists at Los Alamos National Laboratory, a leading scientific and engineering research institution responsible for national security, use 3-D simulations to study nuclear explosions.

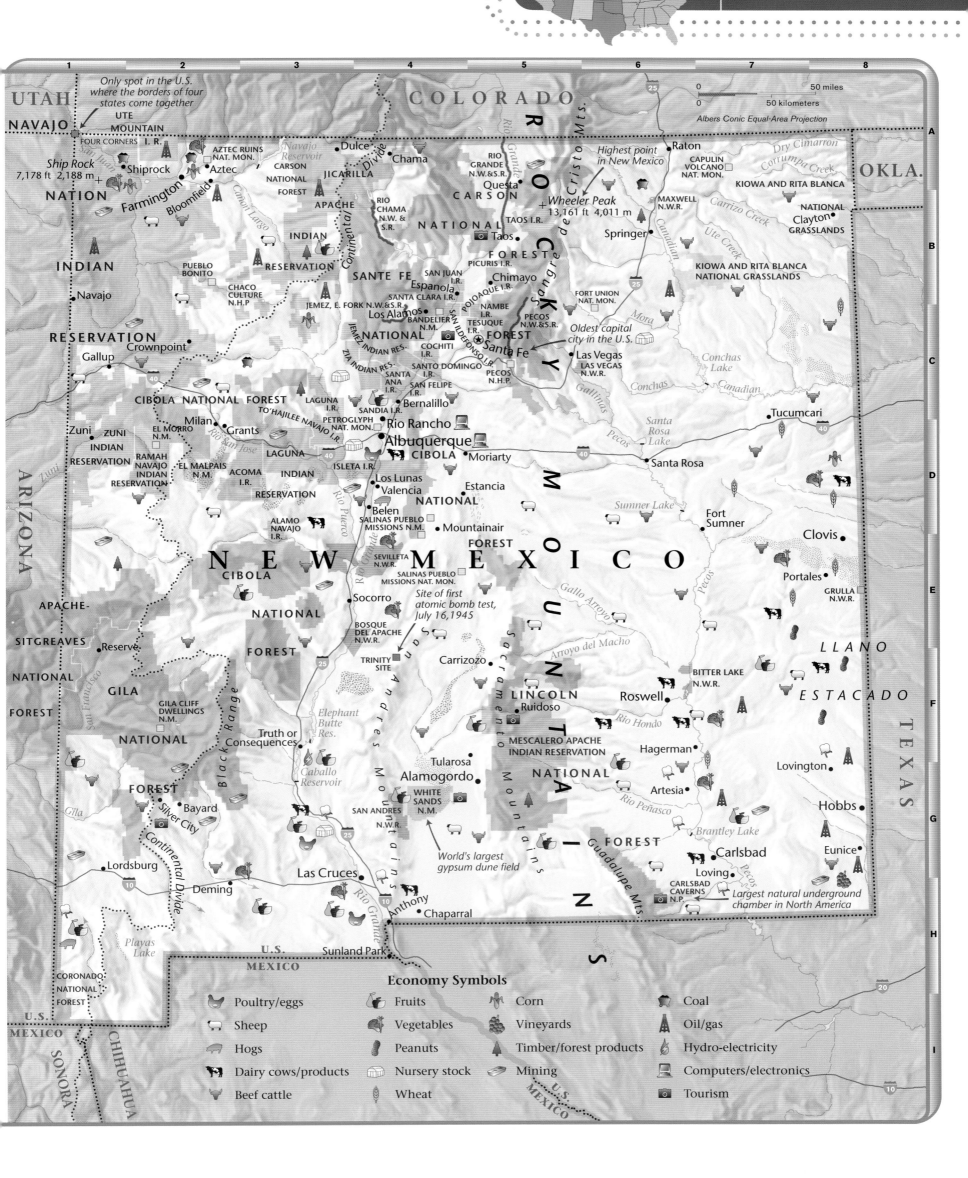

UTAH

NAVAJO

Only spot in the U.S. where the borders of four states come together

UTE MOUNTAIN

FOUR CORNERS I. R.

Ship Rock 7,178 ft 2,188 m

Shiprock

NATION

Farmington
Bloomfield

AZTEC RUINS NAT. MON.
Aztec
CARSON NATIONAL FOREST

Dulce
Chama

COLORADO

Rio Grande

RIO GRANDE N.W.&S.R.
Questa

Raton
CAPULIN VOLCANO NAT. MON.

Dry Cimarron

Corrumpa Creek

OKLA.

INDIAN

Navajo

PUEBLO BONITO
CHACO CULTURE N.H.P.

JICARILLA

APACHE

INDIAN

RESERVATION

Continental Divide

RIO CHAMA N.W. & S.R.

CARSON

NATIONAL

Wheeler Peak 13,161 ft 4,011 m

Highest point in New Mexico

MAXWELL N.W.R.

Springer

KIOWA AND RITA BLANCA NATIONAL
Clayton
GRASSLANDS

Carrizo Creek

Ute Creek

KIOWA AND RITA BLANCA NATIONAL GRASSLANDS

RESERVATION

Gallup

Crownpoint

SANTE FE

Espanola

SAN JUAN I.R.

Chimayo
PICURIS I.R.
POJOAQUE I.R.

TAOS I.R.
Taos

FOREST

NAMBE I.R.
TESUQUE I.R.

PECOS N.W.&S.R.

FORT UNION NAT. MON.

Oldest capital city in the U.S.

Sangre de Cristo Mts.

Canadian

Mora

R O C K Y

ROCKY

Conchas Lake

Tucumcari

ZUNI

Zuni

ZUNI INDIAN RESERVATION

RAMAH NAVAJO INDIAN RESERVATION

CIBOLA NATIONAL FOREST

EL MORRO N.M.

Milan
Grants

EL MALPAIS N.M.

Rio San Jose

TO'HAJIILEE NAVAJO I.R.

JEMEZ, E. FORK N.W.&S.R.
Los Alamos
BANDELIER N.M.

ZIA INDIAN RES.

JEMEZ INDIAN RES.

SANTA ANA I.R.

LAGUNA I.R.

SANTA CLARA I.R.

SAN ILDEFONSO I.R.

COCHITI I.R.

SANTO DOMINGO I.R.

SAN FELIPE I.R.

SANDIA I.R.

PETROGLYPH NAT. MON.

Bernalillo

Rio Rancho

Albuquerque

Santa Fe

Las Vegas

LAS VEGAS N.W.R.

PECOS N.H.P.

Gallinas

Conchas

Santa Rosa Lake

Canadian

ACOMA I.R.

ACOMA INDIAN RESERVATION

LAGUNA INDIAN RESERVATION

ISLETA I.R.

CIBOLA

Los Lunas
Valencia

Moriarty

Estancia

NATIONAL

Pecos

Santa Rosa

ARIZONA

APACHE-

SITGREAVES

NATIONAL

FOREST

Reserve

GILA

FOREST

NATIONAL

GILA CLIFF DWELLINGS N.M.

FOREST

Gila

Silver City
Bayard

ALAMO NAVAJO I.R.

Belen

SALINAS PUEBLO MISSIONS N.M.

Mountainair

N E W   M E X I C O

CIBOLA

NATIONAL

FOREST

Socorro

SEVILLETA N.W.R.

SALINAS PUEBLO MISSIONS NAT. MON.

Rio Grande

Rio Puerco

BOSQUE DEL APACHE N.W.R.

Site of first atomic bomb test, July 16, 1945

TRINITY SITE

San Francisco

San Andres Mountains

Black Range

Truth or Consequences

Elephant Butte Res.

Caballo Reservoir

Continental Divide

Lordsburg

Deming

Las Cruces

Rio Grande

Anthony

Chaparral

SAN ANDRES N.W.R.

Carrizozo

Tularosa

Alamogordo

WHITE SANDS N.M.

World's largest gypsum dune field

Sumner Lake

Fort Sumner

Clovis

Portales

GRULLA N.W.R.

L L A N O

E S T A C A D O

M O U N T A I N S

Gallo Arroyo

Arroyo del Macho

LINCOLN

Ruidoso

MESCALERO APACHE INDIAN RESERVATION

NATIONAL

FOREST

Roswell

BITTER LAKE N.W.R.

Rio Hondo

Hagerman

Artesia

Sacramento Mountains

Rio Peñasco

Guadalupe Mts.

Brantley Lake

Pecos

CARLSBAD CAVERNS N.P.

Carlsbad

Loving

Largest natural underground chamber in North America

Lovington

Hobbs

Eunice

TEXAS

Sunland Park

U.S. MEXICO

CORONADO NATIONAL FOREST

U.S. MEXICO

Playas Lake

SONORA

CHIHUAHUA

U.S. MEXICO

Economy Symbols

Poultry/eggs
Sheep
Hogs
Dairy cows/products
Beef cattle

Fruits
Vegetables
Peanuts
Nursery stock
Wheat

Corn
Vineyards
Timber/forest products
Mining

Coal
Oil/gas
Hydro-electricity
Computers/electronics
Tourism

0   50 miles
0   50 kilometers
Albers Conic Equal-Area Projection

1 2 3 4 5 6 7 8
A B C D E F G H I

OKLAHOMA

THE BASICS

STATS

Area
69,898 sq mi (181,036 sq km)

Population
3,617,316

Capital
Oklahoma City
Population 537,734

Largest city
Oklahoma City
Population 537,734

Ethnic/racial groups
78.3% white; 8.0% Native American;
7.8% African American; 1.7% Asian.
Hispanic (any race) 6.9%.

Industry
Manufacturing, services, government,
finance, insurance, real estate

Agriculture
Cattle, wheat, hogs, poultry, nursery
stock

Statehood
November 16, 1907; 46th state

GEO WHIZ

An area of Oklahoma City has earned the nickname Little Saigon. In the 1960s the city opened its doors to tens of thousands of refugees from Vietnam. Today, the area is a thriving business district that includes people of other Asian nationalities.

"Hillbilly Speed Bump" is one of several nicknames for the armadillo. Native to South America, large populations of this armor-plated mammal are found as far north as Oklahoma.

Before it became a state in 1907, Oklahoma was known as Indian Territory. Today 39 tribes, including Cherokees, Osages, Creeks, and Choctaws, have their headquarters in the state.

SCISSOR-TAILED
FLYCATCHER

MISTLETOE

OKLAHOMA

The U.S. government declared most of present-day Oklahoma Indian Territory in 1834. To reach this new homeland, southeastern Indians were forced to travel the Trail of Tears, named for its brutal conditions. By 1889 areas were opened for white homesteaders who staked claims in frenzied land runs. White and Indian lands were combined to form the state of Oklahoma in 1907. During the 1930s, many Okies fled drought and dust storms that smothered everything in sight. Some traveled as far as California in search of work. Better farming methods and the return of rain helped agriculture recover, and today cattle and wheat are the chief products. Oil and natural gas wells are found throughout the state. The Red River, colored by the region's iron-rich soils, marks the state's southern boundary. Along the eastern border, the Ozark Plateau and Ouachita Mountains form rugged bluffs and valleys. To the west, rolling plains rise toward the High Plains in the state's panhandle.

COLORADO

NEW MEXICO

Black Mesa
4,973 ft
1,516 m

Boise City

Highest point in Oklahoma

KIOWA AND
RITA BLANCA
NATIONAL GRASSLAND

Cimarron

Guymon

OPTIMA
N.W.R.

Optima Lake

Beaver

Beaver

HIGH

PLAINS

1 2 3 4

⇧ NATURAL LANDSCAPE. A bison herd grazes in the Tallgrass Prairie Preserve, near Pawhuska. In years when rain is abundant, the grasses can grow as tall as 8 feet (2.5 m). Tallgrass prairie once covered 140 million acres (57 million ha), extending from Minnesota to Texas, but today less than 10 percent remains because of urban sprawl and cropland expansion.

WEATHER ALERT

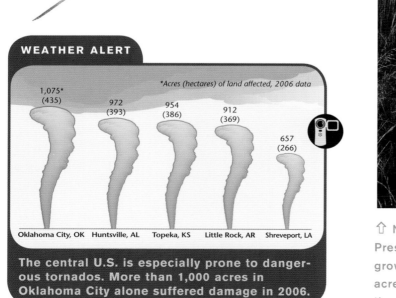

*Acres (hectares) of land affected, 2006 data

1,075*
(435)

972
(393)

954
(386)

912
(369)

657
(266)

Oklahoma City, OK   Huntsville, AL   Topeka, KS   Little Rock, AR   Shreveport, LA

The central U.S. is especially prone to dangerous tornados. More than 1,000 acres in Oklahoma City alone suffered damage in 2006.

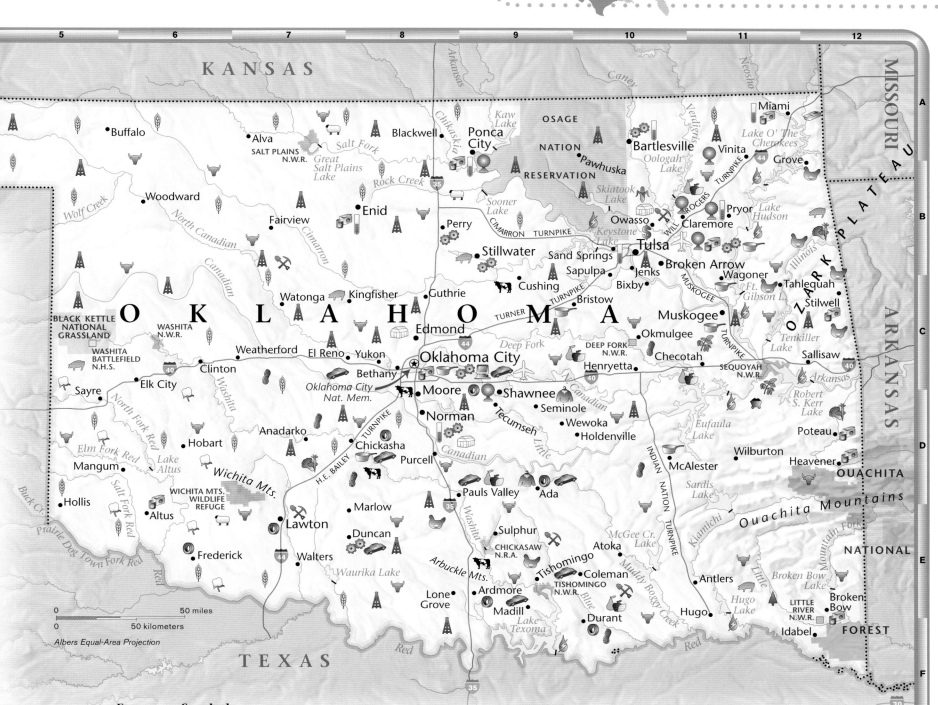

KANSAS

Buffalo · Alva · SALT PLAINS N.W.R. · Blackwell · Ponca City · OSAGE NATION · Bartlesville · Vinita · Lake O' The Cherokees · Grove · Miami

Woodward · Great Salt Plains Lake · Salt Fork · Pawhuska · RESERVATION · Oologah Lake · TURNPIKE · 44

Fairview · Enid · Rock Creek · Perry · Sooner Lake · Skiatook Lake · Keystone Lake · Owasso · Pryor · Lake Hudson

Watonga · Kingfisher · Guthrie · CIMARRON TURNPIKE · Stillwater · Sand Springs · WILL ROGERS · Claremore

O K L A H O M A · Cushing · Sapulpa · Tulsa · Broken Arrow · Wagoner · Tahlequah · Stilwell

BLACK KETTLE NATIONAL GRASSLAND · WASHITA N.W.R. · Weatherford · El Reno · Yukon · Edmond · Bristow · Muskogee · Okmulgee · Checotah · Sallisaw

WASHITA BATTLEFIELD N.H.S. · Clinton · Bethany · Oklahoma City · Deep Fork · DEEP FORK N.W.R. · Henryetta · SEQUOYAH N.W.R.

Sayre · Elk City · Oklahoma City Nat. Mem. · Moore · Shawnee · Seminole · McAlester · Wilburton · Heavener · OUACHITA

Mangum · Hobart · Anadarko · Norman · Tecumseh · Wewoka · Holdenville · Poteau · Ouachita Mountains

Hollis · Altus · WICHITA MTS. WILDLIFE REFUGE · Chickasha · Purcell · Pauls Valley · Ada · Eufaula Lake · Sardis Lake · NATIONAL

Frederick · Lawton · Marlow · Duncan · Sulphur · CHICKASAW N.R.A. · Atoka · Antlers · Broken Bow Lake · Broken Bow · FOREST

Walters · Waurika Lake · Arbuckle Mts. · Tishomingo · Coleman · Hugo Lake · LITTLE RIVER N.W.R. · Idabel

Lone Grove · Ardmore · Madill · TISHOMINGO N.W.R. · Durant · Hugo · Lake Texoma

TEXAS

50 miles / 50 kilometers / Albers Equal-Area Projection

Economy Symbols

Poultry/eggs · Sheep · Hogs · Dairy cows/products · Beef cattle · Fruits · Vegetables · Peanuts · Nursery stock · Wheat · Corn · Soybeans · Cotton · Stone/gravel/cement · Mining

Coal · Oil/gas · Hydro-electricity · Machinery · Metal products · Motor vehicles/parts · Rubber/plastics · Chemistry · Food processing · Clothing/textiles · Electrical equipment · Computers/electronics · Aircraft/parts · Finance/insurance

⇩ HISTORY IN THE AIR. Tulsa's mayor pilots one of the Spirit of Tulsa Squadron's vintage PT-17 airplanes above the city. In 1990 the squadron became part of the Commemorative Air Force, a national organization committed to preserving aviation history by restoring and flying World War II aircraft.

THE LONE STAR STATE:
TEXAS

TEXAS

1   2

Huge size, geographic diversity, and rich natural resources make Texas seem like its own country. In fact, it was an independent republic after throwing off Mexican rule in 1836. A famous battle in the fight for independence produced the Texan battle cry "Remember the Alamo!" In 1845 Texas was annexed by the United States. Texas is the second largest state (behind Alaska) and the second most populous (behind California). It is a top producer of many agricultural products, including cattle, sheep, cotton, citrus fruits, vegetables, rice, and pecans. It also has huge oil and natural gas fields and is a manufacturing powerhouse. Pine forests cover East Texas, the wettest region. The Gulf Coast has swamps and extensive barrier islands. Grassy plains stretch across the northern panhandle, while the rolling Hill Country is famous for beautiful wildflowers. Mountains, valleys, and sandy plains sprawl across dry West Texas. The Rio Grande, sometimes barely a trickle, separates Texas and Mexico.

⇧ BLACK GOLD. Workers plug an oil well. Discovery of oil early in the 20th century transformed life in Texas. Today, the state leads the U.S. in oil and natural gas production.

THE BASICS

STATS

Area
268,581 sq mi (695,624 sq km)

Population
23,904,380

Capital
Austin
Population 709,893

Largest city
Houston
Population 2,144,491

Ethnic/racial groups
82.7% white; 11.9% African American; 3.4% Asian; .7% Native American. Hispanic (any race) 35.7%.

Industry
Chemicals, machinery, electronics and computers, food products, petroleum and natural gas, transportation equipment

Agriculture
Cattle, sheep, poultry, cotton, sorghum, wheat, rice, hay, peanuts, pecans

Statehood
December 29, 1845; 28th state

GEO WHIZ

The Fossil Rim Wildlife Research Center in the Texas Hill Country is breeding black rhinos and other endangered African animals. The goal is to reintroduce offspring into the wild in their native environment. Meanwhile, visitors get a chance to see a bit of Africa in Texas.

Six national flags have flown over Texas during the course of its history— the Spanish, French, Mexican, Texan, Confederate, and American.

Texas has a long history of Bigfoot sightings. The ape-man creature was part of local Indian lore, and white settlers told stories about a wild woman along the Navidad River. The Texas Bigfoot Research Center has collected hundreds of eyewitness reports, footprint casts, and hair samples of what locals call Wooly Booger.

MOCKINGBIRD
BLUEBONNET

ROUNDUP

2007 data

14 million cattle — Texas
6.6 million cattle — Nebraska
6.4 million cattle — Kansas
5.5 million cattle — California
5.2 million cattle — Oklahoma

Texas has more cattle than most states have people. Only California, Texas, New York, and Florida have larger human populations.

⇨ BORDERLAND RELIC. Los Ebanos Ferry, which takes its name from a grove of ebony trees growing nearby, is the last remaining government-licensed, hand-pulled ferry on any U.S. border. The privately owned ferry, near Mission, Texas, can carry three cars at a time across the Rio Grande.

(Map labels:)
Chamizal National Memorial
NEW MEXICO
U.S.
MEXICO
El Paso
GUADALUPE MTS. N.P.
YSLETA DEL SUR I.R.
Fabens
+ Guadalupe Peak 8,749 ft 2,667 m
Highest point in Texas
CHIHUAHUA
Rio Grande
Pecos
ROCKY MTS.
Davis Mts.
FORT DAVIS N.H.S.
Alpine
Marfa
Presidio
BIG NATIO PAR

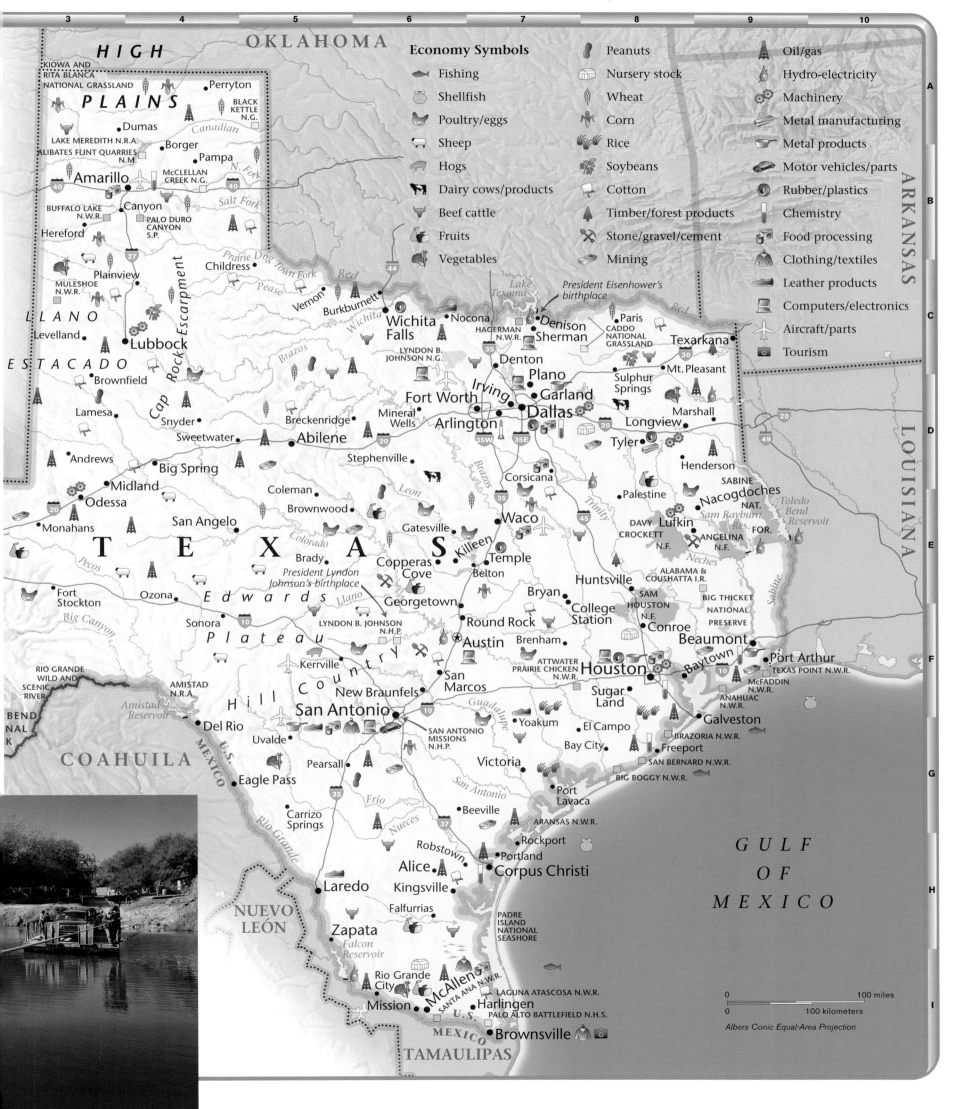

The West

PHYSICAL

Total area
1,635,555 sq mi
(4,236,083 sq km)

Highest point
Mount McKinley (Denali),
AK: 20,320 ft (6,194 m)

Lowest point
Death Valley, CA:
-282 ft (-86 m)

Longest rivers
Missouri, Yukon,
Rio Grande, Colorado

Largest lakes
Great Salt, Iliamna,
Becharof

Vegetation
Needleleaf, broadleaf, and mixed
forest; grassland; desert; tundra
(Alaska); tropical (Hawai'i)

Climate
Mild along the coast, with warm
summers and mild winters; semiarid
to arid inland; polar in parts of
Alaska; tropical in Hawai'i

POLITICAL

Total population
61,788,280

States (11):
Alaska, California, Colorado, Hawai'i,
Idaho, Montana, Nevada, Oregon,
Utah, Washington, Wyoming

Largest state
Alaska: 663,267 sq mi
(1,717,862 sq km)

Smallest state
Hawai'i: 10,931 sq mi (28,311 sq km)

Most populous state
California: 36,553,215

Least populous state
Wyoming: 522,830

Largest city proper
Los Angeles, CA: 3,849,378

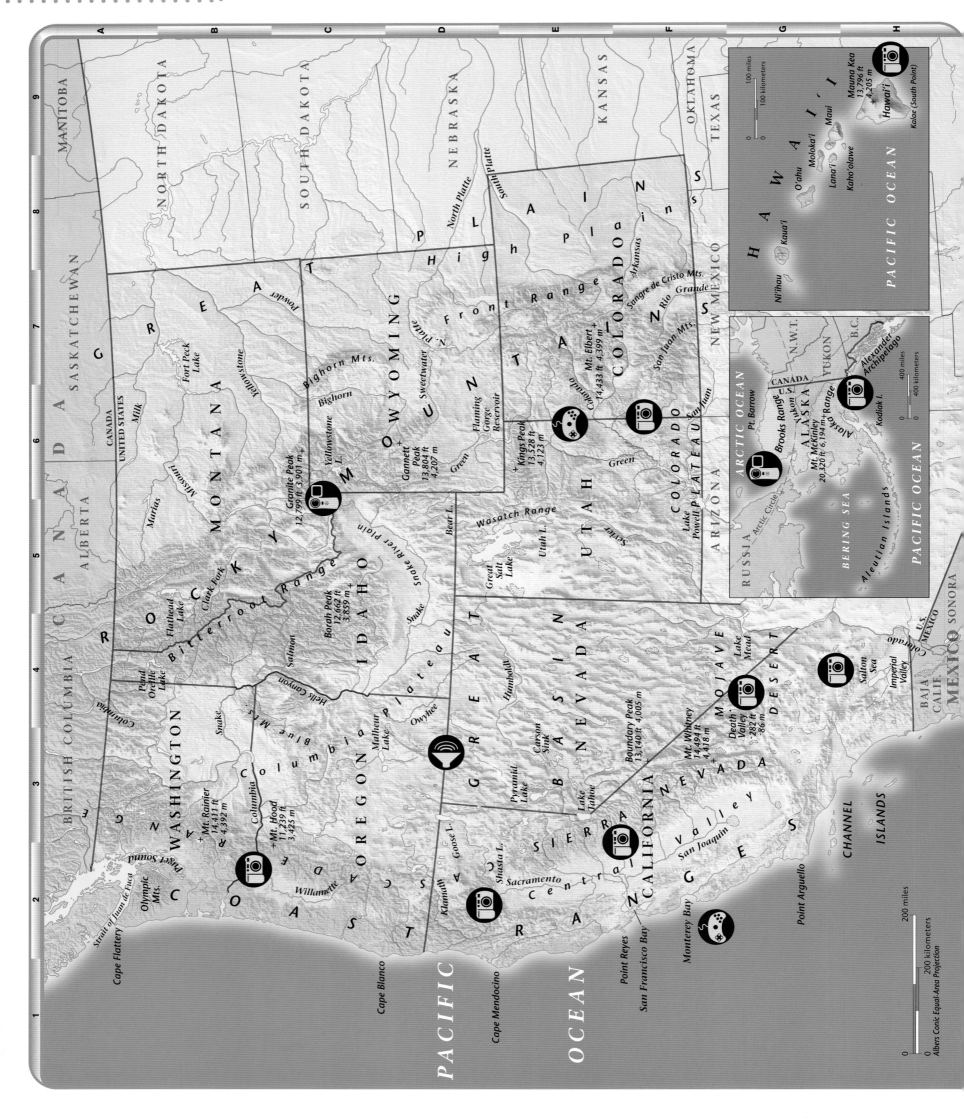

MANITOBA

SASKATCHEWAN

ALBERTA

BRITISH COLUMBIA

C A N A D A

CANADA
UNITED STATES

NORTH DAKOTA

SOUTH DAKOTA

NEBRASKA

KANSAS

OKLAHOMA

TEXAS

G R E A T

P L A I N S

High Plains

Front Range

COLORADO

NEW MEXICO

Sangre de Cristo Mts.

Rio Grande

San Juan Mts.

Arkansas

Mt. Elbert +
14,433 ft 4,399 m

Kings Peak
13,528 ft
4,123 m

San Juan

COLORADO PLATEAU

Lake
Powell

ARIZONA

MONTANA

Milk

Missouri

Marias

Musselshell

Fort Peck
Lake

Yellowstone

Powder

Bighorn Mts.

Bighorn

WYOMING

R O C K Y

M O U N T A I N S

Granite Peak
12,799 ft 3,901 m +

Yellowstone
L.

Sweetwater

N. Platte

Green

Gannett
Peak
13,804 ft
4,207 m

Flaming
Gorge
Reservoir

Green

Colorado

North Platte

South Platte

UTAH

Wasatch Range

Bear L.

Utah L.

Great
Salt
Lake

Sevier

FLATHEAD
Lake

Clark Fork

Bitterroot Range

Pend
Oreille
Lake

Columbia

IDAHO

Salmon

Snake River Plain

Borah Peak
12,662 ft
3,859 m +

Snake

Snake

Hells Canyon

OREGON

Blue Mts.

Malheur
Lake

Owyhee

Columbia Plateau

G R E A T

B A S I N

Humboldt

Carson
Sink

Pyramid
Lake

NEVADA

Boundary Peak
13,140 ft 4,005 m +

Lake
Tahoe

Colorado

Lake
Mead

Salton
Sea

MOJAVE

DESERT

Imperial
Valley

BAJA
CALIF.

MEXICO

SONORA

U.S.
MEXICO

Death
Valley
-282 ft
-86 m

Mt. Whitney
14,494 ft
4,418 m +

S I E R R A

N E V A D A

C O A S T

R A N G E S

Central

Valley

San Joaquin

CALIFORNIA

Sacramento

Shasta L.

Klamath

Goose L.

WASHINGTON

Mt. Rainier +
14,411 ft
4,392 m

Mt. Hood +
11,239 ft
3,425 m

Columbia

Willamette

Puget Sound

Olympic
Mts.

Strait of Juan de Fuca

Cape Flattery

Cape Blanco

Cape Mendocino

Point Reyes

San Francisco Bay

Monterey Bay

Point Arguello

CHANNEL

ISLANDS

P A C I F I C

O C E A N

P A C I F I C   O C E A N

H A W A I ' I

Ni'ihau

Kaua'i

O'ahu

Moloka'i

Lāna'i

Maui

Kaho'olawe

Hawai'i

Mauna Kea
13,796 ft
+ 4,205 m

Kalae (South Point)

PACIFIC OCEAN

100 miles
100 kilometers

ARCTIC OCEAN

Pt. Barrow

RUSSIA

Arctic Circle

Yukon

Brooks Range

Mt. McKinley
20,320 ft 6,194 m + Range

ALASKA
U.S.

Kodiak I.

BERING SEA

Aleutian Islands

PACIFIC OCEAN

CANADA

N.W.T.

YUKON

B.C.

Alexander
Archipelago

400 miles
400 kilometers

200 miles
200 kilometers

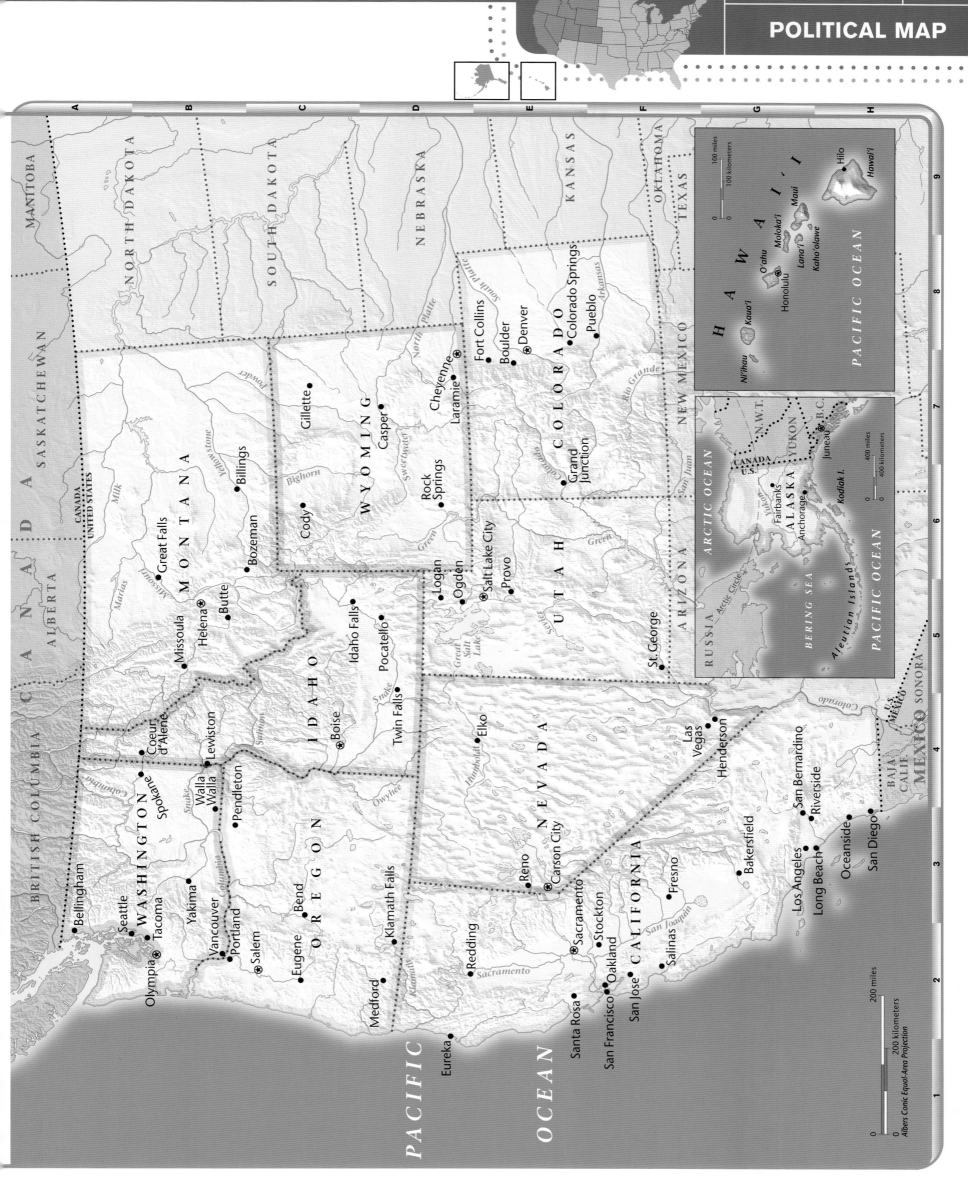

⇨ OLD AND NEW. A cable car carries passengers on a steep hill in San Francisco. In the background modern buildings, including the Transamerica Pyramid, rise above older neighborhoods in this earthquake-prone city.

The West

THE HIGH FRONTIER

The western states, which make up almost half of the country's land area, have diverse landscapes and climates, ranging from the frozen heights of Denali, in Alaska, to the desolation of Death Valley, in California, and the lush, tropical islands of Hawai'i. More than half the region's population lives in California, and the Los Angeles metropolitan area is second only to New York City. Yet many parts of the region are sparsely populated, and much of the land is set aside as parkland and military bases. The region also faces many natural hazards— earthquakes, landslides, wild-fires, and even volcanic eruptions.

⇨ NORTHERN GIANT. Mount McKinley, called Denali—the "High One"— by native Athabascans, is North America's highest peak, rising more than 20,000 feet (6,100 m) in the Alaska Range. The same tectonic forces that trigger earthquakes in Alaska are slowly pushing this huge block of granite ever higher.

WHERE THE PICTURES ARE

Wheat farm p. 152
Seattle skyline p. 152
Astoria Column p. 148
Sea stacks p. 148
Log walker p. 133
Giant sequoia p. 136
Open-pit mine p. 147
Trolley car p. 132
Golden Gate Bridge p. 136
0   200 miles

Mount McKinley p. 132
0   400 mi
Fishing grizzly p. 134
0   100 mi
Anchorage p. 134
Honolulu skyline p. 140
Outrigger canoe p. 133

Logger p. 142
Sheepherders pp. 142-143
Mountain lake p. 145
Potatoes p. 143
Cowboys and cattle p. 144
Hot spring pp. 132-133
Old Faithful p. 155
Pronghorn p. 154
Barn with horse p. 154
Skier p. 138
Mountain lion p. 133
Ancient pueblo p. 138
Delicate Arch pp. 150-151
Mormon temple p. 150
Las Vegas hotel pp. 146-147
Desert scene p. 146
Erupting volcano p. 141

⇧ ELUSIVE PREDATOR. Known by many names, including cougar and mountain lion, these big cats are found mainly in remote mountainous areas of the West, where they hunt deer and smaller animals.

⇦ STEAMY BATH. Colorful, mineral-rich hot springs are just one geothermal feature of Yellowstone National Park. Runoff from rain and snowmelt seeps into cracks in the ground, sinking to a depth of 10,000 feet (3,050 m), where it is heated by molten rock before rising back to the surface.

⇩ BALANCING ACT. For many years, rivers have been used to move logs from forest to market, taking advantage of the buoyancy of logs and the power of moving water. A logger stands on a floating log raft in Coos Bay, Oregon.

⇧ TRADITIONAL SAILING CRAFT. A Hawaiian outrigger canoe on Waikiki Beach promises fun in the surf for visitors to the 50th state. An important part of Polynesian culture, the canoes were once used to travel from island to island.

THE LAST FRONTIER STATE:
ALASKA

ALASKA

Alaska—from *Alyeska*, an Aleut word meaning "great land"—was purchased by the U.S. from Russia in 1867 for just two cents an acre. Many people thought it was a bad investment, but it soon paid off when gold was discovered, and again when major petroleum deposits were discovered in 1968. Today, an 800-mile- (1,287-km-) long pipeline links North Slope oil fields to the ice-free port at Valdez, but opponents worry about long-term environmental impact.

Everything is big in Alaska. It is the largest state, with one-sixth of the country's land area; it has the highest peak in the U.S., Mt. McKinley (Denali); and the largest earthquake ever recorded in the U.S.—a 9.2 magnitude—occurred there in 1964. It is first in forestland, a leading source of seafood, and a major oil producer. Alaska's population includes a higher percentage of native people than that of any other state.

⇧ TIME FOR LUNCH. A grizzly bear wades into the rushing waters of Brooks Falls, in Katmai National Park, to catch a leaping salmon.

THE BASICS

STATS

Area
663,267 sq mi (1,717,862 sq km)

Population
683,478

Capital
Juneau
Population 31,187

Largest city
Anchorage
Population 278,700

Ethnic/racial groups
70.7% white; 15.4% Native American; 4.6% Asian; 3.7% African American. Hispanic (any race) 5.6%.

Industry
Petroleum products, government, services, trade

Agriculture
Shellfish, seafood, nursery stock, vegetables, dairy products, feed crops

Statehood
January 3, 1959; 49th state

GEO WHIZ

During the summer humpback whales migrate to Alaskan waters, where they work together to catch fish. While swimming in circles, the whales blow bubbles that form a net around schools of herring. Each whale can eat hundreds of fish in one gulp.

Global warming and population growth are changing the route of the Iditarod, the world's most famous sled-dog race. Since 2002 lack of snow in Wasilla has forced the starting point for the competition to move 30 miles (48 km) farther north to Willow.

The Tongass National Forest, where conservationists are battling to stop the harvesting of 1,000-year-old trees, is the largest national forest in the United States.

WILLOW PTARMIGAN
FORGET-ME-NOT

C H U K C H I
S E A

RUSSIA
U.S.
RUSSIA

Bering Strait
Little Diomede I.

Cape Prince of Wales
only 2.5 miles from Russia

Nome

St. Lawrence I.

Yukon Delta
Emmonak
Mountain Village

St. Matthew I.
ALASKA MARITIME N.W.R.
Hooper Bay
YUKON D

Nelson I.
NAT I

WILDL

Nunivak I.
RE

B E R I N G
S E A

St. Paul
Pribilof Islands
ALASKA MARITIME N.W.R.

A L E U T I A N   I S L A N D S
IZEMBEK N.W.R.
Unimak I.
A l a
ALASK

Unalaska I.
Dutch Harbor
ALEUTIAN WORLD WAR II N.H.A.
Unalaska
Sanak I.

Umnak I.
Yunaska I.
Islands of Four Mountains
ALASKA   MARITIME   NATIONAL   WILDLIFE

⇐ NORTHERN METROPOLIS. Anchorage, established in 1915 as a construction port for the Alaska Railroad, sits in the shadow of the snow-covered Chugach Mountains.

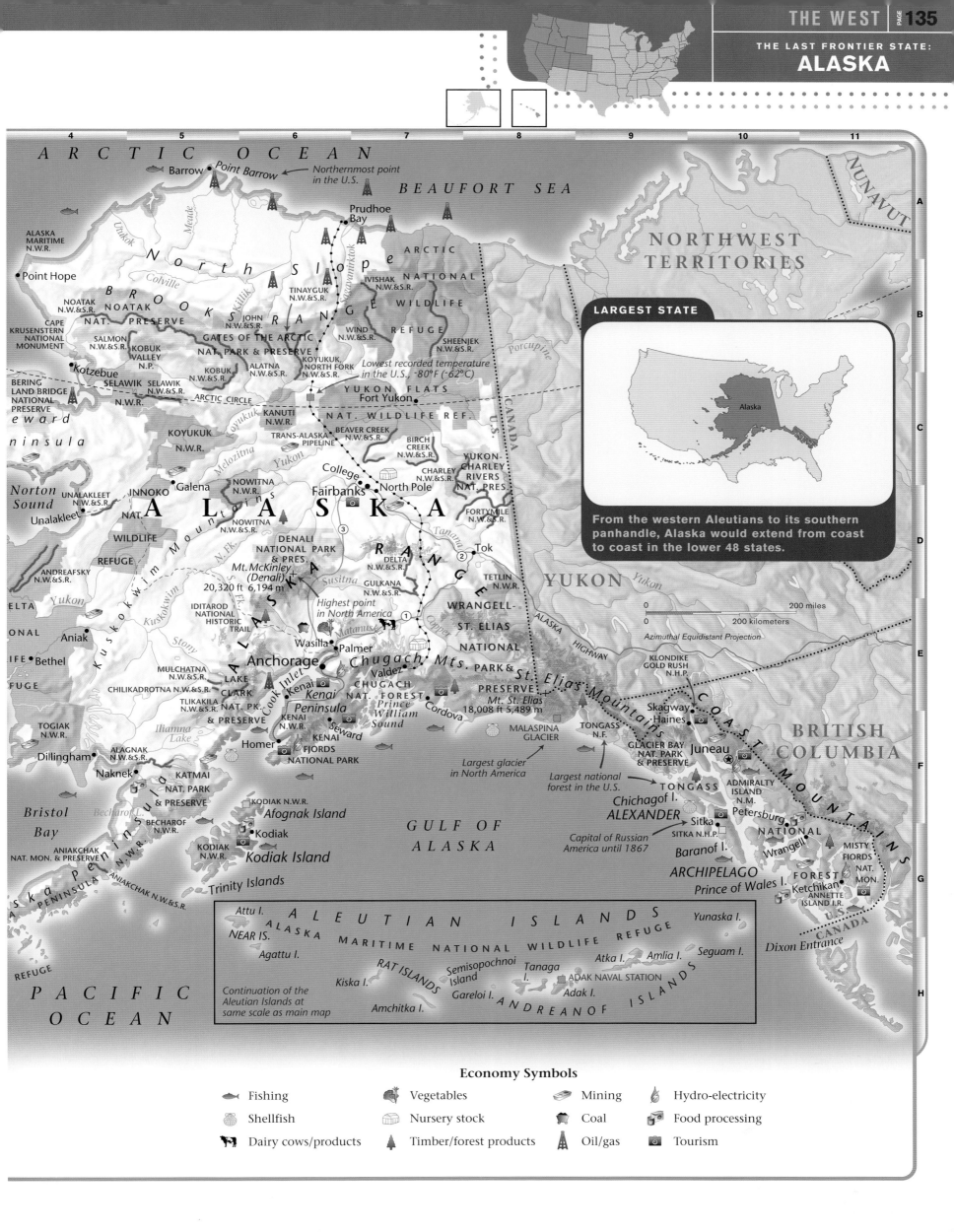

LARGEST STATE

From the western Aleutians to its southern panhandle, Alaska would extend from coast to coast in the lower 48 states.

Economy Symbols

Fishing · Vegetables · Mining · Hydro-electricity
Shellfish · Nursery stock · Coal · Food processing
Dairy cows/products · Timber/forest products · Oil/gas · Tourism

CALIFORNIA REPUBLIC

THE BASICS

STATS

Area
163,696 sq mi (423,972 sq km)

Population
36,553,215

Capital
Sacramento
Population 453,781

Largest city
Los Angeles
Population 3,849,378

Ethnic/racial groups
76.9% white; 12.4% Asian; 6.7% African
American; 1.2% Native American.
Hispanic (any race) 35.9%.

Industry
Electronic components and equipment,
computers and computer software,
tourism, food processing, entertainment,
clothing

Agriculture
Fruits and vegetables, dairy products,
cattle, forest products, commercial fishing

Statehood
September 9, 1850; 31st state

GEO WHIZ

Every December one of the largest
gatherings of northern elephant
seals in the world converges on
the beaches of Año Nuevo State
Reserve, south of San Francisco, to
rest, mate, and give birth.

The Monterey Bay Aquarium has
been working to save endangered
sea otters for 20 years.
Rescued animals that
cannot be rehabilitated for
re-release into the wild find a
permanent home at the aquarium.

Castroville, known as the Artichoke
Capital of the World, crowned
future movie legend Marilyn Monroe
its first-ever artichoke queen in 1947.

CALIFORNIA QUAIL
GOLDEN POPPY

CALIFORNIA

The coast of what is now California was visited by Spanish and English explorers in the mid-1500s, but colonization did not begin until 1769 when the first of 21 Spanish missions was established at San Diego. The missions, built to bring Christianity to the many native people living in the area, eventually extended up the coast as far as Sonoma along a road known as El Camino Real. The U.S. gained control of California in 1847, following a war with Mexico. The next year gold was discovered near Sutter's Mill, triggering a gold rush and migration from the eastern U.S. and around the world. Today, California is the most populous state, and its economy ranks above that of most of the world's countries. It is a major source of fruits, nuts, and vegetables, accounting for more than half of the U.S. output. The state is an industrial leader, producing jet aircraft, ships, and high-tech equipment. It is also a center for the entertainment industry.

⇧ ENGINEERING WONDER. Stretching more than a mile (1.6 km) across the entrance to San Francisco Bay, the Golden Gate Bridge opened to traffic in 1937. The bridge is painted vermilion orange, a color chosen in part because it is visible in fog.

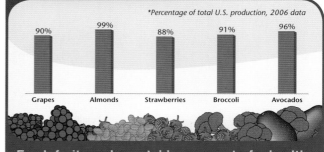

BOUNTIFUL HARVEST

*Percentage of total U.S. production, 2006 data

Grapes	Almonds	Strawberries	Broccoli	Avocados
90%	99%	88%	91%	96%

Fresh fruits and vegetables are part of a healthy
diet. California leads the country in the overall
production of these beneficial crops.

⇦ FOREST GIANT. Sequoias in Yosemite National Park's Mariposa Grove exceed 200 feet (61 m), making them the world's tallest trees. The trees, some of which are 3,000 years old, grow in isolated groves on the western slopes of the Sierra Nevada.

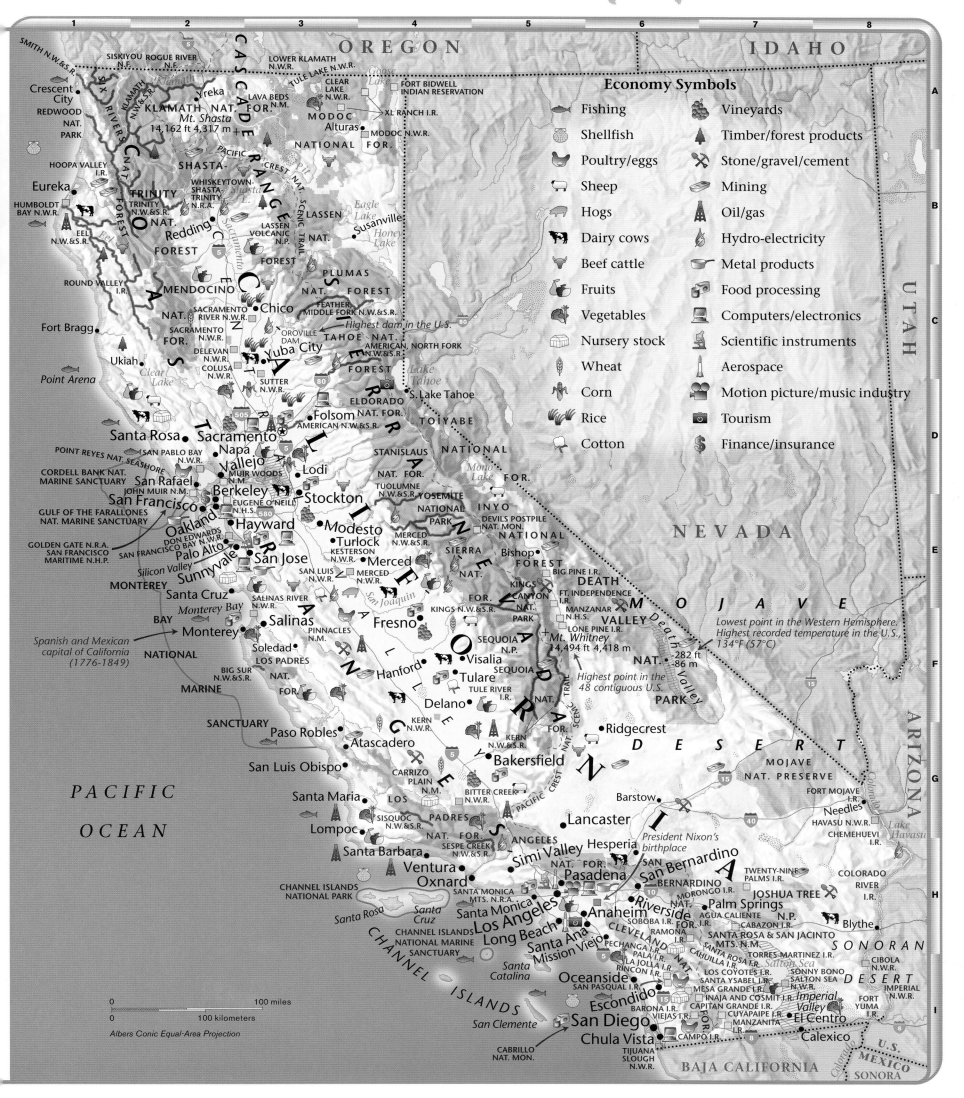

THE BASICS

STATS

Area
104,094 sq mi (269,602 sq km)

Population
4,861,515

Capital
Denver
Population 566,974

Largest city
Denver
Population 566,974

Ethnic/racial groups
90.1% white; 4.1% African American; 2.6% Asian; 1.1% Native American. Hispanic (any race) 19.7%.

Industry
Real estate, government, durable goods, communications, health and other services, nondurable goods, transportation

Agriculture
Cattle, corn, wheat, dairy products, hay

Statehood
August 1, 1876; 38th state

GEO WHIZ

The Black Canyon of the Gunnison is one of the newest national parks in the Rockies. As it flows through the canyon, the Gunnison River drops an average of 95 feet (29 m) per mile—one of the steepest descents in North America. The craggy rock walls are a mecca for rock climbers.

Colorado's lynx population is making a comeback, thanks to a program that releases wild cats captured in Canada into Colorado's southern Rockies. The population in the wild has gone from 1 in 1973 to 170 in 2006.

LARK BUNTING
COLUMBINE

COLORADO

Indians were the earliest inhabitants of present-day Colorado. Some were cliff dwellers; others were plains dwellers. Spanish explorers arrived in Colorado in 1541. In 1803 eastern Colorado became U.S. territory as part of the Louisiana Purchase. Gold was discovered in 1858, and thousands were attracted by the prospect of quick wealth. The sudden jump in population led to conflict with native Cheyennes and Arapahos over control of the land, but the settlers prevailed. Completion of the transcontinental railroad in 1869 helped link Colorado to the eastern states and opened its doors for growth. Cattle ranching and farming developed on the High Plains of eastern Colorado, while the mountainous western part of the state focused on mining. Today, mining is still important in Colorado, but the focus has shifted to energy resources—oil, natural gas, and coal. Agriculture generates more than $15 billion each year, mostly cattle and dairy products. And Colorado's majestic mountains attract thousands of tourists each year.

⇑ THRILLING SPORT. Colorado's snow-covered mountains attract winter sports enthusiasts from near and far. In the past skis were used by gold prospectors. Today skiing and snowboarding are big moneymakers in the state's recreation and tourism industry.

⇐ ANCIENT CULTURE. Ancestral Puebloans lived from about A.D. 600 to A.D. 1300 in the canyons that today are a part of Mesa Verde National Park. More than 600 stone structures were built on protected cliffs of the canyon walls; others were located on mesas. These dwellings hold many clues to a past way of life.

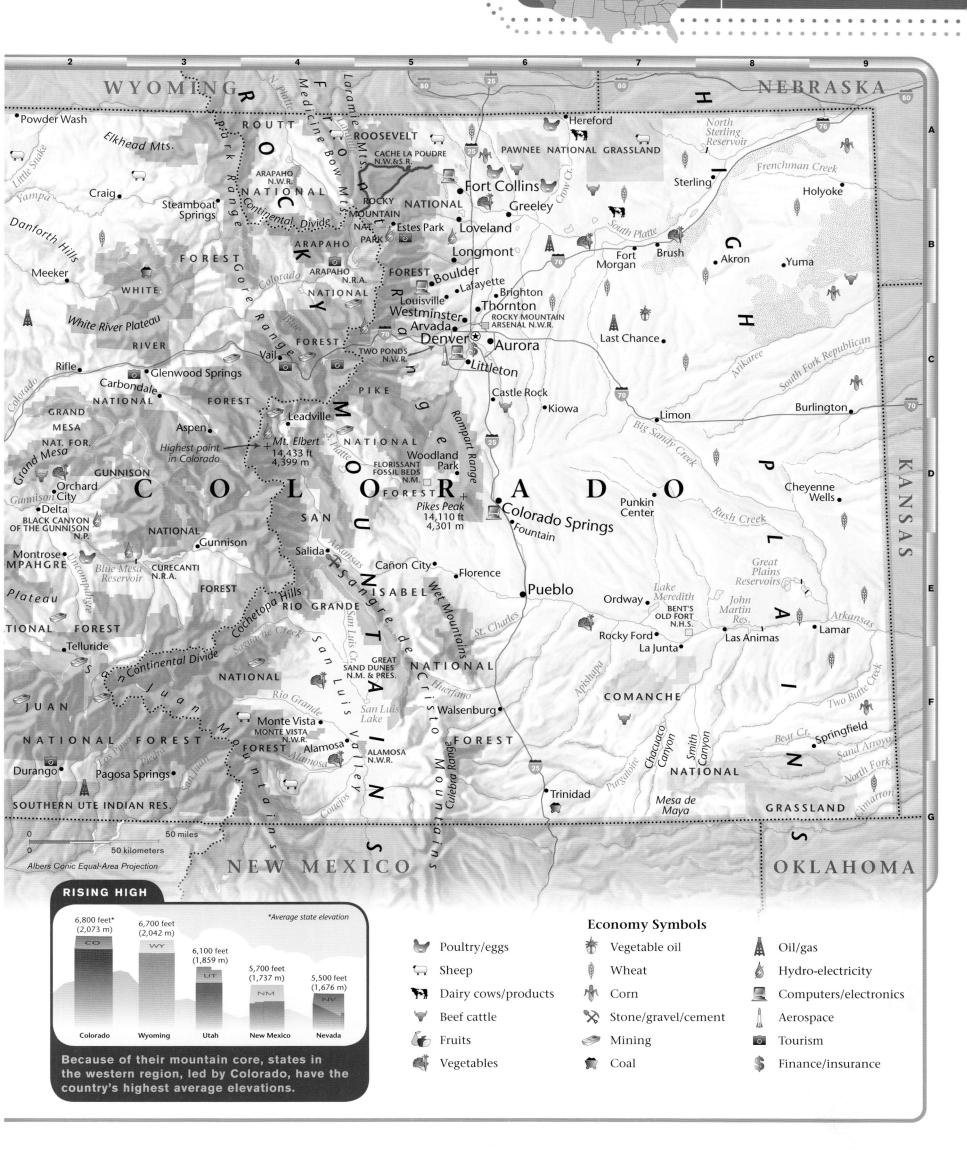

2   3   4   5   6   7   8   9

WYOMING   NEBRASKA

- Powder Wash
Little Snake
Elkhead Mts.
ROUTT
Yampa
- Craig
Danforth Hills
- Steamboat Springs
- Meeker
ARAPAHO N.W.R.
NATIONAL
Park Range
FOREST
WHITE
White River Plateau
RIVER
Continental Divide
Colorado
- Rifle
NATIONAL
- Carbondale
- Glenwood Springs
Colorado
GRAND MESA
NAT. FOR.
Grand Mesa
FOREST
- Aspen
BLACK CANYON OF THE GUNNISON N.P.
Orchard City
- Delta
- Montrose
UNCOMPAHGRE
Plateau
Gunnison River
NATIONAL
Blue Mesa Reservoir
CURECANTI N.R.A.
- Gunnison
SAN
NATIONAL FOREST
NATIONAL FOREST
- Telluride
San Miguel
San Juan
Continental Divide
JUAN
San Juan Mountains
NATIONAL FOREST
- Durango
- Pagosa Springs
Los Pinos
Piedra
SOUTHERN UTE INDIAN RES.
San Juan

ROCKY
N. Platte
Laramie
Medicine Bow Mts.
Front Range
Laramie Mts.
ROOSEVELT
CACHE LA POUDRE N.W.&S.R.
ARAPAHO N.W.R.
NATIONAL
ROCKY MOUNTAIN NAT. PARK
Estes Park
ARAPAHO N.R.A.
NATIONAL
FOREST
Colorado
Gore Range
Blue
FOREST
- Vail
MOUNTAIN
Continental Divide
- Leadville
+ Mt. Elbert 14,433 ft 4,399 m
Highest point in Colorado
S. Platte
NATIONAL
FLORISSANT FOSSIL BEDS N.M.
FOREST
Rampart Range
Woodland Park
Pikes Peak 14,110 ft 4,301 m
SAN
Arkansas
- Salida
Cochetopa Hills
San Luis Cr.
RIO GRANDE
NATIONAL
Saguache Creek
ISABEL
Front Range
PIKE

NATIONAL

- Fort Collins
- Greeley
- Loveland
- Longmont
- Boulder
- Lafayette
- Louisville
Westminster
Arvada
- Brighton
- Thornton
ROCKY MOUNTAIN ARSENAL N.W.R.
TWO PONDS N.W.R.
Denver ★
- Aurora
Littleton
- Castle Rock
- Kiowa

- Hereford
PAWNEE NATIONAL GRASSLAND
- Sterling
North Sterling Reservoir
Frenchman Creek
- Holyoke
Crow Cr.
South Platte
- Fort Morgan
- Brush
- Akron
- Yuma
HIGH
- Last Chance
Arikaree
South Fork Republican
- Limon
- Burlington
Big Sandy Creek
Rush Creek
- Cheyenne Wells
PLAINS
- Punkin Center
Great Plains Reservoirs
John Martin Res.
- Lamar
Arkansas
- Ordway
Lake Meredith
BENT'S OLD FORT N.H.S.
- Rocky Ford
- Las Animas
- La Junta
Great Plains
COMANCHE
Bear Cr.
- Springfield
Two Butte Creek
Sand Arroyo
North Fork
NATIONAL
Chacuaco Canyon
Smith Canyon
GRASSLAND
Cimarron

KANSAS

COLORADO
MOUNTAINS
Range
- Cañon City
- Florence
- Pueblo
St. Charles
Wet Mountains
Huerfano
Sangre de Cristo
- Colorado Springs
- Fountain
Apishapa

GREAT SAND DUNES N.M. & PRES.
Rio Grande
San Luis Valley
San Luis Lake
- Monte Vista
MONTE VISTA N.W.R.
- Alamosa
ALAMOSA N.W.R.
Alamosa
Conejos
NATIONAL
Culebra Range
FOREST
- Walsenburg
Purgatoire
- Trinidad
Mesa de Maya

NEW MEXICO   OKLAHOMA

0   50 miles
0   50 kilometers
Albers Conic Equal-Area Projection

Economy Symbols

Poultry/eggs	Vegetable oil
Sheep	Wheat
Dairy cows/products	Corn
Beef cattle	Stone/gravel/cement
Fruits	Mining
Vegetables	Coal

Oil/gas
Hydro-electricity
Computers/electronics
Aerospace
Tourism
Finance/insurance

HAWAI'I

1   2

Some 1,500 years ago, Polynesians traveling in large canoes arrived from the south to settle the volcanic islands that make up Hawai'i. In 1778 Captain James Cook claimed the islands for Britain, and soon Hawai'i became a center of the whaling industry and a major producer of sugarcane. The spread of sugarcane plantations led to the importation of workers from Asia. Hawai'i became a U.S. territory in 1900. Naval installations, established as fueling depots and to protect U.S. interests in the Pacific, were attacked by the Japanese in 1941, an act that officially brought the U.S. into World War II. In 1959 Hawai'i became the 50th state. Tourism, agriculture, and the military, with bases centered on O'ahu's Pearl Harbor, are the cornerstone of Hawai'i's economy today. Jet airline service makes the distant islands accessible to tourists from both the mainland U.S. and Asia as well as from Australia and New Zealand. Hawai'i is still a major producer of sugarcane, along with nursery products and pineapples.

THE BASICS

STATS

Area
10,931 sq mi (28,311 sq km)

Population
1,283,388

Capital
Honolulu
Population 377,357

Largest city
Honolulu
Population 377,357

Ethnic/racial groups
40.0% Asian; 28.6% white; 9.1% Hawaiian/Pacific Islander; 2.5% African American. Hispanic (any race) 7.8%.

Industry
Tourism, trade, finance, food processing, petroleum refining, stone, clay, glass products

Agriculture
Sugarcane, pineapples, nursery stock, tropical fruit, livestock, macadamia nuts

Statehood
August 21, 1959; 50th state

GEO WHIZ

The shallow waters off the coast of Hawai'i are home to some of the world's most interesting sea creatures: marine worms. They were among the first sea animals more than 500 million years ago.

Hawai'i is the most isolated population center on Earth. It is more than 2,300 miles (3,700 km) from California, 3,850 miles (6,196 km) from Japan, and 4,900 miles (7,886 km) from China.

Everywhere else in the world caterpillars feed on plants. In Hawai'i there are 20 species that eat meat. Scientists have recorded the world's only known carnivorous caterpillars munching on ants.

You can ski two different ways on the same day in Hawai'i: on water at the beach and on snow on the slopes of Mauna Kea, a 13,796-foot- (4,205-m-) high volcano on the Big Island.

HAWAIIAN GOOSE (NENE)
HIBISCUS

One of the world's rainiest spots

KAUA'I
Princeville   KILAUEA POINT N.W.R.
HANALEI N.W.R.
Wai'ale'ale
5,148 ft
1,569 m
Kapa'a
Hanama'ulu
Lehua I.
Kaulakahi Channel
Kekaha
Lihu'e
Pu'uwai
Kalaheo
NI'IHAU

⇧ ISLAND PARADISE. High-rise hotels light up Waikiki, the center of Honolulu's tourist industry. Thousands of visitors flock to the islands each year to enjoy the warm climate, sandy beaches, and rich, multicultural heritage of Hawai'i.

Kure Atoll   Midway Islands
Pearl and Hermes Atoll
N O R T H W E S T E R N   H A W A I
Lisianski I.   Laysan I.
Maro Reef

0   400 miles
0   400 kilometers
Oblique Mercator Projection

DANGER FROM BELOW

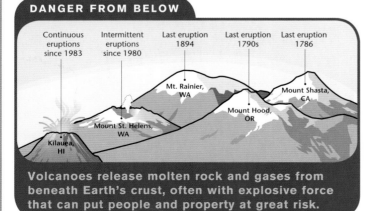

Continuous eruptions since 1983
Intermittent eruptions since 1980
Last eruption 1894
Last eruption 1790s
Last eruption 1786

Mt. Rainier, WA
Mount Hood, OR
Mount Shasta, CA
Mount St. Helens, WA
Kilauea, HI

Volcanoes release molten rock and gases from beneath Earth's crust, often with explosive force that can put people and property at great risk.

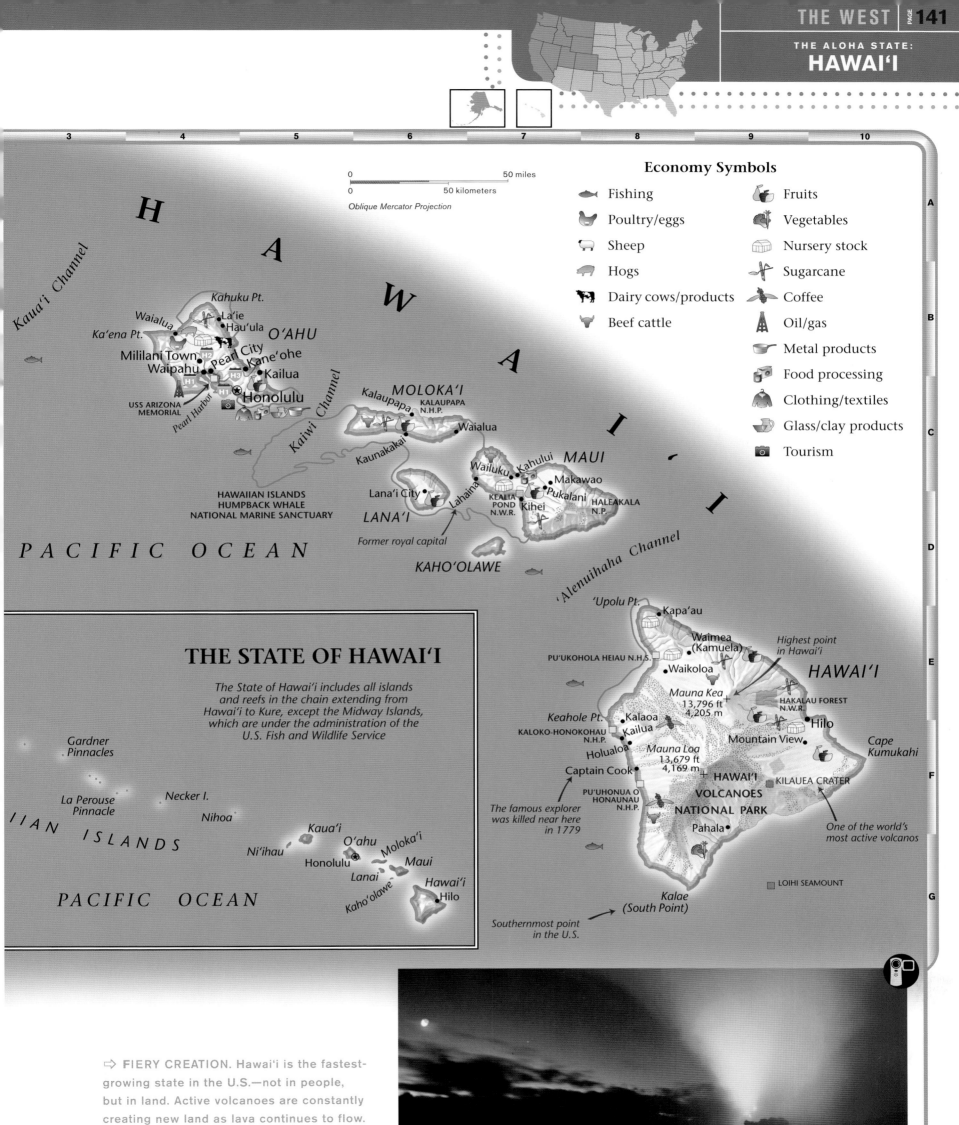

3 4 5 6 7 8 9 10

0 _____ 50 miles
0 _____ 50 kilometers
Oblique Mercator Projection

Economy Symbols

- Fishing
- Poultry/eggs
- Sheep
- Hogs
- Dairy cows/products
- Beef cattle
- Fruits
- Vegetables
- Nursery stock
- Sugarcane
- Coffee
- Oil/gas
- Metal products
- Food processing
- Clothing/textiles
- Glass/clay products
- Tourism

H A W A I I

Kaua'i Channel

Kahuku Pt.
Waialua
La'ie
Ka'ena Pt.
Hau'ula
O'AHU
Mililani Town
Pearl City
Kane'ohe
Waipahu
H2
H3
Kailua
H1
USS ARIZONA MEMORIAL
Honolulu
Pearl Harbor
Kaiwi Channel

MOLOKA'I
Kalaupapa
KALAUPAPA N.H.P.
Waialua
Kaunakakai

HAWAIIAN ISLANDS HUMPBACK WHALE NATIONAL MARINE SANCTUARY

Wailuku
Kahului
MAUI
Makawao
Lana'i City
Pukalani
Lahaina
KEALIA POND N.W.R.
Kihei
HALEAKALA N.P.

LANA'I

PACIFIC OCEAN

Former royal capital

KAHO'OLAWE

'Alenuihaha Channel

'Upolu Pt.
Kapa'au
Waimea (Kamuela)
Highest point in Hawai'i
PU'UKOHOLA HEIAU N.H.S.
Waikoloa
HAWAI'I
Mauna Kea
13,796 ft
4,205 m
HAKALAU FOREST N.W.R.
Keahole Pt.
Kalaoa
KALOKO-HONOKOHAU N.H.P.
Kailua
Mountain View
Hilo
Cape Kumukahi
Holualoa
Mauna Loa
13,679 ft
4,169 m
Captain Cook
HAWAI'I VOLCANOES NATIONAL PARK
KILAUEA CRATER
PU'UHONUA O HONAUNAU N.H.P.
The famous explorer was killed near here in 1779
Pahala
One of the world's most active volcanos
LOIHI SEAMOUNT
Kalae (South Point)
Southernmost point in the U.S.

THE STATE OF HAWAI'I

The State of Hawai'i includes all islands and reefs in the chain extending from Hawai'i to Kure, except the Midway Islands, which are under the administration of the U.S. Fish and Wildlife Service.

Gardner Pinnacles

La Perouse Pinnacle
Necker I.
Nihoa

Kaua'i
Ni'ihau
O'ahu
Moloka'i
Honolulu
Lanai
Maui
Kaho'olawe
Hawai'i
Hilo

IIAN ISLANDS

PACIFIC OCEAN

⇨ FIERY CREATION. Hawai'i is the fastest-growing state in the U.S.—not in people, but in land. Active volcanoes are constantly creating new land as lava continues to flow. The Pu'u 'O'o vent on Kīlauea has added more than 568 acres (230 ha) of new land since it began erupting in 1983.

THE GEM STATE:
IDAHO

IDAHO

Some of the earliest Native American sites in what is now Idaho date back 10,000 to 12,000 years. In the 18th and early 19th centuries, contact between native people and Europeans brought not only trade and cultural change but also diseases that wiped out many native groups. Present-day Idaho was part of the 1803 Louisiana Purchase, and in 1805 it was explored during the famous Lewis and Clark expedition. In 1843 wagons crossed into Idaho on the Oregon Trail. The arrival of white settlers brought conflict with the Indians, which continued until 1890 when Idaho became a state. Today, farming plays an important role in Idaho's economy. More than one-fifth of the land is planted with crops, especially wheat, sugar beets, barley, and potatoes. The state supports the use of alternative sources of energy, including geo-thermal, ethanol, wind, and biomass. The economy has diversified to include manufacturing and high-tech industries. The state's rugged natural beauty also attracts tourists year-round.

⇧ WOOLLY RUSH HOUR. Sheep fill a roadway in Idaho's Salmon River Valley. The herds move twice a year. In the spring they migrate north to mountain pastures. In the fall they return to the Snake River plains in the south.

ANCIENT STAPLE FOOD

Annual harvest, 2006 data

121 million hundredweight — Idaho
89 million hundredweight — Washington
29 million hundredweight — Wisconsin
25 million hundredweight — North Dakota
22 million hundredweight — Colorado

Potatoes were first cultivated by Indians in the mountains of South America. Today, Idaho leads in U.S. potato production.

⇧ TIMBER! More than 40 percent of Idaho's land area is tree-covered, much of it in national forests. Lumber and paper products, most of which are sold to other states, are important to the state economy.

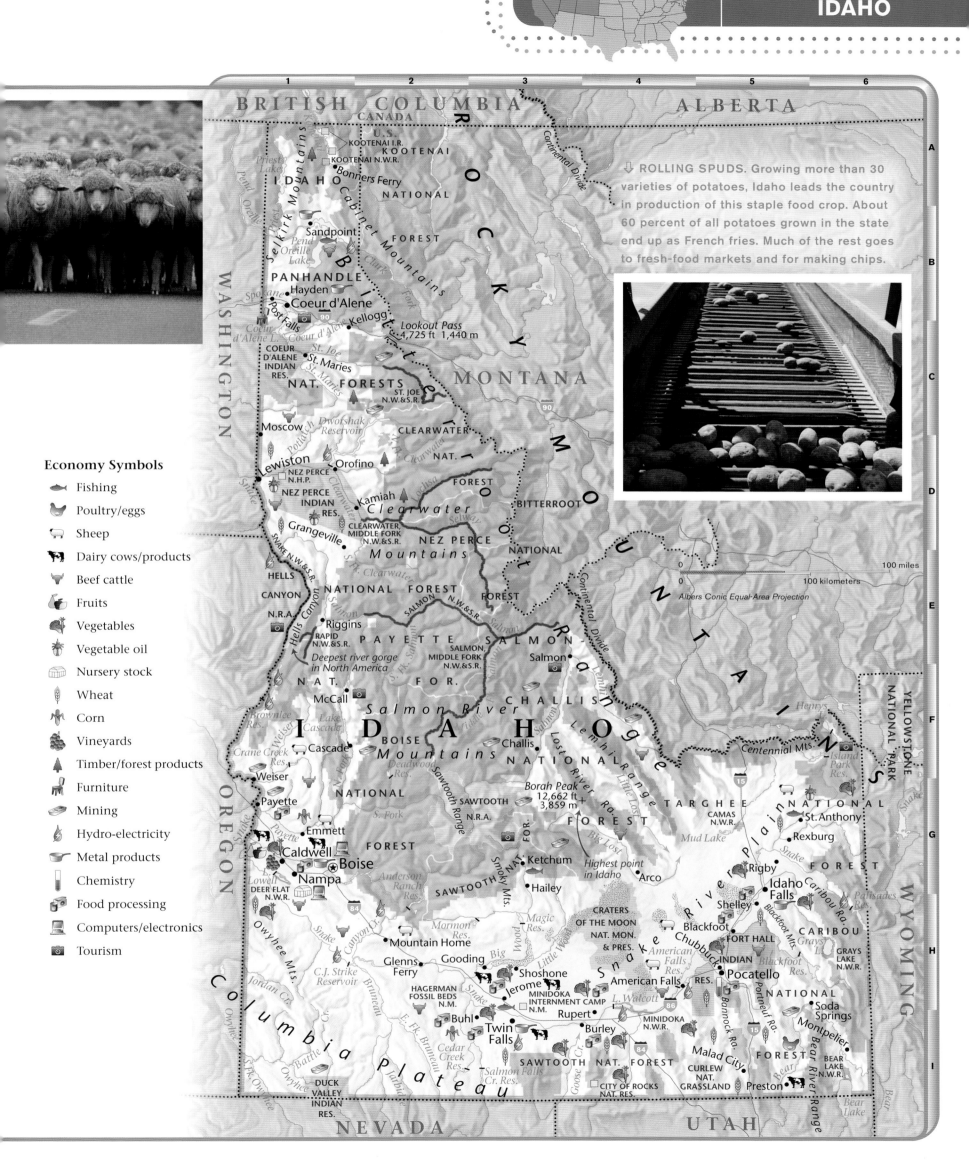

⬇ ROLLING SPUDS. Growing more than 30 varieties of potatoes, Idaho leads the country in production of this staple food crop. About 60 percent of all potatoes grown in the state end up as French fries. Much of the rest goes to fresh-food markets and for making chips.

Economy Symbols

- 🐟 Fishing
- 🐓 Poultry/eggs
- 🐑 Sheep
- 🐄 Dairy cows/products
- 🐂 Beef cattle
- 🍎 Fruits
- 🥬 Vegetables
- 🌻 Vegetable oil
- Nursery stock
- 🌾 Wheat
- 🌽 Corn
- 🍇 Vineyards
- 🌲 Timber/forest products
- 🪑 Furniture
- Mining
- Hydro-electricity
- Metal products
- 🧪 Chemistry
- 📷 Food processing
- 💻 Computers/electronics
- 📷 Tourism

THE TREASURE STATE: MONTANA

MONTANA

Long before the arrival of Europeans, numerous native groups lived and hunted in the plains and mountains of present-day Montana. While contact between European explorers and Native Americans was often peaceful, Montana was the site of the historic 1876 Battle of the Little Bighorn, in which Lakota (Sioux) and Cheyenne warriors defeated George Armstrong Custer's troops. In the mid-19th century the discovery of gold and silver attracted many prospectors, and later cattle ranching became big business, adding to tensions with the Indians. Montana became the 41st state in 1889. Today, Indians still make up more than 6 percent of the state's population—only four other states have a larger percent. Agriculture is an important part of the economy, producing wheat, hay, and barley as well as beef cattle. Mining and timber industries have seen a decline, but service industries and tourism are growing. Montana's natural environment, including Glacier and Yellowstone National Parks, remains one of its greatest resources.

THE BASICS

STATS

Area
147,042 sq mi (380,840 sq km)

Population
957,861

Capital
Helena
Population 26,718

Largest city
Billings
Population 100,148

Ethnic/racial groups
90.8% white; 6.4% Native American. .6% Asian; .4% African American. Hispanic (any race) 2.5%.

Industry
Forest products, food processing, mining, construction, tourism

Agriculture
Wheat, cattle, barley, hay, sugar beets, dairy products

Statehood
November 8, 1889; 41st state

GEO WHIZ

The fossil of a dinosaur about the size of a large turkey is being called the missing link between Asian and North American horned dinosaurs. Paleontologist Jack Horner, who served as the model for the character of Alan Grant in the *Jurassic Park* movies, discovered the fossil while sitting on it during a lunch break at a dig near Choteau.

Montana is the only state with river systems that empty into the Gulf of Mexico, Hudson Bay, and the Pacific Ocean.

Grasshopper Glacier is littered with the bodies of thousands of grasshoppers that became trapped in the ice sometime before the species became extinct 200 years ago.

WESTERN MEADOWLARK

BITTERROOT

⇧ STEP BACK IN TIME. Just like in the past, Montana ranchers move their cattle herds from low winter pastures to higher elevations for summer grazing. Some ranches allow adventurous tourists to participate in the drives.

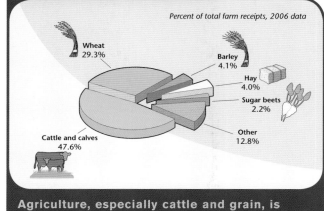

ECONOMIC CORNERSTONE

Percent of total farm receipts, 2006 data

- Wheat 29.3%
- Barley 4.1%
- Hay 4.0%
- Sugar beets 2.2%
- Other 12.8%
- Cattle and calves 47.6%

Agriculture, especially cattle and grain, is important in Montana's economy, adding more than $2 billion to the state income each year.

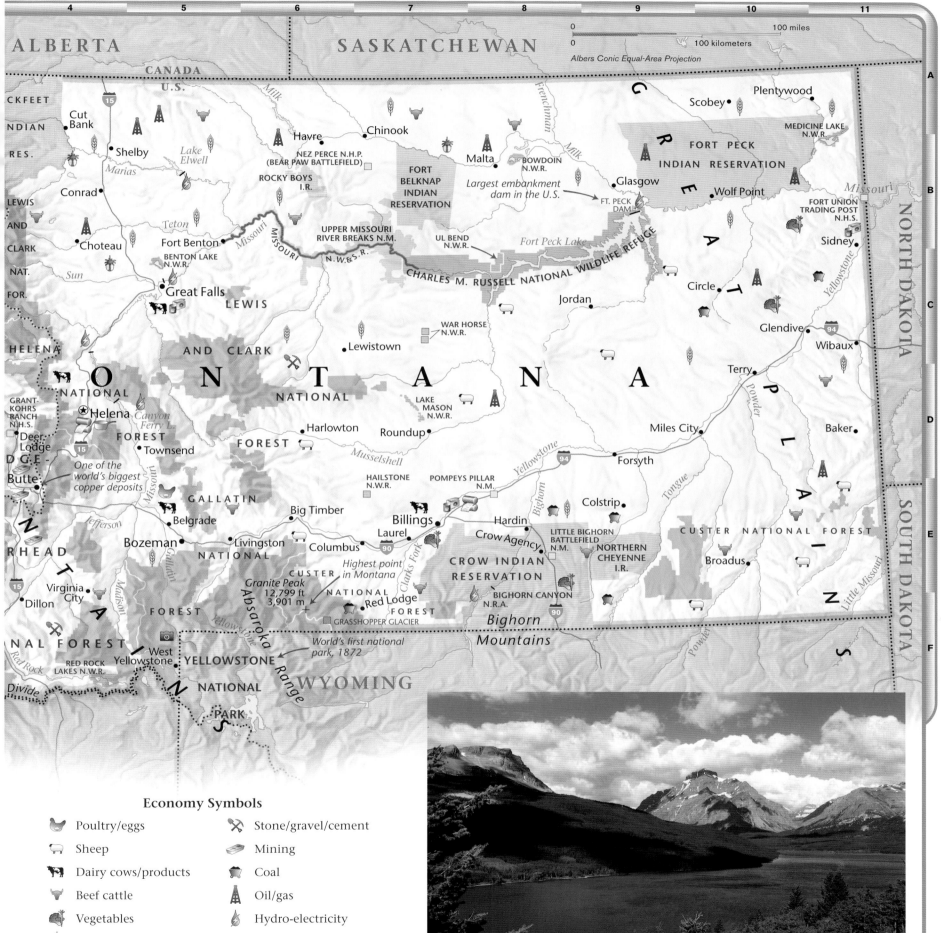

ALBERTA

SASKATCHEWAN

0   100 miles
0   100 kilometers
Albers Conic Equal-Area Projection

CANADA
U.S.

CKFEET
NDIAN
RES.

Cut Bank
Shelby
Conrad

Lake Elwell
Marias

LEWIS
AND
CLARK
NAT.
FOR.

Choteau

Teton

Fort Benton
BENTON LAKE N.W.R.

Sun

Great Falls

Havre
Chinook

NEZ PERCE N.H.P.
(BEAR PAW BATTLEFIELD)
ROCKY BOYS I.R.

Milk

FORT BELKNAP INDIAN RESERVATION

Malta

UPPER MISSOURI RIVER BREAKS N.M.
N.W.&S.R.

Missouri

BOWDOIN N.W.R.

UL BEND N.W.R.

Frenchman

Milk

Largest embankment dam in the U.S.

Glasgow
FT. PECK DAM

Fort Peck Lake

Scobey
Plentywood

MEDICINE LAKE N.W.R.

FORT PECK INDIAN RESERVATION

Wolf Point

FORT UNION TRADING POST N.H.S.

Missouri

Sidney

Circle

Yellowstone

CHARLES M. RUSSELL NATIONAL WILDLIFE REFUGE

Jordan

LEWIS

AND CLARK

MONTANA

NATIONAL

WAR HORSE N.W.R.

Lewistown

LAKE MASON N.W.R.

Glendive
Wibaux

NORTH DAKOTA

Terry

Powder

HELENA

NATIONAL

Helena

Canyon Ferry L.

FOREST

Townsend

Harlowton

Roundup

Musselshell

FOREST

Miles City

Forsyth

Baker

GREAT PLAINS

SOUTH DAKOTA

GRANT-KOHRS RANCH N.H.S.
Deer Lodge

DGE-
Butte

One of the world's biggest copper deposits

15

Jefferson

Madison

N

HAILSTONE N.W.R.

GALLATIN

Belgrade

Bozeman

Gallatin

NATIONAL

Big Timber

Livingston

Columbus

POMPEYS PILLAR N.M.

Billings

Laurel

Yellowstone

94

Tongue

Colstrip

Hardin

Crow Agency

LITTLE BIGHORN BATTLEFIELD N.M.

NORTHERN CHEYENNE I.R.

Bighorn

CUSTER NATIONAL FOREST

Broadus

Little Missouri

RHEAD

15

Virginia City

Dillon

FOREST

Clarks Fork

CUSTER

NATIONAL

FOREST

Red Lodge

Highest point in Montana
Granite Peak
12,799 ft
3,901 m

GRASSHOPPER GLACIER

Absaroka Range

CROW INDIAN RESERVATION

BIGHORN CANYON N.R.A.

Bighorn
Mountains

90

Powder

Red Rock

Divide

NAL FOREST

RED ROCK LAKES N.W.R.

West Yellowstone

YELLOWSTONE

NATIONAL

PARK

World's first national park, 1872

Yellowstone

WYOMING

Economy Symbols

- Poultry/eggs
- Sheep
- Dairy cows/products
- Beef cattle
- Vegetables
- Vegetable oil
- Nursery stock
- Wheat
- Timber/forest products
- Printing/publishing
- Stone/gravel/cement
- Mining
- Coal
- Oil/gas
- Hydro-electricity
- Metal manufacturing
- Metal products
- Food processing
- Tourism

⇧ NATURAL BEAUTY. The rugged mountains and glacier-fed rivers of Montana offer many opportunities to outdoor lovers, including hiking and backpacking as well as fishing in summer, skiing in winter, and year-round wildlife viewing.

THE BASICS

STATS

Area
110,561 sq mi (286,352 sq km)

Population
2,565,382

Capital
Carson City
Population 55,311

Largest city
Las Vegas
Population 552,539

Ethnic/racial groups
81.7% white; 7.9% African American;
6.0% Asian; 1.4% Native American.
Hispanic (any race) 24.4%.

Industry
Tourism and gaming, mining, printing
and publishing, food processing,
electrical equipment

Agriculture
Cattle, hay, dairy products

Statehood
October 31, 1864; 36th state

GEO WHIZ

Lehman Caves, in Great Basin
National Park, contains the best
collection of shield, or angel wing,
formations in the country.

The Applegate Trail, named for two
brothers who first traveled it in 1846,
offered a shorter alternative to
the Oregon Trail. The trail
headed south from Idaho,
across Nevada's Black Rock
Desert into northern California
and then north into Oregon.

So many people claim to have seen
extraterrestrials along a 98-mile
(158-km) stretch of Nevada Highway
375 that the state transportation
board named it Extraterrestrial
Highway in 1996.

MOUNTAIN BLUEBIRD
SAGEBRUSH

NEVADA

Nevada's earliest settlers were native people about whom little is known. Around two thousand years ago, they began establishing permanent dwellings of clay and stone perched atop rocky ledges in what is today the state of Nevada. This was what Spanish explorers saw when they arrived in 1776. In years following, many expeditions passing through the area faced challenges of a difficult environment and native groups protecting their land. In the mid-1800s, gold and silver were discovered. In 1861, the Nevada Territory was created, and three years later statehood was granted. Today, the Nevada landscape is dotted with ghost towns—places once prosperous, but now abandoned except for curious tourists. Mining is now overshadowed by other economic activities. Casinos, modern hotels, and lavish entertainment attract thousands of visitors each year. Hoover Dam, on the Colorado River, supplies water and power to much of Nevada as well as two adjoining states. But water promises to be a challenge to Nevada's future growth.

⇧ TURNING BACK TIME. The Luxor, recreating a scene from ancient Egypt, is one of the many hotel-casinos that attract thousands of tourists to the four-mile (7-km) section of Las Vegas, known as the Strip.

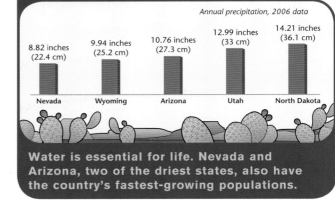

THIRSTY LAND

Annual precipitation, 2006 data

Nevada	Wyoming	Arizona	Utah	North Dakota
8.82 inches (22.4 cm)	9.94 inches (25.2 cm)	10.76 inches (27.3 cm)	12.99 inches (33 cm)	14.21 inches (36.1 cm)

Water is essential for life. Nevada and Arizona, two of the driest states, also have the country's fastest-growing populations.

⇦ PRICKLY GARDEN. Nevada's desert environment includes many varieties of cactuses. Saguaro and aloe plants as well as other xerophytes—plants that tolerate very dry conditions—thrive in this rocky garden.

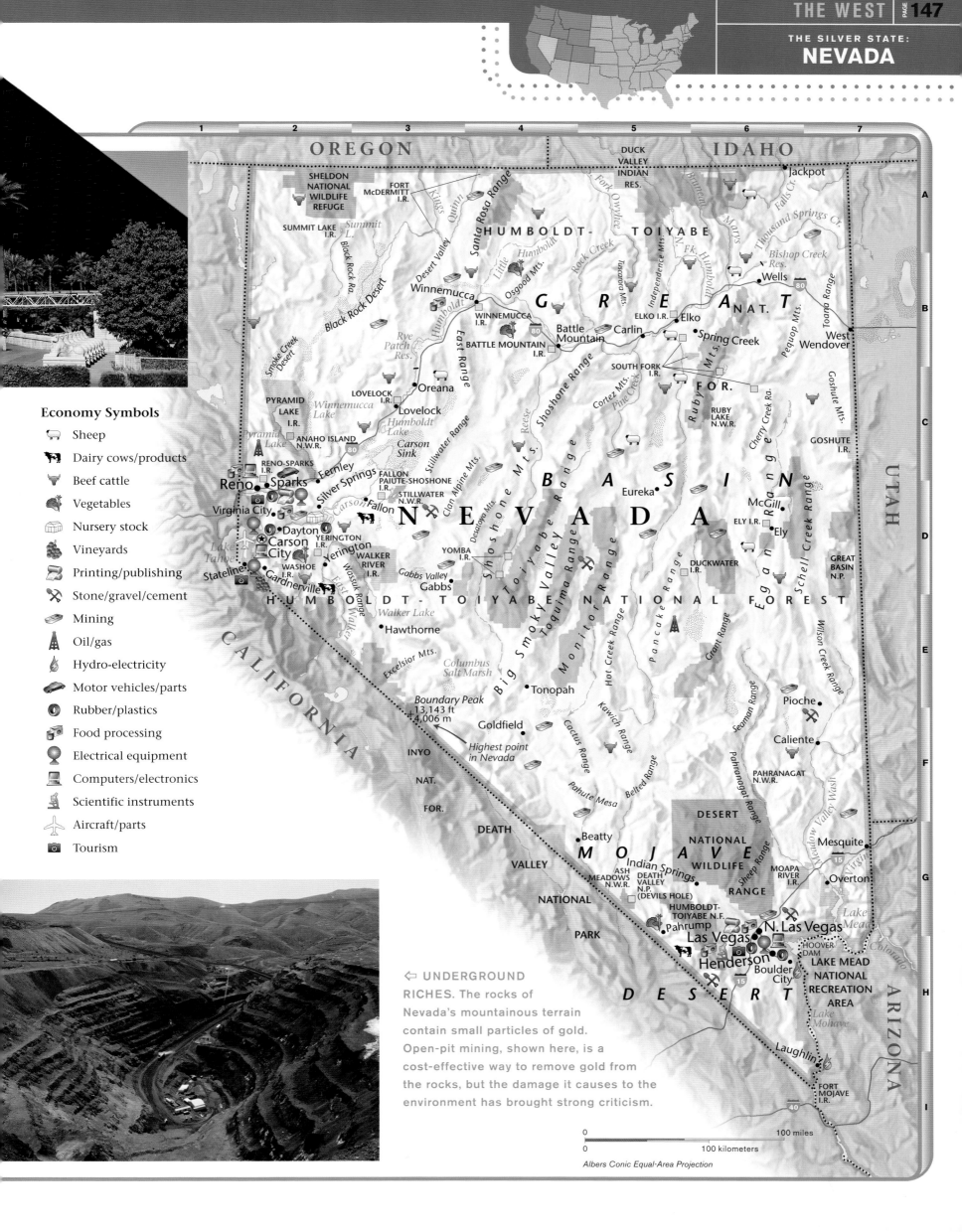

OREGON   DUCK   IDAHO
                                          VALLEY
                                          INDIAN
                                          RES.   • Jackpot

SHELDON   Falls Cr.
NATIONAL   FORT   Thousand Springs Cr.
WILDLIFE   McDERMITT   N. Fk. Humboldt
REFUGE   I.R.   Kings R.   Owyhee

SUMMIT LAKE   Summit   Quinn R.   Wells •
I.R.   L.   Bishop Creek
                       Santa Rosa Range   HUMBOLDT- TOIYABE   Res.
Black Rock Ra.   Independence Mts.
                          Little   Humboldt   Toana Range
Black Rock Desert   Desert Valley   Humboldt   G   R   E   A   T   N   A   T.
                                                    Rock Creek
Smoke Creek   Winnemucca •   Tuscarora Mts.
Desert   Osgood Mts.   ELKO I.R. Elko •   West
                     Humboldt R.   WINNEMUCCA   Carlin • • Spring Creek   Wendover
Rye   East Range   I.R.   Battle   FOR.   •
Patch   BATTLE   Mountain •   SOUTH FORK   Goshute Mts.
Res.   LOVELOCK   MOUNTAIN   I.R.   Cortez Mts.   Cherry Creek Ra.
PYRAMID   I.R.   Oreana •   I.R.   Pine Creek   Ruby
LAKE   Lovelock •   Reese R.   Shoshone Range   RUBY   GOSHUTE
I.R.   Winnemucca   Humboldt   B A S I N   LAKE   I.R.
Pyramid Lake   ANAHO ISLAND   Lake   Ruby Range N.W.R.
       N.W.R.   Carson   Clan Alpine Mts.
RENO-SPARKS   Sink   Stillwater Mts.   N E V A D A
Reno • Sparks • Fernley   Eureka •   McGill •
Virginia City • Silver Springs FALLON   STILLWATER   ELY I.R.
         • Dayton PAIUTE-SHOSHONE N.W.R.   • Ely
Lake   Carson Fallon I.R. STILLWATER   Toiyabe Range
Tahoe   City   YERINGTON I.R.   Shoshone Mts.   Egan Range GREAT
Stateline • • Yerington   YOMBA   Toquima Range   BASIN
Gardnerville   WASHOE WALKER I.R.   Big Smoky Valley   Schell Creek Range N.P.
         I.R.   RIVER   Gabbs Valley   Monitor Range   DUCKWATER
East Walker R.   I.R.   Gabbs •   I.R.
HUMBOLDT- TOIYABE   Walker Lake   N A T I O N A L   F O R E S T
         • Hawthorne   Pancake Range   Grant Range
Walker Lake   Wilson Creek Range
Excelsior Mts.   Columbus   Hot Creek Range
         Salt Marsh   Kawich Range   Seaman Range
Boundary Peak   • Tonopah   • Pioche
13,143 ft   Belted Range
↖ 4,006 m   Goldfield •   Cactus Range   • Caliente
Highest point   Pahute Mesa   PAHRANAGAT
in Nevada   N.W.R.
INYO   Pahranagat Range
         • Beatty   DESERT   Meadow Valley Wash
NAT.   NATIONAL
                         WILDLIFE   • Mesquite
FOR.   Indian Springs •   MOAPA
DEATH   ASH   DEATH   Sheep Range   RIVER
VALLEY   MEADOWS VALLEY   I.R.   • Overton
         N.W.R.   N.P.   M O J A V E RANGE   Lake
NATIONAL   (DEVILS HOLE)   HUMBOLDT-   Mead
                         TOIYABE N.F.   HOOVER
PARK   D E S E R T   Pahrump • N. Las Vegas DAM
                              Las Vegas • LAKE MEAD
⇐ UNDERGROUND   Henderson • NATIONAL
RICHES. The rocks of   Boulder RECREATION
Nevada's mountainous terrain   City •   AREA
contain small particles of gold.   Lake
Open-pit mining, shown here, is a   Mohave
cost-effective way to remove gold from   • Laughlin
the rocks, but the damage it causes to the   ARIZONA
environment has brought strong criticism.   FORT
                                   MOJAVE
                                   I.R.

CALIFORNIA

Economy Symbols

- Sheep
- Dairy cows/products
- Beef cattle
- Vegetables
- Nursery stock
- Vineyards
- Printing/publishing
- Stone/gravel/cement
- Mining
- Oil/gas
- Hydro-electricity
- Motor vehicles/parts
- Rubber/plastics
- Food processing
- Electrical equipment
- Computers/electronics
- Scientific instruments
- Aircraft/parts
- Tourism

0   100 miles
0   100 kilometers
Albers Conic Equal-Area Projection

STATE OF OREGON
1859

THE BASICS

STATS

Area
98,381 sq mi (254,806 sq km)

Population
3,747,455

Capital
Salem
Population 152,239

Largest city
Portland
Population 537,081

Ethnic/racial groups
90.5% white; 3.6% Asian; 1.9% African American; 1.4% Native American. Hispanic (any race) 10.2%.

Industry
Real estate, retail and wholesale trade, electronic equipment, health services, construction, forest products, business services

Agriculture
Nursery stock, hay, cattle, grass seed, wheat, dairy products, potatoes

Statehood
February 14, 1859; 33rd state

GEO WHIZ

To recover wetlands and save two endangered fish species, 100 tons of explosives were used to blast through levees so that water from the Williamson River could again flow into Upper Klamath Lake.

Crater Lake, at 1,943 feet (592 m), is the deepest in the United States. It fills a depression created when an eruption caused the top of a mountain to collapse. Wizard Island, at the center of the 6-mile- (10-km-) wide lake, is the top of a volcano.

Snow-covered Mount Hood dominates the Portland skyline. The peak is one of the most active volcanoes in the Cascade Range. Its last eruption occurred just a few years before Lewis and Clark reached the region.

WESTERN MEADOWLARK
OREGON GRAPE

OREGON

Long before the Oregon Trail brought settlers from the eastern U.S., Indians fished and hunted in Oregon's coastal waters and forested valleys. Spanish explorers sailed along Oregon's coast in 1543, and in the 18th century fur traders from Europe set up forts in the region. In the mid-1800s settlers began farming the rich soil of the Willamette Valley. Oregon achieved statehood in 1859, and by 1883 Oregon was linked to the East by railroad, and Portland had become an important shipping center. Today, forestry, fishing, and agriculture make up an important part of the state's economy, but Oregon is making an effort to diversify into manufacturing and high-tech industries, as well. Dams on the Columbia River generate inexpensive electricity to support energy-hungry industries, such as aluminum production. Computers, electronics, and research-based industries are expanding. The state's natural beauty—snow-capped volcanoes, old-growth forests, and rocky coastline—makes tourism an important growth industry.

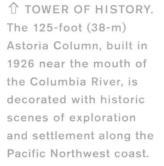

⇧ TOWER OF HISTORY. The 125-foot (38-m) Astoria Column, built in 1926 near the mouth of the Columbia River, is decorated with historic scenes of exploration and settlement along the Pacific Northwest coast.

⇦ CHANGING LANDSCAPE. Oregon's Pacific coast is a lesson on erosion and deposition. Rocky outcrops called sea stacks are leftovers of a former coastline that has been eroded by waves. The sandy beach is a result of eroded material being deposited along the shore.

PACIFIC OCEAN

Astoria
FT. CLATSOP NAT. MEM.
Seaside
CAPE MEARES N.W.R.
Tillamook
Trask
GRAND RONDE I.R.
Lincoln City
SIUSLAW
SILETZ I.R.
Newport
NATIONAL
FOREST
Florence
OREGON DUNES
N.R.A.
Reedsport
Umpqua
COOS, LOWER, UMPQUA, AND SUISLAW I.R.
Coos Bay
North Bend
Coos Bay
COQUILLE I.R.
Coos
Coquille
BANDON MARSH N.W.R.
Cape Blanco
ELK N.W.&S.R.
ROGUE N.W.&S.R.
Rogue
SISKIYOU
ILLINOIS N.W.&S.R.
Illinois
Gold Beach
NATIONAL
CHETCO N.W.&S.R.
Chetco
SMITH, N. FORK N.W.&S.R.
Brookings
FOREST
COAST

THE BEAVER STATE:
OREGON

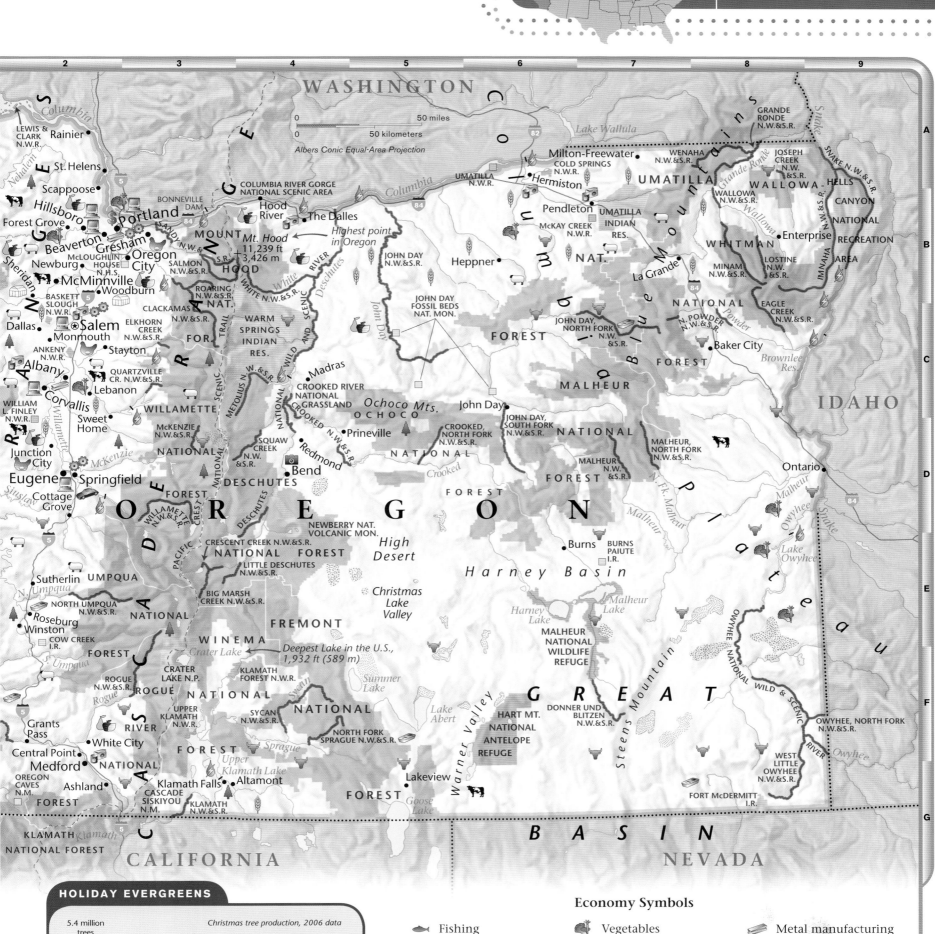

HOLIDAY EVERGREENS

Christmas tree production, 2006 data

- 5.4 million trees — Oregon
- 2.5 million trees — North Carolina
- 1.5 million trees — Michigan
- 1 million trees — Pennsylvania
- .5 million trees — Washington

Oregon's marine west coast climate provides an ideal environment for growing firs and spruce for the lucrative Christmas tree market.

Economy Symbols

- Fishing
- Shellfish
- Poultry/eggs
- Sheep
- Dairy cows/products
- Beef cattle
- Fruits
- Vegetables
- Nursery stock
- Wheat
- Timber/forest products
- Mining
- Hydro-electricity
- Machinery
- Metal manufacturing
- Motor vehicles/parts
- Food processing
- Computers/electronics
- Tourism
- Finance/insurance

THE BEEHIVE STATE: UTAH

UTAH

THE BASICS

STATS

Area
84,899 sq mi (219,888 sq km)

Population
2,645,330

Capital
Salt Lake City
Population 178,858

Largest city
Salt Lake City
Population 178,858

Ethnic/racial groups
93.5% white; 2.0% Asian; 1.3% Native American; 1.0% African American. Hispanic (any race) 11.2%.

Industry
Government, manufacturing, real estate, construction, health services, business services, banking

Agriculture
Cattle, dairy products, hay, poultry and eggs, wheat

Statehood
January 4, 1896; 45th state

GEO WHIZ

A giant, duck-billed dinosaur is among the many kinds of dinosaur fossils that have been found in the Grand Staircase-Escalante National Monument. Scientists think the plant eater was at least 30 feet (9 m) long and had a mouthful of 300 teeth.

Drought has caused the level of Lake Powell to drop by more than 100 feet (30 meters), revealing much of the spectacular scenery of Glen Canyon that was drowned in 1963 when a dam created the lake.

Great Salt Lake is the largest natural lake west of the Mississippi River. The lake, which has a high level of evaporation, is about eight times saltier than the ocean.

CALIFORNIA GULL
SEGO LILY

For thousands of years, present-day Utah was populated by Native Americans living in small hunter-gatherer groups, including the Utes for whom the state is named. Spanish explorers passed through Utah in 1776, and in the early 19th century trappers came from the East searching for beavers. In 1847, the arrival of Mormons seeking freedom to practice their religion marked the beginning of widespread settlement of the territory. They established farms and introduced irrigation. Discovery of precious metals in the 1860s brought miners to the territory. Today, almost 70 percent of Utah's land is set aside by the federal government for use by the military and defense industries and as national parks, which attract large numbers of tourists annually. As a result, government is a leading employer in the state. Another important force in Utah is the Church of Latter-day Saints (Mormons), which has influenced culture and politics in the state for more than a century. More than half the state's population is Mormon.

⇧ NATURE'S HANDIWORK. Arches National Park includes more than 2,000 arches carved by forces of water and ice, extreme temperatures, and the shifting of underground salt beds over a period of 100 million years. Delicate Arch stands on the edge of a canyon, with the La Sal Mountains in the distance.

SPREADING THE FAITH

Mormon Church membership, 2006 data

Utah	California	Idaho	Arizona	Texas
1,789,707	750,024	392,782	361,817	260,076

From a colony of believers who settled in Utah's Salt Lake basin in the 1840s, followers of the Mormon faith have expanded into nearby states.

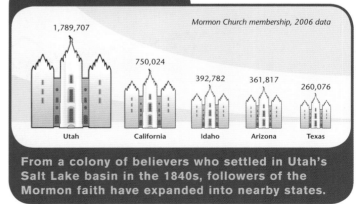

⇦ MONUMENT TO FAITH. Completed in 1893, the Salt Lake Temple is where Mormons gather to worship and participate in religious ceremonies. Church members regard temples as the most sacred places on Earth.

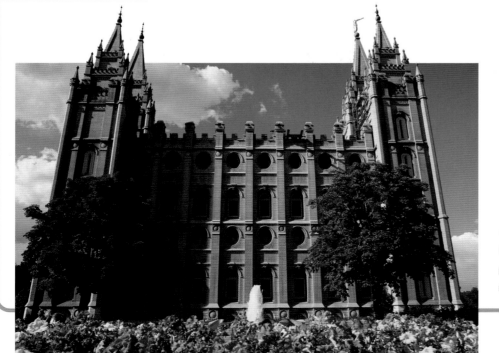

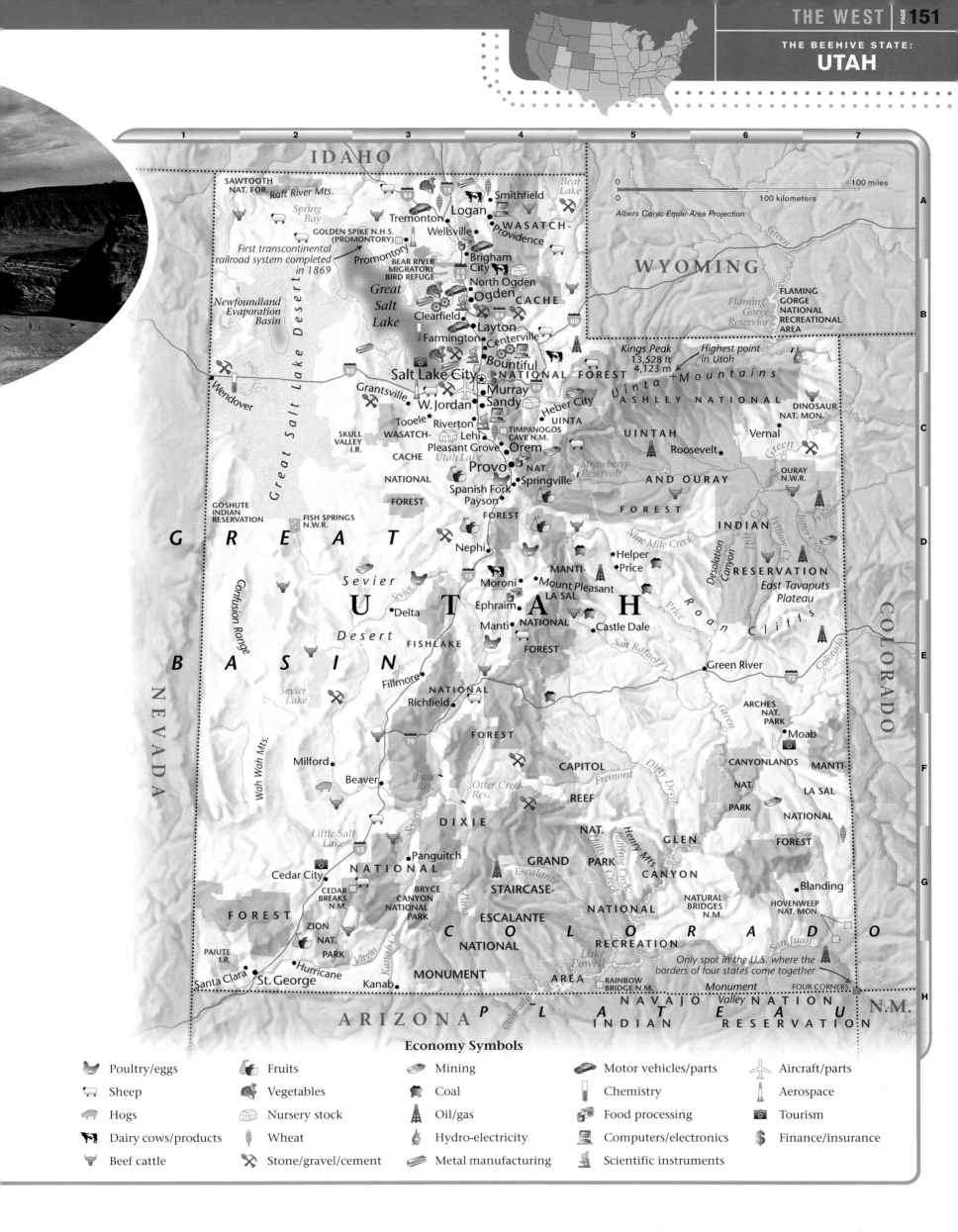

IDAHO

WYOMING

SAWTOOTH
NAT. FOR. Raft River Mts.

Spring Bay

Smithfield

Tremonton

Logan

Bear Lake

0   100 miles
0   100 kilometers

Albers Conic Equal-Area Projection

WASATCH-

Wellsville

Providence

GOLDEN SPIKE N.H.S.
(PROMONTORY)

First transcontinental
railroad system completed
in 1869

Promontory

BEAR RIVER
MIGRATORY
BIRD REFUGE

Brigham
City

North Ogden

CACHE

FLAMING
GORGE
NATIONAL
RECREATIONAL
AREA

*Newfoundland
Evaporation
Basin*

*Great
Salt
Lake*

Ogden

*Flaming
Gorge
Reservoir*

Clearfield

Layton

Farmington

Centerville

Kings Peak
13,528 ft
4,123 m

Highest point
in Utah

Bountiful

NATIONAL FOREST

Uinta Mountains

ASHLEY NATIONAL

Salt Lake City

Murray

Sandy

Heber City

DINOSAUR
NAT. MON.

Grantsville

W. Jordan

UINTA

UINTAH

Vernal

Tooele

Riverton

Lehi

WASATCH-

SKULL
VALLEY
I.R.

TIMPANOGOS
CAVE N.M.

Pleasant Grove

Orem

*Strawberry
Reservoir*

AND OURAY

OURAY
N.W.R.

CACHE

Utah Lake

Provo

Springville

NAT.

FOREST

INDIAN

GOSHUTE
INDIAN
RESERVATION

Spanish Fork

Payson

FOREST

NATIONAL

FISH SPRINGS
N.W.R.

FOREST

Nephi

Nine Mile Creek

Helper

Price

RESERVATION

East Tavaputs
Plateau

GREAT

Sevier

UTAH

Confusion Range

Sevier

Moroni

MANTI-

Mount Pleasant

LA SAL

*Desolation
Canyon*

Roan

Cliffs

Delta

Ephraim

NATIONAL

Castle Dale

Price

Milford

FISHLAKE

Manti

FOREST

San Rafael

Desert

BASIN

*Sevier
Lake*

Fillmore

NATIONAL

Green River

Richfield

FOREST

ARCHES
NAT.
PARK

NEVADA

Wah Wah Mts.

Beaver

*Piute
Res.*

FOREST

CAPITOL

Fremont

Dirty Devil

Moab

CANYONLANDS

NAT.

MANTI-

LA SAL

REEF

PARK

NATIONAL

*Little Salt
Lake*

Panguitch

DIXIE

NAT.

GLEN

FOREST

Cedar City

CEDAR
BREAKS
N.M.

NATIONAL

BRYCE
CANYON
NATIONAL
PARK

Escalante

GRAND

STAIRCASE-

ESCALANTE

Bullfrog Creek

Henry Mts.

CANYON

NATURAL
BRIDGES
N.M.

HOVENWEEP
NAT. MON.

Blanding

FOREST

ZION
NAT.
PARK

COLORADO

NATIONAL

PAIUTE
I.R.

Virgin

NATIONAL

Kanab Cr.

RECREATION

*Lake
Powell*

San Juan

Only spot in the U.S. where the
borders of four states come together

Santa Clara

Hurricane

MONUMENT

St. George

Kanab

AREA

RAINBOW
BRIDGE N.M.

Monument

Valley

FOUR CORNERS

ARIZONA

PLATEAU

NAVAJO NATION

N.M.

COLORADO

INDIAN RESERVATION

Economy Symbols

- Poultry/eggs
- Sheep
- Hogs
- Dairy cows/products
- Beef cattle
- Fruits
- Vegetables
- Nursery stock
- Wheat
- Stone/gravel/cement
- Mining
- Coal
- Oil/gas
- Hydro-electricity
- Metal manufacturing
- Motor vehicles/parts
- Chemistry
- Food processing
- Computers/electronics
- Scientific instruments
- Aircraft/parts
- Aerospace
- Tourism
- Finance/insurance

THE EVERGREEN STATE: WASHINGTON

THE BASICS

STATS

Area
71,300 sq mi (184,666 sq km)

Population
6,468,424

Capital
Olympia
Population 43,963

Largest city
Seattle
Population 582,454

Ethnic/racial groups
84.8% white; 6.6% Asian; 3.6% African American; 1.6% Native American. Hispanic (any race) 9.1%.

Industry
Aerospace, tourism, food processing, forest products, paper products, industrial machinery, printing and publishing, metals, computer software

Agriculture
Seafood, apples, dairy products, wheat, cattle, potatoes, hay

Statehood
November 11, 1889; 42nd state

GEO WHIZ

The forests of the Olympic Peninsula are among the world's rainiest places. The Hoh Rain Forest is one of the planet's few temperate rain forests.

Mount St. Helens, the most active volcano in the lower 48 states, is close to both Seattle and Portland, Oregon. The eruption in May 1980 reduced its elevation by 1,314 feet (401 m), triggering the largest landslide in recorded history.

Orcas, also known as killer whales, are the world's largest dolphins. The 90 or so that call the waters of Puget Sound home have been placed on the government's Endangered Species List.

AMERICAN GOLDFINCH

COAST RHODODENDRON

WASHINGTON

Long before Europeans explored the coast of the Pacific Northwest, Native Americans inhabited the area, living mainly off abundant seafood found in coastal waters and rivers. In the late 18th century, first Spanish sailors and then British explorers, including Captain James Cook, visited the region. Under treaties with Spain (1819) and Britain (1846), the U.S. gained control of the land, and in 1853 the Washington Territory was formally separated from the Oregon Territory. Settlers soon based their livelihood on fishing, farming, and lumbering. Washington became the 42nd state in 1889. The 20th century was a time of growth and development in Washington. Seattle became a major Pacific seaport. The Grand Coulee Dam, completed in 1941, provided the region with inexpensive electricity. Today, manufacturing, led by Boeing and Microsoft, is a mainstay of the economy. Washington leads the country in production of apples and sweet cherries, and the state is home to the headquarters of the popular Starbucks chain of coffee shops.

⇩ HARVEST TIME. Once a semiarid grassland, the Palouse region north of the Snake River in eastern Washington is now a major wheat-producing area.

⇧ PACIFIC GATEWAY. The city of Seattle, easily recognizable by its distinctive Space Needle tower, is a major West Coast port and home to the North Pacific fishing fleet.

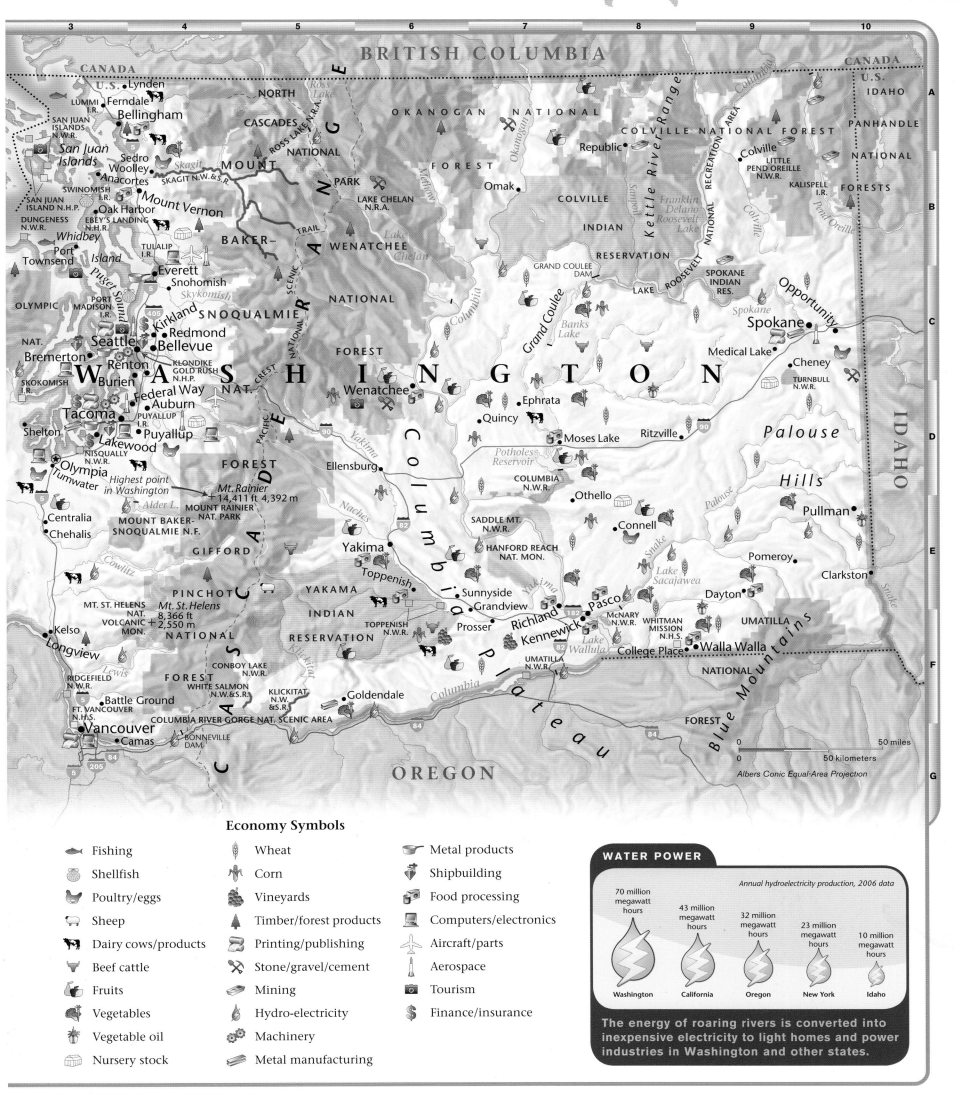

BRITISH COLUMBIA

CANADA
U.S.

CANADA
U.S.
IDAHO

PANHANDLE

NORTH
CASCADES
N.R.A.

Lynden
Ferndale
LUMMI I.R.
Bellingham
SAN JUAN ISLANDS N.W.R.
San Juan Islands
SAN JUAN ISLAND N.H.P.
Sedro Woolley
Anacortes
SWINOMISH I.R.
Oak Harbor
Mount Vernon
DUNGENESS N.W.R.
EBEY'S LANDING N.H.R.
Whidbey Island
Port Townsend
OLYMPIC NAT.
TULALIP I.R.
Everett
Snohomish
Skykomish
PORT MADISON I.R.
Kirkland
Redmond
Seattle
Bellevue
Bremerton
Renton
SKOKOMISH I.R.
Burien
KLONDIKE GOLD RUSH N.H.P.
Federal Way
Auburn
PUYALLUP I.R.
Puyallup
Shelton
Tacoma
Lakewood
NISQUALLY N.W.R.
Olympia
Tumwater
Centralia
Chehalis

MOUNT BAKER–SNOQUALMIE N.F.

SNOQUALMIE NATIONAL FOREST

Highest point in Washington
Mt. Rainier
14,411 ft 4,392 m
Alder L.
MOUNT RAINIER NAT. PARK

Ross Lake
Skagit N.W. & S.R.
Lake Chelan
LAKE CHELAN N.R.A.
Methow
WENATCHEE NATIONAL FOREST
Columbia

OKANOGAN NATIONAL FOREST
Republic
Omak
Okanogan

COLVILLE NATIONAL FOREST
Colville
LITTLE PEND OREILLE N.W.R.
KALISPELL I.R.
NATIONAL FORESTS

Kettle River Range
Sanpoil
Columbia
Pend Oreille

COLVILLE INDIAN RESERVATION
FRANKLIN DELANO ROOSEVELT LAKE
GRAND COULEE DAM
Grand Coulee
Banks Lake
LAKE ROOSEVELT
SPOKANE INDIAN RES.
Spokane
Opportunity
Medical Lake
Cheney
TURNBULL N.W.R.

WASHINGTON

Wenatchee
Ephrata
Quincy
Moses Lake
Ritzville
Potholes Reservoir
COLUMBIA N.W.R.
Othello
Connell
Palouse Hills
Pullman
Pomeroy
Clarkston

Ellensburg
Naches
Yakima
YAKAMA INDIAN RESERVATION
Toppenish
TOPPENISH N.W.R.
SADDLE MT. N.W.R.
HANFORD REACH NAT. MON.
Sunnyside
Grandview
Prosser
Richland
Kennewick
Pasco
McNARY N.W.R.
WHITMAN MISSION N.H.S.
Dayton
Lake Sacajawea
Snake
UMATILLA
Walla Walla
College Place
UMATILLA N.W.R.
Lake Wallula

MT. ST. HELENS NAT. VOLCANIC MON.
Mt. St. Helens
8,366 ft
2,550 m
GIFFORD PINCHOT NATIONAL FOREST
Kelso
Longview
Lewis
RIDGEFIELD N.W.R.
Battle Ground
FT. VANCOUVER N.H.S.
Vancouver
Camas
CONBOY LAKE N.W.R.
WHITE SALMON N.W. & S.R.
KLICKITAT N.W. & S.R.
Goldendale
COLUMBIA RIVER GORGE NAT. SCENIC AREA
BONNEVILLE DAM
Columbia

CASCADE RANGE
MOUNT BAKER–SNOQUALMIE
PACIFIC CREST NATIONAL SCENIC TRAIL

Puget Sound
Cowlitz
Yakima
Columbia Plateau
Blue Mountains
NATIONAL FOREST

OREGON

NORTH CASCADES NATIONAL PARK
MOUNT BAKER–SNOQUALMIE N.F.
BAKER-

0   50 miles
0   50 kilometers
Albers Conic Equal-Area Projection

Economy Symbols

- Fishing
- Shellfish
- Poultry/eggs
- Sheep
- Dairy cows/products
- Beef cattle
- Fruits
- Vegetables
- Vegetable oil
- Nursery stock

- Wheat
- Corn
- Vineyards
- Timber/forest products
- Printing/publishing
- Stone/gravel/cement
- Mining
- Hydro-electricity
- Machinery
- Metal manufacturing

- Metal products
- Shipbuilding
- Food processing
- Computers/electronics
- Aircraft/parts
- Aerospace
- Tourism
- Finance/insurance

WATER POWER

Annual hydroelectricity production, 2006 data

70 million megawatt hours	43 million megawatt hours	32 million megawatt hours	23 million megawatt hours	10 million megawatt hours
Washington	California	Oregon	New York	Idaho

The energy of roaring rivers is converted into inexpensive electricity to light homes and power industries in Washington and other states.

WYOMING

When Europeans arrived in the 18th century in what would become Wyoming, various native groups were already there, living as no mads following herds of deer and bison across the plains. In the early 19th century fur traders moved into Wyoming, and settlers followed later along the Oregon Trail. Laramie and many of the state's other towns developed around old army forts built to protect wagon trains traveling through Wyoming. Today, fewer than 600,000 people live in all of Wyoming. The state's economy is based on agriculture—mainly grain and livestock production—and mining, especially energy resources. The state has some of the world's largest surface coal mines. In addition, it produces petroleum, natural gas, industrial metals, and precious gems. The natural environment is also a major resource. People come to Wyoming for fishing and hunting, for rodeos, and for the state's majestic mountains and parks. Yellowstone, established in 1872, was the world's first national park.

⬆ **WANT TO RACE?** Unique to the High Plains of the West, the pronghorn can sprint up to 60 miles per hour (97 kmph).

⬇ **DRAMATIC LANDSCAPE.** Rising more than 13,000 feet (3,900 m), the jagged peaks of the Tetons, one of the youngest mountain ranges of the West, tower over a barn on the valley floor.

THE BASICS

STATS

Area
97,814 sq mi (253,337 sq km)

Population
522,830

Capital
Cheyenne
Population 54,374

Largest city
Cheyenne
Population 54,374

Ethnic/racial groups
94.5% white; 2.5% Native American; .9% African American; .7% Asian. Hispanic (any race) 6.9%.

Industry
Oil and natural gas, mining, generation of electricity, chemicals, tourism

Agriculture
Cattle, sugar beets, sheep, hay, wheat

Statehood
July 10, 1890; 44th state

GEO WHIZ

The successful reintroduction of wolves into Yellowstone National Park, a program that began in the mid-1990s, has become a model for saving endangered carnivores around the world. In 2001 there were 37 wolves in the Druid Peak pack, making it the largest known pack in history.

The National Elk Refuge, in Jackson Hole, provides a winter home for some 7,500 elk. The herd's migration from the refuge to their summer home in Yellowstone National Park is the longest elk herd migration in the lower 48 states.

Devils Tower, a huge formation of igneous rock near Sundance, was the country's first national monument. It was featured in the science-fiction classic *Close Encounters of the Third Kind*.

WESTERN MEADOWLARK
INDIAN PAINTBRUSH

HOME ON THE RANGE

Farmland usage, 2002 data

Pasture 88%

Cropland 9%

Other uses 3%

More than half of Wyoming's land is in agriculture, mainly pasture. Cattle account for almost 75 percent of the state's agriculture income.

Madison R

YELLOWSTONE

Yellowstone Lake
OLD FAITHFUL

NAT. PARK

TARGHEE

JOHN D. ROCKEFELLER, JR. MEM. PKWY.

BRIDG

GRAND TETON

Jackson L.

NATIONAL

NATIONAL PARK

IDAHO

FOREST

NATIONAL ELK REFUGE

Jackson

TETO

Gros Ventre

CARIBOU

Wyoming Range

NAT.

NATIONAL

Afton

FOREST

Continental Divide

Greys

Bear

Green

Fontenelle Reservoir

FOSSIL BUTTE NAT. MON.

Kemmerer

Hams Fork

UTAH

Evanston

Lyman

Blacks Fork

WASATCH-CACHE NATIONAL FOREST

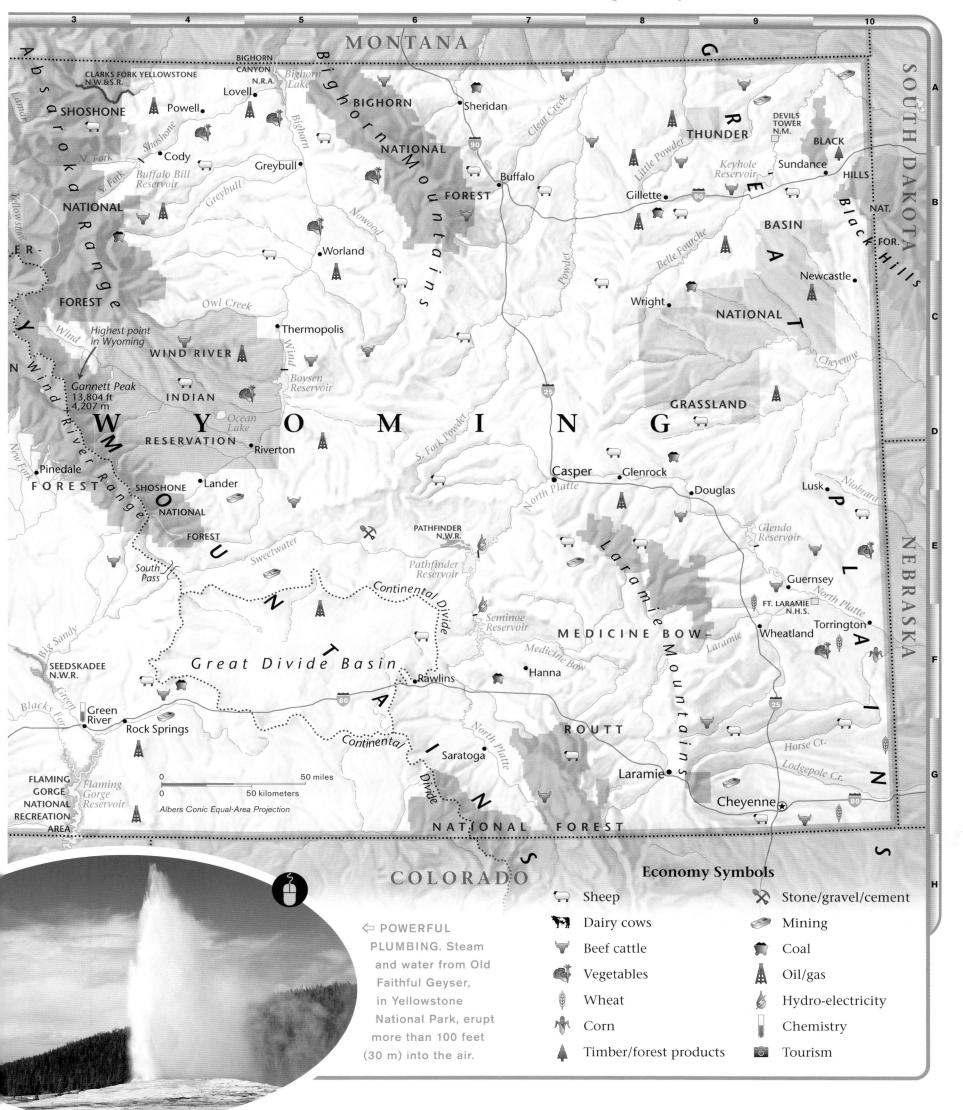

MONTANA

3 4 5 6 7 8 9 10

A

CLARKS FORK YELLOWSTONE
N.W.&S.R.

BIGHORN
CANYON
N.R.A.

Bighorn
Lake

Absaroka Range

SHOSHONE

Powell

Lovell

BIGHORN

Sheridan

GREAT

DEVILS
TOWER
N.M.

BLACK

THUNDER

B

NATIONAL

Cody

Greybull

Shoshone

S. Fork

V. Fork

Buffalo Bill
Reservoir

Bighorn

Greybull

NATIONAL

FOREST

Buffalo

90

Little Powder

Gillette

90

Keyhole
Reservoir

Sundance

HILLS

Black Hills

NAT.
FOR.

SOUTH DAKOTA

NATIONAL

Yellowstone

Nowood

Powder

Belle Fourche

BASIN

Newcastle

C

FOREST

Owl Creek

Worland

Wright

Cheyenne

NATIONAL

ER-

Wind

Thermopolis

Highest point
in Wyoming

Wind

WIND RIVER

Boysen
Reservoir

GRASSLAND

Wind River Range

Gannett Peak
13,804 ft
4,207 m

W Y O M I N G

D

INDIAN

Ocean
Lake

RESERVATION

Riverton

S. Fork Powder

Casper

Glenrock

Douglas

Lusk

Niobrara

New Fork

Pinedale

SHOSHONE

Lander

NATIONAL

FOREST

North Platte

PATHFINDER
N.W.R.

Pathfinder
Reservoir

Glendo
Reservoir

Guernsey

FT. LARAMIE
N.H.S.

Torrington

North Platte

E

Sweetwater

M O U N T A I N S

South
Pass

Continental Divide

Seminoe
Reservoir

Laramie

MEDICINE BOW-

Medicine Bow

Laramie

Wheatland

P L A I N S

F

Big Sandy

SEEDSKADEE
N.W.R.

Great Divide Basin

Rawlins

Hanna

North Platte

ROUTT

25

Horse Cr.

Blacks Fork

Green

Green
River

Rock Springs

80

Continental

Saratoga

North Platte

Laramie

Lodgepole Cr.

80

G

FLAMING
GORGE
NATIONAL
RECREATION
AREA

Flaming
Gorge
Reservoir

Continental

Divide

0   50 miles

0   50 kilometers

Albers Conic Equal-Area Projection

NATIONAL FOREST

Cheyenne

NEBRASKA

H

COLORADO

Economy Symbols

⇐ POWERFUL
PLUMBING. Steam
and water from Old
Faithful Geyser,
in Yellowstone
National Park, erupt
more than 100 feet
(30 m) into the air.

Sheep

Dairy cows

Beef cattle

Vegetables

Wheat

Corn

Timber/forest products

Stone/gravel/cement

Mining

Coal

Oil/gas

Hydro-electricity

Chemistry

Tourism

The Territories

ACROSS TWO SEAS

Listed below are the 5 largest of the 14 U.S. territories, along with their flags and key information. Two of these are in the Caribbean Sea, and the other three are in the Pacific Ocean. Can you find the other 9 U.S. territories on the map?

U.S. CARIBBEAN TERRITORIES

PUERTO RICO

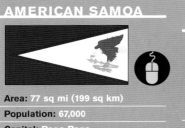

Area: 3,508 sq mi (9,086 sq km)

Population: 3,929,000

Capital: San Juan
Population 2,605,000

Languages: Spanish, English

U.S. VIRGIN ISLANDS

Area: 149 sq mi (386 sq km)

Population: 109,000

Capital: Charlotte Amalie
Population 52,000

Languages: English, Spanish or Spanish Creole, French or French Creole

U.S. PACIFIC TERRITORIES

AMERICAN SAMOA

Area: 77 sq mi (199 sq km)

Population: 67,000

Capital: Pago Pago
Population 55,000

Language: Samoan

GUAM

Area: 217 sq mi (561 sq km)

Population: 171,000

Capital: Hagåtña (Agana)
Population 144,000

Languages: English, Chamorro, Philippine languages

NORTHERN MARIANA ISLANDS

Area: 184 sq mi (477 sq km)

Population: 82,000

Capital: Saipan
Population 75,000

Languages: Philippine languages, Chinese, Chamorro, English

OTHER U.S. TERRITORIES

Baker Island, Howland Island, Jarvis Island, Johnston Atoll, Kingman Reef, Midway Islands, Navassa Island, Palmyra Atoll, Wake Island

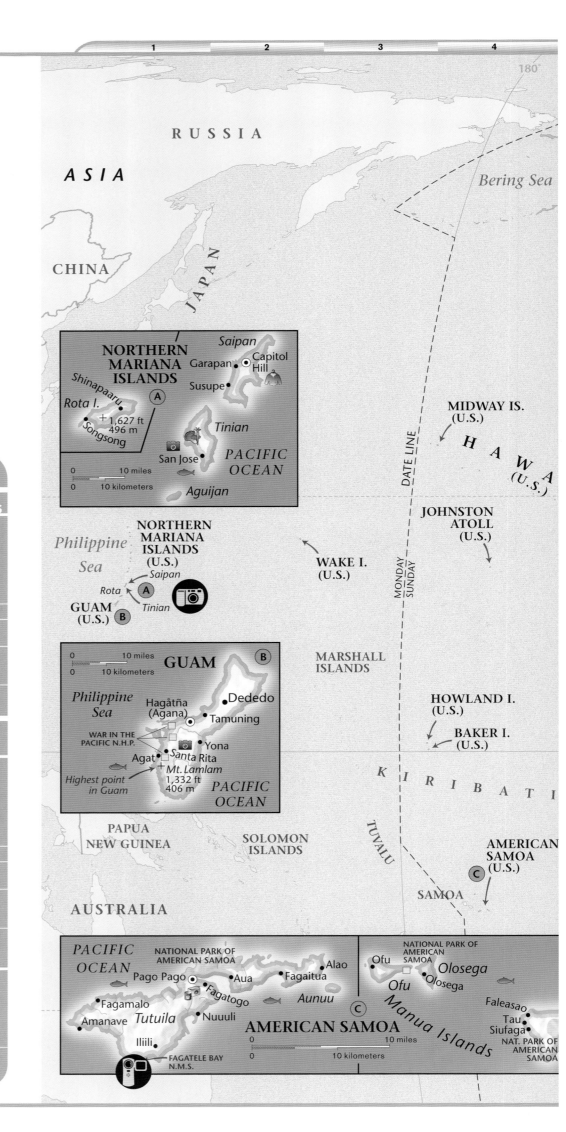

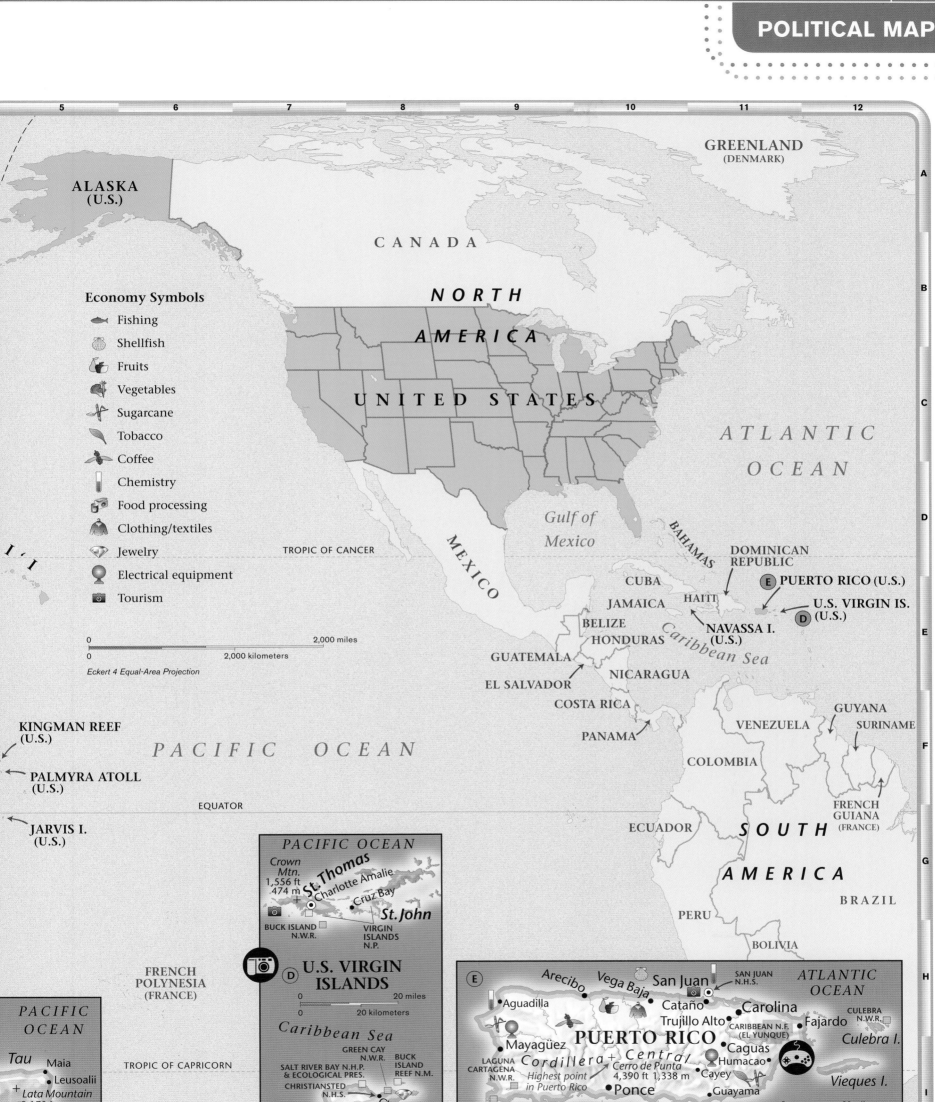

GREENLAND
(DENMARK)

ALASKA
(U.S.)

CANADA

NORTH

AMERICA

UNITED STATES

ATLANTIC

OCEAN

Economy Symbols

Fishing
Shellfish
Fruits
Vegetables
Sugarcane
Tobacco
Coffee
Chemistry
Food processing
Clothing/textiles
Jewelry
Electrical equipment
Tourism

Gulf of
Mexico

MEXICO

TROPIC OF CANCER

BAHAMAS

DOMINICAN
REPUBLIC

CUBA

PUERTO RICO (U.S.)

HAITI

JAMAICA

U.S. VIRGIN IS.
(U.S.)

BELIZE

NAVASSA I.
(U.S.)

HONDURAS

Caribbean Sea

0   2,000 miles

0   2,000 kilometers

Eckert 4 Equal-Area Projection

GUATEMALA

NICARAGUA

EL SALVADOR

COSTA RICA

GUYANA

VENEZUELA

SURINAME

KINGMAN REEF
(U.S.)

PACIFIC OCEAN

PANAMA

COLOMBIA

PALMYRA ATOLL
(U.S.)

FRENCH
GUIANA
(FRANCE)

EQUATOR

JARVIS I.
(U.S.)

ECUADOR

SOUTH

PACIFIC OCEAN

Crown
Mtn.
1,556 ft
474 m

St. Thomas

Charlotte Amalie

AMERICA

Cruz Bay

PERU

BRAZIL

St. John

BUCK ISLAND
N.W.R.

VIRGIN
ISLANDS
N.P.

FRENCH
POLYNESIA
(FRANCE)

U.S. VIRGIN
ISLANDS

BOLIVIA

Arecibo

Vega Baja

San Juan

SAN JUAN
N.H.S.

ATLANTIC
OCEAN

20 miles

Aguadilla

Cataño

Carolina

CULEBRA
N.W.R.

PACIFIC
OCEAN

20 kilometers

Caribbean Sea

Trujillo Alto

CARIBBEAN N.F.
(EL YUNQUE)

Fajardo

Culebra I.

GREEN CAY
N.W.R.

BUCK
ISLAND
REEF N.M.

Mayagüez

PUERTO RICO

Tau

Maia

TROPIC OF CAPRICORN

SALT RIVER BAY N.H.P.
& ECOLOGICAL PRES.

LAGUNA
CARTAGENA
N.W.R.

Cordillera Central

Cerro de Punta
4,390 ft 1,338 m
Highest point
in Puerto Rico

Humacao

Cayey

Leusoalii

CHRISTIANSTED
N.H.S.

Guayama

Vieques I.

Lata Mountain
3,170 ft
966 m

Frederiksted

Christiansted

CABO ROJO
N.W.R.

Ponce

Guayama

20 miles

St. Croix

Caribbean Sea

20 kilometers

⇨ PRESERVING TRADITION. Young dancers from American Samoa, dressed in costumes of feathers and pandanus leaves, prepare to perform in the Pacific Arts Festival, which is held once every four years to promote Pacific cultures.

The Territories
ISLANDS IN THE FAMILY

Fourteen territories and commonwealths scattered across the Pacific and Caribbean came under U.S. influence after wars or various international agreements. Because they are neither states nor independent countries, the U.S. government provides economic and military aid. Puerto Rico's nearly four million residents give it a population greater than that of 24 U.S. states. Many tourists seeking sunny beaches visit the Virgin Islands, purchased from Denmark for $25 million in 1917. American Samoa, Guam, and the Northern Mariana Islands in the Pacific have sizable populations, but several tiny atolls have no civilian residents and are administered by the U.S. military or government departments. In most cases, citizens of these territories are also eligible for American citizenship.

⇧ RELIC OF THE PAST. Sugar mill ruins on St. John, in the U.S. Virgin Islands, recall a way of life that dominated the Caribbean in the 18th and 19th centuries. Plantations used slave labor to grow cane and make it into sugar and molasses.

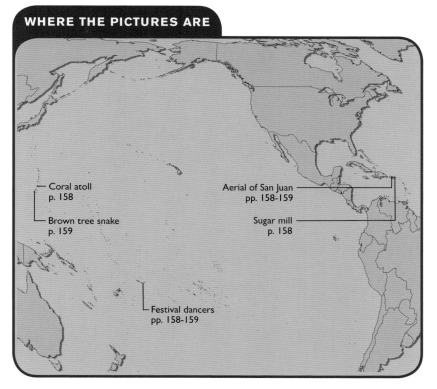

WHERE THE PICTURES ARE

Coral atoll
p. 158

Brown tree snake
p. 159

Festival dancers
pp. 158-159

Aerial of San Juan
pp. 158-159

Sugar mill
p. 158

← PACIFIC JEWEL. Managaha Island sits in the blue-green waters of a lagoon formed by a long reef along Saipan's western coast. Marine biologists fear that portions of the reef are dying due to pollution. The lagoon holds wrecks from battles fought in Northern Mariana waters during World War II.

← ATLANTIC PLAYGROUND. Modern hotels, catering to 2.5 million tourists annually, rise above sandy beaches in San Juan, Puerto Rico. Founded in 1521, the city has one of the best natural harbors in the Caribbean.

⇩ UNWELCOME STOWAWAY. The brown tree snake probably arrived in Guam on cargo ships in the 1950s. The snake has greatly reduced the island's bird and small mammal populations and causes power outages when it climbs electric poles.

U.S. FACTS & FIGURES

THE COUNTRY

STATS

Founding
1776

Area
3,794,083 sq mi (9,826,675 sq km)

Population (January 2008)
303,269,000

Capital
Washington, D.C.

Population
581,530

Largest city
New York

Population
8,214,426

Ethnic/racial groups
80.1% white; 12.8% African American;
4.4% Asian; 1.0% Native American.
Hispanic (any race) 14.8%.

Languages
(most widely spoken)
English, Spanish

Economy
Services: 78.2% of GDP
Industry: 20.9% of GDP
Agriculture: .9% of GDP

BALD EAGLE,
NATIONAL SYMBOL

Top States

Listed below are major farm products, fish, and minerals and the states that currently lead in their production. Following each list is a ranking of the top states in each category.

Farm Products

Cattle and calves: Texas, Nebraska, Kansas, California

Dairy products: California, Wisconsin, New York, Pennsylvania

Soybeans: Iowa, Illinois, Minnesota, Indiana

Corn for grain: Iowa, Illinois, Nebraska, Minnesota

Hogs and pigs: Iowa, North Carolina, Minnesota, Illinois

Broiler chickens: Georgia, Arkansas, Alabama, North Carolina

Wheat: Kansas, North Dakota, Montana, Washington

Cotton: Texas, California, Georgia, Mississippi

Eggs: Iowa, Ohio, Pennsylvania, Indiana

Hay: Texas, California, Pennsylvania, Idaho

Tobacco: North Carolina, Kentucky, Tennessee, South Carolina

Turkeys: Minnesota, North Carolina, Arkansas, Virginia

Oranges: Florida, California, Texas, Arizona

Potatoes: Idaho, Washington, Wisconsin, Colorado

Grapes: California, Washington, New York, Pennsylvania

Tomatoes: Florida, California, Ohio, Georgia

Rice: Arkansas, California, Louisiana, Missouri

Top Ten in Farm Products (by net farm income)

1. California
2. Texas
3. North Carolina
4. Iowa
5. Minnesota
6. Georgia
7. Florida
8. Nebraska
9. Arkansas
10. Kentucky

Fish

Shrimp: Louisiana, Texas, Florida, Alabama

Crabs: Alaska, Louisiana, Oregon, Maryland, California

Lobsters: Maine, Massachusetts, Florida, Rhode Island

Salmon: Alaska, Washington, Oregon, California

Pollock: Alaska, Massachusetts, Maine, New Hampshire

Top Five in Fisheries (by value of catch)

1. Alaska
2. Massachusetts
3. Maine
4. Louisiana
5. Texas

Minerals

Crude oil: Texas, Alaska, California, Louisiana, Oklahoma

Natural gas: Texas, Wyoming, Oklahoma, New Mexico, Louisiana

Coal: Wyoming, West Virginia, Kentucky, Pennsylvania

Crushed stone: Texas, Florida, Pennsylvania, Missouri

Copper: Arizona, Utah, New Mexico, Nevada

Cement: California, Texas, Pennsylvania, Florida

Construction sand and gravel: California, Arizona, Texas, Michigan

Gold: Nevada, Utah, Alaska, Colorado, Montana

Iron ore: Minnesota, Michigan, California

Clay: Georgia, South Carolina, Alabama, Arkansas

Phosphate rock: Florida, North Carolina, Idaho, Utah

Lime: Missouri, Kentucky, Alabama, Ohio, Texas

Salt: Louisiana, Texas, New York, Ohio

Sulfur: Louisiana, Texas

Top Ten in Minerals

1. Arizona
2. California
3. Nevada
4. Florida
5. Utah
6. Texas
7. Minnesota
8. Missouri
9. Georgia
10. Colorado

Extremes

World's Strongest Surface Wind
231 mph (372 kph), Mount Washington, New Hampshire, April 12, 1934

World's Tallest Living Tree
"Hyperion," a coast redwood in Redwood National Park, California, 379.1 ft (115.55 m) high

World's Oldest Living Tree
Methuselah bristlecone pine, California; 4,789 years old

World's Largest Gorge
Grand Canyon, Arizona; 290 mi (466 km) long, 600 ft to 18 mi (183 m to 29 km) wide, 1 mile (1.6 km) deep

Highest Temperature in U.S.
134°F (56.6°C), Death Valley, California, July 10, 1913

Lowest Temperature in U.S.
Minus 80°F (-62.2°C) at Prospect Creek, Alaska, January 23, 1971

Highest Point in U.S.
Mount McKinley (Denali), Alaska; 20,320 ft (6,194 m)

Lowest Point in U.S.
Death Valley, California; 282 feet (86 m) below sea level

Longest River System in U.S.
Mississippi-Missouri; 3,710 mi (5,971 km) long

Rainiest Spot in U.S.
Wai'ale'ale (mountain), Hawai'i: average annual rainfall 460 in (1,168 cm)

Metropolitan Areas with More Than Five Million People
A metropolitan area is a city and its surrounding suburban areas. (2006 data)

1. New York, pop. 21,976,224
2. Los Angeles, pop. 17,775,984
3. Chicago, pop. 9,725,317
4. Washington, D.C., pop. 8,211,213
5. Boston, pop. 7,465,634
6. San Francisco, pop. 7,228,948
7. Philadelphia, pop. 6,382,714
8. Dallas-Fort Worth, pop. 6,359,758
9. Houston, pop. 5,641,077
10. Atlanta, pop. 5,478,667
11. Detroit, pop. 5,410,014

GLOSSARY

aquaculture raising fish or shellfish in controlled ponds or waterways for commercial use

atoll a circular coral reef enclosing a tropical lagoon

arid climate type of dry climate in which annual precipitation is often less than 10 inches (25 cm)

biomass total weight of all organisms found in a given area

bituminous coal a soft form of coal used in industries and power plants

bog a poorly drained area with wet, spongy ground

broadleaf forest trees with wide leaves that are shed during the winter season

butte a high, steep-sided rock formation created by the erosion of a mesa

canal an artificial waterway that is used by ships or to carry water for irrigation

center-pivot irrigation an irrigation system that rotates around a piped water source at its middle, often resulting in circular field patterns

continental climate temperature extremes with long cold winters and heavy snowfall

continental divide an elevated area that separates rivers flowing toward opposite sides of a continent; in the U.S. this divide follows the crest of the Rocky Mountains

copra dried coconut meat from which oil is extracted to make a variety of products, including soap, candles, and cosmetics

Creole a simplified or modified form of a language, such as French or Spanish, used for communication between two groups; spoken in some Caribbean islands

delta lowland formed by silt, sand, and gravel deposited by a river at its mouth

desert vegetation plants such as cactus and dry shrubs that have adapted to conditions of low, often irregular precipitation

fork in a river, the place where two streams join

Fortune 500 company ranking of the top 500 U.S. companies based on total revenue

fossil remains of or an impression left by the remains of plants or animals preserved in rock

geothermal energy a clean, renewable form of energy derived from heat that flows continuously from Earth's interior

grassland areas with medium to short grasses; found where precipitation is not sufficient to support tree growth

gross domestic product (GDP) the total value of goods and services produced in a country in a year

highland climate found in association with high mountains where elevation affects temperature and precipitation

hundredweight in the U.S., a commercial unit of measure equal to 100 pounds

ice age a very long period of cold climate when glaciers often cover large areas of land

intermittent river/lake a stream or lake that contains water only part of the time, usually after heavy rain or snowmelt

lava molten rock from Earth's interior that flows out on the surface during volcanic activity

levee an embankment, usually earth or concrete, built to prevent a river from overflowing

lignite low-grade coal used mainly to produce heat in thermal-electric generators

marine west coast climate type of mild climate found on the mid-latitude West Coast of the U.S.

Mediterranean climate type of mild climate found on the West Coast of the U.S., south of the marine west coast climate

mesa an eroded plateau, broader than it is high, that is found in arid or semiarid regions

metropolitan area a city and its surrounding suburbs or communities

mild climate moderate temperatures with distinct seasons and ample precipitation

nursery stock young plants, including fruits, vegetables, shrubs, and trees, raised in a greenhouse or nursery

pinnacle a tall pillar of rock standing alone or on a summit

plain a large area of relatively flat land that is often covered with grasses

plateau a relatively flat area, larger than a mesa, that rises above the surrounding landscape

population density the average number of people living on each square mile or square kilometer of a specific land area

precipitate process of depositing dissolved minerals as water evaporates, as in limestone caves

rangeland areas of grass prairie that are used for grazing livestock

reactor a device that uses controlled nuclear fission to divide an atomic nucleus to generate power

Richter scale ranking of the power of an earthquake; the higher the number, the stronger the quake

Rust Belt a region made up of northeastern and midwestern states that have experienced a decline in heavy industry and an out-migration of population

scale on a map, a means of explaining the relationship between distances on the map and actual distances on Earth's surface

stalactite column of limestone hanging from the ceiling of a cave that forms as underground water drips down and evaporates, leaving dissolved minerals behind

stalagmite column of limestone that forms on the floor of a cave when underground water drips down and evaporates, leaving dissolved minerals behind

staple main item in an economy; also, main food for domestic consumption

Sunbelt a region made up of southern and western states that are experiencing major in-migration of population and rapid economic growth

territory land that is under the jurisdiction of a country but that is not a state or a province

tropical zone the area bounded by the Tropic of Cancer and the Tropic of Capricorn, where it is usually warm year-round

tundra vegetation plants, often stunted in size, that have adapted to periods of extreme cold and a short growing season; found in polar regions and high elevations

urban areas in which natural vegetation has been replaced by towns or cities, where the main economic activity is nonagricultural

volcanic pipe a vertical opening beneath a volcano through which molten rock has passed

wetland land that is either covered with or saturated by water; includes swamps, marshes, and bogs

OUTSIDE WEB SITES

The following Web sites will provide you with additional valuable information about various topics discussed in this atlas. You can find direct links to each by going to the atlas URL (www.nationalgeographic.com/kids-usa-atlas) and clicking on "Resources."

General information:
States: www.state.al.us (This is for Alabama; for each state insert the two-letter state abbreviation where "al" is now.)

D.C. and the Territories:
Washington, D.C.: http://kids.dc.gov/kids_main_content.html
American Samoa: www.samoanet.com
Guam: http://ns.gov.gu/
Northern Marianas: www.saipan.com/gov
Puerto Rico: www.prstar.net
U.S. Virgin Islands: www.gov.vi

Natural Environment:
Biomes: http://www.blueplanetbiomes.org
Climate: http://www.eoearth.org/
Global Warming: http://www.nrdc.org/globalWarming/

Climate:
http://www.noaa.gov/climate.html
http://www.worldclimate.com (for cities)
http://www.cpc.noaa.gov/

Natural Hazards:
General: http://www.usgs.gov/hazards/
Droughts: http://www.drought.unl.edu/DM/monitor.html
Earthquakes: http://earthquake.usgs.gov/
Hurricanes: http://hurricanes.noaa.gov/
Tornados: http://www.tornadoproject.com/
Tsunamis: http://www.noaa.gov/tsunamis.html
Volcanoes: http://www.geo.mtu.edu/volcanoes
Wildfires: http://www.nifc.gov/ and http://www.fs.fed.us/fire/

Population:
States: http://quickfacts.census.gov/qfd/
Cities: http://www.city-data.com/
Population migration: http://www.census.gov/prod/2001pubs/p23-204.pdf
Hispanic population: http://www.census.gov/prod/2003pubs/p20-545.pdf

Getting Green:
http://www.epa.gov/
http://www.earthday.net/Footprint/index.asp
http://www.footprintnetwork.org/index.php

Bird sounds:
http://www.animalbehaviorarchive.org/loginPublic.do

Mapping site:
http://earth.google.com/

PLACE-NAME INDEX

Map references are in boldface (**50**) type. Letters and numbers following in lightface (D12) locate the place-names using the map grid. (Refer to page 7 for more details.)

Beulah — Cascade

Cascade Range — Crossville

Crow Agency — Fall

Fall Line — Green River

Jamestown — Little Deschutes N.W.&S.R.

Little Diomede Island — Mio

Mishawaka — Odessa

Odessa — Potomac

Potomac — Sandstone

Sandusky — Stilwell

Stockbridge — Waikoloa

Wailuku — Zuni

Published by the National Geographic Society

John M. Fahey, Jr.
President and Chief Executive Officer

Gilbert M. Grosvenor
Chairman of the Board

Tim T. Kelly
President, Global Media Group

Nina D. Hoffman
Executive Vice President; President, Book Publishing Group

Prepared by the Book Division

Nancy Laties Feresten,
Vice President, Editor in Chief, Children's Books

Bea Jackson, Director of Design and Illustrations, Children's Books

Jennifer Emmett, Executive Editor, Reference, Children's Books

Amy Shields, Executive Editor, Series, Children's Books

Carl Mehler, Director of Maps

Staff for this book

Suzanne Patrick Fonda, Project Editor

Bea Jackson, Art Director and Book Design

Ruthie Thompson, Thunder Hill Graphics, Designer

Sven M. Dolling, Laura Exner, Thomas L. Gray,
Nicholas P. Rosenbach, Map Editors

Matt Chwastyk, Sven M. Dolling, Steven D. Gardner,
Michael McNey, Gregory Ugiansky, Mapping Specialists, and
XNR Productions, Map Research and Production

Tibor G. Tóth, Map Relief

Priyanka Lamichhane, Editor

Lori Epstein, Illustrations Editor

Martha B. Sharma, Consultant

Martha B. Sharma, Timothy J. Hill, Writers

Stuart Armstrong, Graphics Illustrator

Chelsea M. Zillmer, Researcher

Dan Sherman, Web Page Design

Jennifer Kirkpatrick, Web Page Editor

Mark H. Bockenhauer, Clean Reader

Sandi Owatverot, Production Design Assistant

Stacy Gold, Nadia Hughes, Illustrations Research Editors

Rebecca Baines, Editorial Assistant

Debbie Guthrie Haer, Copy Editor

Lewis R. Bassford, Production Project Manager

Jennifer A. Thornton, Managing Editor

Grace Hill, Associate Managing Editor

R. Gary Colbert, Production Director

Susan Borke, Legal and Business Affairs

Manufacturing and Quality Management

Christopher A. Liedel, Chief Financial Officer

Phillip L. Schlosser, Vice President

Chris Brown, Technical Director

Nicole Elliott, Manager

Founded in 1888, the National Geographic Society is one of the largest nonprofit scientific and educational organizations in the world. It reaches more than 285 million people worldwide each month through its official journal, NATIONAL GEOGRAPHIC, and its four other magazines; the National Geographic Channel; television documentaries; radio programs; films; books; videos and DVDs; maps; and interactive media. National Geographic has funded more than 8,000 scientific research projects and supports an education program combating geographic illiteracy.

For more information, please call 1-800-NGS LINE (647-5463) or write to the following address:

NATIONAL GEOGRAPHIC SOCIETY
1145 17th Street N.W., Washington, D.C. 20036-4688 U.S.A.

Visit us online at www.nationalgeographic.com/books

For information about special discounts for bulk purchases, please contact National Geographic Books Special Sales: ngspecsales@ngs.org

For rights or permissions inquiries, please contact National Geographic Books Subsidiary Rights: ngbookrights@ngs.org

Teachers and librarians go to ngchildrensbooks.com

Printed in China

Illustrations Credits

Abbreviations for terms appearing below: (t)-top; (b)-bottom; (l)-left; (r)-right; NGS = National Geographic Image Collection; iS = iStockphoto.com; SH = Shutterstock.com

Art for state flowers and state birds by Robert E. Hynes

Locator globe page 16 created by Theophilus Britt Griswold

Front cover, Tibor G. Tóth.

Back cover (t–b), FloridaStock/SH; Peder Digre/SH; Lou Ann M. Aepelbacher/SH; Olga Lyubkina/SH

Front of the Book

2 (l–r), Freerk Brouwer/SH; PhotoDisc; Brandon Laufenberg/iS; Richard Nowitz/NGS; 3 (l–r), Joel Sartore/NGS; Jeremy Edwards/iS; Eileen Hart/iS; PhotoDisc; 4 (l), PhotoDisc; 4 (r), Brian J. Skerry/NGS; 4–5, Lenice Harms/SH; 5 (l), italianestro/SH; 5 (r), James Davis Photography/Alamy; 5 (b), Digital Stock; 11 (t–b), Lane V. Erickson/SH; Elena Elisseeva/SH; SNEHIT/SH; Nic Watson/SH; FloridaStock/SH; Sai Yeung Chan/SH; TTphoto/SH; 12 (l) Lowell Georgia/NGS; 12 (r), NASA; 14 (l–r), George F. Mobley/NGS; Skip Brown/NGS; Jan Brons/SH; Michelle Pacitto/SH; Tammy Bryngelson/iS; 15 (l–r), Carsten Peter/NGS; Mark Thiessen/NGS; Michael Nichols/NGS; Steven Collins/SH; Robert Madden/NGS; 18, Ira Block/NGS; 20 (t), Penny de los Santos; 20 (bl), Steven Clevenger/Corbis; 20–21, Sarah Leen/NGS; 22 (l), Marcelo Piotti/iS; 22–23, Jim Richardson/NGS; 23 (r), Sorin Alb/iS; 24, PhotoDisc; 24–25, PhotoDisc; 25 (t), L. Kragt Bakker/SH; 25 (b), EyeWire.

The Northeast

30 (bl), Rudi Von Briel/Photo Edit; 30 (br), Les Byerley/SH; 30–31 (t), Michael Melford/NGS; 30–31 (b), Tim Laman/NGS; 31 (t), Donald Swartz/iS; 32 (both), David L. Arnold/NGS; 33, Catherine Karnow/NGS; 34 (bl), Kevin Fleming/NGS; 34 (br), Stephen R. Brown/NGS; 34–35, Stephen St. John/NGS; 36 (b), iS; 36–37, PhotoDisc; 37 (b), Roy Toft/NGS; 38 (t), Jeremy Edwards/iS; 38 (b), Justine Gecewicz/iS; 39, James L. Stanfield/NGS; 40 (t), Sarah Leen/NGS; 40 (b), Tim Laman/NGS; 41, Darlyne A. Murawski/NGS; 42 (t), Medford Taylor/NGS; 42–43, Steven Phraner/iS; 43 (t), Richard Nowitz/NGS; 44 (t), Richard Nowitz/NGS; 44 (bl), Iconica/Getty Images; 44 (br), Matt Rainey/Star Ledger/Corbis; 44–45, Mike Derer/Associated Press; 46 (t), Glenn Taylor/iS; 46 (b), James P. Blair/NGS; 47, Kenneth Garrett/NGS; 48 (t), Kenneth Garrett/NGS; 48 (b), Jeremy Edwards/iS; 49, William Albert Allard/NGS; 50 (t), Todd Gipstein/NGS; 50 (b), Onne van der Wal/Corbis; 50–51, Ira Block/NGS; 52, Michael S. Yamashita/NGS; 52–53, David McLain/Aurora/Getty Images; 53, Daniel W. Slocum/SH.

The Southeast

58 (t), Klaus Nigge/NGS; 58 (bl), Tyrone Turner/NGS; 58 (br), Richard Nowitz/Corbis; 58–59, Skip Brown/NGS; 59 (t), Raymond Gehman/NGS; 59 (b), Robert Clark/NGS; 60 (t), Raymond Gehman/NGS; 60 (b), Richard Nowitz/NGS; 62 (t), Harrison Shull/Aurora/Getty Images; 62 (b), Joel Sartore/NGS; 63, Cary Wolinsky/NGS; 64 (t), David Burnett/NGS; 64 (b), Brian J. Skerry/NGS; 64–65, Otis Imboden/NGS; 66 (tl), NGS; 66 (tr), PhotoDisc; 66 (b), Michael Melford/NGS; 68, Melissa Farlow/NGS; 69, Randy Olson/NGS; 70 (t), Tyrone Turner/NGS; 70 (b), Jason Major/iS; 72 (t), William Albert Allard/NGS; 72 (b), Ira Block/NGS; 73, Elena Vdovina/iS; 74 (l), Jack Fletcher/NGS; 74 (r), Pete Souza/NGS; 75, Raymond Gehman/NGS; 76, Terry Healy/iS; 76–77, Annie Griffiths Belt/NGS; 77, Raymond Gehman/NGS; 78, Melissa Farlow/NGS; 79 (t), Dennis R. Dimick/NGS; 79 (b), Jodi Cobb/NGS; 80 (t), Robert Clark/NGS; 80 (b), Richard Nowitz/NGS; 80–81, Medford Taylor/NGS; 82 (t), James L. Stanfield/NGS; 82 (b), Joel Sartore/NGS; 83, Robert Pernell/SH.

The Midwest

88 (t), James L. Stanfield/NGS; 88 (b), Jim Richardson/NGS; 88–89, NGS; 89 (tl), Nadia M. B. Hughes/NGS; 89 (tr), Sean Martin/iS; 89 (b), Aga/SH; 90 (t), Chas/SH; 90 (b), Jenny Solomon/SH; 90–91 (b), Lenice Harms/SH; 92–93 (t), iS; 92–93 (b), Melissa Farlow/NGS; 94 (t), Joel Sartore/NGS; 94 (b), Madeleine Openshaw/SH; 95, Tom Bean/NGS; 96, Cotton Coulson/NGS; 97, Phil Schermeister/NGS; 98 (t), Kevin Fleming/Corbis; 98 (b), Vince Ruffa/SH; 99, Geoffrey Kuchera/SH; 100 (t), Joel Sartore/NGS; 100 (b), Medford Taylor/NGS; 101, Lawrence Sawyer/iS; 102, Phil Schermeister/NGS; 102–103 (b), PhotoDisc; 103, Sarah Leen/NGS; 104 (both), Joel Sartore/NGS; 105, Sarah Leen/NGS; 106 (t), Farrell Grehan/NGS; 106 (b), Beverley Vycital/iS; 107, Annie Griffiths Belt/NGS; 108 (t), PhotoDisc; 108 (bl), Weldon Schloneger/SH; 108 (br), Robert J. Daveant/SH; 110, Peter Digre/SH; 111, Dan Westergren/NGS; 112 (t), Paul Damien/NGS; 112 (b), PhotoDisc; 112–113 Medford Taylor/NGS.

The Southwest

118 (t), Joseph H. Bailey/NGS; 118 (b), Penny de los Santos; 118–119, Anton Folton/iS; 119 (t), Chih Hsueh Tseng/SH; 119 (b), Joel Sartore/NGS; 120 (t), Joel Sartore/NGS; 120 (b), George Burba/SH; 122 (tl), James P. Blair/NGS; 122 (tr), italianestro/SH; 122 (b), Lynn Johnson/NGS; 124, Joel Sartore/NGS; 125, Annie Griffiths Belt/NGS; 126 (t), Sarah Leen/NGS; 126–127, Diane Cook & Len Jenshel/NGS.

The West

132 (both), PhotoDisc; 132–133, Digital Stock; 133 (t), Phillip Holland/SH; 133 (bl), Joel Sartore/NGS; 133 (br), Digital Stock; 134 (t), Joel Sartore/NGS; 134 (b), PhotoDisc; 136 (t), PhotoDisc; 136 (b), Randy Olson/NGS; 138 (both), PhotoDisc; 140, PhotoDisc; 141, Frans Lanting/NGS; 142 (b), Joel Sartore/NGS; 142–143, Michael Melford/NGS; 143 (r), J. Cameron Gull/SH; 144 (b), William Albert Allard/NGS; 145, SH; 146 (b), Sam Abell/NGS; 146–147, Andy Z./SH; 147 (b), Raymond Gehman/NGS; 148 (t), Jennifer Lynn Arnold/SH; 148 (b), Peter Kunasz/SH; 150 (b), Digital Stock; 150–151, PhotoDisc; 152 (l), PhotoDisc; 152 (r), Digital Stock; 154 (t), Michael Rubin/SH; 154 (b), Digital Stock; 155, PhotoDisc.

The Territories and Back of the Book

158 (l), Kendra Nielsam/SH; 158–159 (t), James Davis Photography/Alamy; 158–159 (b), Ira Block/NGS; 159 (t), VisionsofParadise.com/Alamy; 159 (b), Gerry Ellis/Minden/Getty Images; 160, SH.

Map Acknowledgments

2–3, 26–27, 54–55, 84–85, 114–115, 128–129, Blue Marble: Next Generation NASA Earth Observatory; 12–13, climate data adapted from Peel, M. C., Finlayson, B. L., and McMahon, T. A.: Updated world map of the Köppen-Geiger climate classification, Hydrol. Earth Syst. Sci., 11, 1633–1644, 2007; 14–15, data from Billion Dollar Weather Disasters 1980–2007 (map), NOAA's National Climatic Data Center (NCDC); 18–19, data from Center for International Earth Science Information Network (CIESIN), Columbia University, and Centro Internacional de Agricultura Tropical (CIAT), 2005. Gridded Population of the World Version 3 (GPWv3): Population Density Grids—World Population Density, 2005 (map). Palisades, New York: Socioeconomic Data and Applications Center (SEDAC), Columbia University. Accessed October 2007. Available at http://sedac.ciesin.columbia.edu/gpw; 20–21, United States Atlas of Renewable Resources, National Renewable Energy Laboratory; 22–23, U.S. Census Bureau, Census 2000 Redistricting Data (PL 94–171) Summary File, Population Division.

Metric Conversion Tables

CONVERSION TO METRIC MEASURES

SYMBOL	WHEN YOU KNOW	MULTIPLY BY	TO FIND	SYMBOL
LENGTH				
in	inches	2.54	centimeters	cm
ft	feet	0.30	meters	m
yd	yards	0.91	meters	m
mi	miles	1.61	kilometers	km
AREA				
in^2	square inches	6.45	square centimeters	cm^2
ft^2	square feet	0.09	square meters	m^2
yd^2	square yards	0.84	square meters	m^2
mi^2	square miles	2.59	square kilometers	km^2
––	acres	0.40	hectares	ha
MASS				
oz	ounces	28.35	grams	g
lb	pounds	0.45	kilograms	kg
––	short tons	0.91	metric tons	t
VOLUME				
in^3	cubic inches	16.39	milliliters	mL
liq oz	liquid ounces	29.57	milliliters	mL
pt	pints	0.47	liters	L
qt	quarts	0.95	liters	L
gal	gallons	3.79	liters	L
ft^3	cubic feet	0.03	cubic meters	m^3
yd^3	cubic yards	0.76	cubic meters	m^3
TEMPERATURE				
°F	degrees Fahrenheit	5/9 after subtracting 32	degrees Celsius (centigrade)	°C

CONVERSION FROM METRIC MEASURES

SYMBOL	WHEN YOU KNOW	MULTIPLY BY	TO FIND	SYMBOL
LENGTH				
cm	centimeters	0.39	inches	in
m	meters	3.28	feet	ft
m	meters	1.09	yards	yd
km	kilometers	0.62	miles	mi
AREA				
cm^2	square centimeters	0.16	square inches	in^2
m^2	square meters	10.76	square feet	ft^2
m^2	square meters	1.20	square yards	yd^2
km^2	square kilometers	0.39	square miles	mi^2
ha	hectares	2.47	acres	––
MASS				
g	grams	0.04	ounces	oz
kg	kilograms	2.20	pounds	lb
t	metric tons	1.10	short tons	––
VOLUME				
mL	milliliters	0.06	cubic inches	in^3
mL	milliliters	0.03	liquid ounces	liq oz
L	liters	2.11	pints	pt
L	liters	1.06	quarts	qt
L	liters	0.26	gallons	gal
m^3	cubic meters	35.31	cubic feet	ft^3
m^3	cubic meters	1.31	cubic yards	yd^3
TEMPERATURE				
°C	degrees Celsius (centigrade)	9/5 then add 32	degrees Fahrenheit	°F